Rewriting Identities in Contemporary Germany

Studies in German Literature, Linguistics, and Culture

Rewriting Identities in Contemporary Germany

Radical Diversity and Literary Interventions

Edited by
Selma Rezgui, Laura Marie Sturtz,
and Tara Talwar Windsor

Rochester, New York

Copyright © 2024 by the Editors and Contributors

All Rights Reserved. Except as permitted under current legislation, no part of this work may be photocopied, stored in a retrieval system, published, performed in public, adapted, broadcast, transmitted, recorded, or reproduced in any form or by any means, without the prior permission of the copyright owner.

First published 2024 by Camden House

Camden House is an imprint of Boydell & Brewer Inc.
668 Mt. Hope Avenue, Rochester, NY 14620, USA
and of Boydell & Brewer Limited
PO Box 9, Woodbridge, Suffolk IP12 3DF, UK
www.boydellandbrewer.com

ISBN-13: 978-1-64014-155-1

Library of Congress Cataloging-in-Publication Data

CIP data is available from the Library of Congress.

Chapter 10, "Seen as Friendly, Seen as Frightening? A Conversation on Visibilities, Kinship, and the Right Words with Mithu Sanyal" is included with permission from Faculty Ethics Assessment Committee Humanities at Utrecht University (reference number 22-181-01), and has been edited for length and clarity. Open Access License: CC BY-NC. Funding body: Dutch Research Council (NWO): Vl.Veni.211C.012.

The publisher has no responsibility for the continued existence or accuracy of URLs for external or third-party internet websites referred to in this book, and does not guarantee that any content on such websites is, or will remain, accurate or appropriate.

To the writers who are changing Germany and the world

Contents

Acknowledgments   ix

Introduction   1
   Selma Rezgui, Laura Marie Sturtz, and Tara Talwar Windsor

Part I.
Subjectivities, Solidarities, Genealogies

1: Acting from Within: Inclusive Literature and the Power of Writing. A Conversation with Sasha Marianna Salzmann   37
   Selma Rezgui and Laura Marie Sturtz

2: Twin Novels: Renegotiating Self and Other in Sasha Marianna Salzmann's *Außer sich* and Olivia Wenzel's *1000 Serpentinen Angst*   56
   Laura Marie Sturtz

3: New Black German Subjectivity in the Twenty-First Century   83
   Priscilla Layne

4: Talking Back, Paying Forward: Dialogism and Literary Genealogies in May Ayim and Olivia Wenzel   109
   Selma Rezgui

5: Black Poetry Matters: A Conversation with Stefanie-Lahya Aukongo   135
   Jeannette Oholi and Nadiye Ünsal

Part II.
Disruptions, Subversions, Interactions

6: Subversive Aesthetics, Embodied Language, and the Politics of Literature: A Conversation with Özlem Özgül Dündar   145
   Joseph Twist

7: Deintegrative Rewriting of the Bildungsroman:
   Social Criticism from a Postmigrant Perspective in
   Fatma Aydemir's *Ellbogen* (2017) 162
   Lea Laura Heim

8: Reorienting Knowledge of Structural Systems of
   Violence in Sharon Dodua Otoo's *Adas Raum* and
   Antje Rávik Strubel's *Blaue Frau* 187
   Alrik Daldrup

9: Epistolary Interventions, Epistemic Insurrections:
   Creative Writers, Open Letters, and Solidarity with the
   "Womxn, Life, Freedom" Movement in Contemporary
   Postmigrant Germany 209
   Tara Talwar Windsor

10: Seen as Friendly, Seen as Frightening? A Conversation on
    Visibilities, Kinship, and the Right Words with Mithu Sanyal 241
    Leila Essa

Afterword: Rewriting Identities: Conversations about
What Might Be 255
   Sarah Colvin

Notes on the Contributors 261

Index 265

Acknowledgments

This volume has been made possible by our network of partners and collaborators, with whom we have been lucky enough to exchange ideas throughout the long writing and editing process. We are immensely grateful to Jim Walker of Camden House for his guidance, patience, enthusiasm, and all-round encouragement (we almost forgot that last Oxford comma, though). Thanks also to Jane Best, Julia Cook, Chris Adler-France, and the Camden House production team for making the creation of a real (!) book possible, and to the anonymous readers who provided invaluable constructive feedback on the first version of our manuscript. We are deeply grateful for the vital intellectual and financial support we received from Professor Dirk Niefanger, Professor Antje Kley, and the DFG Research Training Group *Literatur und Öffentlichkeit in differenten Gegenwartskulturen* at the Friedrich-Alexander-University Erlangen-Nuremberg, as well as from Dr Charlotte Lee, the Schröder Fund managers, and colleagues in the Faculty of Modern and Medieval Languages and Linguistics at the University of Cambridge.

Professor Sarah Colvin has accompanied this project from its earliest stages, and it is difficult to find words to express the extent of our gratitude for her ongoing support, reassurance, and generosity, not to mention everything she has done for the field of German studies. Many contributions to this book originated from papers given at the Sichtbarkeit*en* conference, which Laura and Selma organized in Oxford in July 2021. Professor Georgina Paul was not only a wonderful supervisor and mentor but also encouraged us to organize a "mini conference" that grew into something much bigger. Dr Veronika Schuchter, Professor Barry Murnane, and the Decolonial Discourses and German Studies Program were on board with our ideas right away. St Hilda's College also provided generous support. We would like to thank everyone who presented, attended, and took part in discussions during that conference, including Fatma Aydemir for her reading, as well as her coeditor Hengameh Yaghoobifarah and the essayists featured in their anthology *Eure Heimat ist unser Albtraum* for inspiring us in the first place.

We are very grateful to Jennifer Petzen and Catriona Corke for their translations, and to Catriona for taking on the mammoth task of indexing the book. Particular thanks must of course go to Alrik Daldrup, Leila Essa, Lea Laura Heim, Priscilla Layne, Jeannette Oholi, Joseph Twist, and Nadiye Ünsal for their brilliant contributions to this volume and to our interview partners Özlem Özgul Dündar, Stephanie-Lahya Aukongo, Sasha Marianna Salzmann, and Mithu Sanyal for making this volume into a very special conversation. Miriam Schwarz, Maha El Hissy, and Jeannette Oholi have been invaluable sounding boards and offered intellectual and emotional support at every stage. None of this work would have been possible without the love, support, patience (and sometimes welcome distractions) of our friends, partners, parents, (chosen) families, and communities—thank you! Finally, we would like to thank each other. This book is the product of genuine teamwork and friendship, and we are proud to have made this happen together.

Selma Rezgui, Laura Marie Sturtz, Tara Talwar Windsor
Berlin, Nuremberg, Cambridge
March 2024

Introduction

Selma Rezgui, Laura Marie Sturtz, and Tara Talwar Windsor

> There's a very clear idea of what belongs to whom, of what counts as German. That only became clear to me when I came into the literary scene myself. I thought, "oh, so this is an intervention. It's seen as an intervention that I'm here." The literature scene sees itself as something that defines Germany. That definition is changing completely, but it's slow, and Germany's idea of itself is like a boulder that we have to chip away at bit by bit with little hammers....
>
> And that, I think, is what we are doing with literature every single day. And that's why it's considered an attack on Germany, as though Germany is being rewritten.
>
> —Sasha Marianna Salzmann[1]

THIS VOLUME IS CONCEIVED OF as a conversation. Or rather, multiple conversations: among us as editors and contributors and the authors featured in this volume; between us and the German cultural and literary landscape as an ever-increasing number of creative writers intervene in the public sphere; and between us and you, our readers, as fellow participants in these ongoing academic and political discussions. The book presents essays on authors such as Fatma Aydemir, Shida Bazyar, Asal Dardan, Sharon Dodua Otoo, Antje Rávik Strubel, Noah Sow, Jackie Thomae, and Olivia Wenzel, as well as original interviews with Stefanie-Lahya Aukongo, Özlem Özgül Dündar, Sasha Marianna Salzmann, and Mithu Sanyal. The quotation above is taken from one of those original interviews—conducted in Summer 2022 with Sasha Marianna Salzmann, which appears as the first contribution to the book following this introduction—and illustrates several key premises of our book. As Salzmann suggests, the prevailing notion of Germanness is an idea rather than a reality. In this context, the very presence of literary and cultural actors who do not appear to conform to that idea is immediately seen as an intervention, an interruption perhaps. Salzmann points to the central role ascribed to

---

1 Quoted from Selma Rezgui and Laura Marie Sturtz, "Acting from Within: Inclusive Literature and the Power of Writing; A Conversation with Sasha Marianna Salzmann," chapter 1 in this volume.

literature in both constructing and challenging dominant ideas, captured in the metaphorical "boulder" of identity. This boulder may appear fixed and insurmountable, but it can in fact be broken down, albeit gradually, by authors who employ alternative narratives and aesthetic strategies as tools—"little hammers," as Salzmann puts it—to craft new formations. In this volume, we bring together scholars and contemporary authors to discuss whose writing is considered part of German literature, and how contemporary writing and writers in Germany contribute to and intervene in public discourses, often from marginalized perspectives that enable radical redefinitions and resignifications of identity, subjectivity, and community. Through their literary interventions, we contend, these minoritized authors write radical diversity into the dominant culture; they show the complexity of German identities by creating fluid, transgressive, and diverse representations of belonging and identity, counteracting essentialist ideas of Germanness and the uniformity of identity itself.

Literary explorations of Germany's radical diversity and creative expressions of solidarity and alliance-building have increased both in range and urgency in recent years, amid ever-louder appeals to regressive ideas of a homogenous German nation and European continent in the political domain. In 2019, Fatma Aydemir and Hengameh Yaghoobifarah published the first edition of their now seminal anthology of essays *Eure Heimat ist unser Albtraum*.[2] According to the editors, the immediate motivation for curating that collection was Minister of the Interior Horst Seehofer's renaming of his ministry as the Bundesministerium des Innern, für Bau und Heimat—often referred to informally as the "Heimatministerium"—in March 2018. In their foreword, Aydemir and Yaghoobifarah draw attention to the violent history and exclusionary connotations of the concept of "Heimat," which they argue were normalized with the rebranding of the ministry.[3] In the meantime, those connotations have been reconfirmed in the self-rebranding of the neo-Nazi Nationaldemokratische Partei Deutschlands as Die Heimat, which recently lost the financial support usually afforded to political parties by the state for a period six years because of its racist, antidemocratic

---

2   Fatma Aydemir and Hengameh Yaghoobifarah, eds., *Eure Heimat ist unser Albtraum* (Berlin: Ullstein fünf, 2019). The first edition has also appeared in English translation. See Fatma Aydemir, Jon Cho-Polizzi, Hengameh Yaghoobifarah, eds., *Your Homeland Is Our Nightmare: An Antifascist Essay Collection* (Berlin: Literarische Diverse Verlag, 2022). A new, extended edition of the German version appeared in February 2024.

3   Fatma Aydemir and Hengameh Yaghoobifarah, "Vorwort," in *Eure Heimat ist unser Albtraum*, ed. Fatma Aydemir and Hengameh Yaghoobifarah (Berlin: Ullstein fünf, 2019), 9–10.

ideology.[4] In January 2024, investigative journalists in the nonprofit organization "Correctiv" revealed that members of the Far Right party Alternative für Deutschland (AfD)—which has been gaining traction and votes since its foundation in 2013—had attended a meeting in November 2023, together with "neo-Nazis and other extremists," to discuss plans for "the mass deportation of migrants, asylum seekers and German citizens of foreign origin deemed to have failed to integrate."[5] These extremist plans have provoked widespread outrage and mass protests against right-wing politics across the Federal Republic, with more than one hundred thousand participants in Munich, Hamburg, and Berlin; there were also protests in smaller cities where approval rates for the AfD are high.[6] However, an ongoing political and discursive shift to the Right is also evident in the policies of the seemingly moderate and liberal parties, epitomized in a much-discussed cover of the current affairs journal *Der Spiegel* featuring an image of Chancellor Olaf Scholz with the heading, a quotation from Scholz, "Wir müssen endlich im großen Stil abschieben" (We finally need to deport on a large scale).[7] At the same time, newly founded parties are entering the political field, including the so-called "WerteUnion," formerly associated with the Christian Democrats (CDU/CSU), which has formed around Hans-Georg Maaßen, the ex-head of the Federal Office for the Protection of the Constitution,[8] as well as the "Bündnis Sahra Wagenknecht," which positions itself as "left-right,"[9] advocating for restrictive migration politics and rapprochement with Russia.

4   "Die Partei Die Heimat (vormals NPD) ist für die Dauer von sechs Jahren von der staatlichen Parteienfinanzierung ausgeschlossen," Pressemitteilung Nr. 9/2024, January 23, 2024, https://www.bundesverfassungsgericht.de/SharedDocs/Pressemitteilungen/DE/2024/bvg24-009.html.
5   Kate Connolly, "Turmoil in Germany over neo-Nazi mass deportation meeting—explained," *Guardian*, January 19, 2024, https://www.theguardian.com/world/2024/jan/19/turmoil-in-germany-over-neo-nazi-mass-deportation-meeting-explained.
6   "Bundesweit neue Demos gegen Rechtsextremismus," tagesschau.de, February 4, 2024, https://www.tagesschau.de/inland/gesellschaft/demos-gegen-rechtsextremismus-106.html.
7   Christoph Hickmann and Dirk Kurbjuweit, "Olaf Scholz: Neue Härte in Der Flüchtlingspolitik: 'Wir müssen endlich im großen Stil abschieben.'" *Der Spiegel*, October 20, 2023, https://www.spiegel.de/politik/deutschland/olaf-scholz-ueber-migration-es-kommen-zu-viele-a-2d86d2ac-e55a-4b8f-9766-c7060c2dc38a.
8   "Verein um Maaßen: WerteUnion als Partei gegründet," tagesschau.de, February 17, 2024, https://www.tagesschau.de/inland/werteunion-partei-maassen-100.html.
9   "Bündnis Sahra Wagenknecht: Hier links, da rechts," Deutschlandfunk, January 27, 2024. https://www.deutschlandfunk.de/wagenknecht-partei-buendnis-gruendung-100.html#:~:text=B.

What might appear as the worrying reemergence of regressive rhetoric and policies for some is experienced by others as the continuation and intensification of long-standing phenomena. When the public sphere is steeped in discursive violence, moreover, acts of physical violence are never far away. As Maha El Hissy has shown, numerous recent literary works and critical collections respond directly to deadly attacks such as the racist murders carried out by the *Nationalsozialistischer Untergrund* in the 2000s, as well as the attacks in Halle in 2019 and Hanau in February 2020, highlight continuities in right-wing violence perpetrated across Germany since at least the 1990s.[10] "Wenn Hanau eine Zäsur war," the writer Shida Bazyar pointedly asks, "was war denn Halle? Was war Mölln, was Solingen? Was waren Nürnberg, München, Hamburg, Rostock, Dortmund, Kassel, Heilbronn, Köln, was war Dessau?" (If Hanau was a caesura, what was Halle? What was Mölln, what about Solingen? What were Nuremberg, Munich, Hamburg, Rostock, Dortmund, Heilbronn, Cologne, what was Dessau?)[11] In her foreword to the anthology of letters *anders bleiben: Briefe der Hoffnung in verhärteten Zeiten*, Selma Wels looks further back at Germany's violent past and acknowledges clear differences between the systematic killing under Nazism and the seemingly arbitrary attacks that take place in democratic Germany. "Aber dennoch müssen wir uns bewusst werden," Wels continues, "dass wir nach 86 Jahren wieder an einem Punkt in der Geschichte stehen, an dem Menschen in Deutschland um ihr Leben fürchten müssen, weil sie anderen nicht 'deutsch' genug erscheinen" (But we nonetheless have to be honest with ourselves that after eighty-six years we have once again reached a point where people in Germany have to fear for their lives because they do not appear "German" enough in the eyes of others).[12]

In addition to drawing attention to long-term continuities in right-wing violence, minoritized writers and editors often find themselves compelled to underscore discrepancies between the lasting effects that such violent attacks have on marginalized communities and the failure of

---

10 Maha El Hissy, "Literarisches Schreiben post Hanau," *Internationales Archiv für Sozialgeschichte der deutschen Literatur* 4, no. 2 (2023): 398–416, esp. 405–9. In addition to her own analysis of Bazyar's *Drei Kameradinnen*, El Hissy mentions as examples Dardan's *Betrachtungen einer Barbarin* (2021), Sanyal's *Identitti* (2021), Aydemir's *Dschinns* (2022), Lena Gorelik's *Wer wir sind* (2022), and Emine Sevgi Özdamar's *Ein Schatten von begrenzter Raum* (2021).

11 Shida Bazyar, "Ein Moment der Schwere," contribution to "Zwei Jahre nach Hanau: Nicht nur erinnern, sondern handeln!" *Berliner Zeitung*, February 2, 2022, https://www.berliner-zeitung.de/wochenende/wie-sollten-wir-der-anschlaege-von-hanau-gedenken-li.211975. See also El Hissy, "Literarisches Schreiben post Hanau," 407.

12 Selma Wels, "Vorwort," in *anders bleiben: Briefe der Hoffnung in verhärteten Zeiten*, ed. Selma Wels (Hamburg: Rowohlt, 2023), 10.

dominantly positioned actors to confront the implications of those acts of violence directly. As Marina Chernivsky and Hannah Peaceman state in their opening editorial of a recent edition of the Jewish journal *Jalta: Positionen zur jüdischen Gegenwart*, poignantly titled "Nachhalle"—a wordplay that can mean both "Echoes" and "After Halle":

> Botschaftstaten, die sich gezielt gegen Menschen und Gruppen richten, haben ein verheerendes traumatisches Potenzial. Sie teilen die Zeit in davor und danach und wirken lange weiter. Erfahrungen, die damit verbunden sind, schichten sich übereinander und ritzen sich ins Gedächtnis von Minderheiten ein. . . . Die sie umgebende Gesellschaft leistet sich demgegenüber die Distanz.
> . . . Denn seit Jahrzehnten zeigt sich in Deutschland die kollektive Unfähigkeit, die historische und gesellschaftliche Kontinuität rechter Ideologien anzuerkennen und dagegen zu handeln. Stattdessen prägen die Historisierung und Entpolitisierung rechter Gewaltgeschichte, . . . sowie das Beharren auf der These der "Einzeltaten" den gesellschaftspolitischen Umgang mit Gewaltphänomenen und verdecken ihre Relevanz für die Gegenwartsgesellschaft.[13]

> [Acts carrying messages that are specifically directed against people and groups have a devastating traumatic potential. They divide time into a before and an after and have long-lasting continuing effects. Experiences associated with them form layers upon layers and carve themselves into the memory of minorities . . . The surrounding society, in contrast, affords itself distance.
> . . . For decades, Germany has shown a collective inability to acknowledge the historical and social continuity of right-wing ideologies and act against them. Instead, the sociopolitical treatment of violent phenomena is characterized by historicization and depoliticization of the history of right-wing violence, . . . as well as the insistence on the theory of "individual acts," masking their relevance in contemporary society.]

The creative literary interventions explored in the present volume expose and push back against the kinds of societal tendencies described here: firstly, the tendency to overlook structural discrimination and the conditions that enable acts of symbolic and physical violence; second, to then downplay collective responsibility when such things occur and, moreover, reoccur. If the presence of increasingly diverse literary actors is seen by

---

13 Marina Chernivsky and Hannah Peaceman, "Nachhalle," thematic issue of *Jalta: Positionen zur jüdischen Gegenwart* 8 (2023): 4–5.

some as an "attack on Germany,"[14] as Sasha Marianna Salzmann suggests in the opening epigraph, the literary assertion of the kinds of radically diverse subjectivities and solidarities presented in our book can also be understood as artistic "Gegenstrategien" (counterstrategies)[15] developed in response to real dangers and to disrupt the complicitous "Tradition des Wegschauens" (tradition of looking away).[16]

This volume focuses on literary interventions in the German context since 2018. As many of our contributions show, however, discussions and renegotiations of German identity are deeply entwined with wider transnational developments and take shape against the backdrop of a political landscape that is constantly and rapidly shifting, often in quite dramatic ways. Since we began working on this book, the already fraught discourse on German identity and purportedly German values has become still more fractious in the wake of ongoing global events such as the Russian invasion of Ukraine in February 2022, the eruption of popular protests in Iran later that year and—most recently, at the time of writing—Hamas's attack on Israel on October 7, 2023, and the subsequent war in Gaza. The latter is a case in point: although the immediate events have taken place elsewhere, their effects have divided time into "davor und danach" (before and after), to borrow from Chernivsky and Peaceman, for minoritized groups in Germany. On the one hand, they have been retraumatizing for many German Jews and have led to a sharp rise in antisemitic violence (in Germany as elsewhere): in just over one hundred days following October 7, more than two thousand antisemitic hate crimes were recorded by the Bundeskriminalamt.[17] On the other hand, they have fueled anti-Muslim and anti-Arab racism, renewed blanket accusations of antisemitism against migrant groups, and exposed the lack of room for Palestinian voices in the German public sphere.[18] Writing in early January 2024 about the

---

14   Salzmann in Rezgui and Sturtz, "Acting from Within."
15   Chernivsky and Peacemann, "Nachhalle," 4.
16   Wels, "Vorwort," 11.
17   "So stark ist die Zahl antisemitischer Straftaten seit dem 7. Oktober gestiegen," *Der Spiegel*, January 25, 2024, https://www.spiegel.de/politik/deutschland/antisemitismus-so-stark-sind-antisemitische-straftaten-seit-dem-7-oktober-angestiegen-a-f104451d-992f-4592-8fe9-f08133854c98.
18   Claudia Mende, interview with Esra Özyürek, "Wir müssen Antisemitismus und Islamfeindlichkeit gemeinsam bekämpfen," *qantara.de*, November 21, 2023, https://qantara.de/artikel/esra-%C3%B6zy%C3%BCrek-%C3%BCber-die-deutsche-debatte-wir-m%C3%BCssen-antisemitismus-und-islamfeindlichkeit; Esra Özyürek, *Subcontractors of Guilt: Holocaust Memory and Muslim Belonging in Postwar Germany* (Stanford, CA: Stanford University Press, 2023); Sarah El Bulbeisi, "Über den Schmerz des Verschweigens. Palästinenser:innen in Deutschland und in der Schweiz," geschichte der gegenwart, September 17, 2023, https://geschichtedergegenwart.ch/

fallout of October 7 in Germany, Sasha Marianna Salzmann commented on the violent atmosphere and existential threats faced by marginalized groups who are hesitant or unable to speak out: "Man möchte nicht—schon wieder—die Minderheit mit dem Problem sein. Und wenn es uns, Jüdinnen und Juden, so geht, frage ich mich, wie es um die anderen Minderheiten in Deutschland bestellt ist. Jene Minderheiten, für die sich keine prominenten Fürsprecherinnen und Fürsprecher vor der Kamera starkmachen." (You don't want to be the minority with the problem—again. And if things are like that for us Jews, I wonder what the situation is like for the other minorities in Germany. Those minorities who don't have prominent advocates to stand up for them in front of the camera.)[19] Salzmann also points to the tendency of leading German politicians to sort individual communities into seemingly clear positions—"bedrohte Arten, Aggressoren und die zu Vernachlässigenden" (threatened species, aggressors, and neglectables)—and to determine political discourse in a manner that not only overlooks but actively diverts attention away from the complicity of representatives of dominant German society: "Im Zuge dieser Sortierung," Salzmann continues, "entsteht perfideweise der Eindruck, Antisemitismus ließe sich in andere Länder abschieben. Wie viele Deutsche müssten dann gehen?" (In the course of this sorting, the perfidious impression arises that antisemitism can be exported to other countries. How many Germans would then have to leave?)[20]

In refocusing on Germany's responsibility to protect all minorities, Salzmann signals a reaffirmation of the kinds of alliances and solidarities explored in this volume, which are in any case fragile and fraught,[21] but which have been placed under more severe pressure than ever by this most recent conflict in the Middle East. A similar kind of cautious regrouping was evident at an event titled "Zerreißproben. Schreiben, Gewalt, Gesellschaft" (Crucial Tests: Writing, Violence, Society) in the Literarisches Colloquium Berlin (LCB), which sought to create space for four authors with diverse backgrounds and perspectives—Dana Vowinckel, Sandra Hetzl, Tomer Dotan-Dreyfus, and Mohamed Amjahid[22]—to

---

ueber-den-schmerz-des-verschweigens-palaestinenserinnen-in-deutschland-und-in-der-schweiz/.

19   Sasha Marianna Salzmann, "An der Formel stimmt etwas nicht," *Süddeutsche Zeitung*, January 4, 2024, http://www.sz.de/1.6327884.

20   Salzmann, "An der Formel stimmt etwas nicht."

21   Deniz Utlu, "Sensitive Solidarities: Notes on the Fragility of Alliances," in *A Congress on Contemporary Jewish Positions, 6–8 May 2016, Maxim Gorki Theatre, Studio Я*, ed. Max Czollek and Sasha Marianna Salzmann (Bielefeld: Kerber, 2017), 73–84.

22   Vowinkel is a German Jewish novelist (*Gewässer im Ziplock* [Frankfurt am Main: Suhrkamp, 2023]); Hetzl is a writer and translator from Arabic into German (editor of the volume *In der Zukunft schwelgen* [Bielefeld: transcript, 2022]);

discuss the impact of the war between Israel and Hamas on their writing.[23] The event can also be seen as an attempt to accommodate some of the radically diverse positions that exist within groups often assumed to be homogenous by mainstream society, not least the Jewish community in Germany, which is divided in opinion on many matters, including Israel and Palestine. The literary interventions explored in this volume predate these latest discussions; however, the polarization of German and international public discourse underscores the timeliness of our ongoing conversations about radical diversity and the political potential of literary and cultural production. To paraphrase a German radio commentary on the aforementioned evening in the LCB: "Am Ende [bleibt] die Zuversicht, dass die Literatur der aufgeheizten Debatte differenzierte Perspektiven entgegensetzen kann." (In the end, we remain confident that literature can counter heated debate by offering differentiated perspectives.)[24]

Radical Diversity and Dominant Culture

The idea of radical diversity has gained increasing currency in German cultural discourse since 2016 through the work of writers and artists associated with the Jewish journal *Jalta* and the Maxim Gorki Theater in Berlin; it has also subsequently gained traction in scholarly research on contemporary German culture. Maria Roca Lizarazu and Moritz Schramm both explain the close relationship between radical diversity and the programmatic notion of "Desintegration" developed and popularized by the poet and publicist Max Czollek in cooperation with Salzmann and others. As Roca Lizarazu argues, radical diversity "entails not only the recognition of the existing complexity and diversity of Jewish and other minority identities, but a more general acknowledgement of the fact that we all are composed of multiple and shifting aspects and attachments and that we all simultaneously belong and do not belong."[25] Building on this, Schramm similarly notes that "the critical practice of de-integration

---

Dotan-Dreyfus is a German-Israeli novelist and translator (*Birobidschan* [Berlin: Voland & Quist, 2023]); and Mohamad Amjahid is a German-Moroccan Journalist and author (*Der weiße Fleck* [Munich: Piper, 2021]; *Let's talk about Sex, Habibi* [Munich: Piper, 2022]).

23   "Zerreißproben. Schreiben, Gewalt, Gesellschaft," January 17, 2024, https://lcb.de/programm/zerreissproben/.

24   Cornelius Wüllenkemper, "Ein Berliner Diskussionsabend über Nah-Ost-Polarisierung in der Literatur," Deutschlandfunk, January 18, 2024, https://www.deutschlandfunk.de/ein-berliner-diskussionsabend-ueber-nah-ost-polarisierung-in-der-literatur-dlf-68cad2d7-100.html.

25   Maria Roca Lizarazu, "'Integration ist definitiv nicht unser Anliegen, eher schon Desintegration.' Postmigrant Renegotiations of Identity and Belonging in Contemporary Germany," *humanities* 9, no. 42 (2020): 5.

can be read as an attempt to reject and reshuffle predefined roles and positions and thus, by doing so, open up a broader diversity of subject positionings, which are not restricted to essentialized or culturalized identity groups."[26] At the same time, the program of "deintegration" is by no means a call for disintegration into hyperindividualism but promotes the establishment of new "Allianzen" (alliances) based on radical diversity: "In contrast to homogenous 'in-'/'out'-groups, the alliance implies a spontaneous, ephemeral, and diverse mix. It is furthermore a coalition based on shared interests and a common purpose, rather than a shared essence, in the form of, for example, ethnicity."[27] Deintegration is about "how society itself can come to be recognized as a *place of radical diversity*"[28] with a view to establishing "new forms of 'being-allied' based on political friendship rather than commonly shared origins or experiences."[29] Far from re-essentializing marginalized subjects as automatically virtuous or subversive and disruptive of all dominant power relations, Schramm emphasizes, moreover, that radical diversity must always comprise "an element of self-critical reflection on one's own possible or real involvement in discriminating structures and actions—regardless of one's own background, heritage or origin."[30]

In the German context, the alliances at the heart of radical diversity and deintegration are conceived of in opposition to the notion of *Leitkultur*, the prescriptive and homogenizing ideal of a national culture in which there is little or no diversity of sexuality, religion, gender, or other identity categories that are conspicuous in their noncompliance to a white, male, heterosexual, Christian norm. This projected idea of Germanness demands the assimilation or integration of minoritized groups according to "soziale Gewohnheiten" (social customs),[31] which the defenders of Leitkultur imagine to be traditionally and quintessentially German. Calls

---

26   Moritz Schramm, "Postmigrant Perspectives: Radical Diversity as Artistic-Political Intervention," *Crossings* 14, no. 1 (2023): 93.
27   Roca Lizarazu, "Integration Ist Definitiv Nicht Unser Anliegen," 5–6. See also Max Czollek and Sasha Marianna Salzmann, eds., *Desintegration: Ein Kongress Zeitgenössischer Jüdischer Positionen* (Bielefeld: Kerber Verlag, 2017); Micha Brumlik, Marina Chernivsky, Max Czollek and Hannah Peaceman, Anna Schapiro, and Lea Wohl von Haselberg, "Desintegration," thematic issue of *Jalta: Positionen zur jüdischen Gegenwart* 2 (2017); Micha Brumlik et al., "Allianzen," thematic issue of *Jalta: Positionen zur jüdischen Gegenwart* 1 (2018); Max Czollek, *Desintegriert Euch!* (Munich: Carl Hanser Verlag, 2018).
28   Czollek, as quoted in Schramm, "Postmigrant Perspectives," 94.
29   Schramm, "Postmigrant Perspectives," 97.
30   Schramm, "Postmigrant Perspectives," 96.
31   Thomas de Maizière, "'Wir sind nicht Burka': Innenminister will deutsche Leitkultur," ZEIT ONLINE, April 30, 2017, https://www.zeit.de/politik/deutschland/2017-04/thomas-demaiziere-innenminister-leitkultur.

for the reinvigoration of this supposed Leitkultur have sparked considerable public debate over recent decades and are frequently revived, most recently (at the time of writing) in the revised political program of the CDU, which states: "Alle, die hier leben wollen, müssen unsere Leitkultur ohne Wenn und Aber anerkennen . . . Nur wer sich zu unserer Leitkultur bekennt, kann sich integrieren und deutscher Staatsbürger werden." (All those who want to live here should recognize our Leitkultur without ifs and buts . . . Only those who are committed to our Leitkultur can integrate and become German citizens.)[32]

The dynamic of increasing exclusion and doubling down on ethnic homogeneity and "traditional" values as markers of national identity are by no means unique to Germany. In her book *European Others*, the historian Fatima El-Tayeb posits that Europe as a whole seeks to exclude the (nonwhite, migrant) Other, and is "arguably invested in 'whiteness' as the norm against which ethnicization is read as a tool of differentiation between insiders and outsiders."[33] El-Tayeb draws on the French philosopher Etiénne Balibar, who describes the "'fictive ethnicity' on which all nation-states are built" and which is "constructed via two primary tools, language and race."[34] In her 2016 study *Undeutsch*, El-Tayeb specifically emphasizes the interplay between national and transnational issues, situating developments in Germany within wider trends in Western Europe since the start of the twenty-first century. It is not only in Germany that a desire for cultural and ethnic uniformity has been consolidated in response to global developments that lie outside the control of the standardized center, such as terror attacks, perceived Muslim antisemitism, and increased migration into Europe.[35] The German context is intimately intertwined with the Eurocentrism of the West in general. Writing shortly after the start of the so-called "Flüchtlingskrise" (refugee crisis), as it was termed in much of German press, El-Tayeb describes worrying trends repeated across Western Europe, citing increasing political

---

32 Katharina James, "CDU: Friedrich Merz 'Dankbar' Für Leitkultur Im CDU-Programmentwurf," *Die Zeit*, February 28, 2024. https://www.zeit.de/politik/deutschland/2024-02/friedrich-merz-bedeutung-leitkultur-cdu-grundsatzprogramm; See also Ozan Zakariya Keskinkılıç, "Wem gehört die 'Leitkultur'? Islamdebatten und Almanyas verborgene Erinnerungen," in *Erinnerungskämpfe: Neues deutsches Geschichtsbewusstsein*, ed. Jürgen Zimmerer (Leipzig: Reclam, 2023).

33 Fatima El-Tayeb, *European Others: Queering Ethnicity in Postnational Europe* (Minneapolis: University of Minnesota Press, 2011), xiv.

34 El-Tayeb, *European Others*, xiii. See also: Etiénne Balibar and Emmanuel Wallerstein, *Race, Nation, Class: Ambiguous Identities* (London: Verso, 1991), 224.

35 Fatima El-Tayeb, *Undeutsch: Die Konstruktion des Anderen in der postmigrantischen Gesellschaft* (Bielefeld: transcript, 2016), 11, 17, 206.

concessions made to nationalist and far-right movements and ever-more restrictive asylum and integration laws: "kurz, Europa scheint sich wieder einmal erfolgreich gegen ein chaotisches Außen abgeschirmt zu haben"[36] (in short, Europe once again seems to have successfully shielded itself from a chaotic outside). This supposed crisis is seen as being produced elsewhere and brought into Europe by racialized and migrantized populations. El-Tayeb identifies Western Europe as a hostile environment, which insists on itself as a progressive, civilized center; voices critical of this narrative of progress are projected outside Europe, reproducing long-standing binaries between "the West and the Rest."[37]

In this context, radical diversity allows for a rewriting of already fictive ethnicities and enables resistance to rigid conditions of inclusion/exclusion in the (German) nation or (European) culture. As Schramm shows, the notion of radical diversity has become inseparable from the practice of "artistic-political intervention," which directly challenges the ideas and narratives underpinning the kind of fictive ethnicity encapsulated in the imagined German Leitkultur by shifting focus onto and, crucially, enacting "interrelations and alliances between different minoritized persons."[38] Following on from the "Desintegrationskongress" organized by Czollek and Salzmann in 2016,[39] for example, the Gorki collective initiated the "Tage der jüdisch-muslimischen Leitkultur" (Days of Jewish-Muslim Leitkultur), a series of events that took place from October 3 to November 9, 2020, which was stylized as the beginning of a new social imaginary underpinned by "Radikale Vielfalt und Gegenwartsbewältigung" (radical diversity and coming to terms with the present) in place of "deutsche Leitkultur und Integration" (prescriptive German culture and integration).[40] Under the banner of a Jewish-Muslim alliance, the organizers described their initiative as an "Intervention in die deutsche Dominanzkultur" (intervention in the German dominant culture), situating their artistic initiative in the academic field of critical

---

36   El-Tayeb, *Undeutsch*, 208.
37   El-Tayeb, *Undeutsch*, 208. See also Stuart Hall, "The West and the Rest: Discourse and Power [1992]," in *Stuart Hall, Essential Essays, Volume 2: Identity and Diaspora*, ed. David Morley (Durham, NC: Duke University Press, 2018), 141–84.
38   Schramm, "Postmigrant Perspectives," 98.
39   "Themenseite Festival Desintegration: Ein Kongress zeitgenössischer jüdischer Positionen kuratiert von Max Czollek und Sasha Marianna Salzmann," accessed June 14, 2023, https://www.gorki.de/de/themenseite-festival-desintegration. A book based on the congress was also published by Kerber Verlag the following year.
40   Tage der jüdisch-muslimischen Leitkultur, accessed April 6, 2024, https://www.gorki.de/de/tdjml. See also Schramm, "Postmigrant Perspectives," 95.

diversity studies. The concept of "Dominanzkultur" was introduced and developed in the German context by Birgit Rommelspacher and other social scientists at the Alice Salomon Hochschule Berlin.[41] It describes the idea "daß unsere ganze Lebensweise, unsere Selbstinterpretation sowie die Bilder, die wir vom Anderen entwerfen, in Kategorien der Über- und Unterordnung gefaßt sind" (that our entire way of living, our self-understanding, and the images we conjure of Others are all contained in categories of domination and subordination).[42] Drawing on both Rommelspacher and Czollek, Miriam Schwarz points out that the idea of *Leitkultur* is indeed better understood as *Dominanzkultur*: "rather than a majority, it in fact represents the sum of dominant ideas and practices."[43] Moreover, as a multidimensional web of reciprocal power relations, the dominant culture is characterized by its all-pervasiveness and therefore relative invisibility. Creative interventions like the "Tage der jüdisch-muslimischen Leitkultur" simultaneously expose this unquestioned omnipresence—for instance, by reappropriating the historically laden dates of October 3 and November 9 and satirically reimagining iconic sites of power in Berlin[44]—and give visibility and voice to alternative identities and alliances. In doing this, they open the way for a reappraisal of dominant conceptions and narratives of Germanness.

41 Birgit Rommelspacher, *Dominanzkultur: Texte zu Fremdheit und Macht* (Berlin: Orlanda-Frauenverlag, 1995); Iman Attia, Swantje Köbsell, and Nivedita Prasad, eds., *Dominanzkultur reloaded: Neue Texte zu gesellschaftlichen Machtverhältnissen und ihren Wechselwirkungen* (Bielefeld: transcript, 2015).

42 Rommelspacher, *Dominanzkultur*, 21. This is also related to Gramsci's concept of hegemony on which Hall builds in his work. See Stuart Hall, "Domination and Hegemony," in *Cultural Studies 1983: A Theoretical History*, ed. Jennifer Daryl Slack and Lawrence Grossberg (Durham, NC: Duke University Press, 2016), 169–71.

43 Miriam Schwarz, "Relational Epistemologies: Friendship and Reading in Shida Bazyar's *Drei Kameradinnen*," *Forum for Modern Language Studies* 60, no. 2 (2024): 219–38.

44 Max Czollek (@rubenmcloop), "Die Tage der Jüdisch-Muslimischen Leitkultur beginnen heute mit einem Paukenschlag: dem History Special der @jewsnews_today (link unten). Ihr könnt die jüdisch-muslimische Leitkultur supporten, indem ihr dieses original Archivfoto teilt. Und eure eigenen Erfahrungen unter #tdjml," Twitter, September 26, 2020, 8:21 a.m., https://twitter.com/rubenmcloop/status/1309845575517581320; jewsnewstoday, "Jews News Today History Special," September 26, 2020, YouTube video, 5:58, https://www.youtube.com/watch?v=41R_X9ZjHRA&t=23s.

On Visibility, Audibility, and Resonances

This collection expands on the notions and practices of radical diversity explored above. It grew out of a conference titled Sichtbarkeit*en* organized by Laura Marie Sturtz and Selma Rezgui at the University of Oxford in July 2021,[45] which took Salzmann's essay "Sichtbar" (Visible) as a cue to discuss tensions between the visibility and invisibility of marginalized identities in contemporary German literature and culture. Salzmann's much-cited essay reflects on the conspicuousness, indeed hypervisibility, of being a queer, nonbinary, Jewish person and, at the same time, the lack of representation and recognition of such identity categories in a German society where those things fall outside the omnipresent (because unmarked and therefore invisible) social norm.[46] The strategic addition and italicization of the plural ending -*en* in the conference title highlights multiple (in)visibilities, which permeate creative and theoretical writing on experiences of marginalization and which we interrogate further throughout this book. In their study of Jewish identity and antisemitism in the context of what they call "Gojnormativität" (Goy normativity), Judith Coffey and Vivien Laumann expand on critical whiteness theory to explain that invisibility can sometimes be seen as an ambivalent privilege for some minoritized groups—for example, Jews who are read as white, or queer people who might hide their queerness—because it can lessen the potential for "Anfeindungen und Übergriffen" (hostilities and attacks).[47] On the other hand, forms of involuntary invisibility imposed by the norms of hegemonic groups result in the suppression of minoritized identities and experiences, which in turn makes the quest for greater visibility a question of empowerment—"ein selbstbewusstes und selbstbestimmtes Nach-Außen-Treten" (a confident and self-assertive stepping-out).[48] Highlighting further intersecting dimensions of (in)visibility, joseph kebe-nguema's recent study of Sharon Dodua Otoo's novella *Synchronicity* draws on DisCrit (an approach that blends disability studies and critical race theory) to

---

45 The conference included a keynote lecture by Sarah Colvin, six papers by students from across Europe and the United States, and a reading by Fatma Aydemir. See St. Hilda's College, Oxford University, accessed June 28, 2023, https://www.st-hildas.ox.ac.uk/content/sichtbarkeiten-conference.

46 Sasha Marianna Salzmann, "Sichtbar," in *Eure Heimat ist unser Albtraum* ed. Fatma Aydemir and Hengameh Yaghoobifarah (Berlin: Ullstein fünf, 2019), 13; see also Judith Coffey and Vivien Laumann, *Gojnormativität: Warum wir anders über Antisemitismus sprechen müssen* (Berlin: Verbrecher Verlag, 2021), 98–99.

47 Judith Coffey and Vivien Laumann, *Gojnormativität*, 95. See their chapter "Sichtbarkeiten und Unsichtbarkeiten von Juden_Jüdinnen," 95–114.

48 Coffey and Laumann, *Gojnormativität*, 95.

underscore that "Blackness is socially both extremely visible and invisible" in the German context: "on the one hand, [it] has been associated with Otherness and constructed as the antithesis of Germanness since at least the Third Reich; on the other hand, the existence of Black people on German soil . . . was barely acknowledged until extremely recently."[49] This "double problem of perception," as kebe-nguema puts it, "contributes simultaneously to the homogenisation of Blackness and the erasure of Black people with [visible or nonvisible] dis/abilities."[50] Through the depiction of her Black female protagonist's experience of a temporary nonvisible impairment, Otoo's novella—in a manner similar to the literary interventions featured in our book—engages thematically, formally, and aesthetically with such dominant perceptions and processes of exclusion, homogenization, and erasure, both in order to make them more transparent and to counteract them.

The question of visibility is inseparable from, and in some cases even superseded by, the question of audibility. The literary author and cultural scholar Mithu Sanyal sums this up in the final interview featured in this book:

> I don't really use the word visibility as much as "becoming a voice." To me it's more about being audible, being listened to. I always felt visible in a way. You can't do anything against that, but in the past, I couldn't speak with my own voice and had others speak about me. Of course, this dynamic also fueled my literature.[51]

What Sanyal describes here is a form of structural silencing and epistemic violence similar to that highlighted by postcolonial theorist Gayatri Chakravorty Spivak when she asked "Can the Subaltern Speak?"[52] In her exploration of postcolonial approaches in the German context, Hito Steyerl—another artist whose work traverses the theoretical—has pointed out that it is not enough to ask "Can the subaltern speak?" or "Can the subaltern speak German?" but rather, "even if he or she has been talking

---

49 joseph kebe-nguema, "Blackness and Dis/ability in the Afrofuturist Christmas Novella *Synchronicity* (2015) by Sharon Dodua Otoo," *German Life and Letters* 77, no. 1 (2024): 37.

50 kebe-nguema, "Blackness and Dis/ability," 36–37.

51 Mithu Sanyal in Leila Essa, "Seen as friendly, seen as frightening? A Conversation on Visibilities, Kinship, and Finding the Right Words with Mithu Sanyal," chapter 10 in this volume.

52 Gayatri Chakravorty Spivak, "Can the Subaltern Speak?" in *Marxism and the Interpretation of Culture*, ed. Cary Nelson and Lawrence Grossberg (Urbana: University of Illinois Press, 1988), 271–313.

on for centuries—why didn't anybody listen?"[53] Not listening, silencing, and/or speaking on someone else's behalf are practices—or dysfunctions—that uphold what the philosopher José Medina calls "epistemologies of ignorance" (drawing on Charles W. Mills and other philosophers of race). Racial oppression, for example, conceals the experiences and meanings of racialized subjects, making them "invisible, inaudible, or simply unintelligible in certain locations and for certain perspectives that protect themselves from facing their involvement in racial oppression with a shield of *active* ignorance."[54] The dominant "white epistemology of ignorance"[55] that underpins structural racism arguably correlates with the invisible omnipresence of the *Dominanzkultur* discussed in the section above. According to Medina, the "epistemic dysfunctions that are constitutive of racial ignorance … produce the phenomenon of *epistemic hiding*—that is, of making subjects and their experiences and perspectives invisible and inaudible, or visible and audible only precariously and in a distorted way."[56] The imperative to talk *with* rather than simply *about* contemporary German authors—to enable them to speak in their own voices and words with academic interlocutors—is a key motivation behind our inclusion of conversations with Aukongo, Dündar, Sanyal, and Salzmann, alongside the more conventional scholarly chapters in this volume.

To make themselves heard and to make others listen, contemporary writers representing marginalized communities are increasingly claiming space in the public domain by staging events that enact a kind of interventionist praxis. The "Tage der jüdisch-muslimischen Leitkultur" discussed in the previous section is a good example of this. Another more recent intervention is the Black literary festival, Resonanzen, curated by Sharon Dodua Otoo as part of the annual Ruhrfestspielen at Recklinghausen for the first time in 2022.[57] This has been followed by second and third iterations in 2023 and 2024, for which Otoo has been joined as cocurator by

---

53 Hito Steyerl, "Can the Subaltern speak German? Postkoloniale Kritik," *transversal texts*, accessed January 28, 2024, https://transversal.at/transversal/0902/steyerl/de.

54 José Medina, "Epistemic Injustice and Epistemologies of Resistance," in *The Routledge Companion to the Philosophy of Race*, ed. Paul Taylor, Linda Alcoff, and Luvell Anderson (New York: Routledge, 2017), 248. Emphasis in original.

55 Charles W. Mills, "White Ignorance," in *Race and Epistemologies of Ignorance*, ed. Shannon Sullivan and Nancy Tuana (Albany: State University of New York Press, 2007), 35.

56 Medina, "Epistemic Injustice and Epistemologies of Resistance," 249.

57 "Resonanzen–Schwarzes Literaturfestival," accessed March 10, 2024, https://www.ruhrfestspiele.de/programm/2022/resonanzen-schwarzes-literaturfestival-2.

the screenwriter and novelist Patricia Eckermann.[58] The conception and organization of this event as "ein Festival im Festival" (a festival within the festival)[59] points to the incursion of hitherto marginalized actors into established cultural spaces in order to change the structural composition of such events from within. The introduction to the documentation of the first *Resonanzen* festival, cowritten by Otoo and literary scholar Jeannette Oholi, is pointedly titled "Interventionen und Institutionen—Auf der Suche nach Resonanz" (Interventions and Institutions—In Search of Resonance). In it, Otoo and Oholi explain that Black people are often denied resonance in white-dominated spaces and that this also applies to the reception of Black German literature and Black German studies; despite the formation of long-standing literary, as well as scholarly, traditions, these are overlooked, misrepresented, or erased altogether in the German context.[60] One of the overarching aims of the Resonanzen festival was and is to counteract that erasure by highlighting the rich traditions and heterogeneity of Black literatures and identities in the past, the present, and the future, emphasizing how Black German authors "schreiben aus vielfältigen Perspektiven und lassen sich nicht allein auf ein deutsches *oder* afrikanisches Erbe festschreiben. Vielmehr positionieren sie sich selbst" (Black authors write from diverse perspectives and don't allow themselves to be pinned down to either a German or an African heritage. Rather, they position themselves as themselves).[61]

Elsewhere, Otoo has described the festival as a space where multiple connected themes and voices of Black literature harmonize with each other. Importantly, the festival name originated in the realm of grassroots activism. Otoo acknowledges Katja Kinder—a founding member of the Black feminist group ADEFRA[62]—as inspiration, who speaks of the need for "Resonanzräume" (resonance chambers) and stresses that is

---

58 "Resonanzen–Schwarze Literatur und Lesearten," accessed March 10, 2024, https://www.ruhrfestspiele.de/programm/2023/resonanzen-schwarze-literatur-und-lesarten; "Resonanzen–Schwarzes Internationales Literaturfestival," accessed March 10, 2024, https://www.ruhrfestspiele.de/programm/2024/resonanzen-schwarzes-internationales-literaturfestival. Eckermann had already been involved at the inaugural festival in 2022 as a PR consultant.

59 "Resonanzen–Schwarzes Literaturfestival," accesssed March 10, 2024, https://www.ruhrfestspiele.de/programm/2022/resonanzen-schwarzes-literaturfestival-2.

60 Otoo and Oholi, "Interventionen und Institutionen," 6–10.

61 Sharon Dodua Otoo and Jeannette Oholi, "Interventionen und Institutionen. Auf der Suche nach Resonanz," in *Resonanzen: Schwarzes Literaturfestival—Eine Dokumentation* (Leipzig: Spector Books, 2022), 10.

62 For a detailed account of ADEFRA's formation and activism, see Tiffany Florvil, *Mobilizing Black Germany: Afro-German Women and the Makings of a Transnational Movement* (Urbana: University of Illinois Press, 2020), 77–104.

not enough "dass ein Schwarzes Gesicht irgendwo sitzt und dann ist die Diversität des Raumes gewährleistet, sondern dass es darum geht, dass das was wir beizugetragen haben, wirklich Resonanz findet" (for a Black face to be present in the room in order to guarantee its diversity, but rather the goal has to be that our contributions find real resonance).[63] In the context of this volume, the idea of resonance—in both its musical and its activist connotations—is an important conceptual extension of the notions of visibility and audibility; indeed, it is a more inclusive concept since resonances can also be sensed through vibration and it implies ongoing reverberation that is more lasting than tokenistic diversity initiatives, which perpetuate (in)visibilities and power imbalances determined by the dominant culture.

The quest for belated resonance across time and space is also evident in relation to other minoritized literatures. The poet and political scientist Ozan Zakariya Keskinkılıç has reflected on the heterogeneity and ambiguity of what he calls "poetischer Islam" (poetic Islam), looking to the Quran and early Persian, Arab, and Indian poets, as well as forward to a new generation of Muslim voices writing in various contexts around the world.[64] Their poetic interventions contradict the kinds of fundamentalist, racist, and sexist interpretations that emerge from the dominant culture's tendency to "*mis*hear certain voices and perspectives and to *dis*believe' their contributions."[65] The creative resistance of these Muslim writers inspires Keskinkılıç's own writing as a means of challenging what he calls the "Klischee-Korsett" of German debates about Islam and Leitkultur: "Indem sie an Altes erinnern und Neues gestalten, entfaltet sich in ihren Versen die Kraft des poetischen Vokabulars, um Gesellschaft anders denken zu können. Ob in den vergangenen oder zeitgenössischen Gedichten, diese Dichter:innen bilden nicht 'den' Islam ab. Das ist gar nicht der Anspruch. Stattdessen unterlaufen sie den Drang nach Absolutheit mit Pluralität." (In reminding us of the old and creating new, their verses open up the power of poetic vocabulary to conceive of a different society. Whether in past or contemporary poems, these poets do not represent "one" Islam. That is not their intention. Instead, they subvert the desire for absolutes with plurality.)[66] Like the curators of the Resonanzen festival, Keskinkılıç insists on literature as a way of introducing multivocality

---

63   Sharon Dodua Otoo in Selma Rezgui and Laura Sturtz, "Literatur, Aktivismus, Archiv. Ein Gespräch mit Nouria N. Asfaha und Sharon Dodua Otoo," in *Schwarze deutsche Literatur: Ästhetische und politische Interventionen von den 1980er Jahren bis heute*, ed. Jeannette Oholi (Bielefeld: transcript, forthcoming 2025).

64   Ozan Zakariya Keskinkılıç, *Muslimaniac. Die Karriere eines Feindbildes* (Berlin: Verbrecher Verlag), 153–60.

65   Medina, "Epistemic Injustice and Epistemologies of Resistance," 249.

66   Keskinkılıç, *Muslimaniac*, 160–61, 164–65.

and writing against stereotypes and homogenizing attributions. They all make the point that the work of Muslim or Black writers respectively does not represent those groups in one particular way, but instead rejects a "desired communal uniformity"[67] through texts that are plural in form, aesthetics, and content.

By doubling down on efforts to highlight plurality within minoritized groups and emphasizing their indebtedness to longer-standing traditions, the writers featured in our volume push back against inappropriate or reductive categorizations that often render the complexity of their role models invisible, inaudible, and unintelligible. Referring to the work of Emine Sevgi Özdamar, Rafik Schami, SAID, Aras Ören, May Ayim, and many others, the literary critic and scholar Maryam Aras has pointed out:

> Es gibt diese Tradition von deutschsprachiger Literatur, die aus marginalisierter Perspektive vielstimmig und ästhetisch innovativ schon lange gegen ein Machtzentrum anschreibt. Das ist nichts Neues. Mit dieser Generation ist aber genau das passiert, was wir nicht wollen—ihnen wurde als Autor*innen von "Migrationsliteratur" eine kleine verstaubte Box im Ordnungssystem der deutschen Literatur zugewiesen.[68]

> [There is this tradition of German-language literature that has long been writing against a powerful center from a marginalized perspective in a multi-voiced, aesthetically innovative way. That's nothing new. What happened to that generation, however, is exactly what we don't want—they were assigned to a small, dusty box in the classification system of German literature labeled "Migrant Literature."]

Honoring the long tradition of literature by marginalized authors in German without reinforcing fixed categorizations is a principal aim of our volume. We seek to examine the heterogeneity within minoritized literary voices and the manifold ways in which they stake their positions as part of German society. The aim is not to re-essentialize all marginalized writers as resistant Others, but to trace connections and resonances—synchronically and diachronically—and explore intersecting counterperspectives and counternarratives presented by a heterogenous "Community

---

67 Joseph Twist and Maria Roca Lizarazu, "Rethinking Community and Subjectivity in Contemporary German Culture and Thought," *Oxford German Studies* 49 (2020): 105.

68 Maryam Aras in Jeannette Oholi, Maha El Hissy, Kyung-Ho Cha, and Maryam Aras, "Postmigration Reloaded," *PS Politisch Schreiben* 7 (2022): 71, https://www.politischschreiben.net/ps-7/postmigration-reloaded-ein-schreibgesprch.

aus Büchern" (community of books), to quote Aras quoting Sanyal.[69] The artists and works we engage with show that there has never been a homogenous, hermetic German culture and that diversity is not only a contemporary phenomenon but has a long and varied history. Their literary expressions of alternative German identities and communities can be understood as doubly in progress: as a post hoc reclaiming of suppressed traditions—staging what Medina, drawing on Foucault, calls the "insurrection of subjugated knowledges"[70]—and as an invention of the traditions to be passed into the future.

New German Studies: Interdisciplinary and Transnational Research

As Maria Roca Lizarazu and Joseph Twist show in their 2020 special issue of *Oxford German Studies*—"Rethinking Community and Subjectivity in Contemporary German Culture and Thought"—the "perennial question 'was ist deutsch?' resounds throughout the 20th and 21st centuries."[71] Our book takes up these ongoing discussions about renegotiations of the German literary canon and the contemporary cultural landscape as laid out in recent collections that present new perspectives on Germanness as an open, evolving category and make visible a German society and literature whose reality is far from monolithic. Contributing to this chorus of work can be understood as an additional level of—academic—intervention that accounts for the need to reshape analytical frames and expand the field of literary studies by engaging with a plurality of literatures and interdisciplinary approaches.

Much of this current research, including ours, is indebted to pioneering work from the 1990s onward that began to challenge the analytical lens and label of "migrant literature," which situated the works of "Gastarbeiter" as well as other minoritized groups outside the German literary landscape and canon. In her seminal work *The Turkish Turn*,[72] for instance, Leslie Adelson introduced a new critical grammar of migration with regard to German-Turkish literature of the 1990s, counteracting

---

69 Maryam Aras in Oholi et al., "Postmigration Reloaded," 71.

70 José Medina, "Toward a Foucaultian Epistemology of Resistance: Counter-Memory, Epistemic Friction and Guerilla Pluralism," *Foucault Studies* 12 (2011): 12–21.

71 See Maria Roca Lizarazu and Joseph Twist, "Rethinking Community and Subjectivity in Contemporary German Culture and Thought," *Oxford German Studies*, 49, no. 2 (2020): 103.

72 Leslie Adelson, *The Turkish Turn in Contemporary German Literature* (New York: Palgrave Macmillan, 2005).

"intercultural" paradigms that center the apparent "in-betweenness" of migrant literature as situated between two discrete cultures.[73] Adelson is highly critical of that paradigm, which, in her opinion, is "ill equipped" to analyze the complexity of German-Turkish literature of the 1990s, as it reduces its place to "a central representative position, not on a vibrating tightrope, but on an inflexible bridge 'between two worlds.' One of these worlds," she continues, "is customarily presumed to be European and the other not, while the space between is cast as a site of discriminatory exclusions or the home of happy hybridity."[74] Instead, Adelson proposes the concept of "touching tales" to foreground the multidirectionality of writing by authors of Turkish descent and its interrelatedness with the dominant German culture.[75]

Building on this, recent publications explicate a theoretical shift toward an intersectional approach to contemporary German literature, focusing on the interrelatedness of artistic strategies employed by minoritized writers. In their above-mentioned special issue, Roca Lizarazu and Twist draw on various scholars and writers[76] who criticize the notion of a homogenous German nation-state and point out that its roots are in "racist colonial structures."[77] The contributions to their special issue explore literary and philosophical ways of relating to the self and Other and investigate alternatives to the dominant paradigm, focusing on the post-reunification period in which an "ethnic, racialized sense of Germanness emerged as one . . . unifying feature, to the exclusion of migrants and ethnic minorities."[78] As Roca Lizarazu and Twist point out, "reconceptualizations of community often come from minorities and (post-)migrants who find themselves in an outsider position."[79] Literature and cultural production by the writers featured in their collection—as well as those in our volume—"seek[s] to re-think community, kinship and togetherness beyond the notions of biologically determined, nationally bounded and monolithic attachments."[80]

---

73   Adelson, *The Turkish Turn*, 14. With regard to the intercultural paradigm, see Norbert Mecklenburg, "Poetik und Hermeneutik der Interkulturalität," in *Tischgespräche: Einladung zu einer Interkulturellen Wissenschaft*, ed. Corinna Albrecht and Andrea Bogner (Bielefeld: transcript, 2017), 31–53; Carmine Chiellino, *Interkulturelle Literatur in Deutschland* (Stuttgart: Metzler, 2000).
74   Adelson, *The Turkish Turn*, 14.
75   Adelson, *The Turkish Turn*, 20.
76   El-Tayeb, *Undeutsch*; Navid Kermani, *Wer ist Wir? Deutschland und seine Muslime* (Munich: Beck, 2009).
77   Roca Lizarazu and Twist, "Rethinking Community and Subjectivity," 105.
78   Roca Lizarazu and Twist, "Rethinking Community and Subjectivity," 104.
79   Roca Lizarazu and Twist, "Rethinking Community and Subjectivity," 108.
80   Roca Lizarazu and Twist, "Rethinking Community and Subjectivity," 110.

Similarly, the editors of the recent volume *Minority Discourses in Germany since 1990* note that "long-standing intersectional collaborative efforts" among minoritized groups in the artistic and activist realms have not always been reflected in the scholarship of "Germanistik and German studies."[81] *Minority Discourses* also establishes reunification as a turning point, "as a critical juncture in German identity, a point where it started being reframed."[82] Their collection points toward the importance of "cross-discipline communication"[83]—particularly across Black German studies, Turkish German studies, and German Jewish studies, building on key research that has been conducted in the respective fields.[84] Through this, they seek to engage in a "dialogue that will both investigate differences and similarities but most importantly consider what we as scholars can learn from each other to work toward an understanding of Germanness as plural, culturally diverse, and multilingual."[85] We see our volume as a continuation and expansion of these dialogues, moving even further into the contemporary, bringing together literary works that reflect the radical diversity of German society and shed light on alliances that have often been overlooked by an academic focus on specific groups.

One concept that has proved productive in this regard and that has gained traction in the academic field over recent years is the notion of postmigration and the postmigrant, which enables the interlinking of research on different minoritized subgroups—for example Jewish-, Turkish-, Afro-German.[86] According to Roca Lizarazu, this offers a more inclusive approach, which represents "intersecting experiences of violent pasts and discriminatory presents, whilst also featuring explorations of common ground on which new futures may be constructed."[87] Postmigration also acts as an important connection point between academic research, cultural production, and public discourse, as it offers ways to think about common strategies of artistic and political intervention that act as a "subversiver Verweis auf die Fluidität von Herkunft, Kultur und die Transformation kollektiver Identität" (a subversive indicator for fluid

---

81 Ela Gezen, Priscilla Layne, and Jonathan Skolnik, "Introduction: Minority Discourses in Germany since 1990," in *Minority Discourses in Germany since 1990*, ed. Ela Gezen, Priscilla Layne, and Jonathan Skolnik (New York/Oxford: Berghahn, 2022), 7–8.
82 Gezen, Layne, and Skolnik, "Introduction," 3.
83 Gezen, Layne, and Skolnik, "Introduction," 2.
84 See Gezen, Layne, and Skolnik, "Introduction," 12–19, for a concise overview of research that has shaped the fields of German Turkish Studies, Black German Studies, and German Jewish Studies respectively.
85 Gezen, Layne, and Skolnik, "Introduction," 4.
86 Roca Lizarazu, "'Integration Ist Definitiv Nicht Unser Anliegen,'" 11; Gezen, Layne, and Skolnik, "Introduction," 10.
87 Roca Lizarazu, "'Integration Ist Definitiv Nicht Unser Anliegen,'" 11.

origins, culture, and the transformation of collective identities),[88] which can lead to the reformulation of the fundamental premises of belonging that underpin cultural and national narratives. Although the concept of the postmigrant was first used in an anthology of British youth culture by Gerd Baumann and Thijl Sunier in 1995,[89] it was popularized in the German context by Shermin Langhoff, a Berlin-based theater director. The term took hold in the 2000s as a subversive strategy of self-labeling to counteract the ongoing "migrantization" of aesthetic productions by the children and grandchildren of immigrants, which perpetuated the process of Othering that situates German-based and/or German-born artists according to their perceived "Migrationshintergrund" (migration background).[90] The postmigrant theater established a "gemeinsamer Raum der Diversität" (shared space of diversity),[91] giving voice to stories yet untold in the sphere of theatrical representation. In the meantime, the term has been readopted and adapted by the social sciences building on postcolonial studies to facilitate a "kritische Auseinandersetzung mit gesellschaftlichen Machtverhältnissen" (critical engagement with social power relations).[92] This positions migration not as a "Sonderfall" (special case) but as a phenomenon at the center of contemporary German society and at the heart of social analysis, understanding postmigration as a perspective or paradigm rather than an object of study.[93] Consequently, the "post" in postmigrant—like the "post" in postcolonial—does not point to an aftermath of migration but rather constitutes an epistemological turn, which interrupts and decenters the dominant white gaze.[94]

As is often the case with popular theoretical concepts, the idea of postmigration has been stretched and, in many cases, deprived of its original "Strahlkraft und Radikalität" (radiating and radical power) as it has been increasingly co-opted for a broad range of migration experiences—or

---

88   Naika Foroutan, *Die Postmigrantische Gesellschaft: Ein Versprechen der pluralen Demokratie* (Bielefeld: transcript, 2021), 49.

89   Gerd Baumann and Thijl Sunier, *Post-Migration Ethnicity: De-Essentializing Cohesion, Commitments, and Comparison* (Amsterdam: Het Spinhuis, 1995).

90   See Lizzie Stewart, *Performing New German Realities: Turkish-German Scripts of Postmigration* (London: Palgrave Macmillan, 2021).

91   Shermin Langhoff, "Die Herkunft spielt keine Rolle–'Postmigrantisches' Theater im Ballhaus Naunynstraße," *bpb.de. Bundeszentrale für politische Bildung*, March 10, 2011. https://www.bpb.de/lernen/kulturelle-bildung/60135/die-herkunft-spielt-keine-rolle-postmigrantisches-theater-im-ballhaus-naunynstrasse/.

92   Erol Yildiz, "Postmigrantisch," *Inventar der Migrationsbegriffe*, 20 January 2022. https://www.migrationsbegriffe.de/postmigrantisch, 7.

93   Regina Römhild, "Beyond the Bounds of the Ethnic: For Postmigrant Cultural and Social Research," *Journal of Aesthetics & Culture* 9, no. 2 (2017): 72.

94   El Hissy, "Literarisches Schreiben post Hanau," 401–2.

other experiences of alienation—in a manner that serves rather than decenters the dominant culture and therefore reproduces "Unsichtbarkeiten" (invisibilities) of precisely "diejenigen marginalisierten Akteur*innen . . ., die im Mittelpunkt stehen sollen" (those marginalized actors who are supposed to be foregrounded).[95] The tendency to dilute and whitewash the concept in the literary and academic fields has been interrogated by Jeannette Oholi, Maha El Hissy, Kyung-Ho Cha, and Maryam Aras in their "Postmigration Reloaded: Ein Schreibgespräch."[96] Their conversation refocuses on the subversive origins, as well as the transnational dimensions and potential of the concept. Drawing on the interconnected work of theorists such as El-Tayeb, Stuart Hall, Edward Said, and Gloria Wekker,[97] they reclaim the radical potential of the postmigrant perspective by emphasizing its relationship with postcolonialism and intersectionality, two fields that are less established, and in some cases systematically dismissed, in the German context.[98] As Oholi points out, "ein intersektionales, postkoloniales und komparatistisches Nachdenken über das Postmigrantische hätte zur Folge, dass Rassifizierungen und Marginalisierungen nicht mehr nur als singulär und ahistorisch sichtbar würden, sondern als Tiefenstrukturen, die Europa zugrunde liegen" (thinking about postmigration in an intersectional, postcolonial, and comparative way would make racializations and marginalizations visible as not just singular and ahistorical, but as deep-seated structures at the heart of Europe).[99] In this sense, postmigration can be recalibrated as a tool for the analysis of literary and cultural interventions that aim to change the German cultural system—and the Eurocentric West more broadly—from within, as they expose and destabilize hegemonic structures while also highlighting the "transformative" and utopian potential for manifold transnational "Allianzen" (alliances) across different groups and subject positions.[100]

In line with these arguments forwarded by Oholi, El Hissy, Cha, and Aras, our book is premised on the assumption that the concept of the postmigrant is most useful when understood as creative agency and

---

95   El Hissy, "Literarisches Schreiben post Hanau," 403.

96   Oholi et al., "Postmigration Reloaded," 62–73.

97   Oholi et al., "Postmigration Reloaded"; El-Tayeb, *Undeutsch*; Stuart Hall, "When was the Post-Colonial? Thinking at the Limit," in *The Post-Colonial Question*, ed. Iain Chambers and Lidia Curti (London: Routledge, 1996), 242–60; Edward Said, *Reflections on Exile and other Literary and Cultural Essays* (London: Granta, 2012); Gloria Wekker, *White Innocence: Paradoxes of Colonialism and Race* (Durham, NC: Duke University Press, 2016).

98   See also El Hissy, "Literarisches Schreiben post Hanau," 401.

99   Oholi in Oholi et al., "Postmigration Reloaded," 64. See also Jeannette Oholi, *Afropäische Ästhetiken* (Bielefeld: transcript, 2024).

100 Oholi in Oholi et al., "Postmigration Reloaded," 64.

resistance to dominant epistemologies. We expand this by drawing on recent research on cultural production and epistemic injustice. This is another field that shifts focus away from fixed ideas of the nation, ethnicity, and migration to global structures of oppression and, crucially, creative resistance to these. In German studies, this emergent "epistemic turn" has been advanced by Sarah Colvin with particular focus on the narrative and aesthetic strategies of Black German writers such as May Ayim, Phillip Khabo Koepsell, Sharon Dodua Otoo, and Olivia Wenzel.[101] Other studies by Cha, El Hissy, and Schwarz have applied related approaches to writing by Deniz Ohde and Shida Bazyar.[102] In their recent volume *Epistemic Justice and Creative Agency*, Sarah Colvin and Stephanie Galasso bring together a global collective of scholars to explore the creative potential of literature and film to "provide new imaginative possibilities, and break down barriers of resistance toward alternative knowledges."[103] Although it is often associated with the philosopher Miranda Fricker,[104] Colvin and Galasso outline the long intellectual history of the concept of epistemic injustice, which has roots in postcolonial, feminist, and critical race theory, and explain how Fricker's ideas on "testimonial" and "hermeneutical" injustice have been developed further by others, most extensively by Medina.[105] In contrast to the "epistemic arrogance," "epistemic laziness," and/or

---

[101] Sarah Colvin, "Talking Back: Sharon Dodua Otoo's Herr Gröttrup setzt sich hin and the Epistemology of Resistance," *German Life and Letters* 73 (2020): 659–79; Sarah Colvin, "Words that Might Save Necks: Phillip Khabo Koepsell, Epistemic Murder and Poetic Justice," *German Life and Letters* 74 (2021): 511–36; Sarah Colvin, "Freedom Time: Temporal Insurrections in Olivia Wenzel's *1000 Serpentinen Angst* and Sharon Dodua Otoo's *Adas Raum*," *German Life and Letters* 75 (2022): 138–65; Sarah Colvin, "May Ayim and Subversive Laughter: The Aesthetics of Epistemic Change," *German Studies Review* 45 (2022): 81–103.

[102] Kyung-Ho Cha, "The Postmigrant Critique of the Bildungsroman and the Epistemic Injustice of the Educational System in Deniz Ohde's Scattered Light," in *Epistemic Justice and Creative Agency: Global Perspectives on Literature and Film*, ed. Sarah Colvin and Stephanie Galasso (New York: Routledge: 2022), 131–47; El Hissy, "Literarisches Schreiben post Hanau"; Schwarz, "Relational Epistemologies."

[103] Sarah Colvin and Stephanie Galasso, "Introduction: Changing the Story? Epistemic Shifts and Creative Agency," in *Epistemic Justice and Creative Agency: Global Perspectives on Literature and Film*, ed. Sarah Colvin and Stephanie Galasso (New York: Routledge: 2022), 7.

[104] Miranda Fricker, *Epistemic Injustice: Power and the Ethics of Knowing* (Oxford: Oxford University Press, 2007).

[105] Colvin and Galasso, "Introduction," 2–7.

"closed-mindedness"[106] often characteristic of dominantly positioned groups, oppressed and marginalized subjects develop and offer alternative epistemic resources, discourses, and practices, thereby exerting "epistemic resistance" to the dominant position of "empowered ignorance" (around such categories as race, gender, sexuality, age, and disability).[107] Like in the "Schreibgespräch" discussed above and in our book as a whole, conversation is important. Drawing on Medina and Jonathan O. Chimakonam, Colvin and Galasso explain that "epistemic resistance gives rise to epistemic friction, which is adversarial without seeking resolution; it is conversational in Chimakonam's sense ('critiquing and correcting; opening but never closing')."[108] According to Chimakonam, conversationalism "does not seek to annihilate epistemic borders, but to build bridges to connect all borders."[109] This kind of epistemic resistance and creative agency is illustrated in many of the writings explored in this volume, which therefore, we suggest, make epistemological interventions that offer readers opportunities to reassess the ways in which (German) literature, culture, and society are understood by academics and wider publics.

Literary Strategies and Interventionist Praxis

This volume explores a range of interventions into the German cultural context that are made from radically diverse perspectives. The contributions pose several central questions relating strategies of literary intervention through subversive aesthetics and the ways in which creative writing can be understood as a form of public intervention: What literary and aesthetic means and media are employed by minoritized writers to center and thematize the radical diversity of experiences and (hi)stories that already shape German society? How do these texts conceive of a new sense of subjectivity and community that transcends narrow frames of identity and belonging? In doing so, what new ways of reconceiving, redefining, rewriting, and perhaps even overturning "Germanness" do they offer? Much of the conceptual framework of our volume departs

---

106 José Medina, *The Epistemology of Resistance: Gender and Racial Oppression, Epistemic Injustice and Resistant Imaginations* (Oxford: Oxford University Press, 2013), 30–31 and 33–34; Colvin and Galasso, "Introduction," 7.

107 Colvin and Galasso, "Introduction," 6–7; see also Mills, "White Ignorance."

108 Colvin and Galasso, "Introduction," 7; here they cite Medina, *The Epistemology of Resistance*, 281, and Jonathan O. Chimakonam, "African Philosophy and Global Epistemic Injustice," *Journal of Global Ethics* 13 (2017): 134.

109 Chimakonam, "African Philosophy," 121; Colvin and Galasso, "Introduction," 7.

from artistic practices and the literary and activist interventions made by authors in the public sphere. To underline this important role of authors as public figures and their central role in (re)framing literary and public discourses, the book contains four original interviews that enter into conversation with the research chapters, highlighting the interconnectedness of the literary, the cultural, and the academic spheres. In this way, we also underline different forms of knowledge production that contribute to the ongoing project of rewriting and transcending the idea of Germany as homogenous and univocal.

The volume is divided into two sections, each of which is bookended with interviews that frame the topics discussed in the respective thematic articles. Sasha Marianna Salzmann opens the first section on "Subjectivities, Solidarities, Genealogies" by entering into conversation with Selma Rezgui and Laura Marie Sturtz on the implications of being a queer, non-binary, Jewish and Post-Soviet German author in contemporary Germany and the act of writing as a means of overcoming and subverting these categories. Following this, the chapters in the first section center on questions of subject formation, belonging, community, and alliance. The works discussed in this section conceive a subversive and transgressive language of identity and belonging that counteracts the "mythical norm"[110] of Germanness that has been hitherto bound to nationality, ethnicity, sexuality, or gender. They do this, for example, by centering previously marginalized perspectives, exploring new ways of understanding the self and the collective, engaging in dialogical writing, and drawing lines to literary ancestors. With this, they claim their place within rather than at the peripheries of the German literary context.

In her chapter "Twin Novels: Re-Negotiating Self and Other in Sasha Marianna Salzmann's *Außer sich* and Olivia Wenzel's *1000 Serpentinen Angst*," Laura Marie Sturtz builds on Deleuze and Guattari's notion of minor literature and the concept of postmigration to underline the potential of self-representation as a form of subversive and interventionist storytelling. Through a combined reading of Salzmann and Wenzel, the article shows the productiveness of highlighting shared strategies of interventionist writing not attributed to a common background of authors or texts. Sturtz engages with the respective protagonists' process of finding a voice that speaks for themselves and against the attributions of "Otherness" in a hegemonic and violent mainstream society. The process of dealing with familial trauma and the loss of their respective twin brothers features prominently in both novels and, ultimately, establishes alternative forms of community.

---

110 Audre Lorde, "Age, Race, Class and Sex: Women Redefining Difference [1980]," in *Sister Outsider* (London: Penguin, 2007), 109.

Priscilla Layne's contribution, "New Black German Subjectivity in the Twenty-First Century," examines the increased prominence of Black literature in Germany and the attention it has received from the majority white publishing industry and *Feuilleton* in recent years, focusing in particular on Noah Sow's *Die Schwarze Madonna* (The Black Madonna, 2019), Jackie Thomae's *Brüder* (Brothers, 2019), and Olivia Wenzel's *1000 Serpentinen Angst* (*1000 Coils of Fear*, 2020). Layne considers these novels in relation to the literary category New Subjectivity, a term coined in the 1970s to describe a focus on introspection, individual concerns, and subjective experiences in German literature. By contextualizing them within the German literary tradition, Layne's article shows how contemporary Black German writing is similar to and expands New Subjectivity, counteracting the assumption that Black German authors have more in common with diasporic authors than with non-Black German authors.

In her article "Talking Back, Paying Forward: Dialogism and Literary Genealogies in May Ayim and Olivia Wenzel," Selma Rezgui investigates dialogism and conversation as a means of Black German literary subject formation. Rezgui's contribution draws genealogical lines that acknowledge similarities and differences in the approaches of two authors who represent different phases and generations of Black German writing. Her chapter explores the ways in which Wenzel's and Ayim's texts speak to each other, tracing collaborative and dialogic processes of Afro-German subject formation that depart from conventional notions of national, ethnic, and linguistic affiliations, in order to forge and perpetuate alternative senses of home, belonging, and identity.

The closing interview of this section, "Black Poetry Matters: A Conversation with Stefanie-Lahya Aukongo," takes up the genealogical lines and the transnational, transtemporal, and intertextual subjectivities apparent in the works discussed in this section. In their conversation, Jeannette Oholi, Nadiye Ünsal, and Aukongo highlight how Aukongo's work reflects intersecting subjectivities in a multilayered way, as she makes her experiences and the plurality of Black identities visible through poetry, while denouncing the invisibility of German colonial history and a heteronormative social norm that excludes all those who do not conform to it.

The second section of the volume—"Disruptions, Subversions, Interactions"—opens with an interview by Joseph Twist with the poet Özlem Özgul Dündar on "Subversive Aesthetics, Embodied Language, and the Politics of Literature." The conversation grapples with the politics of the literary imagination, especially with regard to the (in)visibility of victims of racism in the German memory landscape. It highlights the subversiveness of embodied and affective language as well as multilingualism as key elements of Dündar's poetry and radio plays. Following this, the section assembles essays that account for a variety of interventionist practices, as an ever-increasing number of minoritized authors disrupt the status quo of who is seen and heard, and who interacts in negotiations of public opinion in postmigrant Germany. These practices include the appropriation of dominant and canonized genres, experimenting with narrative voice, characterization, and representation, and (re-)inscribing a plurality of perspectives and (hi)stories. In her chapter "Deintegrative Rewriting of the Bildungsroman: Social Criticism from a Postmigrant Perspective in Fatma Aydemir's *Ellbogen* (2017)," Lea Laura Heim explores how the novel voices social criticism by adapting and appropriating the genre to expose mechanisms of marginalization and challenge structures of discrimination inherent in the *Dominanzkultur*. Aydemir's novel harnesses and transforms the canonical authority of the Bildungsroman, thus questioning the persistent (mis-)perception of a supposedly homogeneous national literature in a country shaped by immigration. Drawing on Czollek's notion of "deintegration" and Bourdieu's theory of "symbolic violence," Heim shows how Aydemir's use of an antagonistic protagonist resists what Kobena Mercer terms the "burden of representation" often imposed on minoritized subjects.

Alrik Daldrup's essay "Reorienting Knowledge of Structural Systems of Violence in Sharon Dodua Otoo's *Adas Raum* and Antje Rávik Strubel's *Blaue Frau*" draws on Sara Ahmed's discussion of structural violence and James Odhiambo Ogone's notion of "representational epistemic injustice" to analyze processes of Othering that work to legitimize marginalized subjects as targets of violent practices. Daldrup considers how these processes are counteracted in the literary texts written by a Black feminist and a queer feminist respectively, showing how they stage the resistance of the imagined "Other(s)," who talk back to those who misrepresent them.

In her chapter "Epistolary Interventions, Epistemic Insurrections: Creative Writers, Open Letters, and Solidarity with the 'Womxn, Life, Freedom' Movement in Contemporary Postmigrant Germany," Tara Talwar Windsor explores the idea of open letters as forms of literary activism and instruments of intellectual intervention, which advance the transformative potential of the postmigrant perspective and enact transnational feminist alliances. Focusing on letters circulated by Shida Bazyar and Asal Dardan, the chapter highlights strategies employed by authors to adopt, adapt, and subvert the genre at a time when its usefulness had been called into question. Windsor argues that these epistolary interventions generate epistemic friction and instigate acts of what José Medina calls "epistemic insurrection" by mobilizing the genre's dual mode of address to both named recipient(s) and wider reading public(s), amplifying marginalized voices, and exposing ambivalent positionalities, thereby challenging mainstream perspectives and disrupting Western-centric epistemologies in a German public sphere shaped by global events.

The section closes with an interview between Leila Essa and Mithu Sanyal titled "Seen as Friendly, Seen as Frightening? Visibilities, Kinship, and Finding the Right Words." In their conversation, Essa and Sanyal rethink the role of authors as public figures navigating intervention and friendliness, rupture and relation. Their conversation probes how we must rethink this role in the face of marginalized authors' strategies for discursive interventions, which also entail "collective choices, collective intentions." The conversation also grapples with questions of who is visible or rather who is being listened to, the responsibilities that audibility brings, and the uses of the terms "postmigrant" and "postcolonial" in German public discourse, thus drawing together many themes of the volume as a whole.

Bibliography

Adelson, Leslie. *The Turkish Turn in Contemporary German Literature.* New York: Palgrave Macmillan, 2005.

Albrecht, Corinna, and Andrea Bogner, eds. *Tischgespräche: Einladung zu einer interkulturellen Wissenschaft.* Bielefeld: transcript, 2017.

Attia, Iman, Swantje Köbsell, and Nivedita Prasad, eds. *Dominanzkultur reloaded: Neue Texte zu gesellschaftlichen Machtverhältnissen und ihren Wechselwirkungen.* Bielefeld: transcript, 2015.

Aydemir, Fatma, and Hengameh Yaghoobifarah, eds. *Eure Heimat ist unser Albtraum.* Berlin: Ullstein, 2019.

Aydemir, Fatma, John Cho-Polizzi, and Hengameh Yaghoobifarah. *Your Homeland Is Our Nightmare: An Antifascist Essay Collection.* Berlin: Literarische Diverse Verlag, 2022.

Baumann, Gerd, and Thijl Sunier. *Post-Migration Ethnicity: De-Essentializing Cohesion, Commitments, and Comparison.* Amsterdam: Het Spinhuis, 1995.

Bazyar, Shida. "Ein Moment der Schwere," in "Zwei Jahre nach Hanau: Nicht nur erinnern, sondern handeln!" *Berliner Zeitung*, February 2, 2022. https://www.berliner-zeitung.de/wochenende/wie-sollten-wir-der-anschlaege-von-hanau-gedenken-li.211975.

Bertram, Ingrid. "Verein um Maaßen: WerteUnion als Partei gegründet." tagesschau.de. February 17, 2024. https://www.tagesschau.de/inland/werteunion-partei-maassen-100.html.

"Bündnis Sahra Wagenknecht: hier links, da rechts." Deutschlandfunk, January 27, 2024. https://www.deutschlandfunk.de/wagenknecht-partei-buendnis-gruendung-100.html#:~:text=B.

Cha, Kyung-Ho. "The Postmigrant Critique of the Bildungsroman and the Epistemic Injustice of the Educational System in Deniz Ohde's Scattered Light." In *Epistemic Justice and Creative Agency: Global Perspectives on*

Literature and Film, edited by Sarah Colvin and Stephanie Galasso, 131–47. New York: Routledge: 2022.

Chambers, Iain, and Lidia Curti, eds. *The Post-Colonial Question: Common Skies, Divided Horizons*. London: Routledge, 1996.

Chernivsky, Marina, and Hannah Peaceman. "Nachhalle." Thematic issue of *Jalta: Positionen zur jüdischen Gegenwart* no. 8 (2023).

Chiellino, Carmine. *Interkulturelle Literatur in Deutschland*. Stuttgart: Metzler, 2000.

Chimakonam, Jonathan O. "African Philosophy and Global Epistemic Injustice." *Journal of Global Ethics* 13, no. 2 (2017): 120–37.

Coffey, Judith, and Vivien Laumann. *Gojnormativität: Warum wir anders über Antisemitismus sprechen müssen*. Berlin: Verbrecher Verlag, 2021.

Colvin, Sarah. "Freedom Time: Temporal Insurrections in Olivia Wenzel's *1000 Serpentinen Angst* and Sharon Dodua Otoo's *Adas Raum*." *German Life and Letters* 75, no. 1 (January 2022): 138–65.

———. "May Ayim and Subversive Laughter: The Aesthetics of Epistemic Change." *German Studies Review* 45, no. 1 (2022): 81–103.

———. "Talking Back: Sharon Dodua Otoo's *Herr Göttrup setzt sich hin* and the Epistemology of Resistance." *German Life and Letters* 73, no. 4 (October 2020): 659–79.

———. "Words That Might Save Necks: Philipp Khabo Koepsell, Epistemic Murder and Poetic Justice." *German Life and Letters* 74, no. 4 (October 2021): 511–36.

Colvin, Sarah, and Stephanie Galasso. *Epistemic Justice and Creative Agency: Global Perspectives on Literature and Film*. 1st ed. New York: Routledge, 2022.

Connolly, Kate. "Turmoil in Germany over Neo-Nazi Mass Deportation Meeting—Explained." *Guardian*, January 19, 2024. https://www.theguardian.com/world/2024/jan/19/turmoil-in-germany-over-neo-nazi-mass-deportation-meeting-explained.

Czollek, Max. *Desintegriert euch!* Munich: Carl Hanser Verlag, 2018.

Czollek, Max, Hannah Peaceman, and Lea Wohl von Haselberg. "Allianzen." Thematic issue of *Jalta: Positionen zur jüdischen Gegenwart* no. 3 (2018).

———. "Desintegration." Thematic issue of *Jalta: Positionen zur jüdischen Gegenwart* no. 2 (2017).

De Mazière, Thomas. "'Wir sind nicht Burka': Innenminister will deutsche Leitkultur." ZEIT ONLINE. April 30, 2017. https://www.zeit.de/politik/deutschland/2017-04/thomas-demaiziere-innenminister-leitkultur.

"Die Partei Die Heimat (vormals NPD) ist für die Dauer von sechs Jahren von der staatlichen Parteienfinanzierung ausgeschlossen." Pressemitteilung no. 9/2024, January 23, 2024. https://www.bundesverfassungsgericht.de/SharedDocs/Pressemitteilungen/DE/2024/bvg24-009.html.

El Bulbeisi, Sarah. "Über den Schmerz des Verschweigens. Palästinenser:innen in Deutschland und in der Schweiz." geschichte der gegenwart. September 17, 2023, https://geschichtedergegenwart.ch/ueber-den-

schmerz-des-verschweigens-palaestinenserinnen-in-deutschland-und-in-der-schweiz/.
El Hissy, Maha. "Literarisches Schreiben post Hanau." *Internationales Archiv für Sozialgeschichte der deutschen Literatur* 48, no. 2 (2023): 398–416.
El-Tayeb, Fatima. *European Others: Queering Ethnicity in Postnational Europe*. Minneapolis: University of Minnesota Press, 2011.
———. *Undeutsch: Die Konstruktion des Anderen in der postmigrantischen Gesellschaft*, Bielefeld: transcript, 2016.
Florvil, Tiffany. *Mobilizing Black Germany: Afro-German Women and the Makings of a Transnational Movement*. Urbana: University of Illinois Press, 2020.
Foroutan, Naika. *Die Postmigrantische Gesellschaft: Ein Versprechen der pluralen Demokratie*. Bielefeld: transcript, 2021.
Fricker, Miranda. *Epistemic Injustice: Power and the Ethics of Knowing*. Oxford: Oxford University Press, 2007.
Gezen, Ela, Priscilla Layne, and Jonathan Skolnik, eds. *Minority Discourses in Germany since 1990*. New York: Berghahn, 2022.
Hall, Stuart. "Domination and Hegemony." In *Cultural Studies 1983: A Theoretical History*, edited by Jennifer Daryl Slack and Lawrence Grossberg, 169–71. Durham, NC: Duke University Press, 2016.
Hickmann, Christoph, and Dirk Kurbjuweit. "Olaf Scholz: Neue Härte in Der Flüchtlingspolitik: 'Wir Müssen Endlich Im Großen Stil Abschieben.'" *Der Spiegel*, October 20, 2023. https://www.spiegel.de/politik/deutschland/olaf-scholz-ueber-migration-es-kommen-zu-viele-a-2d86d2ac-e55a-4b8f-9766-c7060c2dc38a.
James, Katharina. "CDU: Friedrich Merz 'Dankbar' Für Leitkultur Im CDU-Programmentwurf." *Die Zeit*, February 28, 2024. https://www.zeit.de/politik/deutschland/2024-02/friedrich-merz-bedeutung-leitkultur-cdu-grundsatzprogramm.
kebe-nguema, joseph. "Blackness and Dis/ability in the Afrofuturist Christmas Novella *Synchronicity* (2015) by Sharon Dodua Otoo." *German Life and Letters* 77, no. 1 (2024): 33–50.
Kemani, Navid. *Wer ist wir? Deutschland und seine Muslime*. Munich: Beck, 2009.
Keskinkılıç, Ozan Zakariya. *Muslimaniac: Die Karriere eines Feindbildes*. Berlin: Verbrecher Verlag, 2021.
Langhoff, Shermin. "Die Herkunft spielt keine Rolle—'Postmigrantisches' Theater im Ballhaus Naunynstraße." bpb.de. Bundeszentrale für politische Bildung. March 10, 2011. https://www.bpb.de/lernen/kulturelle-bildung/60135/die-herkunft-spielt-keine-rolle-postmigrantisches-theater-im-ballhaus-naunynstrasse/.
Lorde, Audre. "Age, Race, Class and Sex: Women Redefining Difference [1980]." In *Sister Outsider*, 107–16. London: Penguin, 2007.
Medina, José. "Epistemic Injustice and Epistemologies of Resistance." In *The Routledge Companion to the Philosophy of Race*, edited by Paul Taylor,

Linda Alcoff, and Luvell Anderson, 247–60. New York: Routledge, 2017.

———. "Toward a Foucaultian Epistemology of Resistance: Counter-Memory, Epistemic Friction and Guerilla Pluralism." *Foucault Studies* no. 12 (2011): 9–35.

Mende, Claudia. "Wir müssen Antisemitismus und Islamfeindlichkeit gemeinsam bekämpfen." Qantara.de. November 21, 2023. https://qantara.de/artikel/esra-%C3%B6zy%C3%BCrek-%C3%BCber-die-deutsche-debatte-wir-m%C3%BCssen-antisemitismus-und-islamfeindlichkeit.

Mills, Charles W. "White Ignorance." In *Race and Epistemologies of Ignorance*, edited by Shannon Sullivan and Nancy Tuana, 13–38. Albany: State University of New York Press, 2007.

Nelson, Cary, and Lawrence Grossberg, eds. *Marxism and the Interpretation of Culture*. Urbana: University of Illinois Press, 1988.

Oholi, Jeannette. *Afropäische Ästhetiken*. Bielefeld: transcript, 2024.

———, ed. *Schwarze deutsche Literatur: ästhetische und politische Interventionen von den 1980er Jahren bis heute*. Bielefeld: transcript, forthcoming 2025.

Oholi, Jeannette, Maha El Hissy, Kyung-Ho Cha, and Maryam Aras. "Postmigration Reloaded." *PS Politisch Schreiben* 7 (2022): 62–73.

Otoo, Sharon, and Jeannette Oholi, eds. *Resonanzen: Schwarzes Literaturfestival—eine Dokumentation*. Leipzig: Spector Books, 2022.

Özyürek, Esra. *Subcontractors of Guilt: Holocaust Memory and Muslim Belonging in Postwar Germany*. Stanford, CA: Stanford University Press, 2023.

Roca Lizarazu, Maria. "'Integration Ist Definitiv Nicht Unser Anliegen, Eher Schon Desintegration.'" Postmigrant Renegotiations of Identity and Belonging in Contemporary Germany." *humanities* 9, no. 2 (2020): 42. https://doi.org/10.3390/h9020042.

Roca Lizarazu, Maria, and Joseph Twist. "Rethinking Community and Subjectivity in Contemporary German Culture and Thought." *Oxford German Studies* 49 (2020): 103–16.

Römhild, Regina. "Beyond the Bounds of the Ethnic: For Postmigrant Cultural and Social Research." *Journal of Aesthetics & Culture* 9, no. 2 (2017): 69–75.

Rommelspacher, Birgit. *Dominanzkultur: Texte zu Fremdheit und Macht*. Berlin: Orlanda-Frauenverlag, 1995.

Salzmann, Sasha Marianna. "An der Formel stimmt etwas nicht." *Süddeutsche Zeitung*, January 4, 2024. https://www.sueddeutsche.de/meinung/salzmann-antisemitismus-deutschland-7-oktober-kommentar-1.6327884.

Schramm, Moritz. "Postmigrant Perspectives: Radical Diversity as Artistic-Political Intervention." *Crossings* 14, no. 1 (April 1, 2023): 89–104.

Schwarz, Miriam. "Relational Epistemologies: Friendship and Reading in Shida Bazyar's *Drei Kameradinnen*." *Forum for Modern Language Studies* 60, no. 2: 219–38.

"So stark ist die Zahl antisemitischer Straftaten seit dem 7. Oktober gestiegen." *Der Spiegel*, January 25, 2024. https://www.spiegel.de/politik/

deutschland/antisemitismus-so-stark-sind-antisemitische-straftaten-seit-dem-7-oktober-angestiegen-a-f104451d-992f-4592-8fe9-f0813 3854c98.
Steyerl, Hito. "Can the Subaltern speak German? Postkoloniale Kritik." *transversal* texts. https://transversal.at/transversal/0902/steyerl/de.
Sullivan, Shannon, and Nancy Tuana, eds. *Race and Epistemologies of Ignorance*. Albany: State University of New York Press, 2007.
Taylor, Paul, Linda Alcoff, and Luvell Anderson, eds. *The Routledge Companion to the Philosophy of Race*. New York: Routledge, 2017.
Utlu, Deniz. "Sensitive Solidarities: Notes on the Fragility of Alliances." In *Desintegration: Ein Kongress Zeitgenössischer Jüdischer Positionen*, edited by Max Czollek and Sascha Marianna Salzmann, 73–84. Bielefeld: Kerber Verlag, 2017.
Wels, Selma. *anders bleiben: Briefe der Hoffnung in verhärteten Zeiten*. Hamburg: Rowohlt, 2023.
Wüllenkemper, Cornelius. "Ein Berliner Diskussionsabend über Nah-Ost-Polarisierung in der Literatur." Deutschlandfunk, January 18, 2024. https://www.deutschlandfunk.de/ein-berliner-diskussionsabend-ueber-nah-ost-polarisierung-in-der-literatur-dlf-68cad2d7-100.html.

Part I

Subjectivities, Solidarities, Genealogies

1: Acting from Within: Inclusive Literature and the Power of Writing. A Conversation with Sasha Marianna Salzmann

Selma Rezgui and Laura Marie Sturtz

SASHA MARIANNA SALZMANN'S WORK shapes contemporary discourses in the German literary and cultural sphere through their wide-ranging and prolific artistic interventions as an author of novels as well as essays, a playwright and art director at the Studio R (Gorki Theater), curator of festivals and roundtables and as an editor and cofounder of *freitext*. Their two novels, *Außer sich* (*Beside Myself*, 2018), and *Im Menschen muss alles herrlich sein* (*Glorious People*, 2021), received public, as well as critical interest, shaping debates around multifaceted identities in contemporary German writing. Their first novel, *Außer sich*, which received considerable interest in academic discussions around German-Jewish, postmigrant, and queer literature, subverts narrative categories such as time and space, languages and narrative perspectives, tackling gender identities, migration, and (familial) belonging. Their second novel, *Im Menschen muss alles herrlich sein*, is based on the experience of the perestroika and the disintegration of post-Soviet Russia and Ukraine, exploring transgenerational discords, and mother-daughter-relationships. We met Salzmann at a café in Kreuzberg, Berlin in August 2022, a few months after Russia's full-scale invasion of Ukraine, to have a conversation about radical diversity and intervention through literature, the German cultural sphere, polyphony, and alliances, as well as the quest for more inclusive forms of writing.

Laura Sturtz: Sasha, we're so happy to speak to you today about visibility and representation, political and interventionist writing, and inclusive literature. Our volume is called *Rewriting Identities in Contemporary Germany: Radical Diversity and Literary Intervention*—and part of our project is to think about terms and concepts to make a certain shift visible that is happening in society and on the literary scene. I think it makes sense to begin with these concepts. What does radical diversity mean to you? Perhaps you could tell us what you associate with that term.

Sasha Marianna Salzmann: It's always interesting for me to think in both directions. Firstly, about labeling from outside, and secondly acting from within. Artistic action, if we're talking about literary intervention. From my point of view, it never happens to prove something to anybody—it happens because *we exist*. That alone is a political issue for mainstream society. That's why there is a gaze from outside that brings a certain framing with it. I think that radical diversity is the counterconcept. Radical diversity essentially says that either we're all diverse or nobody is. That's an idea of Max Czollek, who is also part of the Institute for Social Justice and Radical Diversity. As a political scientist, Max thinks a lot about how to abolish "normal." My personal approach is a little different. I don't believe that we will be able to abolish normal. There is a normal and everyone can define that normal if they have to. It doesn't help me to say that it doesn't exist, so I honestly don't even try to ignore it, but just assume that it's there, and I strip it of its power by stripping it of its authority. That's radical diversity in my work.

When I write I never write in order to prove something. If I find myself doing that, I put my pen away, otherwise it just ends up being a bad text; I can feel it. That essentially means you have to get to a point where it doesn't matter what is ascribed to you from the outside. As you can imagine, that's not easy. But it's worth it. It's worth it because it's only then that something happens at your desk. That's why I write and why I perform. That's poetry, that uplifting feeling of "this is art, and no one can take it away from me." No label can diminish what I do. And I think the way to get to that point is daily work, sort of starting from the beginning again and again. Because we all live a life with ascriptions from the outside. Normal people live with ascription too. I think that truly good art comes out of a space where we can free ourselves from it.

I have to say, though; I keep hitting these new starting points or dead ends, because you can't escape it. It always matters; the point will never arrive where it doesn't matter who you are. So how are you supposed to write your way to liberation? I think I work in that tension. I can tolerate both. I can tolerate wanting a creative moment where it's not about my marginalization, where I'm not afraid of someone assuming that I'm writing *because* . . . And at the same time there is and has to be a radical labeling if we want to make progress at all. Maybe I can make that more concrete: I remember when *Außer sich* (Beside myself, 2017) came out and of course people said to me "Ah, you've written a queer novel!" I said, "I've written a *novel*!"

But of course, I still want queer teenagers in small towns who are looking for queer books to find my novel. So, in that regard I think it's right to have this queer literature. I think it's good and right for marketing. I essentially feel fine when I'm put in a Jewish corner or a lesbian corner or a queer corner in bookshops. I just don't want to be thinking about that while I'm writing. If I'm thinking about which corner I'm writing into that's a problem.

Selma Rezgui: That's interesting. Would you say that literary intervention only happens for you after the act of writing? That it's something that happens when the text has been created and is being presented? It sounds as though intervention by a book from a minoritized perspective doesn't belong to the process of creation of a book but happens as it's read and received.

SMS: I think it takes place there, yes. I think literary interventions happen outside. You have to stay true to yourself. Look, Mithu Sanyal has been writing incredible, important texts for over a decade and now she's done it again and only now is it being recognized. That means essentially Mithu hasn't done anything differently, even though her writing is only now being perceived as an intervention. I think that's why *Identitti* has been so successful because this is what she's always done. That's her. What she writes is completely her.

It was interesting for me too because I have a different perspective: I came from the theater onto the German literary scene. I don't know how it is in other countries, but I do find that here the habitus is one of: "language is ours, philosophy is ours. We created the great masters." That's why it's so difficult to fight back; the rhetoric is so rooted in the culture. There's a very clear idea of what belongs to whom, of what counts as German. That only became clear to me when I came onto the scene myself. I thought, "oh, so this is an intervention. It's seen as an intervention that I'm here." The literature scene sees itself as something that defines Germany. That definition is changing completely, but it's slow, and Germany's idea of itself is like a boulder that we have to chip away at bit by bit with little hammers.

SR: We have also thought a lot about these questions of Zeitgeist, and the current book market. Why are specific texts, specific authors, getting attention now in particular? There's a kind of "turn toward" greater visibility for literature by marginalized authors. There are more and more texts that address this subject. More and more authors outside the norm who are positively critically received and are commercially successful. On the other hand, we have to be careful that we don't imply that all these writers appeared on the scene out of nowhere; they've always been there and have always written. Something's shifted, but it's not the literature itself; rather, it's how it's being received.

LS: At the same time, it's an important step that we're talking about it, that it's more visible now. We have to emphasize how important and exciting this literature is. But then we have to weigh up how to talk about it, what to call it. There are certain terms that we might not necessarily want to perpetuate, but as soon as you start searching for new discursive terms, for new ways of talking about these texts, you have to rely on older terminology at least to an extent, even in order to rewrite them and to develop new frames. It's a balance.

SMS: It will always be like that and that's OK. As long as it's always part of a conversation. I've organized so many festivals and literature workshops and that's always been the question. I'll never forget organizing my first literature workshop with Deniz Utlu. We drummed up people like Hakan Savaş Mican, Georgia Doll, Olivia Wenzel. We called the workshop "Neue deutsche Stücke" (New German plays). Tuncay Kuloğlu, who was still dramaturg in the Ballhaus Naunynstraße at the time, said "that's a trap. "Neue Deutsche" is just what Germany wants to hear. Don't do it." And I thought, "But Tuncay, I'm hardly going to call it 'Migranskis.'" I can hear his voice to this day. Then later there was "neue deutsche Medien" (New German media). "New German" became a concept. But what's new about it? Here for five generations and still new or what?

I think Tuncay was right. Maybe the positive thing is the metamorphosis of the terms. It's completely ok if we say we'll try things out until they feel right. I was a foreigner first, then a migrant, then a postmigrant. Why post? I came here when I was ten years old, so it's not really very post. Then "New German." I'm at the point where I feel like saying "how about foreigner?" Let's go back. It's OK for me if others see it differently though; I know that in your field in particular terms have to be watertight.

I already had problems with these fixed terms when I wrote my first novel. I had always written for the stage, which means my texts were always spoken and never read. And I felt like writing a book is so rigid, so fixed, the opposite of fluid. I'm talking about fluidity and I'm writing a *novel* of all things. That's nuts! That's why I made it multilingual, genderfluid, all that. I know that not everyone has the freedom to do that.

LS: Maybe we can think about the concept of intervention in two ways. On the one hand, you write as a public figure, perform as a public figure; you interact with discourses in society and in the literary scene. At the same time, you are finding a literary language, exploring the limits of the sayable, creating representation and visibility for experiences outside the norm. *Außer sich* reflects the search for a self across boundaries that dissolve and subvert clearly delineated categories of belonging like language, nation, religion, family, sexuality, and gender.

SMS: I didn't know how to write a novel. I grew up with books, but a lot of people read and that doesn't mean they know how to write. I didn't know much about the cultural sector either, didn't know how important the German Book Prize is. I didn't know what the difference between Suhrkamp, Fischer, or Rowohlt is. But that also gave me a certain freedom. I just wrote the manuscript and published it. Of course: there are four, five languages in *Außer sich*, but those are the languages I existed in. I wasn't trying to say "hey, multilingualism in the new thing," I was just being honest. Then a lot of things happened with the book—I was accused of jumping on a trendy topic. I thought "this is my life. I'm trendy? Since when has my life been trendy?" Not everyone denied that the book was literary, I think partly because it was published by Suhrkamp, that meant that the publisher believed in me. Suhrkamp was absolutely not interested in whether it was trendy or not trendy. That was cool, because I was really insecure and specifically didn't want to be marketed as a migrant author. They couldn't understand who would be interested in my background, but I told them they just didn't have enough migrants in their repertoire; they just didn't know what they were letting themselves in for. Afterward they saw what I was talking about, and I realized what a wild intervention into the literary scene the whole thing had been. But that wasn't the original intention.

I didn't start writing *Außer sich* thinking it would be a huge intervention; I went to Istanbul and fell so deeply in love with the city that I started writing love letters to Istanbul. I was spending a lot of time with trans women, so what I wrote about Istanbul is set in that scene. It was only partially autofictional; sometimes it was just fictional. I was so swept up in it. At that moment, no one was waiting for my novel. The atmosphere wasn't like it is now, where agents are looking for marginalized voices because they think that's what sells. That's the bitter truth, but back then it wasn't the case yet. No one was telling me that if I don't write this book I'll disappear into irrelevance. I just started writing the book, that's it.

Then everything twisted and suddenly I was in Odesa one hundred years ago. Things got wilder and wilder; I couldn't get a hold on the material. I thought, I don't have to get a hold on it, I just have to try to follow what is being created within me and, in doing so, listen to the advice I've been giving to my writing students for more than a decade; it doesn't matter what you are *trying* to do, you have to follow that inner voice." Only that voice knows. That's what ultimately decides whether you can look at yourself in the mirror when you're finished. I tried to take my own advice.

LS: Your books create a certain publicity and, like so many other authors, you take up a position in the discourse, in media, in Deutschlandfunk or the *Süddeutsche Zeitung*, but also in genres like essays in collected volumes, in curating formats like the Desintegrationskongress[1] or before that with *freitext*.[2] That makes a reclamation of certain descriptions possible: you're not only described, but you also forge your own visibility in the position of speaker, as public intellectuals, like Mithu Sanyal or Sharon Dodua Otoo also do. When you contribute to the cultural discourse in this way you go above and beyond the reception of your texts and target society as a whole, where it goes without saying that migrantized and marginalized people are part of the conversation.

SMS: Definitely. We talk back. That's hugely important and it's why these are better times. In the past we were so desperate to find these voices, and now they're on Deutschlandfunk, the big broadsheets commission pieces from us and give us carte blanche. I don't take that for granted and we have to acknowledge that as a gesture of genuine interest. I want to highlight the positives but stay realistic; these are suboptimal times. We can't let things stay the way they are now.

You can see that from the reception of my novels: *Außer sich* took off in a big way. It was all over the TV, in all the papers. I was passed around this Bundesrepublik—I didn't know Germany before that—in front of all these people who had probably never seen somebody like me before. That was educational. And now I've written *Im Menschen muss alles herrlich sein* (*Glorious People*, 2021) which is deliberately much more conventional, much more heteronormative. Of course, I'm aware of that and it cost me a lot, but that's how it had to be. The second book has already sold twice as many copies as *Außer sich*, even though the first book was incredibly popular and experienced such a strong resonance with journalists and academics. But normal people said "what? Why should I have to get to grips with five languages? Sorry, my life is hard enough as it is." You have to take that into account. But I still asked myself what was wrong with *Außer sich*. Was it too queer? But I actually think queerness was one thing, but maybe not the central thing. It's just too wild, too much. Which continent? What century? Which migrants again? I think

---

1 The festival Desintegration, a "Kongress zeitgenössischer jüdischer Positionen" (congress of contemporary Jewish positions), curated by Max Czollek and Sasha Marianna Salzmann, constituted a forum for the variety of Jewish positions and experiences in contemporary Germany, aiming to counteract predominant ascriptions to Jewish identity in Germany after 1945. See GORKI, Kongress zeitgenössischer jüdischer Positionen, accessed June 14, 2023, https://www.gorki.de/de/themenseite-festival-desintegration. A book based on the congress was also published by Kerber Verlag the following year.

2 A culture journal platforming transcultural perspectives in Germany, *Freitext* appeared between 2003 and 2019. Sasha Marianna Salzmann was part of the editorial team.

it just reflects who is out there, outside our bubble. Those are the facts. Suhrkamp marketed me in exactly the same way for both books; they didn't try less hard with *Außer sich*—in fact that book got more media attention. But the second [more conventional, heteronormative] book sold more.

Talking back is another thing we've always done. I edited *freitext* with colleagues for twelve years. That was our journal, and it was important to us to speak outward, and other communities, always marginalized communities, gave us feedback or wrote for us and we made the magazines together as a collaborative project. And now we're on Deutschlandfunk. That's something we need to reflect on, because at the end of the day we are doing exactly what we've always done. That there's such a strong interest now means it feels more like an intervention, but we have always intervened. I've been organizing events to intervene since I was sixteen. I started Global Open Stage in Hannover when I was a school dropout. I just wanted people to feel safe and to be able to do whatever they want to on stage—and I do exactly that to this day. I think the fact that the culture sector in dominant society is reacting has something to do with the fact that it's popular and it sells, even though they have no real understanding of what we do. When you're actually there in the Deutschlandfunk studio talking to the journalists and they ask you certain questions you realize that they haven't understood. But: our people hear it anyway, so it's worth it. But we still need a huge amount of patience and a thick skin. That's why so many of us won't do it anymore; they say that they can't listen to these same questions after ten, twenty years. They completely retreat. That's also part of our reality.

SR: I'm interested in whether you or others in your writer circles sense a certain burden of representation, especially these days when literature by marginalized authors has a greater reach and, as we have discussed, is very present in the mainstream media. How do you deal with the fact that, for example, *Außer sich* is categorized as queer literature, which means you're then expected—since queer literature unfortunately so rarely receives critical acclaim—to represent all queer literature and queer people to dominant society. How do you avoid tokenism?

SMS: There are strategies for this, and not having any can be debilitating, even dangerous. So, I'd support everything you say. We not only face a burden of representation but also undergo a process of exclusion. It's all about pushing a certain group of othered people further and further away so no one has to bother with them anymore. With *Im Menschen muss alles herrlich sein*, I felt that there aren't many books—that's not to say none at all—written in German by someone my age about these people at that time [the perestroika and the effects on the Soviet people]. And there's a danger that people will think, "oh, I know what it was like because I've read Salzmann." This pushed me to research everything in great detail because even though it's marked as fiction, we all know how it is. As Hannah Arendt put it, we expect truth from writers.[3] But why?

There will always be a burden of representation. I find it helpful to acknowledge it. And I also feel a sense of freedom because I represent such a small group of people. Few already know what queer Jewish "quota refugees" are like and so you can play with that. I weave certain moments into the text; in *Außer sich* there are lots of points where I make fun of the reader. Like when Anton says, "I always wondered why people were prepared to buy these stories about my supposed family—from me, a Russian-Jewish guy from Germany. But at some point, I realized that you can sell people any story. People want to hear stories. And then you get them to pay up. Family tragedies are particularly lucrative." It's literally there in the text. That's how I communicate with people, though obviously it's not a true dialogue. I totally recognize that this is the case with artistic work. Most people do not read into it or are unable or unwilling to reflect on it, as is their right. I believe in infinite freedom when it comes to understanding art.

And then there are strategies for working in the public sphere. Years ago, I developed a strategy that really works. Whenever I receive an invitation, I insist that someone else is also invited who would otherwise not be considered. If they want me, then this person has also got to be invited under the same conditions. They've yet to say no to me. I'm very aware of my privilege and I know that it doesn't always work. But often it does.

SR: At the end of *Im Menschen muss alles herrlich sein* you thank your literary role models "for the polyphony"[4] inherent in your work. Could you tell us more about this concept and what polyphony means in your writing? Do you see yourself as part of a particular tradition extending across the whole twentieth century, including Toni Morrison, Audre Lorde, and all the others you name? What role does this polyphony play in your work?

SMS: "Those who you came with" is an expression from hip hop. I always try to show what I've read. I enter into dialogue with it, and I want that to be crystal clear. Not because I'm afraid someone will accuse me of stealing but because I believe that it's got to be clear that together we form a network, whether we like it or not, and regardless of whether we like each other. No thought is unique, nothing emerges from nowhere.

---

3   See Hannah Arendt, *Denktagebuch* (Munich: Piper Verlag, 2020).
4   Sasha Marianna Salzmann, *Im Menschen muss alles Herrlich sein* (Frankfurt am Mein: Suhrkamp, 2021).

You've got to read a lot to have your own thoughts, you're essentially constructing a work that has already been made. Angela Davis encapsulated it for me once onstage when she began by thanking all the men and women whom she was unable to name but whom she wanted to thank for enabling her to be on that stage at all. That moment has really stayed with me. Of course, I want to thank those whose names I do know, but I also want to thank all those many people whose names I don't know who have made our struggle today a little bit easier. I am inspired by this feeling of gratitude. I don't feel forced to do this work, but reflecting on the work of others, thanking them, even disagreeing with them, is integral to my work. Sometimes you've got to disagree, but that's why I always want to name them. It takes nothing away from the work of art. That's something else that I've come to understand; it's good to know just how many of us there are. We are impressive in number.

LS: Apropos being numerous, networks and community are central to your work. The characters in your novels often form communities of solidarity, adopt family members, and build alliances—all this is also very present as an alternative to familial structures and patriarchal dynamics. Often these communities of solidarity are where the protagonists find understanding, acceptance, and care, and they ultimately serve to anchor them. What role does this strategy of belonging—in the sense of both being and writing—play for you in this form?

SMS: Yes, it's very evident in my work and my mother takes it quite badly. We otherwise have a very good relationship, but she knows what I'm saying. For me personally, it all started with thinking about the body and how it gets categorized; genetics are such a burden. And yet they are this non-negotiable fact of our existence. I'm not going to suggest that none of it exists and that chromosomes are just an invention; science exists, biology exists. Most of the time we need all this knowledge, and I don't have a problem with that. But I feel that it places a burden on marginalized people and many stay in their familial structures because to leave would quite simply mean death. The family is fundamentally envisaged as a support system but that doesn't mean that you'll get the support you need. And so many injuries are also sustained when the support and understanding that you need is withdrawn.

I'm nonbinary and have also accompanied so many trans people through their transitions. Seeing how far all these concepts can be expanded has been part of my reality, as has seeing just how starkly conditions are limited and dictated by external forces to the point that your life, literally your life, is on the line when you challenge any of this. It was interesting to me. People told me I was a girl, that I was from this country, had this passport and that birth certificate, but none of it felt right. Absolutely none of it. Realizing this was an act of liberation, which sounds more glamorous than it is. It's not glamorous to have to free yourself through struggle over and over again. There's this norm that you've got to rebel against in order to live.

LS: In your essay "Sichtbar" (Visible) you also write: "We are the *others* who know that *normal* has nothing to say to us. *Normal* is not an authority for us. . . . But we know about the power of alliances."[5]

SMS: Exactly—I feel like I'm always coming up against a deliberate misinterpretation of gender theory as something that we can just slip into because we feel like it. Today I'm totally down to change my gender because it's the trend. It all comes from a very malicious place. Even in the mainstream, people don't quite get us. I was finally able to explain it to my mother by saying: do you really think that people went into the concentration camps for fun? Do you seriously believe that they would have not been heterosexual if given the choice? And I think that within her Jewish body where she bore her pain, which carries generations of trauma, something suddenly clicked. But many people do not have a wound to which you can speak, a wound that may permit you to explain the loss experienced by so many people on this planet as a result of having grown up in birth families who completely deny them from being who they say they are. And to some extent that was true for me.

I had to completely sever connections with some family members. But I never felt alone. That was the thing. Even before there were words for what we wanted, before the slogans, before *Transparent* came out,[6] the first series for me . . . I know there were a few small things before then, but I wasn't aware of them at the time. I was wild with joy: we were serious! It was official: we were everywhere! We just hadn't known about all the others. Now we're on Netflix, which is a whole other problem . . . But at least word has spread that your birth family is just one choice out of many. I consider that an important step. I think it's quite clear how I incorporate it into my work. First, I make sure my chosen family is seen by naming them at the end. I always do that. Everyone in my acknowledgments is also my chosen family. I also believe that it's totally possible for chosen family to become an established concept. It will never be as strong as your birth family as an idea because of genetics, because of biology, and because it's a marginal experience, of course. But I still believe that it will

---

5 Sasha Marianna Salzmann, "Visible," in *TRANSIT, Your Homeland Is Our Nightmare*, trans. Lou Silhol-Macher, *TRANSIT*, accessed June 22, 2023, https://transit.berkeley.edu/2021/visible/.

6 An American television series that aired from 2014 to 2019 revolving around a family coming to terms with their middle-aged parent coming out as a trans woman.

someday be possible for chosen family to be a fully accepted term that no one questions. It's getting easier and easier—though it's still very hard—for it to be set down in law. I have a lot of contact with Ukrainian refugees and one of the discussions in the community was about how [gay] men sent to the front have no right to see their partners or get any support and that's what they want to change right now. That's a huge step forward, especially now amid the war in Ukraine. In 2017, I was in Odesa with my wife and all our friends told us, "don't hold hands and don't even think about kissing, don't do it. Just no." And now in the middle of the war there's this step forward. So much will become possible.

LS: There's also a sense of momentary utopia in this interweaving of so many perspectives from such a diverse range of people who can extend alliances and solidarity across their differences, who understand what it means to be there for each other. Earlier you mentioned wounds that bring us together and that have the potential to create new connections between us that we couldn't have predicted.

SMS: I think the question of how we can be there for each other without understanding each other has a paradoxical answer. In my essay "Sichtbar," I describe how two men, clearly perceived as Muslim in this country, came to the aid of a lesbian couple. We had so few experiences in common, but they had a wound and I have a wound and they simply called to each other. In simpler words, it's about being able to find connection. And that's why it's so difficult for people without wounds to understand even if they want to. You can't hold it against anyone. I'd much rather everyone bore fewer wounds, you know? I'd hardly insist on someone going out to injure themselves just so they can talk to me. That would be a bit strange. But experience is what brings us together and it's also what sets us apart.

This year I had the most extreme experience of all. I thought I had already reached that limit but no, you can never say for sure that this is the most extreme it will ever get. Never. The war in Ukraine radically cut my world off from so many people in my community. And suddenly it got very unsettling as I realized that this is an experience that will divide us forever. I was completely subsumed by an avalanche and so many people in the community said, well we didn't talk about Afghanistan, we didn't talk enough about Syria, so why should I talk about Ukraine? I'm absolutely prepared to have this discussion. I understand it. And that's when I realized that you can't choose your wounds, you can't choose when to connect with others, but turning this into something productive and progressive will bring those of us with wounds together.

Oh, and I have another nice story. In 2016 and 2017 I was living with several young Syrian men and when the war escalated in Ukraine I thought, I wonder how they are doing? How were they coping with it all? First because of the war, as some people were being retraumatized, and also because people were being welcomed a bit differently compared to how Yazan and Mazen had experienced it back then . . . But they just said, seriously, we really wish everyone all the best. There was clearly no bad blood from their side, it was just stirred up by others. That's the sense I got from my conversations at least, and that was very encouraging.

LS: And it also helps to understand that it's not so simple: We need to envisage who we are as a collective differently. It's got to be more complex, with room for diversity and heterogeneity. This is also part of talking back in literature. It's all about representing a Germany that is not imagined in homogenous terms. And for this we need a common language to serve as a common perspective on the world and who we are—for all this to be conceivable at all. As Toni Morrison said in her Nobel lecture, language determines the system: "Oppressive language does more than represent violence; it is violence; does more than represent the limits of knowledge; it limits knowledge. . . . Sexist language, racist language, theistic language — all are typical of the policing languages of mastery, and cannot, do not permit new knowledge or encourage the mutual exchange of ideas."[7]

SR: And Audre Lorde said, "Name the nameless so it can be thought."[8] We need to find the words to describe ourselves and to make things speakable.

SMS: And that's what makes it all such a tough process: A war has been waged against the gender asterisk for years . . . When I started using the asterisk it was so controversial that I felt that we couldn't just be talking about a little pompom punctuation mark. We were talking about German identity. We were talking about the limits of your imagination. And that's why it felt so existential. That's why I also belong to this fraction that says, "Let's name it!" It's a fight for our identity. It's a fight for everything. Though there are some people who say, "I'm a lesbian, so what?" No, it does matter. The question is how much can you endure? And if you cannot endure it, what does that say about you? There are many lines that I'm obsessed with, and there's that one from Hannah Arendt about how you can identify the essence of a society by how it treats minorities. As Antje Rávic Strubel said, what does it say about you if a gender asterisk makes you mad but a dollar sign doesn't?! Antje was onstage and they

---

7   Toni Morrison, Nobel Lecture December 7, 1993, https://www.nobelprize.org/prizes/literature/1993/morrison/lecture/.

8   Audre Lorde, *Your Silence Will Not Protect You* (London: Silver Press, 2017), 8.

were saying it's a big problem to read and print it. And yet the dollar sign has never been questioned?

And that, I think, is what we are doing with literature every single day. And that's why it's considered an attack on Germany, as though Germany is being rewritten. And from my perspective at least, that's exactly what we are doing.

LS: Rewriting German identities.

SR: I spend a lot of time in German-language literature and German cultural spaces as someone who comes from England and speaks English as my first language. People often want to know what I think because, after all, "in England you don't need the gender asterisk." The English language doesn't explicitly mark gender—using feminine forms is considered outdated and not progressive. An actor is an actor no matter their gender; the term *actress* is redundant. You don't need to indicate the gender of a person in their job title. Whereas in German, as I always try to explain, we're dealing with a completely different language with a much stronger grammatical gender, and it just works differently. It's not about this punctuation mark, but about everything else around it. It's about identity and finding a language that can create a sense of belonging and that is not violent. Yes, it might be different in English, but here we are talking about the German language and German identity.

SMS: I also feel that there are people who have realized that they can make a career out of being against it. Some people are seriously against it. And then there are the people whose very existence depends on being able to be represented in language. We've all got to somehow make it through. And I've got to say that the fact that my voting papers now have the asterisk on them puts me completely at ease with the times in which we are living. Of course, I'm aware that most people are against it. But my voting papers testify to my existence. It really encourages me to go and vote.

SR: Perhaps we could go back to *Im Menschen muss alles herrlich sein* and talk about how—as you've said yourself—it's written in a much more conventional and heteronormative way compared to *Außer sich*?

SMS: Yes, I'm always happy to talk about it, to make clear that it was no coincidence, it was part of a huge process. I mean, when you look at the books, I don't think anyone would think that they were written by different people, but you can see that there is a completely different impetus behind the story. At some point, I realized that I wanted to tell this woman's story. It begins in the seventies in the Soviet Union. She's a lesbian but she doesn't know it and has no words for it. I had to take this perspective and ask how does she perceive women if she doesn't know that she desires them? I basically gave women a sharper outline than men, but it didn't go any further than that. And then that became a point of criticism as soon as the book was released: I mean, of course my male characters are vague, my character is a lesbian! At the same time, I quickly realized that a novel set in the Soviet Union during the seventies, eighties, and into the perestroika era could not use the gender asterisk. It had to be the opposite of fluid. It was a painful yet necessary process. Ultimately, it's not about how I would like the world to have looked, but rather what kind of conditions it might have created for my protagonists. My material led me into this whole ecosystem in which my choices were limited.

It was hard work. I could breathe a little sigh of relief when the daughter's generation arrived in the shape of Edi. Now we could speak as I think. And yet everything was still quite binary; I mean, I was still thinking only in terms of men and women, which is a real contradiction for me. But I knew that these are the people who exist in that story. So, who I am or what I want is of little relevance. But I could get Edi to say things as a commentary on what happened back then. In *Außer sich*, Ali spends all this time reflecting on the uncertainty of whether you are really who other people say you are, whereas Edi can do the same thing from within the very rigid system of the post-Soviet world by realizing that she's got to reject everything with every fiber of her being. And she's got to grapple with blood. That was the conflict I had to embark on. And there are also lots of hints, for me and for the small lesbian community that will pick up on them, like the deep infatuation with Aljona.[9] Or the fact that Edi is simply unaware that her mother is a lesbian. Just think how many daughters are in that position. I mean, it blows my mind that so many children don't know that their parents were or are queer because they themselves lacked the right words. At one of the first readings, I was still a little uncertain about the material and felt that it was rather utopian for both mother and daughter to be lesbians. It seemed wishful thinking on my part. But then a translator came up to me and said, "My daughter is also a lesbian." And I thought, oh my God, of course families like this exist! Why wouldn't they? It was such a relief to think that I can write moments of freedom into dictatorial systems too. And a great moderator once asked me about Aljona as representing the epitome of freedom in the book. Most people never ask about her. This freedom is less about lesbian desire—it's the ultimate escape for her to burn her red pioneer scarf. But I was so happy that it can also be read as such because—quite apart from lesbian or any other desire for that matter—it's all about freedom

---

[9] One of the novel's protagonists, Lena, befriends a girl named Aljona at a pioneer summer camp in the Soviet Union. See Salzmann, *Im Menschen muss alles herrlich sein*, 48.

and deprivation of freedom. And to give in to it under a system where everything else means death. It's not always a choice. Lena often faces no choice at all.

I followed this thread and found it incredibly hard. But an amazing part of the process was interviewing these women for the novel. It was just amazing to sit with them and hear about realities that I could hardly have envisaged. You can't imagine what you don't know exists. I didn't have the right questions. They answered questions that I didn't even have yet. That's the greatest gift of writing: I become so much wiser in the process. It doesn't always have to be biographical or autobiographical, I just get to understand the complexities of other people's lives a little better. And it also makes me take stock. I consider the fact that I know just a fraction of what my mother went through. For her, there was no alternative to so much of what seems like violence to me. Not for her. I feel that these learning processes are interwoven with this material, and they only happen because I look at the truth and don't try to make things seem better than they were.

LS: Part of the underlying theme of *Im Menschen muss alles herrlich sein* is also about these different realities and people's inability to communicate with one another. But you also grant access to these realities through your writing. You have recently developed the concept of inclusive literature, writing that is empathetic to other lived realities—and "maximum honesty" means "being who we are whether we like it or not. It's not about being right or wrong, attributions are no longer relevant."[10]

SMS: Yes, it's both a concept and a process. I mean, I only really believe in temporary autonomous zones, and concepts are also temporary autonomous zones for me. That's why the term *queer* has undergone such a transformation and that's why we are never quite sure what we mean. And to be honest, I find that more comfortable than setting it in stone—you'd have a problem if it no longer fit. And I often think about what it could mean at this point in time. I feel that *Im Menschen muss alles herrlich sein* should be inclusive literature in retrospect. I hoped that the women I interviewed would understand what I wanted. And I'd already experienced this when writing for the stage. I wanted a completely different set of people in the audience. At the time only a small subset of society went to the theater, my own plays included. But I wanted the exact opposite

10   Anja Johannsen and Sasha Marianna Salzmann, "Sasha Marianna Salzmann," *boxenstopp*, a podcast, June 4, 2021, https://podcasters.spotify.com/pod/show/boxenstopp/episodes/Sasha-Marianna-Salzmann-e11tm1u. See also Sasha Marianna Salzmann, "Die bestehende Ordnung der Dinge stören," Deutschlandfunk, June 16, 2021, https://www.deutschlandfunk.de/themenreihe-muss-literatur-politisch-sein-die-bestehende-100.html.

kind of audience. I think that they don't usually come because they are used to not understanding why they are being written about or why someone is walking around naked. So, an image of inclusion emerges from the negative. It may sound like a sociopedagogical term, but I view it as an artistic practice. I love German theater, and its aggressive politics came about because Nazi grandchildren were in the audience, and they needed to be shouted at. Handke wrote *Publikumsbeschimpfungen*[11] because he wanted to attack Nazis and their children. Fair enough. I mean, he could have included himself in that attack, but hey, he was fundamentally going in the right direction. Now there are not only the offspring of Nazi families in the audience and so the politics of it must work differently. We cannot have people sitting there and thinking, "what's it got to do with me? Why are you shouting at me?" And so, I try to write for those who are not necessarily thought of as theater audiences in the first place. Yes, the critics don't always like it; they think that I write that way because I'm from abroad. In *Außer sich* I just didn't think about it, not the critics, not the audience. I didn't think, "oh I'm writing for us or for the community or anything like that." I just wrote. And in *Im Menschen muss alles herrlich sein* I thought, "I don't want to become incomprehensible to the people I interviewed." You'd have to have quite a nerve to go, "great, I'll take your stories, thanks for the interview, now I'm off to turn them into 'high art.'" There was no way I could do that. But it only worked out because I could make it integral to the structure of the story.

There is no singular inclusive literature, but I found *Rombo* by Esther Kinsky thought-provoking. Esther is probably one of the most brilliant authors alive today. There is nothing that she hasn't read. And this novel is written in independent clauses, relatively simple ones at that. It even reads like a children's book at times and yet you know it's seriously great literature. She never tries to prove anything to anyone, and it caused me to have this fleeting thought—I don't know if it's true, it's just a hypothesis really—but I felt this slight pang as I read her book that maybe I write such long sentences because I'm still trying to prove that I can speak German. That's something to work out in the third book.

I can't say what it all means exactly. Not inclusion as a political stance, but rather inclusion as a way of saying that big truths can be contained in complex sentences, but they can also be found in simple sentences. Both are possible. How many people can you actually take with you, and are they the ones you actually want to reach? Novels haven't had an easy time

---

11 Handke's *Publikumsbeschimpfung*, which premièred in 1966, was an innovative play that explicitly addressed the audience, confronting the spectators with their guilt and involvement in the atrocities committed by the Nazis, culminating in insults and abuses on the part of the actors. See Peter Handke, *Publikumsbeschimpfung und andere Sprechstücke* (Berlin: Suhrkamp, 2019).

lately, for good reason. I just felt during the pandemic that you've got to be extremely privileged to be able to read novels. And then with the full-scale war I thought I've only got time to read poetry now. There's nothing stopping anyone from making your work accessible to as many people as possible while telling a very complex story, though it's only recently that I've stopped viewing this as a contradiction. And I think that has a lot to do with inclusion as an aesthetic approach.

LS: Speaking of your aesthetic approach, there's a very interesting part in *Im Menschen muss alles herrlich sein* where Edi discusses the war in Donbas with her uncle at a pretty catastrophic family gathering. And then they talk about this text and about what side the hero of the story is on—he's on neither; and the uncle thinks that you can't write like that, you've got to take a side—anything else is nonsense, rubbish. And when I read that I thought, I don't believe that you believe that yourself. And then I asked myself whether this had changed because of the war in Ukraine.

SMS: Yes, though it's also different for me to read that aloud now. But I find it incredibly important to me personally. Take Serhij Zhadan's novel *Internat* (The orphanage),[12] which I read so many times long before the war started to spread west. He wrote it in 2014 or 2015, I think. To me, he was doing something here that epitomizes good, decidedly political literature. But I wasn't exactly sure how he did it, so I wanted to learn. The novel is set in Donbas, in an occupied area where a man is trying to get his nephew out of an orphanage. The orphanage is suddenly in a war zone and inside is this child who needs to be rescued. Because of the war, it takes days to get to the neighboring town and so the novel takes place over three days. Right up until the end, you don't know whether the protagonist is Russian or Ukrainian, where he is coming from and traveling to. At each checkpoint, you have no idea which language he is speaking and with whom. You don't know the crest on the passport that he has to keep showing. You just have no idea. And I thought, I want to achieve that! I don't exactly know how, but that's exactly what I want. For Zhadan to do that in a super-specific context, having been traipsing from one Ukrainian military base to the next since 2014, to write in this way despite his position being very clear ... That's why I position uncle Valery in such stark opposition. He says "no, of course you've got to take sides, here are the good people, there are the evil ones, and there are blood rights too." I see Zhadan as the opposite of all that. His position as a human and an activist is very clear, but his writing is different. I'm yet to manage it myself but that's what I'm really looking for in my own writing. I don't think it's possible to write in an apolitical way. But literature

---

12   Serhij Zhadan, *Internat*, trans. Juri Durkot und Sabine Stöhr (Berlin: Suhrkamp, 2018).

is also not a political manifesto. My essays are explicitly political, but they can only find expression in a form of poetry that is not explicitly political.

LS: Maybe this partly answers the question of how you can write during war? In an essay you wrote of the impossibility of writing because of the war in Ukraine and quoted the Ukrainian author Lyuba Yakimchuk: "There's no poetry about war. Just decomposition."[13] And yet at the same time literature is always a medium for bearing witness—and that's not easy right now, to continue to bear witness demands a lot from you.

SMS: Yes, I was asked to write an opening speech for the 2022 Acting through Language Festival at the Literary Colloquium Berlin. I agreed to it in January and only started writing in March, by which time I thought, "acting through language?!" It was about the future of reading and literature, and I just thought—"now?"

But then again, we have and always will have literature. People encounter it in prisons, in psychiatric wards, in wars, or while experiencing torture. It doesn't just belong to literary institutes. To me, literature and art are life itself. When art comes into being, it shows that someone is still alive. That's why I'm not concerned about art at all. Art will exist for as long as life itself. It doesn't matter that not everything will be published or shown on a big stage; not everything will be nominated for a Nobel prize. Art remains unaffected and it's a way of life for those who create it, a way of staying alive. I'm not at all worried in that sense but I am worried about everything else. I feel that everything else is ending, nothing is safe. But then so many people manage to write against all odds. Sometimes they are visible, sometimes they are not. Sometimes we get to read their work, sometimes we don't. But still it exists. And in that sense, it's all gonna be alright.

—Translated by Catriona Corke and Selma Rezgui

---

13 Sasha Marianna Salzmann, "Bitte warten Sie," *Süddeutsche Zeitung*, June 22, 2022, https://www.sueddeutsche.de/kultur/sasha-marianna-salzmann-schreiben-krieg-in-der-ukraine-fluechtende-1.5607325.

Bibliography

Arendt, Hannah. *Denktagebuch*. Munich: Piper Verlag, 2020.

Handke, Peter. *Publikumsbeschimpfung und andere Sprechstücke*. Berlin: Suhrkamp, 2019.

Lorde, Audre. *Your Silence Will Not Protect You*. London: Silver Press, 2017.

Morrison, Toni. Nobel Lecture. December 7, 1993. https://www.nobelprize.org/prizes/literature/1993/morrison/lecture/.

Salzmann, Sasha Marianna. *Außer sich*. Berlin: Suhrkamp, 2017.

———. *Beside Myself*. Translated by Imogen Taylor. New York: Other Press, 2019.

———. "Bitte warten Sie." *Süddeutsche Zeitung*, June 22, 2022. https://www.sueddeutsche.de/kultur/sasha-marianna-salzmann-schreiben-krieg-in-der-ukraine-fluechtende-1.5607325.

———. *Im Menschen muss alles Herrlich sein*. Berlin: Suhrkamp, 2021.

———. "Visible." In *TRANSIT, Your Homeland Is Our Nightmare*. Translated by Lou Silhol-Macher. *TRANSIT*. Accessed June 22, 2023. https://transit.berkeley.edu/2021/visible/.

Zhadan, Serhij. *Internat*. Translated by Juri Durkot und Sabine Stöhr. Berlin: Suhrkamp, 2018.

2: Twin Novels: Renegotiating Self and Other in Sasha Marianna Salzmann's *Außer sich* and Olivia Wenzel's *1000 Serpentinen Angst*

Laura Marie Sturtz

> *Ich weiß nicht, wohin es geht, alle anderen wissen es, ich nicht.*[1]
> [I don't know where we're going. All the others know, but I don't.]

> *WO BIST DU JETZT? . . .*
> *WO BIST DU ZUHAUSE? . . .*
> *WO IST DEIN PLATZ? . . .*
> *WO KOMMST DU HER?*[2]
>
> [WHERE ARE YOU NOW? . . . WHERE ARE YOU AT HOME? . . . WHERE DO YOU BELONG? . . . WHERE DO YOU COME FROM?]

SUCH QUESTIONS OF BELONGING weave through both Sasha Marianna Salzmann's novel *Außer sich* (2017; *Beside Myself*, 2019) and Olivia Wenzel's novel *1000 Serpentinen Angst* (2020; *1000 Coils of Fear*, 2022) as they present us with their protagonists' quests for themselves and "another possible community" that subverts the logic of Otherness.[3] Salzmann's novel follows its nonbinary, queer, Soviet-Jewish protagonist Ali on their journey to Istanbul in search of their twin brother Anton, and

---

1 Sasha Marianna Salzmann, *Außer sich* (Frankfurt am Main: Suhrkamp, 2017), 11. Cited in the following as *AS* with page number. Sasha Marianna Salzmann, *Beside Myself*, trans. Imogen Taylor (New York: Other Press, 2019), 3. Cited in the following as *BM* with page number.

2 Olivia Wenzel, *1000 Serpentinen Angst* (Frankfurt am Main: S. Fischer Verlag, 2020), 17–32. Cited in the text as *TSA* with page number. Olivia Wenzel, *1000 Coils of Fear*, trans. Priscilla Layne (London: Dialogue Books, 2022), 9, 23–24. Cited in the text as *CF* with page number.

3 Gilles Deleuze and Felix Guattari, *Kafka: Toward a Minor Literature* (Minneapolis: University of Minnesota Press, 1986), 17.

across one century of Soviet-Jewish family history marked by displacement and violence.[4] Wenzel's novel is concerned with the unnamed protagonist's trauma caused by racism, the suicide of her twin brother, and the experience of being nonwhite as well as GDR-born and queer in contemporary Germany. Both texts portray their protagonists' process of finding a voice to narrate their own story, counteracting the exterior gaze and forging a language and means for self-expression—coming to terms with their own stories by integrating and engaging with their closest Other: their twin brothers. Salzmann and Wenzel make an interesting pairing regarding these similarities, posing questions of belonging as well as challenging the reader with disorienting narratives that transcend any linear or chronological order, mirroring the uprootedness of their protagonists. Building on a combined theoretical framework of Deleuze and Guattari's minor literature and the contemporary concept of postmigrant storytelling, I show how these novels represent narratives of subject formation that transcend narrow frames of a "mythical norm" of Germanness, to borrow Audre Lorde's term, anticipating alternative visions of self and Other, individual and community.[5]

"Another Possible Community": Minor Literature and Postmigrant Storytelling

While the ideas of Deleuze and Guattari were developed some time ago, they have not ceased to provide a fruitful vocabulary regarding the revolutionary potential of the literary text, enabling an eminently political approach. This becomes all the more discernible when adapted to the context of contemporary German literature and the concept of postmigration. These approaches can be brought together productively to highlight the literary intervention imminent in the writings of both Salzmann and Wenzel. As of late, the concept of minor writing has inspired renewed interest, not least in an extensive *Modern Languages Open* special collection edited by Maria Roca Lizarazu and Godela Weiss-Sussex: *Rethinking "Minor Literatures"—Contemporary Jewish Women's Writing in Germany and Austria* (2020). As laid out in the collection's introduction, its aim "is to probe the productivity of . . . 'minor literature' in the context of contemporary Jewish writing in the German-language

---

4   I will be using they/them pronouns when referring to Ali, mirroring the novel's decided transgression of gender binaries and the fluctuation between the use of she/her and he/him pronouns.
5   Audre Lorde, *Your Silence Will Not Protect You: Essays and Poems* (London: Silver Press, 2017), 194.

literary landscape."[6] In reapplying the concept developed by Deleuze and Guattari as a philosophical reading of Kafka's writing as a Jew in Prague, the collection engages with a shift in contemporary German-Jewish literature that addresses themes such as migration and multilingualism and increasingly "tend[s] to question fixed binaries and boundaries, often in terms of national and linguistic belonging."[7] Building on this line of thought, as well as Roca Lizarazu's observation that Salzmann's work is equally relevant to the recent wave of postmigrant writing in German literature,[8] I will show that the applicability of the concept of minor literature is by no means limited to the contemporary German-Jewish context but proves to be productive when brought together and extended in relation to the concept of postmigrant writing, with which it shares an explicit interest in the literary text as a means of social and political intervention from the perspective of those who are marked as Other in the face of an "imagined" majority community.[9] Moreover, a combined reading of Salzmann and Wenzel makes it possible to highlight shared strategies and themes of interventionist writing that are not attributed to a common background of authors or texts—for example, German-Jewish writing—but much rather to their joint addressing the literary, cultural, and political landscape of contemporary Germany, forming part of a current wave of political writing in German that includes many of the authors discussed in this volume.

In *Toward a Minor Literature*, the authors underline that "minor literature doesn't come from a minor language; it is rather that which a minority constructs within a major language."[10] While the linguistic aspect of minor writing, the "deterritorialization of language,"[11] figures most prominently in literary analysis of migrant writing,[12] focusing on the destabilization of meaning-making in the so-called "major" language,

---

6   Maria Roca Lizarazu and Godela Weiss-Sussex, "Introduction: Rethinking 'Minor Literatures'—Contemporary Jewish Women's Writing in Germany and Austria," *Modern Languages Open* 1 (2020): 1–7, 1.
7   Roca Lizarazu and Weiss-Sussex, "Introduction," 2.
8   Maria Roca Lizarazu, "Ec-Static Existences: The Poetics and Politics of Non-Belonging in Sasha Marianna Salzmann's *Außer Sich* (2017)," *Modern Languages Open* 1, no. 10 (2020): 1–19, 16. See also Maria Roca Lizarazu, "'Integration ist definitiv nicht unser Anliegen, eher schon Desintegration.' Postmigrant Renegotiations of Identity and Belonging in Contemporary Germany," *humanities* 9, no 2 (2020): 42.
9   Benedict Anderson, *Imagined Communities: Reflections on the Origin and Spread of Nationalism* (London: Verso Books, 2016).
10 Deleuze and Guattari, *Toward a Minor Literature*, 16.
11 Deleuze and Guattari, *Toward a Minor Literature*, 18.
12 Margaret Littler, "Cramped Creativity: The Politics of a Minor German Literature," in *Aesthetics and Politics in Modern German Culture*, ed. Brigid

my interest lies in the political and social implications of literary writing implicit in Deleuze and Guattari's thinking. The subversive potential of minor writing derives from the ascribed position inside a majority culture, simultaneously partaking in the cultural settings of the majoritarian society *and* being considered as situated outside the common frame of nation and identity: "literature finds itself positively charged with the role and function of collective, and even revolutionary, enunciation. . . . If the writer is in the margins or completely outside his or her fragile community, this situation allows the writer all the more the possibility to express another possible community and to forge the means for another consciousness and another sensibility."[13] Consequently, the notion of the minor is tied to its potential to oppose and subvert common frames of identity, community, and belonging. As such, it constitutes an interesting frame for reading *Außer sich* and *1000 Serpentinen Angst*, both of which bring formerly underrepresented perspectives to the contemporary German literary scene, reflecting on their protagonists' positionalities in contemporary Germany, portraying their struggles for recognition, their vulnerability in the face of physical and psychological violence, and their quest for a representation of the self, which is presented as fluid and multilayered rather than static and fixed, counteracting foreclosing notions of "Germanness" and "normality." It is this potential of political agency of minor literature that Margaret Littler expands on: "*minor* literary production's intervention is of an entirely different order. Rather than 'representing' a people, minor politics is about their *creation*. . . . Minoritarian becomings occur when those who do not conform to the standard change the way that the standard is defined."[14] As Littler stresses, minor literature is essentially about the *intervention* and *transformation* of society, making the writing of Salzmann and Wenzel an imminently political act of aesthetic envisioning from the perspective of those whose writing traditionally has not been considered to be part of the German canon.

While the concept of Deleuze and Guattari is tied to the social position of the minor as situated "in the margins or completely outside his or her fragile community,"[15] perpetuating the idea of a marginalized or minoritized literature that does not belong to the frames of the majoritarian society, I want to stress the subversive potential that literary strategies of those who are marked as Other have inside a majoritarian society still tied to an exclusionary vision of a homogenous community—an approach that can be related to the concept of the postmigrant as a self-labeling act

---

Haines, Stephen Parker, and Colin Riordan (Bern: Internationaler Verlag der Wissenschaften, 2010), 222.

13 Deleuze and Guattari, *Toward a Minor Literature*, 17.
14 Littler, "Cramped Creativity," 224–25.
15 Deleuze and Guattari, *Toward a Minor Literature*, 17.

that opposes foreclosing notions of Germanness. The term was popularized in the 2010s by the Berlin-based theater producer Shermin Langhoff to counteract the label of "migrant theater"—and has since been adopted as an academic perspective of ever-growing interest.[16] Emerging from this artistic context as a self-description, the term *postmigrant* reclaims the subversive potential of storytelling to create a space for the plurality of narratives *within* the German society as a "gemeinsame[r] Raum der Diversität jenseits von Herkunft" (a shared space beyond common origin).[17] Postmigrant storytelling creates visibility as well as audibility for the "radical diversity"[18] of contemporary German identities and intervenes in the dominant collective stories through "practices [that] represent a challenge to ways in which we are accustomed to talking about . . . so-called roots or originary cultural belongings, language, inequality and, of course, identity."[19] Consequently, postmigrant storytelling shares with minor literature the perspective of those who are marked as outsiders by the dominant culture. At the same time it contains the potential of rewriting the very imagery of a homogenous society through "counter-hegemonic knowledge production"[20] and the subversion of "eingespielten Dichotomien 'Wir/Die'" (well-practiced assumptions about Them/Us) and the creation of "eine andere Genealogie der Gegenwart . . .[,] [in der] das etablierte Bild von Gesellschaft, Kultur und Identität . . . einer Prüfung unterzogen wird . . . um mehr Denk- und Deutungsalternativen

---

16   Anne Ring Petersen, Moritz Schramm, and Frauke Wiegand, "Introduction: From Artistic Intervention to Academic Discussion," in *Reframing Migration, Diversity and the Arts: The Postmigrant Condition*, ed. Moritz Schramm, Sten Pultz Moslund, and Anne Ring Petersen (London: Routledge, 2021), 3–11.

17   Shermin Langhoff, Bundeszentrale für politische Bildung, "Die Herkunft spielt keine Rolle—'Postmigrantisches' Theater im Ballhaus Naunynstraße," Bundeszentrale für politische Bildung, March 10, 2011, https://www.bpb.de/lernen/kulturelle-bildung/60135/die-herkunft-spielt-keine-rolle-postmigrantisches-theater-im-ballhaus-naunynstrasse/. (accessed February 28, 2024). Interestingly, the term postmigrant was first mentioned in 1995 by Baumann and Sunier used in 1995 by Baumann and Sunier in their anthology *Post-Migration Ethnicity*, albeit as a descriptive term that was not theorized further. Since being popularized by Shermin Langhoff it has been established as an analytical lens for the German cultural sphere. See Gerd Baumann and Thijl Sunier, *Post-Migration Ethnicity: De-Essentializing Cohesion, Commitments, and Comparison* (Amsterdam: Het Spinhuis Publishers, 1995). See also Anita Rotter and Erol Yildiz, "Postcolonialism and Postmigration: Re-Mapping the Topography of the Possible," *Crossings* 14, no. 1 (2023): 20. All translations are my own unless otherwise stated.

18   Max Czollek. *Desintegriert euch!* (Berlin: Hanser, 2018), 15.

19   Roger Bromley, "A Bricolage of Identifications: Storying Postmigrant Belonging," *Journal of Aesthetics & Culture* 9, no. 2 (2017): 32.

20   Rotter and Yildiz, "Postcolonialism and Postmigration," 20.

zu ermöglichen"[21] (an alternative genealogy of the present . . ., which scrutinizes the established image of society, culture, identity . . . to enable different approaches and interpretations).[22] Brought together with the ideas inherent in Deleuze and Guattari's conception of minor literature, postmigrant storytelling can be thought of as an "intervention of a different order,"[23] underlining the revolutionary and counterhegemonic potential of their artistic practices. Yet, the postmigrant strives to overcome the very notions of Otherness tied to migratory experiences still implicit in Deleuze and Guattari and acts as an emancipatory self-labeling approach that claims its place as part of contemporary German society.

Finding a Voice: Writing the Self in *Außer Sich* and *1000 Serpentinen Angst*

In their essay "Sichtbar," Salzmann reflects on the need for self-representation as a means to counteract the hegemonic interpretative pattern applied from outside: "Ich werde nie wissen, was es heißt, unsichtbar zu sein. . . . Mich in der Menge aufzulösen, ist keine Option für mich. Ich gehöre gleich mehreren Minderheiten an; das kaschieren zu wollen, birgt für mich größere Gefahren, als meine Positionen zu benennen" (I will never know what it means to be invisible. . . . To dissolve in the crowd is not an option for me. I belong to several minority groups at once; to conceal this would entail more dangers for me than to name my positionalities).[24] Drawing on the poetics of Audre Lorde, Salzmann underlines the need to speak for oneself, to oppose the dogma of assimilation and to frame one's existence against a supposed frame of "normality."[25] Formulating one's own position against the dominant culture is a powerful political action, as Audre Lorde expounds in her anthology *Your Silence Will Not Protect You*, arguing for poetry as "a vital necessity of our existence" that gives "name to the nameless so it can be

---

21 Erol Yildiz, "Postmigrantische Lesart: Theoretische und methodisch-methodologische Implikationen," in *Othering in der postmigrantischen Gesellschaft: Herausforderungen und Konsequenzen für die Forschungspraxis*, ed. Irini Siouti et al. (Bielefeld: transcript, 2022), 51.
22 Yildiz, "Postmigrantische Lesart," 51.
23 Littler, "Cramped Creativity," 224.
24 Sasha Marianna Salzmann, "Sichtbar," in *Eure Heimat ist unser Albtraum*, ed. Fatma Aydemir and Hengameh Yaghoobifarah (Berlin: Ullstein fünf, 2019), 13; Sasha Marianna Salzmann, "Visible," in *TRANSIT, Your Homeland Is Our Nightmare*, trans. Lou Silhol-Macher, *TRANSIT*, accessed June 22, 2023, https://transit.berkeley.edu/2021/visible/.
25 Salzmann, "Sichtbar," 14.

thought."[26] Through the act of generating narratives, one's own existence becomes palpable, speaks against the narrow frame of reality and identity in a supposedly white, male, heterosexual society. This creates alternative visions that empower and reclaim the interpretational sovereignty over one's own existence: "Poetry is not a luxury. . . . It forms the quality of light within which we predicate our hopes and dreams towards survival and change, first made into language, then into idea, then into more tangible action. . . . And where that language does not yet exist, it is our poetry which helps to fashion it."[27] With this, Lorde underlines the political power of literary self-representation as a counternarrative to foreclosing notions of identity and as a means of forging a language for the self that overcomes the language of discrimination and enables "survival and change."

"Ein Я konnte ich nicht denken": Poetics of the Self in *Außer sich*

Salzmann's *Außer sich* presents us with a narrative that challenges fixed borders of majoritarian identity and belonging, transcending frames such as nation, genealogy/family, mother tongue, gender—even time and space—deterritorializing and subverting "mythical norms" of Germanness. The point of departure for the nonlinear accounts that constitute the novel is the disappearance of the protagonist's twin Anton, whom they follow to Istanbul. However, Ali's journey evolves into a quest for themselves as they undergo a process of gender transition, which constitutes the novel's plotline in the present. This is complemented with the retracing of their Jewish-Soviet family history across three generations and a multitude of stories shaped by migration and displacement, antisemitic and domestic violence, disintegration, and trauma against which Ali places their own narrative in the form of an ambiguous and fluid becoming. Everything is constantly on the move: characters, destinies and causalities blur, languages intersect, narrative perspectives and pronouns alternate, fluidity and dynamics are proposed in lieu of set meanings and the defining of the "I" as a fixed entity. As Ali states about themselves: "'Ich' ist im Russischen nur ein Buchstabe: 'Я.' Ein einziger Buchstabe in einem dreiunddreißigstelligen Alphabet. . . . Ein 'Я' konnte ich nicht denken" (*AS*, 274; "'I' in Russian is 'Я', the last of thirty-three letters. I couldn't think a 'Я'," *BM*, 236). In this sense, *Außer sich* is explicit about the protagonist's quest for the means to narrate the self,—to say "I" in the face of social norms and languages that do not render themselves speakable because they lack the necessary frames for identification: "Ich . . . fühle mich unfähig, . . . eine Perspektive einzunehmen, eine Stimme

---

26 Lorde, *Your Silence Will Not Protect You*, 8.
27 Lorde, *Your Silence Will Not Protect You*, 9.

zu entwickeln, die nur die meine wäre und für mich sprechen würde" (*AS*, 275; "I feel unable to state anything with certainty, to adopt a point of view, develop a voice of my own, a voice that would speak for me," *BM*, 236). Gender, sexuality, language, homeland, genealogy all appear as questionable in the face of the protagonist's experiences as a nonbinary, queer, German-Post-Soviet-Jewish individual for whom concepts such as "going home" (*AS*, 11) and "mother tongue" (*AS*, 167) can only be put in quotation marks. Their existence seems to take place in-between or beyond any fixed categories that would offer them the means to render themselves describable: "Immer wenn ich merke, dass es für Menschen eine Vorstellung von Welt gibt, auf die sie ohne Zweifel bauen, fühle ich mich allein. Ausgeliefert. . . . Ich weiß ja noch nicht mal, als was ich angesprochen werde . . .—als ein Er oder als eine Sie? Mein Gesicht überrascht mich jeden Morgen im Spiegel, und ich bin skeptisch gegenüber jeder Prognose" (*AS*, 261; "Hearing people talk of the world as if they could rely on it always makes me feel lonely and helpless. . . . I don't even know what I'll be addressed as . . . a he or a she? Each morning I'm surprised by my own face in the mirror, and I'm skeptical about any attempts to predict the future," *BM*, 225). As Maria Roca Lizarazu points out, Judith Butler's notion of the *ec-static* applies to the inability of Salzmann's protagonist to understand themselves as "I," ultimately leading to a constant state of becoming that challenges the very norms that govern our existence by opposing them with another form of reality: "when the unreal lays claim to reality, or enters into its domain, something other than a simple assimilation into prevailing norms can and does take place. The norms themselves can become rattled, display their instability, and become open to resignification."[28] Thus, the quest for the means to narrate an "I" outside these very norms is constitutive for *Außer sich* as an act of literary resistance and interventionist self-expression.

The nonlinear and fragmented structure of the novel mirrors Ali's process making sense of their position: In trying to compose their own story, they turn to the genealogical lines, assembling and listening to the accounts of their family members. This, however, turns out to be equally disorienting: "Zeit ist für mich eine Drehscheibe. Bilder verschwimmen vor meinen Augen und immer wieder aufs Neue stelle ich Vermutungen darüber an, wie irgendetwas vielleicht ausgesehen haben könnte" (*AS*, 275; For me, time is a turntable. Images blur before my eyes, and over and over I guess how things might have looked, *BM*, 236). Time presents itself as a continuum, "ein Heute, von vor hundert Jahren bis jetzt" (*AS*, 7; "The time, then, is a today, from a hundred years ago until now,"

---

28 Judith Butler, "Beside Oneself: On the Limits of Sexual Autonomy," in *Undoing Gender*, ed. Judith Butler (London: Routledge, 2004), 27–28. See also Roca Lizarazu, "Ec-Static Existences," 3–4.

BM, v), a constant blurring of often traumatic familial memories, much less an origin story than another example for the "Kausalitätslosigkeit der Geschichte" (*AS*, 274; "the absence of historical causality," *BM*, 236) that Ali feels. However, as Sarah Colvin elaborates—with regard to *1000 Serpentinen Angst*, which is equally transgressive regarding time, places, and familial memories that are assembled in the protagonist's (inner) conversations—such nonchronological accounts imply the potential for "temporal insurrections": "The narratives . . . not only disrupt linear chronology, but are insurrectionary in (grammatical) mood, exposing the politically immobilising indicative (this is how it was, is, and always will be) and replacing it with subjunctives of possibility (this is how it could have been, or might yet be)."[29] This is also true for Salzmann's text, since filling gaps in the familial stories and imagining alternative visions, is another important feature in Ali's process, as the stories of those who came before them are not offering any pattern they could use to describe their own subjectivity. When they meet Katho, who also undergoes a gender transition and becomes Ali's partner in Istanbul, Ali wonders about the untold story of the queer members of their families, the blank spaces in the family histories, and envisions them as populated by people who are like them, situating them in an imaginary frame of relatedness: "Sie wünschten sich Vorfahren, die so waren wie sie. Onkel mit rasierten Beinen, die nachts ihre Bäuche in Corsagen und Kleider zwängten, Tanten mit Wasserwelle und schwarzem Lippenstift, die in Anzügen durch die Straßen spazierten. Keine dieser Geschichten hatte je ihren Weg in die Erzählungen von Familie gefunden, aber es musste sie doch gegeben haben, also was war falsch daran, sie sich zu erdenken?" (*AS*, 71; "They wished for ancestors like them: uncles who'd shaved their legs and squeezed their bellies into corsages and dresses at night, aunts with shingled hair and black lipstick, strolling through the streets in suits. None of these stories had ever found its way into the annals of family history, but they must have existed, so what was wrong with inventing them?," *BM*, 113). Consequently, inventions of alternative genealogies and creative accounts of the self are essential in filling the gaps of the official accounts of community and family.

Questions of storytelling are therefore at the heart of *Außer sich*. As Annette Bühler-Dietrich so rightly concludes with regard to Ali: "there is no anchor unless it is being found in the very act of telling a story and listening to it."[30] This is also mirrored in Ali's conversation with their

---

29 Sarah Colvin, "Freedom Time: Temporal Insurrections in Olivia Wenzel's *1000 Serpentinen Angst* and Sharon Dodua Otoo's *Adas Raum*," *German Life and Letters* 75, no. 1 (2022): 141.

30 Annette Buehler-Dietrich, "Relational Subjectivity: Sasha Marianna Salzmann's Novel 'Außer Sich,'" *Modern Languages Open* 1, no. 10 (2020): 1–17, 5.

mother Valja. It is through telling her story and being listened to, that Ali's mother is able to literally recompose herself: "meine Mutter . . . war [dabei], sich mit Hilfe von Bruchstücken ihrer Geschichte selbst zusammenzusetzen. . . . Ich war gekommen, um zuzuhören" (*AS*, 259–61; "my mother pieced herself together, . . . I was here to listen," *BM*, 225). Thus, the different storylines of the novel can be read as a way for Ali to recompose themselves, assembling the stories of others, filling the gaps with possibilities and probabilities to tell their story:

> Ich weiß nicht mehr, wie dieser Sichtwechsel kam und wann. Warum ich beschlossen habe, diese Folien und Bilder in meinem Kopf zu ordnen, warum ich angefangen habe, mich als mich zu denken, zu sprechen, sogar zu schreiben. . . . Ich war es damals noch gewohnt, von mir außerhalb meiner selbst, von mir in der dritten Person zu denken, als einer Geschichte, die irgendwem gehört. . . . Ich wusste, ich konnte nicht verlangen, dass sie diese Geschichte verstanden, aber sie hörten mir zu, als ich ihnen von Ali erzählte und wie sie zu Anton wurde. (*AS*, 210)

> [I don't know how or when I began to see things differently—why I decided to put the transparencies and images in my head in some kind of order, why I began to think and speak and even write about myself as me . . . Back then, I was still used to thinking about myself from outside myself, in the third person—a story belonging to somebody else. . . . I knew I couldn't expect them to understand the story, but they listened as I told them about Ali and how she became Anton.] (*BM*, 178)

Telling and listening, which Bühler-Dietrich identifies as the key element of the novel, can then also be expanded to us as readers, as listeners to Ali's stories. Telling one's own story—reimagined, fluid, ambiguous—as an act of constructing oneself is essential for *Außer sich* as it forges a language beyond pregiven categories of identity and self, the possibility of saying "I."

WO BIST *DU*?: Narrative Belonging in *1000 Serpentinen Angst*

1000 Serpentinen Angst portrays the (inner) journey of a Black, female, bisexual, GDR-born protagonist suffering from an anxiety disorder triggered by the constant threat of racist assaults. Wenzel's novel foregrounds the perspective of those marked as Other by taking a decidedly

---

Bühler-Dietrich interestingly connects Cavarero's philosophy of *Relating Narratives* with Salzmann's novel by showing how the telling of stories constitutes the self in relation to others.

inner perspective, addressing the psychological effects of racism and the constant feeling of being vulnerable, adding a pivotal narrative perspective to contemporary German literature. The novel follows the unnamed protagonist on her journey spanning the United States, Berlin, Morocco, Angola, Vietnam, and Thuringia, assembling scraps and pieces, memories and photographs that compose a picture of her experiences as a Black woman born in the GDR, instances of racist violence, her familial relationships, and the suicide of her twin brother. The transitory space of a train station, where the protagonist awaits a train to visit her grandmother, mirrors the situation in which the protagonist finds herself: trying to make sense of her past to come to terms with the present where she tries to anchor herself in the new situation of her pregnancy. The nonchronological and nonlinear accounts of events that constitute the novel are therefore essentially part of an *inner* journey of the protagonist: This also relates to the overall structure of the book taking the form of a dialogue, alternating uppercase and lowercase letters. The capitalized voice investigates the protagonist's thoughts and feelings, printed in regular font with direct speech in italics, and comments on her responses, the aggressiveness of the capitalization underling the power exerted by the interrogating voice. Rather than representing a certain person, it mimics the external world with its stereotypical thinking, also incorporating questionnaires and police interrogations. Wenzel herself has described the origin of the voice as texts coming from everywhere, as questioning authorities, that represent the current discourse, as well as psychological patterns.[31] Accordingly, the dialogical structure underlines internalized modes of thinking, reflecting the constant self-assessment of the marginalized described by W. E. B. Du Bois as "double-consciousness." Coined at the beginning of the last century, it outlines how the Black population in the United States had internalized the hegemonic, racist perception of the white population: "this double-consciousness, this sense of always looking at one's self through the eyes of others, of measuring one's soul by the tape of a world that looks on in amused contempt and pity."[32] The protagonist's way of moving through society is fundamentally shaped by this experience:

1. Öffentlich eine Banane essen als schwarze Person: Rassistische Affenanalogien, *uga uga uga*. *Aua*.

---

[31] Katrin Gottschalk, "Autorin Olivia Wenzel über Identität: 'Coming-out als Nicht-Weiße,'" Taz.de, March 5, 2020, https://taz.de/Autorin-Olivia-Wenzel-ueber-Identitaet/!5666451/.

[32] W. E. B. Du Bois, *The Souls of Black Folk* in *The Oxford W. E. B. Du Bois*, ed. Brent Hayes Edwards (Cary, NC: Oxford University Press, 2007), 3.

2. Eine Banane essen als Ossi: ... Sinnbild für die Unterlegenheit des beigen Ostens gegenüber dem goldenen Westen. ...
3. Eine Banane essen als Frau—Blowjob, dies das. ... *Mach' doch mal Deep-throat, hähähä*. (*TSA*, 49–50)

[If you're Black eating a banana in public: racist ape analogies, ooga ooga ooga. Ouch. If you're East German: ... the banana as a symbol for the inferiority of the beige East in contrast to the golden West. ... If you're a woman eating a banana—blowjob this and that. ... Act out *Deep Throat*, hahaha.] (*CF*, 36)

Relating to the intersectionality of her ascribed identity positions, being Black, born in the GDR and female, this passage points toward the complexity of inner reflections related to as simple an act as eating a banana in public. Being subjected to this exterior gaze is a fundamental experience in the novel, highlighting the destructiveness, the psychological effect it has on those who are marked as Other. Throughout the novel, the protagonist questions her own positionality and sense of belonging, which is as fragmented as the inner dialogues that constitute the book. This interestingly relates to the central question which is posed continuously by the capitalized voice throughout the text: "WO BIST DU JETZT?" (*TSA*, 17; "WHERE ARE YOU NOW?," *CF*, 9). These iterations fulfill a double function: they orientate the reader in the nonlinear narrative lines, indicating the whereabouts of the protagonist, as well as pointing toward deeper questions of affiliation, urging the protagonist to position herself not only in geographical terms but also regarding her origin and belonging.

Like Ali, the protagonist is unable to situate herself in the realm of the family, which does not offer any sense of safety but rather confronts the protagonist with her own Otherness from mainstream white German society:

Wenn ich meine Oma Rita fragen würde, ob sie Parallelen sehen könne, zwischen dem Hass, der mir und meinem Bruder entgegenschlug ... [und] dem Hass, der heute systematisch schwarzen Menschen in den USA entgegenschlägt ..., sie sich vorstellen könnte, ... dass ich am Ende des Tages doch mit diesen Menschen im Alltag viel mehr teile, als mit ihr, meiner Großmutter, nämlich die Tatsache einem Blick ausgeliefert zu sein, der uns ... als das Gleiche markiert, als das Nichtweiße, das Andere, als Beleg einer Idee von Hautfarben und Differenz? ... Was soll mir meine weiße Großmutter antworten auf die Frage, ob sie eine Ahnung hat, was es bedeutet, keinen Ort zu kennen, an dem man selbst die Norm ist? (*TSA*, 80–82)

[If I asked my grandma Rita whether she can see parallels between the hatred . . . my brother and I faced . . . [and] the hatred that Black people face in the U.S. systematically . . . that at the end of the day, in my everyday life, I share more with these people than with her, my grandmother. Namely the fact that I am subjected to the same gaze that perceives us, . . . as marked in the same way, marked as the non-white one, as the Other, as evidence of the notion of race and difference? . . . How is my grandmother supposed to respond to the question of whether she knows what it means to know of no place where you are the norm?] (*CF*, 61–62)

The family constellation in Wenzel's novel—the white grandmother with racist inclinations, the alienation from her (also white) mother, and the physical absence of her father—intensifies her feeling of not belonging rather than presenting her with an affiliation to a system of love and care, and it further complicates her need for positioning herself beyond these relations. Consequently, the central question, "where are you?"— meant literally as well as metaphorically—needs answering on a personal level: not only meaning *where* are you, but also where are *you*, how do you position yourself in all this, as a person, an entity, a subject rather than being governed by the myths and norms that are attributed to you from outside?[33]

This is deeply related to the possibility of her survival in a world that is shaped by racism, leading to the protagonist's anxiety disorder, "ein permanenter Case of Emergency" (*TSA*, 259; "a permanent case of emergency," *CF*, 213), which is furthermore intensified by the traumatic loss of her twin brother. Over and over again is the protagonist faced with situations of imminent violence from racists and Nazis, a constant threat that is contextualized by the recounts of historic violence against Black people in the United States as well as against people of color and immigrants in Germany:

BIST DU SICHER?
Ich bin nie sicher.
Für mich ist es wahrscheinlicher beim Spazierengehen an Brandenburger Seen von drei Nazis krankenhausreif geprügelt zu werden, als . . . Opfer eines islamistischen Anschlags zu werden. . . .

---

[33] In her article "Talking Back, Paying Forward: Dialogism and Literary Genealogies in May Ayim and Olivia Wenzel," Selma Rezgui also explores the multifacetedness and ambiguities of the protagonists' positionalities which are reflected in her inner dialogue: "in illuminating the tension between the narrator's various affiliations—between her privilege and her oppression—Wenzel offers a yet more dialogic subjectivity, which is unstable and ever-shifting in its parameters and its understanding of itself." See chapter 4 of this volume.

WURDEST DU ÜBERHAUPT SCHON MAL VON DREI
NAZIS "KRANKENHAUSREIF" GEPRÜGELT?
Die Angst vor manchen Realitäten kann schlimmer sein als diese
Realitäten selbst. (*TSA*, 85)

[IS IT SAFE TO SAY THAT? It's never safe. In my case, it's more
likely I'll get beaten to a pulp by three Nazis while walking along
a lake in Brandenburg than become the victim of an Islamic terror
attack . . . HAVE YOU ACTUALLY EVER BEEN BEATEN TO A
PULP BY THREE NAZIS? The fear of some realities can be worse
than the realities themselves.] (*CF*, 65)

Instead of foregrounding the physical assault, the novel points toward the underlying dynamics of racism: By focusing on the protagonist's inner voice(s), it highlights the manifold forms of racist violence that are by no means limited to physical violence. As Priscilla Layne points out, Wenzel's narrative does not focus on the "spectacle of racism"[34] but rather on the everyday instances and the constant threat of violence—and its effects on the protagonist: "the silences, the gap in understanding between Black victims and white witnesses. The latter don't even know what they're not seeing or that they're missing anything at all."[35] As Layne stresses, there is a form of resistance in Wenzel's use of autofiction, as it subverts the external gaze and judgments from outside.[36] Moreover, it is also way of reclaiming the narrative perspective, finding the means for self-expression, the language for the experience of those who are not represented on the level of the majoritarian society.

Hence, the novel is essentially about finding means for the Othered self to survive in hostile environments, to transcend the narrow frames of white supremacist thinking as the basis for self-assessment. This is also reflected in the form of the inner narrative; toward the end of the novel the inner voices begin to alternate in the telling of the protagonist's story:

WO IST MEINE MUTTER JETZT?
Deine Mutter?
JA, MEINE MUTTER. . . . ICH LÖSE DICH AB. DU HAST
FÜR DEN MOMENT GENUG.
. . . Okay. (*TSA*, 271)

---

34 Priscilla Layne, "'That's How It Is': Quotidian Violence and Resistance in Olivia Wenzel's *1000 Coils of Fear*," *NOVEL A Forum on Fiction* 55, no. 1 (2022): 46.
35 Layne, "That's How It Is," 46.
36 Layne, "That's How It Is," 49.

[WHERE IS MY MOTHER NOW? Your mother? YES, MY MOTHER.... I'M RELIEVING YOU. YOU'VE HAD ENOUGH FOR NOW.... Okay.] (*CF*, 217)

The inner dialogue is transfigured, the double-consciousness of the beginning, implying an external gaze, is superseded with a more personal self-talk, with the voices eventually converging. The protagonist's inner conversations become clearer as she works through the painful memories of her racist experiences, her brother's suicide, and her dysfunctional family experiences. This could be seen as the prerequisite for the protagonist's ultimate survival, making way for a new form of identity as a means to be able to enter the future, to make it possible "to live":

SO KOMMEN WIR NICHT ANS ZIEL....
Ach so? Was ist denn mein Ziel?
IM LEBEN?
Ja.
ZU LEBEN?
... Ja. (*TSA*, 271)

[WE'RE NEVER GOING TO REACH OUR DESTINATION THIS WAY. What destination? IN LIFE? Yes. TO LIVE? ... Yes.] (*CF*, 215–16)

The I—The Other: Twin Novels

Both novels share another interesting aspect essential for the subject formation of their protagonists—the twin brothers. Twins, a highly investigated motif in literary studies,[37] can be understood as the closest Others, not only in appearance but also regarding the experiences in their families, a theme that runs through both novels. The twin brothers are therefore part of the protagonists' grappling with the family histories while at the same time pointing toward an alternative way of how things could have been or could be, an alternative way of thinking about the self in relation to the closest possible Other.

In *Außer sich* the outward identicalness of the twins is thematized in an interesting scene of transvestism, already pointing toward the ambiguity of gender identities that is at the heart of the novel. While Ali fights to dress up in a golden gown, Anton poses in a childhood picture, juxtaposing their later gender transition: "Ali wollte lieber sterben als es anzuziehen ... es war erst Ruhe, als Anton in das Kleid kletterte, ganz ohne

---

37 Barbara Frey, *Zwillinge und Zwillingsmythen in der Literatur* (Berlin: Iko-Verlag, 2006).

Aufforderung, sogar ... mit den Hüften wackelte, als würde er darin tanzen ..." (*AS*, 36; "Ali would rather have died than wear it; ... Anton climbed into the dress without being asked, ... wiggling his hips as if he were dancing," *BM*, 25). Throughout the novel, Anton is presented as the most intimate counterpart; the protagonist remembers their childhood games as a constant play with each other, copying each other's movements: "Weil sie kaum Spielzeuge hatten, spielten sie mit sich, ... verglichen die Bewegungen des anderen mit den eigenen, froren ein und spiegelten sich" (*AS*, 99; "Because they had hardly any toys, they played with one another, ... comparing each other's movements, freezing and mirroring one another," *BM*, 81). This motif is taken up repeatedly in the novel. Looking at the mirrored ceiling of a bar in Istanbul, Ali seems to be able to spot Anton: "Ali schaute in Antons Gesicht neben sich und lächelte, und Anton lächelte in exakter Spiegelung zurück, sie bewegte ihren kleinen Finger auf dem Sofapolster zu ihm hin in der Hoffnung, seinen Finger zu finden, schaute aber nicht weg, hielt ihn mit ihrem Blick an der Decke fest" (*AS*, 35; "Ali looked into Anton's face beside her and smiled, and Anton smiled back, an exact mirror image. She moved her little finger toward him along the sofa cushions in the hope of finding his finger, but didn't take her eyes off him, keeping him pinned to the ceiling with her gaze," *BM*, 24–25). It takes a moment for the reader to realize that the supposed encounter of the twins is Ali's mirror image. This is taken even further in the most emblematic description of the twin relation taking place after the twins have been beaten up as teenagers by their fellow schoolmates because of their Russian background: "als sie fertig waren, waren die Zwillinge zu einem Körper verschmolzen. ... Sie lagen sich in den Armen. ... Ali lief Sabber aus dem Mund auf Antons Stirn, er wischte ihn mit seinem Hemdsärmel weg, schob sich zu ihr hoch, drückte seine Nasenspitze an ihre, ihre Wimpern verhakten sich, ihre Münder standen offen, sie atmeten ineinander. Erst als Anton Ali küsste, fing sie an zu weinen" (*AS*, 107; "When they were done, the twins had melted into one body. ... They lay in each other's arms. ... Dribble ran out of Ali's mouth onto Anton's forehead; he wiped it away with his shirtsleeve, pushed himself level with her and pressed the tip of his nose against hers. Their eyelashes meshed, their mouths were open, they were breathing into one another. It was only when Anton kissed Ali that she began to cry," *BM*, 87). The incident of xenophobia is juxtaposed with a moment of closest intimacy—or, as Maria Stehle and Beverly Weber would call it, a moment of "precarious intimacy."[38] The scene's meaning remains ambiguous, as the experience of violence blends

---

38 Maria Stehle and Beverly Weber, *Precarious Intimacies: The Politics of Touch in Contemporary Western European Cinema* (Evanston, IL: Northwestern University Press, 2020).

into sibling tenderness and then into a seemingly sexual encounter; the boundaries between them dissolve, leaving "them" as "one" in the face of the assault. The twins merge into one, undistinguishable, the closest person beyond themselves becomes a part of themselves. As Roca Lizarazu puts it, Anton is essential for Ali's self-understanding: "the psychological and physical enmeshment of the twins illustrates quite literally how 'I' am always dependent on an Other to construct a sense of self, to think myself."[39] This can be taken even further, however, when applied to Ali's gender transition: the novel opens up yet another reading of the twin relation with Anton as an embodied and externalized male counterpart of Ali's gender transition process—to the end that Ali *becomes* Anton (which is also their chosen name after the transition). While there is a sequence in the novel in which we supposedly get to know Anton's side of the story, it could be argued that this is part of Ali's imagination: "ich erdenke mir neue Personen, wie ich mir alte zusammensetze. Stelle mir das Leben meines Bruders vor, stelle mir vor, er würde all das tun, wozu ich nicht in der Lage gewesen bin, sehe ihn als einen, der auszieht in der Welt, weil er den Mut besitzt, der mir immer gefehlt hat" (*AS*, 275; "I make up new characters in the same way that I piece together old ones. I imagine my brother's life, imagine him doing all the things I can't do, see him setting off into the world because he has the courage I've always lacked," *BM*, 237). Consequently, the twin appears as an alternative way of being, an alternative story for the self. In the end, the novel evades any form of closure, presenting us with oscillating meanings that exceed predetermined readings and underlining the fluidity of Ali's self-narration, being "Schwester, Bruder, ich" (*AS*, 7; "sister, brother, me," *BM*, iii): nothing is stable, everything remains fluid—and ultimately forms part of a shape-shifting, polysemic self.

 Wenzel's unnamed protagonist also faces the loss of her twin brother who committed suicide. Here, too, the twin brother serves as a counterpart, representing an alternative outcome, the closest Other, with whom the protagonist shares her descent as well as the early experiences of racism, the constant threat and vulnerability. Only by working through the traumatic loss and these shared experiences is the protagonist able to come to terms with their past and to face the future—and survive. As in *Außer sich*, the absence of the twin brother acts as a point of departure for the protagonist's quest for herself: It becomes apparent that she will only be able to recover from her anxiety disorder if she faces her grief—constituting a turning point in the novel. While the protagonist is waiting at the train station the scenery transforms into a dreamlike nonplace where she meets her dead brother who threw himself in front of a train in the ultimate form of self-destruction. In the surreal setting of a deserted

---

39 Roca Lizarazu, "Ec-Static Existences," 11.

train station, the protagonist confronts her trauma through the embodied appearance of her twin, facing the circumstances of racist violence and hatred that might have led to her brother's suicide:

> *ich hatte immer so viele sorgen um dich, . . . wie du damals mit dem messer im bein heimkamst und dich geschämt hast. du warst so klein und die haben dich schon so gehasst.*
> *spring' doch.*
> *jetzt kann dir niemand mehr was tun.*
> *spring' doch.*
> *jetzt kann dir nichts mehr passieren.* (*TSA*, 120)

> [*i was always so worried about you, . . . how you came home one day, with a knife in your leg, and how you were ashamed. you were so small, and they already hated you so much. jump already. now no one else can hurt you. jump already. now nothing else can happen to you.*] (*CF*, 95)

The iterated demand "jump already" echoes an earlier passage in the book referring to the racial assaults against Turkish immigrants in the 1990s in Germany that seem to haunt them and it opens the space for seeing the continuity of racist violence against different migrantized groups in Germany (*TSA* 20). The death of the twin accounts for the ultimate destructiveness of racism. Here we find another representation of racist hatred that not only manifests itself in incidents of actual violence but also causes harm on a different level. While the protagonist comes to terms with the interior voices, finding a voice that belongs to herself rather than being supplemented to the exterior gaze, her brother acts as a negative foil, an alternative—but no less probable—outcome of her own life. In the earlier passages of the book, suicide even seems to be the better option compared to the constant case of emergency, the anxiety attacks and fear that mark her life when she reflects that her brother managed to "ums Leben drumherum gekommen" (*TSA*, 44; avoid life).[40] However, in the end, it seems that the protagonist transcends the destructiveness of interiorized thinking, which also becomes apparent in the imaginative conversation with her twin:

> *wenn ich zaubern könnte, würde ich dir eine andere frisur herbeizaubern!*
> *was stimmt denn nicht mit meinen haaren?*
> *ich denke, du magst die nicht.*

---

40 In the translation of Layne: "Lost his life. Lost track of his life?" (*CF*, 32). I have proposed a slightly more literal translation for the sake of the interpretation here.

ich bin mittlerweile okay mit mir, also mit meinem körper und den haaren.
    seit wann?
seit ich mehr schwarze menschen kenne . . . (*TSA,* 115)

[*if i could do magic, i'd conjure up a new hairdo for you! what's wrong with my hair? i thought you don't like it. meanwhile, i'm okay with myself, with my body and my hair. since when? . . . since i know more black people . . .*] (*CF,* 91)

Here, the potential of self-acceptance and the overcoming of internalized racism becomes palpable: the protagonist finds ways to position herself differently—through the relation with others, the positive feeling of connections—embracing the story of her brother without eclipsing herself and her chance of survival. The protagonist understands that she is not bound to the same destiny as her twin but is a separate entity: "Ich habe nicht mich verloren, ich habe nicht einen Teil von mir verloren, sondern eine andere Person" (*TSA,* 178; "I didn't lose myself, I didn't lose a part of myself, rather, I lost another person," *CF,* 142). Consequently, the protagonist can transform her grief and expand the love for her twin brother to include another being, her own child. This allows the protagonist to create an alternative vision for her*self*, making a future possible: "Du wirst . . . begreifen, dass du den Platz deines Bruders in dir wirst teilen müssen, . . . dass das . . . vielleicht etwas in dir verdoppeln oder ausbreiten oder heilen [wird]. Etwas, das damit einhergeht, eine neue, gesunde Angst in dein Leben zu lassen . . ., eine Angst, gebunden an eine Liebe, so stark wie alles, was du bisher kanntest, mal 1000" (*TSA,* 337; "you'll understand that you'll have to share that spot reserved for your brother inside yourself, . . . that this . . . something inside of you will double or spread out or heal. Something that comes with letting a new healthy fear into your life . . ., a fear tied to a love that's as strong as everything that you have ever known, times a thousand," *CF,* 267–68). By pointing toward the "yet to be,"[41] the potentiality of a different future, the pregnancy symbolizes the protagonist's ability for survival while also situating her in a new set of relations, a queer family constellation that forms part of the novel's envisioning of a different community.

The Rise of the Rhizome: Toward an Alternative Sense of Community

Both *Außer sich* and *1000 Serpentinen Angst* present us with protagonists who deviate from a majoritarian norm regarding their subject

---

41   Colvin, "Freedom Time," 39.

positions—tying in with Deleuze and Guattari's concept of the minor—while also being fractured by dysfunctional family structures that do not offer them a stable anchor for their identity formation. In the end, both protagonists find their own voice and narrative, expounding the subversive potential of self-expression against the "mythical norm" of a majoritarian society that does not provide a sense of belonging that could work for the protagonists, neglecting their existence within the common frames of identity not only through the lack of representation but also through the constant threat of violence, racism, discrimination, resulting in vulnerability and self-neglect. In reframing their positionalities, the protagonists recompose themselves in a new way, relating themselves to others, situated in a network of relationships that undermine the master narrative of family and genealogy, applying strategies of queering heterosexual and patriarchal forms of relations and storytelling—literally envisioning "another possible community."[42] This ties in with another term coined by Deleuze and Guattari that proves to be fruitful in describing the networks of relations that both novels lay out in reflecting on the nature of self and Other: the rhizome. As opposed to the linear and genealogic logic of the family tree, the rhizome is "an anti-genealogy"[43] governed by the "principles of connection and heterogeneity. . . . This is very different from the tree or root, which plots a point, fixes an order."[44] The main features of the rhizome are lines—relations—that link everything—and everyone—together. While the tree follows the "logic of reproduction,"[45] the rhizome follows the principles of interrelatedness regardless of difference, acting as an ideal image for alternative forms of family and alliances that are not governed by principles of homogeny: "We're tired of trees. We should stop believing in trees, roots, and radicles. They've made us suffer too much. . . . Nothing is beautiful or loving or political aside from underground stems and aerial roots, adventitious growths and rhizomes."[46] The rhizome acts as a model that surpasses the idea of a binary, patriarchal model of a tree, being based on connection. These connections, however, do not have to be tied to a shared identity or positionality but rather offer a model of alliance: "the rhizome is alliance, uniquely alliance."[47] The rhizomatic network therefore acts as a perfect image for the idea of "another possible community"[48] not based on foreclosing notions of identity, that is,

42   Deleuze and Guattari, *Toward a Minor Literature*, 17.
43   Deleuze and Guattari, *A Thousand Plateaus*, 11.
44   Deleuze and Guattari, *A Thousand Plateaus*, 8.
45   Deleuze and Guattari, *A Thousand Plateaus*, 8.
46   Deleuze and Guattari, *A Thousand Plateaus*, 15.
47   Deleuze and Guattari, *A Thousand Plateaus*, 25.
48   Deleuze and Guattari, *Toward a Minor Literature*, 17.

nation, family, language—roots—but instead offer ways for the self to be situated in a network of relations including fluid forms such as queer families, friendships, and communities of care.

The normative heterosexual family in *Außer sich* is revealed as essentially dysfunctional, shaped by spirals of patriarchal violence, not offering any models for caring relationships. Ali decidedly puts an end to the cycles of trauma that mark their family chronicles, making *Außer sich* "not so much a Familienroman but a deliberation on the failure of the family novel," as Roca Lizarazu puts it.[49] Instead, the novel presents other forms of relationality, replacing reproductivity and bloodlines with emotional bonds and alliances. It is alternative forms of belonging—enveloping Ali in a web of substitute relatives and friends that understand them and recognize their fluid gender identity—that offer them a place in the world. This is true for their adopted uncle Cemal in Istanbul and their best friend and flatmate Elyas. While fleeing their family, Ali creates a sense of home that transcends the narrow frames of familial belonging and heteronormative relationships. When Elyas and Ali first meet, they find themselves being drawn to each other in a crowd of people, queering a love-at-first-sight moment: "Ali und Elyas begegneten sich mit Blicken im Raum, die sich zögernd streiften. . . . Sie steuerten aufeinander zu, langsam, . . . es gab kein Ziel, sie wussten nicht, was sie voneinander wollten, das Übliche jedenfalls nicht. . . . Sie atmeten nebeneinander, unschlüssig, ob sie sich küssen sollten . . . aber was sie stattdessen machen sollten, wussten sie nicht. Küssen wäre sicher einfacher gewesen" (*AS*, 211–13; "They headed toward one another, slowly, . . . they had no purpose; they didn't know what they wanted of each other, but not the usual, that was for sure. They lay there breathing, uncertain whether to kiss; . . . but they didn't really know what else to do. Kissing would definitely have been easier," *BM*, 181). Challenging heteronormative storytelling and sexual attraction as a framework, they initiate a relationship of care, moving in together and sharing their lives. Similarly, Ali builds a relation with Cemal, Elyas's uncle, with whom they spend most of their time in Istanbul. Cemal never asks about Ali's gender identity and accepts their gender-fluid partner Katho without questioning: he offers Ali a place to come for shelter whenever they need it, being there for them unconditionally. The striking contrast between the biological and the alternative family members becomes visible in the following passage, when Ali tries to tell their mother about their gender transition, imagining how it would feel to be recognized and understood by their blood family:

---

49 Roca Lizarazu, "Ec-Static Existences," 10.

Ali . . . stellte sich vor, wie [their mother] sein Gesicht fassen und . . . streicheln würde, unbeirrt von den Stoppeln auf der Oberlippe, von den Pickeln auf dem Hals. Wie seine Mutter seine Augenlider küssen würde, seinen Kopf gegen ihre Schulter drücken . . . würde. . . . Das Bild hielt nicht an, er versuchte es wieder zusammenzusetzen, aber er kam nicht mal bis zu der Stelle mit der Oberlippe. . . . Er hörte Cemal ins Zimmer schlurfen, . . . Cemal griff ihn unter den Achseln wie ein Kleinkind und legte ihn aufs Sofa. . . . Cemal streichelte Alis Bauch in kreisenden Bewegungen, tätschelte seinen Oberschenkel, fuhr über die roten, entzündeten Beulen auf seinen Waden. . . . (*AS*, 344)

[Ali . . . imagined those hands clasping his face, stroking it with their thumbs, undeterred by the stubble on his upper lip, the pimples on his throat. He imagined his mother kissing his eyelids, pressing his head against her shoulder. . . . The image didn't hold; he tried to piece it back together again, but he didn't even get as far as the bit with his upper lip. . . . He heard Cemal shuffle into the room . . . Cemal grabbed him under his arms like a toddler and laid him on the sofa. . . . Cemal stroked Ali's belly in circling movements, patted his thighs, ran his fingers over the red, inflamed boils on his calves.] (*BM*, 297–98)

Even in Ali's imagination, the connection between mother and child seems to fail. Instead, Cemal acts as a counterimage to the biological parental figure, treating them with motherly tenderness, representing an alternative vision of kinship that is based on recognition, acceptance, and kindness. Following Kate Weston's assessment that "chosen families . . . undercut procreation's status as a master term imagined to provide the template for all possible kinship relations,"[50] *Außer sich* offers an alternative vision for relations of care beyond the family tree.

This is also true for *1000 Serpentinen Angst:* Here, the family also fails to sustain the protagonist with any sense of belonging and frame for their subject formation, leading her to the conclusion that she has "keine richtige Familie, also im biologischen Sinne" (*TSA*, 41; "I don't really have family, at least biologically," *CF*, 30) but instead believes in "soziale Beziehungen" (*TSA* 41, "social relations," *CF*, 29). As in *Außer sich*, the dysfunctional family is replaced by an alternative network of relations: The chosen family is the protagonist's anchor—it is this network that sustains the protagonist throughout her weakest moments and her anxiety disorder: Burhan, a psychiatrist, whose mother fled to Germany,

---

50 Kate Weston, "The Politics of Gay Families," in *Rethinking the Family: Some Feminist Question,* ed. Barrie Thorne and Marilyn Yalom (Boston: Northeastern University Press, 1992), 137.

offers the protagonist a place to stay, urging her to take medication and see a therapist; Luise, a single mother with her daughter, also forms part of the network, represented in the following scene of a shared dinner, an alternative image to the stereotypical ideal of a family meal:

> Am Abend, an dem ich zum ersten Mal wieder allein in meiner Wohnung schlafe, besuchen mich Luise, Milli und Burhan. . . . Sie [haben] . . . eine Gemüselasagne dabei, Burhan . . . Tiramisu. . . . Als Vorspeise serviere ich eine Karottenkokossuppe, es ist das einzige Rezept, das ich auswendig kann; jede Freundin und jeder Freund hat sie schon mindestens dreimal gegessen. (*TSA*, 208)
>
> [On the first evening that I sleep in my apartment alone, Luise, Milli, and Burhan pay me a visit. . . . She has vegetarian lasagna with her. Burhan . . . brings tiramisu . . . [;] he sits down at the table with us. I serve carrot-and-coconut soup as an appetizer. It's the only recipe that I know by heart; every friend of mine has eaten it at least three times.] (*CF*, 167)

Furthermore, there is Kim, her Vietnamese on-off-girlfriend with whom the protagonist tries to rebuild their relationship, which fell apart over the inability of the protagonist to come to terms with the emotional baggage of her family—namely, her twin and her mother: "Kim hat . . . gesagt, sie werde . . . mich . . . immer lieben. Aber es gehe in meinem Leben zu viel um mich und meine Vergangenheit. Gegen die zwei habe sie keine Chance" (*TSA*, 84; "Kim told me that she . . . would always love me. But that my life is too consumed with myself and my past. And she doesn't have a chance against those two," *CF*, 65). In the end, the protagonist finds a way to work through and integrate her familial past in a new life and a coparenting relationship with Kim. With this, they establish an alternative form of family that explicitly aims to counteract the idea of a heterosexual family picture—or, as the protagonist puts it: "*Aber ich will jetzt nicht so happy Hetero-Kernfamilie spielen*" (*TSA*, 315; "*But I don't want to suddenly play happy hetero-nuclear family now*," *CF*, 251). As Berghahn points out, queer defines "itself against the normal and the normative, of which the heterosexual is but one particular normative. . . . Queerness therefore implies transgression, subversion and dissent."[51] While Ali in *Außer sich* decides to renunciate the principle of reproduction with their gender transition, stating the "Desinteresse meines Uterus" (*AS*, 262; "my uninterested uterus," *BM*, 226) as a

---

51   Daniela Berghahn, "Queering the Family of Nation: Reassessing Fantasies of Purity, Celebrating Hybridity in Diasporic Cinema," *Transnational Cinemas* 2, no. 2 (2012): 133.

disallowance of the patterns of heteronormative and biological family,[52] *1000 Serpentinen Angst* subverts the logics of genealogy through queering the family. Instead of sticking to the fixed frames of family, kinship, and belonging, both novels transcend these lines, offering the future perspective of flexible and caring connections. This adds another layer to how *Außer sich* and *1000 Serpentinen Angst* offer a literary model that intervenes in common social images by tying in with practices of queering kinship and family to shape alternative visions of self and Other, individual and community: "the queer aesthetic, frequently contains blueprints and schemata of a forward-dawning futurity . . . queer aesthetics map future social relations. . . . Queerness is essentially about the rejection of a here and now and an insistence on potentiality or concrete possibility for another world."[53]

Conclusion

Außer sich and *1000 Serpentinen Angst* widen the scope of contemporary German literature by contributing stories of those who hitherto have been denied a place in the German canon. Both novels create multilayered and intersectional visions of subjectivity, epitomizing an aesthetic intervention that implicates the subversive potential laid out by Deleuze and Guattari's notion of minor literature by disrupting dominant narratives from the perspective of those who are marked as Other. Moreover, the protagonists reclaim the interpretational sovereignty over their own (hi)stories and experiences in a narrative that opts for "survival and change"[54] instead of being subjected to or silenced by the destructiveness of discrimination and violence. The novels literarily conceive of a narrative self-expression that mirrors the self-designatory approach that lies at the heart of postmigrant storytelling, counteracting the external gaze with the internal reflections and narrative quests for identity and self. At the same time, they tackle themes such as familial relationships and trauma, most emblematically through the twin brothers, and they open up a space to create the self anew as part of "another possible community"[55] that transcends the genealogical family tree by queering the family and building rhizomatic relationships that are not based on a shared identity but on solidarity and alliance. With this, *Außer sich* and *1000 Serpentinen Angst* form part of a current wave of novels that represent the many layers and

52   Roca Lizarazu "Ec-static Existence," 13.
53   José Esteban Muñoz, *Cruising Utopia, 10th Anniversary Edition: The Then and There of Queer Futurity* (New York: New York University Press, 2020), 1.
54   Lorde, *Your Silence Will Not Protect You*, 9.
55   Deleuze and Guattari, *Toward a Minor Literature*, 17.

struggles of a postmigrant and radically diverse present in the form of complex and multilayered narratives that claim their part in the contemporary German landscape.

Bibliography

Primary Texts

Salzmann, Sasha Marianna. *Außer sich*. Frankfurt am Main: Suhrkamp, 2018.
———. *Beside Myself*. Translated by Imogen Taylor. Melbourne: Text Publishing, 2019.
Wenzel, Olivia. *1000 Serpentinen Angst*. Frankfurt am Main: S. Fischer Verlag, 2020.
———. *1000 Coils of Fear*. Translated by Priscilla Layne. London: Dialogue Books, 2023.

Secondary Texts

Anderson, Benedict. *Imagined Communities: Reflections on the Origin and Spread of Nationalism*. London: Verso Books, 2016.
Baumann, Gerd, and Thijl Sunier. *Post-Migration Ethnicity: De-Essentializing Cohesion, Commitments, and Comparison*. Amsterdam: Het Spinhuis, 1995.
Berghahn, Daniela. "Queering the Family of Nation: Reassessing Fantasies of Purity, Celebrating Hybridity in Diasporic Cinema." *Transnational Cinemas* 2, no. 2 (2012): 129–46. https://doi.org/10.1386/trac.2.2.129_1.
Buehler-Dietrich, Annette. "Relational Subjectivity: Sasha Marianna Salzmann's Novel 'Außer Sich.'" *Modern Languages Open* 1, no. 10 (2020): 1–17. https://doi.org/10.3828/mlo.v0i0.287.
Butler, Judith. "Beside Oneself: On the Limits of Sexual Autonomy." In *Undoing Gender*, edited by Judith Butler, 17–39. London: Routledge, 2004.
Bromley, Roger. "A Bricolage of Identifications: Storying Postmigrant Belonging." *Journal of Aesthetics & Culture* 9, no. 2 (2017): 36–44. https://doi.org/10.1080/20004214.2017.1347474.
Colvin, Sarah. "Freedom Time: Temporal Insurrections in Olivia Wenzel's *1000 Serpentinen Angst* and Sharon Dodua Otoo's *Adas Raum*." *German Life and Letters* 75, no. 1 (2022): 138–65. https://doi.org/10.1111/glal.12323.
Czollek, Max. *Desintegriert euch!* Berlin: Hanser, 2018.
Deleuze, Gilles, and Felix Guattari. *Kafka: Toward a Minor Literature*. Minneapolis: University of Minnesota Press, 1986.
———. *A Thousand Plateaus*. London: Bloomsbury Academic, 2013.

Du Bois, W. E. B. *The Souls of Black Folk*. In *The Oxford W. E. B. Du Bois*, edited by Brent Hayes Edwards. Cary, NC: Oxford University Press, 2007.

Frey, Barbara. *Zwillinge und Zwillingsmythen in der Literatur*. Berlin: Iko-Verlag, 2006.

Gottschalk, Katrin. "Autorin Olivia Wenzel über Identität: '"Coming-out als Nicht-Weiße."' Taz.de. March 5, 2020. https://taz.de/Autorin-Olivia-Wenzel-ueber-Identitaet/!5666451/.

Layne, Priscilla. "'That's How It Is': Quotidian Violence and Resistance in Olivia Wenzel's *1000 Coils of Fear*." *NOVEL A Forum on Fiction* 55, no. 1 (2022): 38–60. https://doi.org/10.1215/00295132-9614973.

Littler, Margaret. "Cramped Creativity: The Politics of a Minor German Literature." In *Aesthetics and Politics in Modern German Culture*, edited by Brigid Haines, Stephen Parker, and Colin Riordan, 221–35. Bern: Internationaler Verlag der Wissenschaften, 2010.

Lorde, Audre. *Your Silence Will Not Protect You: Essays and Poems*. London: Silver Press, 2017.

Muñoz, José Esteban. *Cruising Utopia, 10th Anniversary Edition: The Then and There of Queer Futurity*. New York: New York University Press, 2020.

Roca Lizarazu, Maria. "Ec-Static Existences: The Poetics and Politics of Non-Belonging in Sasha Marianna Salzmann's Außer Sich (2017)." *Modern Languages Open* 1, no. 10 (2020): 1–19. https://doi.org/10.3828/mlo.v0i0.284.

———. "'Integration ist definitiv nicht unser Anliegen, eher schon Desintegration.' Postmigrant Renegotiations of Identity and Belonging in Contemporary Germany." *humanities* 9, no 2 (2020): 42. https://doi.org/10.3390/h9020042.

Roca Lizarazu, Maria, and Godela Weiss-Sussex. "Introduction: Rethinking 'Minor Literatures'—Contemporary Jewish Women's Writing in Germany and Austria." *Modern Languages Open* 1 (2020): 1–7. https://doi.org/10.3828/mlo.v0i0.285.

Salzmann, Sasha Marianna. "Sichtbar." In *Eure Heimat ist unser Albtraum*, edited by Fatma Aydemir and Hengameh Yaghoobifarah, 13–27. Berlin: Ullstein fünf, 2019.

———. "Visible." In *TRANSIT, Your Homeland Is Our Nightmare*, translated by Lou Silhol-Macher. *TRANSIT*. Accessed June 22, 2023. https://transit.berkeley.edu/2021/visible/.

Ring Petersen, Anne, Moritz Schramm, and Frauke Wiegand. "Introduction: From Artistic Intervention to Academic Discussion." In *Reframing Migration, Diversity and the Arts: The Postmigrant Condition*, edited by Moritz Schramm, Sten Pultz Moslund, and Anne Ring Petersen, 3–11. London: Routledge, 2021.

Rotter, Anita, and Erol Yildiz. "Postcolonialism and Postmigration: Re-Mapping the Topography of the Possible." *Crossings* 14, no. 1 (2023): 19–35. https://doi.org/10.1386/cjmc_00072_1.

Stehle, Maria, and Beverly Weber. *Precarious Intimacies: The Politics of Touch in Contemporary Western European Cinema*. Evanston, IL: Northwestern University Press, 2020.

Langhoff, Shermin, and Bundeszentrale für politische Bildung. "Die Herkunft spielt keine Rolle—'Postmigrantisches' Theater im Ballhaus Naunynstraße." Bundeszentrale für politische Bildung. March 10, 2011. https://www.bpb.de/lernen/kulturelle-bildung/60135/die-herkunft-spielt-keine-rolle-postmigrantisches-theater-im-ballhaus-naunynstrasse/.

Yildiz, Erol. "Postmigrantische Lesart: Theoretische und methodisch-methodologische Implikationen." In *Othering in der postmigrantischen Gesellschaft: Herausforderungen und Konsequenzen für die Forschungspraxis*, edited by Irini Siouti, Tina Spies, Elisabeth Tuider, Hella von Unger and Erol Yildiz, 31–57. Bielefeld: transcript, 2022.

Weston, Kate. "The Politics of Gay Families." In *Rethinking the Family: Some Feminist Questions*, edited by Barrie Thorne and Marilyn Yalom, 119–39. Boston: Northeastern University Press, 1992.

3: New Black German Subjectivity in the Twenty-First Century

Priscilla Layne

WE ARE EXPERIENCING a renaissance of Black German literature. This is not to say that there is necessarily more Black German writing at present or that it is qualitatively better than Black German writing in the past. The main difference has to do with structural changes, both within the publishing industry and in opposition to it. The Black German poet, dramatist, and activist, Philipp Khabo Koepsell, has adamantly insisted that Black German literature did not begin in the 1980s, despite how important the publication of *Farbe bekennen* (1986; *Showing Our Colors*, 1992) was to the then-burgeoning Second Black German Movement. In the essay "The Invisible Archive" Koepsell traces several earlier instances of Black German writing stretching back as far as the Weimar Republic—for example, Dualla Misipo's novel *Der Junge aus Duala* or the short-lived magazine *Elolombé ya Kamerun* (Sun of Cameroon, 1908), which was published in both German and Duala and included articles "questioning the morality of colonial rule."[1] Furthermore, one could possibly go back even further and attempt to integrate the work of Black German philosopher of West African descent Anton Wilhelm Amo (ca. 1703–59) into the narrative of Black German writing as well, which several scholars recently attempted with the publication of *The Faculty of Sensing—Thinking, With, Through, and by Anton Wilhelm Amo*, edited by Bonaventure Soh Bejeng Ndikung, Nele Kaczmarek, and Jule Hillgärtner.

---

1 Philipp Khabo Koepsell, "The Invisible Archive. A Historical Overview of Black Literature Production in Germany," in *AfroFictional In[ter]ventions: Revisiting the BIGSAS Festival of African (-Diasporic) Literatures, Bayreuth 2011–2013*, ed. by Susan Arndt and Nadja Ofuatey-Alazard (Münster: edition assemblage, 2014), 121. *Elolombé ya Kamerun* was intended to be published monthly, but only one issue was published, in January 1908. Perhaps the short life of the journal can be explained by the fact that Mpundo's criticism of colonialism "intensified the antagonism he experienced in Germany and revived earlier plans of deporting the irritating African." See Axel Stähler, *Zionism, the German Empire and Africa: Jewish Metamorphoses and the Colors of Difference* (Berlin: De Gruyter, 2019), 279.

So what is it about the present moment that has resulted in a flurry of Black German publications and attention given to Black German writing? On the one hand, Black German writers have recently been receiving increasing attention from major publishers. Both Sharon Dodua Otoo and Olivia Wenzel recently published novels with Fischer Verlag (Frankfurt am Main)—*Adas Raum* (2021) and *1000 Serpentinen Angst* (2020), respectively. An equally respected publisher, Rowohlt Verlag (Hamburg) published Jasmina Kuhnke's novel *Ein Schwarzes Herz* (2021). A few literary texts have been published by the academic press Unrast, including Olumide Popoola's first novel *this is not about sadness* (2010), Philipp Khabo Koepsell's collection of poetry *Die Akte James Knopf* (2010), and Michael Götting's debut novel *Contrapunctus*. A press that has focused on publishing Black German literary works in English is edition assemblage, which, under the "Witnessed" series, has published Olumide Popoola's play *Also by Mail* (2015), Anja Saleh's *Soon, The Future of Memory* (2021), the collection of short stories *Winter Shorts* (2015) edited by Otoo and Clementine Ewokolo Burnley, and several novels written by Otoo, including *the things i'm thinking while smiling politely* (2012) and *Synchronicity* (2015). Some examples of literary works that have been published by smaller presses are Noah Sow's *Die schwarze Madonna* (2019) and SchwarzRund's *Biskaya* (2020), published by Books on Demand, and Koepsell's *Afro Shop* (2014), which was published by epubli.

While these are by no means all the books by Black German authors published by major German publishers, they represent a sample of some of the most recent publications. Anke Biendarra's study of contemporary German literature, globalization, and publishing may offer some insight into why, even within a majority white publishing industry like Germany's, Black German authors have an increasing chance of getting published. As Biendarra writes:

> The most significant feature that sets Germany's publishing field apart from those in other European countries and the United States is that since the eighteenth century, Germany's literary field has been shaped by an active *Feuilleton*, i.e. the arts and leisure sections of newspapers, that provide a forum for public discussion, launch debates and create trends (see Todorov). Furthermore, the literary scene is characterized by the fostering of literary talent through countless prizes and contests, as well as television formats and professional writers' workshops.[2]

---

2   Anke S. Biendarra, *Germans Going Global: Contemporary Literature and Cultural Globalization* (Berlin: De Gruyter, 2012), 19.

One example of how this culture can work to support racialized writers and help move their work into the mainstream is the Adelbert von Chamisso Prize, which was established by the Robert Bosch Stiftung in 1985 and was awarded to works by authors whose mother tongue was not German. However, in 2016 the Bosch Stiftung decided to end the prize, giving the justification that it had fulfilled its purpose, as previous winners like Feridun Zaimoğlu, Yoko Tawada, and Saša Stanišić had long found success in mainstream German publishing. Even though a small number of authors who are nonnative speakers of German have indeed broken into the mainstream, it's questionable whether that really means there is no need for state-funded support of those who are still trying to get published and get publicity. Nevertheless, even if the prize were to continue to be awarded, it would not necessarily help Black German authors without a background of migration.[3]

Otoo, who was born in England to Ghanaian parents, has spoken publicly about how difficult it was in the past to gain the attention of major German publishers. She has also insisted that she believes that, had she not won the Ingeborg Bachmann Prize in 2016, a major publisher like Fischer would not have been interested in her writing, and certainly would not have allowed her to write such an unconventional, nonlinear narrative as she did with *Adas Raum*.[4] Prior to publishing *Adas Raum*, Otoo had only ever published with edition assemblage, including the aforementioned fiction works and a collection of essays she coedited, *The Little Book of Big Visions* (2012).

The fact that authors like Otoo and Wenzel have had major success in the mainstream market does not mean they do not continue to work outside of it. An excellent example is the recent Black German literary festival *Resonanzen*, which in part came about because Kuhnke was not feeling supported by the Frankfurt Book Fair, having expressed concerns about her safety owing to the presence of right-wing publishers at the fair in 2021. In response, Black German activists and artists responded not only on social media and in national newspapers but also by organizing and participating in the three-day *Resonanzen* festival in May 2022. As described on the festival website, the festival was "a cooperation between the Ruhrfestspiele and writer and political activist Sharon Dodua Otoo. It aimed to rethink, reimagine and further develop perspectives and

---

3 In the essay "Internationalität ≠ Interkultur. Eine Schwarze deutsche Kritik" (Internationalism ≠ interculturalism: A Black German critique), Black German dramatist, director, and performer Simone Dede Ayivi discusses how problematic it is that white Germans in charge of funding theater projects, for example, seem to think that the solution to addressing racism and representation is to invite more Black performers from abroad.

4 Sharon Dodua Otoo in discussion with the author, Women in German Conference, October 2021.

experiences within the German-language literary scene."[5] One of the keys to this description is that *perspectives* and *experiences* are mentioned in the plural, suggesting it is important for Germans to recognize that writing in the Black German community reflects a variety of differences. This is something Otoo addressed directly when she gave the annual speech at the Bachmann Prize in 2020, a talk titled "Können Schwarze Blumen malen?" (Can Blacks paint flowers?). Otoo considered what kinds of difficulties marginalized artists have to contend with when they are trying to find time to create their art—including a lack of childcare, financial needs, health risks, and racist aggression. Otoo states:

> Many Black artists work under these or similar constraints. Even if we want, our art doesn't stand on its own—it becomes the representation of an entire community. How do we deal with that? There are Black German authors who do not even address being Black in their work. Others may write Black main protagonists, but consciously choose not to place violent experiences of discrimination at the center of the story. Jackie Thomae expressly did not want to write a book about racism with *Brüder*. And still other authors describe in detail the various realities of life of their Black characters. The novel *1000 Serpentinen Angst* by Olivia Wenzel, published in the spring, reflects the story of a Black East German queer woman. There must be room for these various novels—and also for those by Chantal-Fleur Sandjon, Schwarz-Rund, Noah Sow, Zoe Hagen, Michael Götting, and many more. Because through the reception of a whole range of works, positions and problems will become clearer, more complicated, and more challenging.[6]

Otoo's remarks here are an important jumping-off point for my reflection on Black German literature at the present. She suggests, if one were to ask her what is *Black* about Black German literature, that she would have to offer a variety of examples because the Black German community is not a monolith and likewise the authors from the community have diverse ways of approaching literature. In fact, it would be more accurate to refer to *Black German communities,* as a number of different communities have emerged around intersecting identities.[7] I find it useful to consult Stuart Hall's influential essay "What is the Black in Black

---

5 "Resonanzen—Schwarzes Literaturfestival," Ruhrfestspiele, May 19–22, 2022, https://www.ruhrfestspiele.de/en/program/2022/resonanzen-schwarzes-literaturfestival-2.

6 Otoo, "Können Schwarze Blumen malen?," 45. All quotations from German language texts are translated into English by the author.

7 See the essays by trans and non-binary Black German folx in the volume *Spiegelblicke*.

Popular Culture?" as a follow-up to Otoo's comments. In this essay, Hall argues that Blackness is a construct and that, as such, how Blackness is understood, including who and what is considered Black, is dependent on time and place. Thus, if we were to ask ourselves what is unique about Black German literature, we are really asking what is Black German literature *today*. In this essay, by drawing on examples from three novels—Olivia Wenzel's (*1000 Coils of Fear*, Jackie Thomae's *Brüder* (*Brothers*, 2019), and Noah Sow's *Die Schwarze Madonna* (*The Black Madonna*, 2019)—I make the following three claims regarding what is characteristic about more recent Black German literature. First of all, Black German literature does not seek to describe racism; rather, Black German literature provides an intersectional critique of racism. Secondly, Black German literature emphasizes *both* local and global connections while negotiating them vis-à-vis the national. And finally, Black German literature indicates a turn inward, but unlike the literary phenomenon of "new subjectivity," this is a turn inward that is still constantly aware of positionality and intersectionality, *and* aware that white people are also fragmented, even if they don't have the added layer of double consciousness that Black Germans experience.

The first claim, the insistence on not just describing racism, already makes things more difficult for Black German authors seeking to publish their work. In "Dürfen Schwarze Blumen malen," Otoo addresses a multitude of challenges confronting Black German authors in today's publishing market and one of them is, in a literary market dominated by white authors, publishers, and critics, there is a tendency of approaching Black German literature as if it were homogenous rather than appreciating its diversity. Instead of accepting that authors like Thomae, Wenzel, and Sow each have something unique to contribute to the landscape, the market wants to place restrictions on authors and compare them to each other, as if there were only room for a single Black German narrative. Frequently, the sole questions the literary market asks of Black German books is, is this a narrative about racism or not? But this is not an easy question to answer about any of these novels. Take, for example, Thomae's novel.

In *Brüder*, the two brothers in the novel's title are biracial Black East Germans: Mick and Gabriel. They are actually half-brothers who not only have never met, but don't even know of each other's existence. What they share is an absent father, Idris, a Senegalese student who studied medicine in the GDR, had an affair with Monika (Mick's mother) in East Berlin and later with Gabriele (Gabriel's mother) in Leipzig. Idris left East Germany to pursue more opportunities in the West, which is why he did not take part in either of his sons' upbringing. To reiterate, in her speech, Otoo says of Thomae's novel: "Mit 'Brüder' wollte Jackie Thomae ausdrücklich kein 'Rassismusbuch' schreiben" (Jackie Thomae expressly did not want to write a book about racism).[8] But what exactly is a book about racism, or a *Rassismusbuch*, as Otoo states in German? It is not the case that Thomae's novel doesn't address racism *at all*. We learn, for example, that Mick had difficulties as a child, which, the narrator implies, may have something to do with the trauma of being the only Black kid in his class *and* that his Black father was not present for him to confide in about this. Mick spends his adulthood chasing enlightenment on trips to the Caribbean, India, and Thailand. Gabriel, on the other hand, tries to avoid most conversations about race and Blackness. He moves to London to be invisible, so he can disappear in a sea of diverse faces. When he is himself accused of bias, it comes as a shock to his system. Gabriel, who is on the brink of a midlife crisis and a nervous breakdown, catches a young Black woman letting her dog defecate outside of his house. He overreacts, chasing her down with the feces in his hand, ultimately smearing her with it by accident. He soon learns that she is actually a student from his class at university where he teaches architecture. When the student tells the press about the incident, they uncover other unflattering forms of behavior of Gabriel's. For example, he once made fun of this same student to his colleagues, questioning whether she was a good fit for their program. Gabriel is shocked how this single incident has not only turned him into a predator but stripped him of his racial identity. He laments: "Und plötzlich war ich weiß. Ich. Es war nicht die einzige Verdrehung von Tatsachen an diesem Tag, aber die absurdeste. Nicht, dass die Tabloids mich explizit als weiß bezeichnet hätten. Das war nicht nötig. Ich wurde weiß, indem sie darauf verzichteten zu schreiben, dass ich es nicht war" (And suddenly I was white. Me. It wasn't the only distortion of facts that day, but it was the most absurd. Not that the tabloids explicitly called me white. That was not necessary. I became white by refraining from writing that I wasn't).[9] And so Gabriel, the Black German man who never wanted people to focus on his Blackness, now finds himself in a situation where he needs people to see his Blackness to understand why he is innocent of bias. He insists that he would never commit a hate crime against someone else. But for the student, he was neither a Black nor a biracial man; he was an older man, a man of a particular class, and a man with certain privileges and authority over her. And the truth is, from an intersectional perspective, Gabriel does have more power and privilege than this Black woman. But he had never thought of it like that. Only now does he realize: "Gender, Bildungssystem, Klasse, Hautfarbe, alles kam aufs Tapet . . . Mir wurden mehr Macht, mehr Geld und mehr Einfluss unterstellt, als ich je erreichen werde" (Gender, education, class, race, everything was relevant . . . I was accused of having more power, more money and more influence than I

8   Otoo, "Dürfen Schwarze Blumen malen?," 45.
9   Jackie Thomae, *Brüder* (Munich: Hanser Verlag, 2019), 219.

will ever achieve).[10] Thus, it is not that Thomae's novel *doesn't* address racism at all. Perhaps what Otoo really means is, Thomae didn't want to write a book with the sole task of *describing racism*. Because Thomae's book *does* in fact discuss race, just not in the simplified way white German audiences might expect and desire.[11]

In *Dear Science*, Katherine McKittrick questions the motivation of academic work about Black people that simply describes their oppression. McKittrick writes,

> Description is not liberation. Methodology that is relational, intertextual, interdisciplinary, interhuman, and multidisciplinary honors black studies. Methodology that is relational, intertextual, interdisciplinary, interhuman, and multidisciplinary provides an intellectual framework through which the study of black life cannot be reduced to authentic biological data (biologized-identity-discipline) that emanates some kind of truth about racial oppression (black people are abject) and a solution to repair that truth (we must fix [correct], fix [designate and detain], and get rid of the abject).[12]

To bring up a common interlocutor in Black German Studies, Audre Lorde once said,

> It appears as understandable that Black people in general are not seen as having full lives. Black people are not seen as having relationships, loves, intricate and complex family relationships. We are seen as sociological examinations of psychological depravation, as triumph of whatever, not as human.[13]

This is what Thomae meant when she said she did not want to write a *Rassismusbuch*. She did not intend to write a book whose sole purpose was to describe "some kind truth of about racial oppression." Instead, Thomae gives us complex characters who are Black, and whose experience demands an analysis that is "relational, intertextual, interdisciplinary,

---

10   Thomae, *Brüder*, 220.

11   Here the title of Alice Hasters's book comes to mind, *Was weisse Menschen nicht über Rassimus hören wollen, aber wissen sollten* (What white people don't want to hear about racism, but should know, 2019). Hasters's title implies that while some white Germans may like to think of themselves as anti-racist, there are ultimately topics that they don't feel comfortable discussing.

12   Katherine McKittrick, *Dear Science and Other Stories* (Durham, NC: Duke University Press, 2021), 44.

13   Audre Lorde, *Audre Lorde: Dream of Europe: Selected Seminars and Interviews: 1984–1992*, edited by Mayra A. Rodriguez Castro and Dagmar Schultz (Chicago: Kenning Editions, 2020), 36.

interhuman, and multidisciplinary." And this, arguably, is not just what Black literature and Black studies do, but what Black *German* literature does and what the study of Black German literature *should do*.

In the United States, we have several pioneering scholars to thank for helping to define Black German literature and proposing that Germanists include it for our teaching and our research—for example, Leroy Hopkins, Sara Lennox, Michelle Wright and Fatima El-Tayeb. Hopkins wrote some of the first essays attempting to define Black German literature. While recently revisiting his essay, "Speaks so I Might See You" (1995), one of the things that struck me was his use of African American models to understand Black German literature.[14] This is not surprising. We know that for decades, African American culture, including literature, has had a strong influence in the Black German community. One need only think of examples such as Audre Lorde, Maya Angelou, and Toni Morrison, each of whose writings have profoundly influenced the Black German community. In his essay, Hopkins compares Black German literature to the slave narrative, "in which the dehumanized object is empowered by relating his story."[15] And we know how important this notion of conveying one's narrative has been for Black Germans, particularly those born since World War II, beginning with the publication of *Farbe bekennen (Showing Our Colors)*.[16] But I worry there is a danger in viewing Black German literature as simply a response to or only inspired by African American literature. In her monograph *African Diasporas*, Aija Poikane-Daumke justifies her comparison of African American literature and Black German literature by saying both groups are "united by the struggle against racism and marginalization which has led to the creation of a separate literature."[17] But what if we were to view Black German literature as *a part of* rather than *separate from* German literature as a whole? Could we then challenge the assertion that, in Poikane-Daumke's words, "African American literature presided over the birth of Afro-German literature"?[18]

Poikane-Daumke is right to allege that Black German identity is a construction, inasmuch as *all* our identities in this modern age are constructions. But what I'd like to challenge is the suggestion that the Black German identities we encounter in recent novels are constructed

---

14   Aija Poikane-Daumke takes a similar approach to comparing Black German and African American literature in *African Diasporas*.

15   Leroy Hopkins, "Speak, so I Might See You!: Afro-German Literature," *World Literature Today* 69, no. 3 (1995): 534.

16   See May Ayim, Katharina Oguntoye, and Dagmar Schultz, eds., *Farbe bekennen: Afro-deutsche Frauen auf den Spuren ihrer Geschichte* (Berlin: Orlanda Verlag, [1986] 2020).

17   Aija Poikane-Daumke, *African Diasporas: Afro-German Literature in the Context of the African American Experience* (Berlin: Lit, 2006), 3–4.

18   Poikane-Daumke, *African Diasporas*, 4.

primarily vis-à-vis African and African American identities. In my discussion of these novels I demonstrate that these Black German protagonists on the one hand see themselves as part of a greater Diaspora, but they also see that, as Black Germans, and Black Germans of a particular class, they have a unique position vis-à-vis other racialized groups. As Stuart Hall says, identity "is a construction, a process never completed—always 'in process.'. . . identification is in the end conditional, lodged in contingency. Once secured it does not obliterate difference. The total merging it suggests is, in fact, a fantasy of incorporation."[19]

It is important to contextualize Black German literature both within the diaspora and within German literary history, because doing so helps resist the tendency of viewing Black German literature as *Nischenliteratur* or "niche literature." In another poignant essay called "Vor der Grenze" (Before the border), which discusses race and literary translation, Sharon Dodua Otoo states:

Und dann gibt es das Problem, dass deutschsprachige Literatur von Schwarzen Menschen, zumindest bis vor kurzem, eher als Nischenliteratur angesehen wurde. Nicht wenige Rezensionen der Romane "1000 Serpentinen Angst" von Olivia Wenzel oder "Brüder" von Jackie Thomae drehten sich um die vorhandenen oder fehlenden Rassismuserfahrungen der Protagonist*innen und wie zugänglich oder nachvollziehbar diese für nicht-Schwarze Lesende seien. Als würde es bei der Schilderung solcher Erfahrungen darum gehen, ausschließlich andere Menschen dafür zu sensibilisieren.

[And then there is the problem that German-language literature from Black people, was, at least until recently, viewed as niche literature. Quite a few reviews of the novels *1000 Coils of Fear* by Olivia Wenzel or *Brothers* by Jackie Thomae revolved around the existing or missing racism experiences of the protagonists and how accessible or understandable these are for non-Black readers. It's as if describing such experiences has the sole purpose of sensitizing people toward it.][20]

In a manner reminiscent of the points made in her Klagenfurt speech, Otoo is saying here that Black German authors should not all be expected to do the same thing. They should not be expected to convey experiences

---

19 Stuart Hall, "Introduction: Who Needs 'Identity'" in *Questions of Cultural Identity*, edited by Stuart Hall and Paul du Gay (London: SAGE, 1996), 2–3.
20 Sharon Dodua Otoo, "Vor der Grenze: Über einen Übersetzungsstreit," 54 Books, March 29, 2021 https://www.54books.de/vor-der-grenze-ueber-einen-uebersetzungsstreit/.

with racism as though the sole function of Black literature were to educate white people about racism. Following Otoo's lead, I am not interested in whether or not these novels address racism, but rather in *how they approach Black subjectivity* and more specifically in how this approach to subjectivity can be considered a literary movement. If critics notice certain similarities among these three books, instead of pitting them against each other by suggesting one author does something better or is copying another, why not take the approach we would typically take toward non-racialized authors and group them together within a literary movement? Specifically, I think it is worth considering how these novels could be contextualized against the German literary phenomenon of new subjectivity, most often associated with the 1970s.

When considering what these three novels have in common, what strikes me is a certain turn inward: Black characters who not only grapple with their experience of a racist society but who have additional personal concerns that have to do with how they relate to others. Sometimes those others are family members. The narrator in Wenzel's novel, for example, is constantly taking stock of her relationship with her mother and grandmother. In Sow's novel, the protagonist Fatou reflects on her lack of a relationship with her biological mother, her evolving relationship with her surrogate mother, and her challenging relationship with her daughter. And in *Brothers*, Gabriel's and Mick's lack of relationship to their biological father has had a significant impact on their lives, whether or not they want to admit it. This focus on the family in Black German literature is not new. We find it in May Ayim's poetry, in Ika Hügel-Marshall's *Daheim unterwegs* (*Invisible Woman*), and in Hans-Jürgen Massaquoi's *Destined to Witness*.[21] What *is* new is how central it has become for Black German characters to consider their positionality vis-à-vis other racialized and oppressed groups. In *1000 Coils of Fear*, the narrator's travels to the United States, Vietnam, and Morocco prompt her to think about her privilege as a German citizen. In *The Black Madonna*, Fatou tries to solve a crime that has taken place in her provincial, Bavarian hometown; she is aided by Grace, a West African refugee who frequently checks Fatou's German privilege. And, as indicated in my discussion of *Brothers* above, Gabriel is surprised that a Black female student would accuse him of a hate crime and view him as just another male predator, regardless of his racialized identity. The key word in all these examples is *privilege*. As Stuart Hall states, "identification is . . . a process of articulation, a suturing, an overdetermination or a lack, but never a proper fit, a totality" and

---

21 See May Ayim, *Blues in schwarz weiss: Gedichte* (Berlin: Orlanda Frauenverlag, 1995); Ika Hügel-Marshall, *Daheim unterwegs: ein deutsches Leben* (Berlin: Orlanda Frauenverlag, 1998); Hans-Jürgen Massaquoi, *Destined to Witness: Growing up Black in Nazi Germany* (New York: Perennial, 1999).

this is what the protagonists in these novels find as they try to relate to different groups.[22] In each novel, the Black German protagonists understand how racism impacts their lives, but the texts also focus on whether or not they become aware of the power and privilege they themselves have, dependent on citizenship, class, and gender.

New Subjectivity

It is because of the way Black German characters in these novels think of both the "objective" and the "subjective" factor of identity that I would like to consider how Black German literature today is not only similar to but *expands* the literary category of new subjectivity. *New subjectivity* is a term that was proposed by Marcel Reich-Ranicki to describe a direction taken by German literature in the 1970s, where the author "von sich selber redet, von seinem Innenleben berichtet und Intimes nicht ausspart" (speaks about himself, about his inner life and doesn't spare intimate details).[23] After the politicization of the late 1960s, following 1968, the German student movement and the left-wing terrorism of the Red Army Faction, *new subjectivity* marked the moment when German authors turned inward to explore personal dreams and problems, in contrast to the more politically engaged literature of the 68ers.[24] But *new subjectivity* was not apolitical. As Wolfgang Beutin states, "diese Entpolitisierung [enthielt] eine stärkere Betonung individueller Interessen und Motivationen" (this depoliticization meant a stronger emphasis on individual interests and motivations);[25] indeed, as the slogan of the new women's movement claimed, "the personal and the political" were no longer separable. Furthermore, as Leslie Adelson suggests, new subjectivity acknowledged that someone's political identity does *not* have to be tied to a blue-collar identity. Previously, the "fundamental assumption designated the factory as the locus of political identity. Students who wanted to contribute to the socialist revolution were thus expected to fulfill their role as the political vanguard by doing political work at the base."[26]

Today's Black German literature is similar to new subjectivity in that it stresses "self-reflection and self-experience" without negating "history

---

22   Stuart Hall, "Introduction: Who Needs 'Identity'?" 3.
23   Marcel Reich-Ranicki, "Anmerkungen zur deutschen Literatur der siebziger Jahre," *Merkur* 33 (1979): 176.
24   Leslie Adelson, *Crisis of Subjectivity* (Amsterdam: Rodopi, 1984), 2.
25   Wolfgang Beutin et al., *Deutsche Literaturgeschichte: von den Anfängen bis zur Gegenwart* (Stuttgart: Metzler, 2001), 636.
26   Adelson, *Crisis of Subjectivity*, 5.

or politics."[27] For example, the Black German protagonists of these novels frequently attempt to grasp the motivations of the previous generation, in order to better understand themselves. They wonder about Black and white absent parents, why they left and what kinds of hardships they might have dealt with. Part of grappling with subjectivity is a certain negotiation between the local, the national and the global. Furthermore, Black German authors do not romanticize the working class as the "political vanguard" or the only class suffering from oppression. Black German authors write about characters who span a variety of class experiences—from undocumented immigrants to working-class mall detectives and substitute teachers to middle-class architects. And although they acknowledge that the lives of such Black characters can be quite different, they may all still experience anti-Blackness, whether at the hands of the powerful (police, the courts, employers) or at the hands of white people on the margins (unemployed, unhoused, or criminal).

Of all the epochs of German literary history, I choose to situate these Black German novels vis-à-vis new subjectivity, because of its significance for exploring identity. Of course, one could go further back in history to grapple with this same issue, to *Empfindsamkeit* (in English sentimentalism), for example, or *Sturm und Drang*. But "new subjectivity" was a particular iteration of German literature that contended with the individual at a certain place in time; one that particularly grappled with questions of alienation. And as James Snead, another African American Germanist, once said, who has more authority to speak about alienation in the modern world, than Black people?[28]

Linda C. DeMeritt describes protagonists in "new subjectivity" as follows:

> The new subjective protagonist is an alienated individual, someone for whom the patterns, routines, and conventions of society are no longer valid. Accordingly, this individual stands alone and isolated, no longer part of the smoothly functioning whole continuing without interruption for other people. Alienation is often precipitated by the experience of a personal catastrophe....[29]

In contrast, I would argue that for the protagonist of new Black German subjectivity, the experience that precipitates the feeling of alienation is racialization. And it is not that racialization is the *only* trauma. DeMeritt

---

27 Beutin, *Deutsche Literaturgeschichte*, 638.
28 See James Snead, "On Repetition in Black Culture," *African American Review* 50, no. 4 (Winter 2017): 648–56.
29 Linda C. DeMeritt, *New Subjectivity and Prose Forms of Alienation: Peter Handke and Botho Strauss* (New York: P. Lang, 1987), 8.

describes a host of traumas that may affect a protagonist in a new subjective novel:

> New subjective traumas include death, sickness, abandonment, betrayal, and separation. Such traumas destroy the seeming security of the individual's everyday world. The subject is confronted with something inexplicable and meaningless which invalidates all previous patterns of life. Everything which once was taken for granted becomes questionable and uncertain. The alienated individual no longer believes in a meaningful and comprehensive totality which orders and explains the world and the purpose of a single existence within this world.[30]

Just like the protagonists of "new subjectivity," the Black German protagonists I discuss also experience "death, sickness, abandonment, betrayal, and separation." But the thing that makes them doubt a "comprehensive totality which orders and explains the world and the purpose of a single existence within this world" is racialization itself. Thus, the key difference between white German protagonists and Black German protagonists with respect to new subjectivity, is that while white German protagonists are on the search for objective truth, the Black German protagonists never had the naïve perspective that there was objective truth to begin with. They were always already alienated by the system; they are just finally able to see the falseness of race and look beyond the veil.

Furthermore, despite this feeling of alienation, the Black German subjects in these novels do not see themselves as "alone and isolated" from everyone. Rather, they experience Blackness as a constant negotiation between exclusion and inclusion. If being Black in Germany means others conveying to you that you are to be *excluded*, then in the United States or London it means feeling *included*. But this incorporation, as Hall argues, can only ever be partial. Wenzel's protagonist knows she can only feel at home in Black America for the time being, just as Thomae's protagonist Gabriel knows his sense of belonging in London is conditional and Sow's protagonist knows her sense of belonging in Bavaria among white Germans or together with African refugees is also conditional, but for different reasons.

What one can observe in these recent novels is that while the Black German characters desire to stress their *local* belonging to a particular city or region, they often neglect to consider what implications their *national* belonging has for their identities. This observation is not meant to serve as a critique of the characters themselves. I believe these authors intentionally present us with imperfect characters so that we can witness

---

30   DeMeritt, *New Subjectivity and Prose Forms*, 9.

their progression from a lack of awareness of the implications of national belonging to being more fully aware of how the intersection of their identities influences their relationships with others.

Noah Sow's novel *The Black Madonna* literally emphasizes the local in its subtitle—*Afrodeutscher Heimatkrimi* (Afro-German homeland detective novel). In Sow's novel, a Black German mother, Fatou Fall, and her adolescent daughter, Yesim, are spending the summer visiting her "aunt Hortensia" (they have no biological relation), the queer white German woman who raised her together with her life-long partner in the small town of Altötting in Bavaria. By referring to Fatou's nonbiological relative as her "aunt," Sow also stresses queerness by emphasizing that in both Black and queer communities (Black and non-Black), nonbiological chosen family is often key to an individual's survival.[31] Fatou is treating this as an opportunity for Yesim to get to know her Bavarian roots, which is made difficult by the town's rural setting and her aunt's ignorance and insensitivity when it comes to talking about race. As Vanessa Plumly writes about the novel, "Black Germans' presence in smaller cities . . . serves to inscribe them into the national narrative and frame at a regional level."[32] In addition to its small-town setting, another unusual thing about the novel is its genre: a *Krimi*, or detective novel. As such, the novel centers around a crime. During a visit to a local church, specifically *The Church of the Black Madonna*—a reference to the real Shrine of Our Lady in Altötting—Fatou and Yesim happen to witness an apparent "terrorist" attack. Plumly argues that "crime novels and crime television shows might shift the representation and recognition of Black Germans" from the typical representation of them in big cities.[33] Furthermore, since the regional *Krimi* allows for an intimate study of a

---

[31] In *Black Feminist Thought*, Patricia Hill Collins discusses how important nonbiological "other-mothers" have been to the Black diaspora when biological mothers have been absent from a child's life, owing to a variety of reasons from the inhumane conditions of slavery to Black women's domestic work and Black women's imprisonment. Patricia Hill Collins, *Black Feminist Thought* (New York: Routledge, 2009), 192–205. And queer theorist Eve Kosofsky Sedgwick has written about how queer folx have an important role in the life of a child, serving as the queer aunts and uncles whose unconventional lives demonstrate to a child that they do not have to follow the path of heteronormativity. See Eve Kosofsky Sedgwick, "Tales of the Avunculate: Queer Tutelage in *The Importance of Being Earnest*," in *Professions of Desire: Lesbian and Gay Studies in Literature*, ed. George E. Haggerty and Bonnie Zimmerman (New York: Modern Languages Association of America, 1995), 191–209.

[32] Vanessa D. Plumly, "*Auf den Spuren ihrer Geschichte*: Black German Detectives and the Cases of Anäis Schmitz and Fatou Fall," *Seminar: A Journal of Germanic Studies* 57, no. 4 (2021): 420.

[33] Plumly, "*Auf den Spuren ihrer Geschichte*," 403.

place, a *Regionalkrimi* by a Black German author can reveal "how institutional and historically anchored racist structures 'frame' Black German belonging," even in the province.[34]

During the alleged terrorist attack that takes place in the novel, several men wearing ski masks enter the Church of the Black Madonna, and spray paint the following: "ALLAH WAKBA." While the white German witnesses and the police are convinced this is the work of Muslim terrorists, Fatou and Yesim observe that not only is this incorrect Arabic but the men were wearing dark makeup around their eyes as if to camouflage the part of their bodies that the ski masks would otherwise reveal to be white. The rest of the novel follows Fatou as she attempts to discover the true nature of this crime, leading her to uncover corruption among local politicians and church leaders. Throughout the novel, Fatou performs her Bavarianness. She enjoys it when Hortensia cooks the local cuisine. She makes use of local dialect whenever a white German attempts to question her belonging, even if she has long chosen Hamburg as her *Wahlheimat* (chosen home). However, Fatou isn't completely comfortable with how her Heimat may have shaped her. She only relies on her cultural cache when it benefits her, such as when white Germans don't want to take her seriously. In those moments, stressing her local ties allows Fatou to challenge their assumptions about whiteness and German identity. Nevertheless, there are other moments when her comfort in this local setting becomes a problem. Specifically, when she meets Grace Bâ, a West African refugee and activist who has lived in the area for ten years. Grace says several things that make Fatou realize just how much privilege she has and how much the local has shaped her identity. In the following scene, Grace confronts Fatou about her naïve trust in local SPD politicians who may come across as tolerant but are as uninterested in helping immigrants as the local CDU politicians. Fatou states about the SPD mayoral candidate,

"Dabei ist er doch eigentlich einer von den Guten."
Grace sah sie ungläubig von der Seite an. "Er engagiert sich für Jugendliche," sagte Fatou.
"Hast du seine Wahlplakate gesehen?," zischte Grace. Natürlich hatte sie das: Integration fördern, Zuzug regulieren, bla bla bla. Dort hätte auch stehen können: Südeuropäer tolerieren, Roma und Afrikaner nicht reinlassen.
"Na also!," sagte Grace. "Was ist daran denn gut? Dass er schlimmer sein könnte? Das ist das Problem mit euch Deutschen, ihr wollt 'gut' sein, aber ihr haltet immer zusammen."

---

34   Plumly, "*Auf den Spuren ihrer Geschichte.*"

Fatou brauchte ein paar Momente, bis der Inhalt des Satzes bei ihr angekommen war . . . Sie war unter Schock. Wieso hatte Grace sie als 'Deutsche' angegriffen, wo sie doch ebenso eine Schwarze Frau war und deswegen die ganze Zeit für eine Ausländerin gehalten wurde? Das musste Grace doch klar sein . . .

"Ich wollte dich nicht verletzen. Bist du jetzt traurig, dass du Deutsche bist?," fragte Grace.

["But he's actually one of the good guys."

Grace gave her a sideways look in disbelief. "He has a lot of youth initiatives," said Fatou.

"Have you seen his campaign posters?" Grace hissed. Of course she had: promote integration, regulate immigration, blah blah blah. They could also have written: Tolerate Southern Europeans, don't let Roma and Africans in.

"There you go!" said Grace. "What's so good about that? That it could have been worse? That's the problem with you Germans, you want to be 'good,' but you always stick together."

It took Fatou a few moments for the content of the sentence to sink in . . . She was in shock. Why did Grace attack her as a 'German' when she was also a Black woman and was therefore mistaken for a foreigner all the time? Surely Grace must have realized that. Fatou felt unfairly treated . . .

"I didn't mean to hurt you. Are you sad now that you're German?" Grace asked.][35]

This scene reveals just how complex Fatou's identity is. When she was growing up in Altötting, she was the victim of both structural racism (at school for example) and her white German family's ignorance about racism and their lack of understanding about how to best equip her with the skills to survive in a society where the majority is white. In addition to being racialized, there are other parts of her identity that place her in a marginalized and precarious position: she is a single mother and she is recently unemployed. At the same time, she enjoys certain privileges that Grace does not have. Fatou is a citizen who must not worry about fulfilling the requirements of legal residency. After spending her childhood in Altötting, she was able to pick up and move to a more diverse city, Hamburg, where she enjoys living among liberal-minded Germans. For these reasons, Fatou does not immediately see the potential for violence contained in a phrase like "regulate immigration." For her liberal mindset, and from the perspective of someone with German citizenship, this seems like a reasonable approach to immigration. Grace's remarks quickly

---

35 Noah Sow, *Die Schwarze Madonna: Fatou Falls erster Fall* (Norderstedt: BoD—Books on Demand, 2019), 133.

rip her out of this fantasy. This is why Grace tells her "Ein Paar Sachen haben wir gemeinsam. Aber nicht alles. Deine Mentalität" (We have a few things in common. But not everything. Your mentality . . .).[36]

This encounter with Grace sends Fatou into an identity crisis. She has fought her entire life to be recognized as Black *and* German, but when Grace labels her as "German," it is clearly meant as an insult. Grace's comment—"That's the problem with you Germans, you want to be 'good,' but you always stick together"—suddenly places Fatou on the wrong side of history. She is effectively lumped together with all the white Germans who are ashamed of their racist and fascist past and want to be perceived as good because they are "tolerant" of difference, even if they don't challenge engrained prejudices against marginalized groups like Sinti, Roma, and African immigrants. Fatou had always considered herself as existing in solidarity with other Black people; she had never thought about what ways she might be complicit in anti-Blackness and prejudice toward other marginalized groups. Furthermore, Fatou never thought of herself as being ashamed of her African identity, but she is so used to taking a defensive stance when white Germans ask her "Where are you really from?" that when Grace asks where her parents are from she thinks, "Grace musste doch selbst darunter leiden, dass immer eine *Erklärung* von ihr verlangt wurde dafür, dass sie es überhaupt wagte, in Deutschland anwesend zu sein" (Grace must also suffer from always being expected to explain why she even dared to be present in Germany).[37] Grace, however, insists, "Du kannst African Pride haben und trotzdem hier aufgewachsen sein" (You can have African pride and still grow up here).[38] But although Fatou's initial reaction to Grace is defensive, by the end of the novel she takes her new friendship with Grace as an opportunity to reevaluate her relationship to Black culture, which is why the novel ends with her embracing the new short afro Grace recently cut for her in the style of South African singer Miriam Makeba based on a photo Fatou had once seen in a magazine as a child and saved: The novel ends thus: "Sie fuhr die Fensterscheibe hoch und schaltete die Lüftung ein. Seit sie den kurzen Afro trug, gab es keine Strähne mehr, die sie sich aus der Stirn pusten konnte. Sie kämmte sich stattdessen mit großer Geste über die Schläfe. Es fühlte sich gut an" (She rolled up the windowpane and turned on the ventilation. Ever since she's been wearing the short afro, there hasn't been a strand of hair she's had to blow off her forehead. Instead, she smoothed down her edges with a sweeping gesture. It feels good).[39]

36 Sow, *Die Schwarze Madonna*, 134.
37 Sow, *Die Schwarze Madonna*, 175–76.
38 Sow, *Die Schwarze Madonna*, 176.
39 Sow, *Die Schwarze Madonna*, 393.

Similar to how Fatou's relationship with her daughter motivates her rediscovery of her roots, in *1000 Coils of Fear*, the Black German narrator's coming to terms with her background is closely tied to her pregnancy and her hopes and fears surrounding her potential relationship to her future child. This nameless protagonist has an even more complex positionality, as she is also queer and East German, making her a minority even among Black Germans. Another important difference is the style of each novel. Sow chose a familiar genre, the *Regionalkrimi*, as a vehicle for tackling an unfamiliar story—that of a Black German growing up in a Bavarian village. Thus, Sow is able to focus on the particularity of Black German experience, while still insisting on the connections that can be made between Black German experience and regional traditions, history, and identity. Wenzel takes an entirely different approach, using the form of autofiction and nonlinear, dialogic storytelling, which allows her to blend her own biography with the protagonist's, while simultaneously making it unclear how much of the story is fiction and how reliable the narrator is.[40]

What contributes to the reader's disorientation when reading *1000 Coils of Fear*, is how the novel frequently jumps across time, entangling the present with past memories and even incorporating her past, present, and future fantasies. Throughout the novel, she recalls her grandmother's and mother's experiences in the German Democratic Republic and reflects both on how their epigenetic trauma may have shaped her and on how her life differs from theirs—for example, she has so much more mobility than they did. At the same time, it frustrates her that her grandmother doesn't understand that the freedom of mobility that came with a new passport from the Federal Republic of Germany does not negate her experiences with anti-Blackness. She reflects:

> Wenn ich ihr von der Schule erzählen würde, die Refugees in Kreuzberg vor einigen Jahren besetzt haben, wenn ich ihr von dem verzweifelten Mann erzählen würde, der auf dem Dach dieser Schule stand und damit drohte, sich in den Tod zu stürzen, sollte die Schule geräumt werden, weil er lieber sterben wollte, als abgeschoben zu werden, wenn ich meiner Großmutter von dem weißen Polizisten erzählen würde, der auf dem Dach gegenüber stand und erst mit einer Banane, dann mit Handschellen dem Suizidgefährdeten

---

40 Priscilla Layne discusses the importance of autofiction for the novel in "'That's How It Is': Quotidian Violence and Resistance in Olivia Wenzel's *1000 Coils of Fear*." *Novel: A Forum on Fiction* 55, no. 1 (2022): 38–60. Michelle Wright discusses the significance of dialogic storytelling in the poetry of May Ayim in *Becoming Black: Creating Identity in the African Diaspora* (Durham, NC: Duke University Press, 2004).

zuwinkte, was sollte sie erwidern? Wenn ich meine Oma Rita fragen würde, ob sie Parallelen sehen könne zwischen dem Hass, der meinem Vater in der DDR entgegenschlug, auch von ihren Freundinnen, auch von ihren Arbeitskollegen, und dem Hass, der mir und meinem Bruder entgegenschlug, von Mitschülerinnen, Eltern und allen, die sich generell für Hitler begeistern, wenn ich fragen würde, ob sie Parallelen sehen könne zwischen dem Hass, der heute systematisch schwarzen Menschen in den USA entgegenschlägt, und dem Hass, der permanent und weltweit Geflüchteten entgegenschlägt, was sollte sie sagen?[41]

[If I told her about the school that refugees occupied in Kreuzberg a few years ago, if I told her about the desperate man who stood on the roof of that school and threatened to throw himself to his death, if he was evicted from school, because he would rather die than be deported, if I told my grandmother about the white policeman standing across the street on the roof waving first a banana, then handcuffs at the suicidal man, what would she say? If I asked my grandmother Rita whether she could see parallels between the hatred my father faced in the GDR, also from her friends, also from her work colleagues, and the hatred I and my brother faced, from classmates and parents and to all those who are generally enthusiastic about Hitler, if I asked her if she could see parallels between the hatred that is systematically directed at Black people in the USA today and the hatred that is constantly and worldwide directed at refugees, what should she say?] (*1000 C* 61)

In this passage, the narrator realizes that her white grandmother isn't capable of the same intersectional analysis of oppression as she is. She identifies a through line of anti-Blackness between her father's experiences in the GDR and her and her brother's experiences with racism following reunification and the contemporary dehumanization of African refugees. Whereas her grandmother cannot see the connections between these incidents, because she sees her granddaughter as German and as not having anything of significance in common with immigrants, refugees, or African Americans a half a world away. As a white woman, her grandmother has the privilege of not seeing racism or the continuities between intolerant, anti-Black regimes, because that racism does not directly affect her. But this passage also reveals the shortcomings of the narrator. She has yet to better understand her positionality and privilege vis-à-vis other racialized

---

41   Olivia Wenzel, *1000 Serpentinen Angst* (Frankfurt am Main: Fischer, 2020), 80. From here on I will refer to the German edition as *1000 S* and the English edition as *1000 C* in parenthetical citations. See Olivia Wenzel, *1000 Coils of Fear* (New York: Catapult, 2022).

groups. Sometimes these experiences are a result of her travels—she traverses the globe from the US to Morocco and finally to Vietnam. In the United States, she has the following epiphany:

> Und plötzlich begreifst du: diese warme Community schwarzer Menschen, hier in den USA, ist nur möglich, weil sie jahrhundertelang zum Überleben nötig war. Die Basis, auf der sich diese Menschen begegnen und bestärken, war und ist blutig, ungerecht, qualvoll. Du kannst dankbar sein, dass du willkommener Gast in dieser Gemeinschaft bist, eine Touristin dieser auf Schmerz gewachsenen Blackness. Du kannst froh sein, dass dein Herz hier nur temporär ein paar düstere Schläge imitiert. (*1000 S* 312)

> [And suddenly you understand: This warm community of Black people, here in the USA, is only possible because for centuries it was necessary in order to survive. The basis upon which these people meet each other and empower each other was and is bloody, unjust and torturous. You can be thankful that you are just a welcomed guest in this community; a tourist of this Blackness born of pain. You should feel lucky that your heart temporarily attempts a few somber beats only while you're here.] (*1000 C* 249)

She is a "welcomed guest" in the African American community. But the key word here is "guest"; she cannot become a permanent member of this community. Although Black Germans and African Americans may share common experiences of racism, discrimination, and violence, and a past of slavery and colonialism, she knows she did not walk in the same shoes as the African Americans she encounters or their ancestors, and as a result her experience of her Blackness and anti-Black racism often looks much different.

In Morocco, she realizes what kinds of privileges she has as a German citizen when a taxi driver misunderstands a comment she makes about work, and suggests she apply for a position as a member of the cleaning staff in a local hotel:

> Der Fahrer verweist mich an ein Hotel, in dem viele "Schwarzafrikaner" arbeiten. Ich könne dort meinen CV einreichen, wenn ich wolle. Ob ich wisse, was ein CV sei? Das sei das, wo ich mein Leben auflisten würde. Ja, das wisse ich, aber nein nein, sage ich, ich meinte eben: Ich kann auch *von* hier aus arbeiten, nicht: Ich kann ja auch *hier* arbeiten. *Ach* so. Der Taxifahrer wirkt enttäuscht. Ich stelle mir kurz den Alltag als Reinigungskraft in einem marokkanischen Hotel vor, mit kleiner weißer Haube auf dem Kopf in gebückter Haltung, stöhnend oder summend ... Ein anderes Leben, wenige Kilometer entfernt. (*1000 S* 87)

[The driver refers me to a hotel where a lot of "sub-Saharan Africans" work. He suggests I could submit my résumé there if I wanted. *Do you know what a résumé is? It's a piece of paper where you itemize your life.* I say, *Yes, I know, but no no, I just meant: I can also work "from here,"* not: *I can also work here.* The taxi driver seems disappointed. For a minute, I imagine what my daily life would be working as a housekeeper in a Moroccan hotel, with a small white bonnet on my head, bent over, groaning or humming . . . A different life, just a few kilometers away.] (*1000 C 67*)

And finally while in Vietnam, her ex-girlfriend Kim, who is Vietnamese German, accuses her of Eurocentricism, because she views Vietnamese facilities as substandard. In the following dialogue, Kim's speech is indented. The narrator asks, rhetorically:

Das findest du so richtig kacke, oder?
Dass ich mich hier bei diesem Deutschen eingemietet habe?
  Der Typ hat den halben Strand aufgekauft.
Aber die vietnamesische Regierung hat das doch gewollt, mit der Gesetzesänderung, oder? Dass die ausländischen Investoren jetzt loslegen.
  Weißt Du, die Kinder, die jetzt hier selbstverständlich Fußball
  spielen oder Musik hören, die dürfen in zehn Jahren die neuen
  Beach Resorts nicht mehr betreten. Außer sie sind dort angestellt.
Hm.
  Lothar ist vielleicht nett, aber was der hier an Neokolonialismus
  abzieht, geht gar nicht. Diese Bungalows sehen aus wie mini
  Reihenhäuser in Schwaben. Das hat nichts damit zu tun, wie die
  Leute hier leben.
Ich hatte halt Bock auf deutsche Sauberkeit.
Und Erholung.
  Ich weiß (*1000 S 317*)

[You think that's really shitty of me, don't you? That I've rented a place here owned by a German.
  That guy bought up half the beach.
But the Vietnamese government wanted that, with the change in the law, right? They wanted foreign investors to really get going.
  You know, the kids who play soccer or listen to music here without
  a care, ten years from now they won't be able to set foot in the new
  beach resorts. Unless they're employed there.
Hm.
  Lothar might be nice, but this neocolonialism that he's involved in
  here is not okay. These bungalows look like miniature row houses in
  Germany. They have nothing to do with the people who live here.
I was just looking for German cleanliness. And relaxation.
  I know.] (*1000 S 252*)

While the scenes I have thus far depicted all occur while the narrator is traveling abroad, there are also moments in the text that demonstrate how her emerging understanding of privilege changes the way she interacts with other racialized people within Germany as well. For example, in one scene, she is riding her bike through Brandenburg when she happens to meet a young man to whom she takes a liking. The narrator doesn't explicitly racialize him. We only learn his name is Jacob and that the two of them have some banter back and forth and exchange numbers, hoping to meet again later. The only indication that Jacob might be Black comes about when she walks him back to his home and describes his living circumstances. In this excerpt, although the narrator is speaking of herself, she uses the second person address, which is a particular narrative choice Wenzel uses that results in implicating the reader as well:

> Später geht ihr zusammen ein Stück die Landstraße entlang, teil einen Müsliriegel, du fragst nicht nach seiner Herkunft. Schließlich bleibt ihr vor einem großen, eisernen Tor stehen. Dahinter siehst du ein mehrgeschossiges Gebäude, das an eine Scheune und ein Krankenhaus zugleich erinnert. Jacob sagt: *I must go here now*, und sieht traurig aus. In dem Moment fährt ein blauer Trabi die Straße entlang. Der weiße Fahrer kurbelt die Scheibe runter, reckt den Arm raus, formt mit der Hand eine Pistole, zielt auf euch und drückt ab. Jacob sieht es nicht, der Mann fährt hinter seinem Rücken vorbei. (*1000 S* 216)

> [Later, you walk along a stretch of country road together, share a granola bar, and you don't ask him about his ancestry. In the end, you stop in front of a large iron gate. Behind it, you see a multistory building that reminds you of a barn and a hospital simultaneously. Jacob says: *I must go here now*, and looks sad. At exactly this moment, a blue Trabant drives down the street. The white driver rolls down his window, stretches out his arm, turns his hand into a gun, points at you both, and pulls the trigger. Jacob doesn't see it, his back is to the man as he drives by.] (*1000 C* 174–75)

Although the narrator doesn't describe Jacob as a Black refugee, we know this is the case because of three things: first, the white man who drives by pretends to shoot *both* of them. Second, the narrator wishes she could give him her dead brother's passport so he can travel freely. Finally, the building in which Jacob lives, which looks like a prison and a hospital, is an asylum seeker's home. The narrator does not introduce Jacob as a Black refugee living in Brandenburg, because she would like to believe that his citizenship status doesn't influence whether or not she wants to befriend him or date him. That's why she explicitly points out that she does not ask him where he's from. She is attempting to show the readers that there is an important distinction between her and white Germans. But the reality is, even if she can empathize with his struggles with racism, his legal status in Germany limits his mobility in contrast to her and this leaves her feeling guilty:

> Du schlägst verwirrt vor, dass Jacob dich ja mal in Berlin besuchen könne, und ihr tauscht Handynummern. Jedes Mal, wenn er dir in den folgenden Wochen schreibt, weißt du nicht, was du antworten sollst.
> *Hey, girl, have you forgotten about me?*
> . . .
> *Hello?*
> Hättest du Jacob den Pass deines Bruders gegeben, könnte er jetzt vielleicht an einer Straße wohnen, auf der keine Trabis mit pantomimefreudigen Insassen herumtuckern.
> . . .
> *Hey, girl, why don't you answer my—*
> SORRY, BUT I CAN GO WHEREVER I WANT TO, AND YOU CAN GO NOWHERE, BYEEE.
> Irgendwann blockierst du Jacobs Nummer. (*1000 S* 216–17)

> [Confusedly, you suggest that Jacob should come to visit you in Berlin sometime and you exchange cell phone numbers. In the coming weeks, every time he writes to you, you don't know how you should answer.
> *Hey, girl, have you forgotten about me?*
> . . .
> *Hello?*
> If you had given Jacob your brother's passport, maybe he could have now lived on a street without Trabants driven around by pantomime-friendly occupants.
> . . .
> *Hey, girl, why don't you answer my—*
> sorry, but i can go wherever i want to and you can go nowhere, byeee.
> At some point you block Jacob's number.] (*1000 C* 175–76)

To return to the point I made earlier, when the German literary market expects Black German novels to explicitly center racism, it not only places limitations on what we expect from Black German literature but it also too narrowly defines the effects of racism. These three novels are about the development of Black German subjectivity and how this subjectivity is always constructed in relation to others. This is why each novel emphasizes an intersectional approach to understanding Black German identity. Each character's trials and tribulations are about race, but they are also about gender, citizenship, sexuality, and any number of additional identity categories. White Germans' failure to recognize how formative racialization can be causes them to focus too much on racial violence that you can *see* as opposed to the racial violence that's psychological. This is why Wenzel's novel in particular places so much emphasis on mental health. During the course of the novel, the narrator makes several attempts to find a therapist to help her work through her anxiety. Her first attempt fails, largely because the white therapist lacks an understanding of how the experience of racialization affects all aspects of her life. This is one of several moments in the novel, where Wenzel uses italics to differentiate between the narrator's thoughts and speech and the speech of her interlocutor. After the narrator describes her mental state, the therapist responds:

> *Sie fühlen sich zerrissen zwischen den Kulturen. Ich denke, das sind Probleme, die im Hier und Jetzt bestehen, mit der Außenwelt. Mein Therapieangebot richtet sich ja eher an Menschen, die von der Vergangenheit belastet sind . . . Ich denke deshalb, dass ich Ihnen mit meinem Angebot nicht helfen kann. Und Ihre Fragen sind ja im Grunde nicht therapeutisch zu klären.* (*1000 S* 189)

> [*You feel torn between cultures. I think those are problems that exist in the here and now, with the external world. My therapy is directed more toward people who are burdened by the past . . . therefore, I don't think I can offer you any help. And in principle, your questions can't be answered with therapy.*] (*1000 C* 150)

His answer suggests that Black people's problems can only be linked to structural, external, societal issues and do not simultaneously relate to the psyche and trauma. This would assign the space of inward-looking subjectivity to whites only. By proposing the category of new Black German subjectivity, I argue that considering these works as expanding on new subjectivity would help acknowledge that Black people are just as affected by inner conflict as by outside stressors; in fact, the outside stressors of racism and racialization contribute to the inner conflict. Positioning these Black German novels vis-à-vis new subjectivity requires the category to be expanded and insists that we find ways to relate Black German literature nationally to the German canon, not just transnationally to a larger Black diasporic canon.

Bibliography

Adelson, Leslie. *Crisis of Subjectivity*. Amsterdam: Rodopi, 1984.
Ayim, May. *Blues in schwarz weiss: Gedichte*. Berlin: Orlanda Frauenverlag, 1995.
Ayim, May, Katharina Oguntoye, and Dagmar Schultz, eds. *Farbe bekennen: Afro-deutsche Frauen auf den Spuren ihrer Geschichte*. Reprint, Berlin: Orlanda Verlag, 2020.
Ayivi, Simone Dede. "'Internationalität ≠ Interkultur': eine Schwarze deutsche Kritik." In *Allianzen: Kritische Praxis an weissen Institutionen*, edited by Elisa Liepsch, Julian Warner, and Matthias Pees, 74–83. Bielefeld: Transcript, 2018.
Biendarra, Anke S. *Germans Going Global: Contemporary Literature and Cultural Globalization*. Berlin: De Gruyter, 2012.
Bergold-Caldwell, Denise, Laura Digoh, Hadijah Haruna-Oelker, Christelle Nkwendja-Ngnoubamdjum, Camilla Ridha, and Eleonore Wiedenroth-Coulibaly. *Spiegelblicke: Perspektiven Schwarzer Bewegung in Deutschland*. Berlin: Orlanda Verlag, 2017.
Beutin, Wolfgang. *Deutsche Literaturgeschichte: von den Anfängen bis zur Gegenwart*. Stuttgart: Metzler, 2001.
Collins, Patricia Hill. *Black Feminist Thought*. New York: Routledge, 2009.
DeMeritt, Linda C. *New Subjectivity and Prose Forms of Alienation: Peter Handke and Botho Strauss*. New York: P. Lang, 1987.
Götting, Michael. *Contrapunctus*. Münster: Unrast, 2015.
Hall, Stuart. "Introduction: Who Needs 'Identity.'" In *Questions of Cultural Identity*, edited by Stuart Hall and Paul du Gay, 1–17. London: SAGE, 1996.
———. "What Is the 'Black' in Black Popular Culture?" In *Black Popular Culture*, edited by Gina Dent, 21–33. Seattle, WA: Bay Press, 1992.
Haster, Alice. *Was weisse Menschen nicht über Rassimus hören wollen, aber wissen sollten*. Munich: Hanserblau, 2019.
Hillgärtner, Jule, Nele Kaczmarek, Bonaventure Soh Bejeng Ndikung, and Kunstverein Braunschweig. *The Faculty of Sensing—Thinking, With, Through, and by Anton Wilhelm Amo*. Braunschweig: Milano Mousse Publishing and Kunstverein Braunschweig, 2021.
Hopkins, Leroy. "Speak, so I Might See You!: Afro-German Literature." *World Literature Today* 69, no. 3 (1995): 533–38.
Hügel-Marshall, Ika. *Daheim unterwegs: ein deutsches Leben*. Berlin: Orlanda Frauenverlag, 1998.
Koepsell, Philipp Khabo. *Afro Shop*. Berlin: epubli, 2014.
———. *Die Akte James Knopf: afrodeutsche Wort- und Streitkunst*. Münster: Unrast, 2010.
———. "The Invisible Archive. A Historical Overview of Black Literature Production in Germany." In *AfroFictional In[ter]ventions Revisiting the BIGSAS Festival of African(-Diasporic) Literatures, Bayreuth 2011–2013*, edited by Susan Arndt and Nadja Ofuatey-Alazard, 121–34. Münster: edition assemblage, 2014.

Layne, Priscilla. "'That's How It Is': Quotidian Violence and Resistance in Olivia Wenzel's *1000 Coils of Fear*." *Novel: A Forum on Fiction* 55, no. 1 (2022): 38–60.

Lorde, Audre. *Audre Lorde: Dream of Europe: Selected Seminars and Interviews: 1984–1992*. Edited by Mayra A. Rodriguez Castro and Dagmar Schultz. Chicago: Kenning Editions, 2020.

Massaquoi, Hans-Jürgen. *Destined to Witness: Growing up Black in Nazi Germany*. New York: Perennial, 1999.

McKittrick, Katherine. *Dear Science and Other Stories*. Durham, NC: Duke University Press, 2021.

Otoo, Sharon Dodua. "Dürfen Schwarze Blumen malen." In *Herr Gröttrup setzt sich hin: Drei Texte*, 29–47. Frankfurt am Main: Fischer Verlag, 2022.

———. "Vor der Grenze: Über einen Übersetzungsstreit." 54 Books. March 29, 2021. https://www.54books.de/vor-der-grenze-ueber-einen-uebersetzungsstreit/.

Otoo, Sharon Dodua, and Clementine Burnley, eds. *Winter Shorts*. Münster: edition assemblage, 2015.

Plumly, Vanessa D. "*Auf den Spuren ihrer Geschichte*: Black German Detectives and the Cases of Anäis Schmitz and Fatou Fall." *Seminar: A Journal of Germanic Studies* 57, no. 4 (2021): 402–23.

Poikane-Daumke, Aija. *African Diasporas: Afro-German Literature in the Context of the African American Experience*. Berlin: Lit, 2006.

Popoola, Olumide. *Also by Mail*. Münster: edition assemblage, 2015.

Reich-Ranicki, Marcel. "Anmerkungen zur deutschen Literatur der siebziger Jahre." *Merkur* 33 (1979): 169–79.

Saleh, Anja. *The Future of Memory*. Münster: edition assemblage, 2021.

SchwarzRund. *Biskaya: ein Afroqueerer Roman*. Norderstedt: Books on Demand, 2020.

Sedgwick, Eve Kosofsky. "Tales of the Avunculate: Queer Tutelage in *The Importance of Being Earnest*." In *Professions of Desire: Lesbian and Gay Studies in Literature*, edited by George E. Haggerty and Bonnie Zimmerman, 191–209. New York: Modern Languages Association of America, 1995.

Snead, James. "On Repetition in Black Culture." *African American Review* 50, no. 4 (Winter 2017): 648–56.

Sow, Noah. *Die Schwarze Madonna: Fatou Falls erster Fall*. Norderstedt: BoD—Books on Demand, 2019.

Stähler, Axel. *Zionism, the German Empire and Africa: Jewish Metamorphoses and the Colors of Difference*. Berlin: De Gruyter, 2019.

Thomae, Jackie. *Brüder*. Munich: Hanser Verlag, 2019.

Wenzel, Olivia. *1000 Coils of Fear*. New York: Catapult, 2022.

Wright, Michelle. *Becoming Black: Creating Identity in the African Diaspora*. Durham, NC: Duke University Press, 2004.

4: Talking Back, Paying Forward: Dialogism and Literary Genealogies in May Ayim and Olivia Wenzel

Selma Rezgui

BLACK GERMAN CULTURAL PRODUCTION is notably dialogic. It is worth highlighting that Black German identity as we know it today developed mutually and collaboratively across decades through conversations between individuals, consciously built on unconventional "alliances beyond stable identity groups"[1] that did not rely on constructions such as background, nuclear family, or ethnicity in order to forge political, literary, and cultural bonds. I have also observed a dialogic aesthetic in several literary texts by Black German writers who intervene in the public and cultural discourse on Blackness and work to forge a diverse and ever-evolving Black German identity through their articulation of various Black experiences in Germany and elsewhere. May Ayim's 1995 poetry collection *blues in schwarz weiss* (*Blues in Black and White*) is an early example, and has been followed more recently by a wave of publications such as the poetry collection *Buchstabengefühle* (Letter feelings) by Stephanie-Lahya Aukongo (2018), and the novels *1000 Serpentinen Angst* (*1000 Coils of Fear*) by Olivia Wenzel (2020), as well as *Adas Raum* (*Ada's Room*) by Sharon Dodua Otoo (2021). These texts all engage in dialogues in their form and content, thematizing diaspora, memory, and the creation of community across temporal and national boundaries. They also engage with themes of lineage and cultural and literary heritage that are not bound to any nation. Despite differences in genre, form, and narrative, these texts by Black German authors share a focus on exchange, resonance, and callback by more recent works to older texts and traditions. For the purposes of this chapter, I will focus on the aforementioned texts by May Ayim and Olivia Wenzel as examples of a multivocal and multiperspectival Black German literature. These two texts in particular can

---

1 Moritz Schramm, "Postmigrant Perspectives: Radical Diversity as Artistic-Political Intervention," *Crossings: Journal of Migration & Culture* 14, no. 1 (2023): 97.

be described as "doubly dialogic":[2] they represent conversations between narrators and various interlocutors, or use the second person to bring the reader into this formative conversation. Moreover, they use these diegetic dialogues to enact a dialogic process of Black German subject formation and locate themselves in transnational Black literary genealogies.

The poems in *blues in schwarz weiß* address Ayim's experiences of racism, growing up Black in an overwhelmingly white German society, the search for recognition and solidarity as a Black woman, and her experience of German reunification. Wenzel's novel also traces the experience of growing up Black, alienation from family, and feelings of isolation in the midst of a white majority. In both texts, the speakers shift between voices, ventriloquize, and establish a means of communication as Black German literary subject formation. By focusing on two writers who represent two different phases and generations of Black German writing, my chapter draws a genealogical line that acknowledges these authors' different approaches to questions of identity and belonging that nevertheless traces similarities, shared histories, and the ways in which Wenzel's and Ayim's texts speak to each other. I think it is worth reading Wenzel and Ayim together like this: elsewhere in this volume, Priscilla Layne calls for Black German literature not only to be viewed as simply a response to or as having been influenced by African American literature, but for us to view it as "*a part of* rather than *separate from* German literature as a whole."[3] I hope to show how Wenzel's text can be situated in a German literary tradition initiated by Ayim and her contemporaries.

Ayim and Wenzel stage conversations between their speakers and various interlocutors, dramatizing German Blackness by recording experiences of alienation and marginalization at the hands of white German society. Writing from an always-roaming perspective, Ayim and Wenzel destabilize fixed notions of identity while at the same time asserting the validity of Black Germanness as an identity in itself. Through these dialogues, they overcome the "barrier of isolation" and situate their texts and characters in a wider global Black movement. Moreover, these texts affirm conversation, or "talking back," as the expression of a "liberated voice"[4] that is "borderless and brazen,"[5] not beholden to national, lin-

2 Sarah Colvin, "Narrative Pilgrimage and Chiastic Knowledge. Olivia Wenzel's *1000 Coils of Fear* and Sharon Dodua Otoo's *Ada's Room*," in *Epistemic Justice and Creative Agency: Global Perspectives on Literature and Film*, ed. Sarah Colvin and Stephanie Galasso (New York: Routledge, 2023), 180.
3 Priscilla Layne, "New Black German Subjectivity in the Twenty-First Century," chapter 3 in the present volume.
4 bell hooks, *Talking Back: Thinking Feminist, Thinking Black* (Abingdon: Routledge, 2015), 5, 9.
5 May Ayim, "borderless and brazen," in *Blues in Black and White: A Collection of Essays, Poetry and Conversations*, trans. Anne V. Adams (Asmara: Africa

guistic, or even generational affiliations. By focusing on dialogism and dialogues, my reading locates discourses on Blackness in Germany in terms of cross-cultural, temporal, and spatial conversations with the global Black diaspora in the absence of cultural or ethnic homogeneity or common migratory history among Black Germans, highlighting the creation of a hybrid Black German identity that is multivalent, polyphonic, and always in conversation with itself.

Scholars have often remarked that the Black German experience is unusual among other Black diasporic communities. In the translator's afterword to *Showing our Colors*, the English-language translation of the 1986 anthology *Farbe Bekennen: Afro-deutsche Frauen auf den Spuren ihrer Geschichte*, which collected texts, testimonials, interviews, transcripts of conversations, and poetry by Black German women, Anne V. Adams comments that:

> The name Afro-German designates a population native to Germany, raised and enculturated as Germans, with little or no actual contact with their African cultural heritage. The ironic paradox of being viewed and therefore treated as foreigners but having, in most cases, no personal Black reference—conscious or unconscious, individual or collective—within their lives as Germans creates a limbo-life with no analog among Black populations in ex-colonial Europe or in North America.[6]

Similarly, Michelle Wright notes that the Black German identities recorded in *Farbe Bekennen*, and in particular the ways in which these identities are parsed by white Germans, "speak to a unique set of circumstances . . . not found in the diverse array of 19th- and 20th-century African American literature and theory."[7] The Black German experience was atomized, with Black Germans tending to be mixed race, growing up in a majority white environment away from their Black parent, with little access to their African or Black American background.

The position of Black people in Germany is anomalous compared to in the United States or even in other Western European countries like France or Britain because of this widespread isolation of Black individuals, and absence of migrant communities. This constitutes a unique form

---

World Press, 2003), 48. Cited in the following as *BBW* with page number.

6   Anne V. Adams, "Translator's Afterword," in *Showing Our Colors: Afro-German Women Speak Out*, ed. May Ayim (Opitz), Katharina Oguntoye, Dagmar Schultz, trans. Anne V. Adams (Amherst: University of Massachusetts Press, 1986), 236.

7   Michelle Wright, "Others-from-within from without: Afro-German Subject Formation and the Challenge of a Counter-Discourse," *Callaloo* 26, no. 2 (2003): 296.

of racial othering in which Black people in Germany are simultaneously "Others from Within" (physically part of the nation but seen as foreign bodies within it), and "Others from Without" (outside the nation, usually conceptualized as primitive savages living elsewhere).[8] Black Germanness is not recognized within the German cultural consciousness; such is the strength of (white) German conceptions of Germany as an ethnically homogenous white nation that Black Germans are persistently misread. They are not perceived as Germans at all, but as Africans (even if they have never been to Africa, even if they do not actually have African heritage or contact to existing African family). Black Germans are hypervisible within German society as a racial Other, but invisible as *Germans*. As Wright puts it, "Afro-German identity is not the *antithesis* in the dialectic of (white) German subjectivity: *it is simply non-existent*" (italics in original).[9] Fatima El-Tayeb also emphasizes the difference between the German cultural conception of Blackness versus other minorities in Germany:

> In most cases having one white German parent and one Black, non-German parent, and often having grown up in largely white neighborhoods, Afro-Germans are likely the most highly assimilated German minority, according to official standards: "culture," language, education and—last but not least—citizenship. They are, however, also the minority generally perceived as being most "un-German."[10]

Literary representations of Black subjectivity and Black German identity defy white denials of a coexistence of Blackness and Germanness, and of Blackness in Germany. El-Tayeb describes Black Germans' "double-displacement," referring to the way Black Germans' presence is seen as "oxymoronic" within the nation and similarly disjunctive within the African diaspora.[11] This doubly displaced position contributes to a critical distance from fixed, essentialist notions of nation, home, roots, and origins in Black German community building and writing. New conceptions of home and memory are cumulatively and collaboratively developed, along with frameworks of belonging that are not reliant on common ancestry, national or ethnic origin, or even language.

It is the heterogeneity that contributes to Black German literature's representation of a conception of identity (or identities) that is expansive

---

8   Wright, "Others-from-within from without," 297.
9   Wright, "Others-from-within from without," 298.
10 Fatima El-Tayeb, "Blackness and its (Queer) Discontents," in *Remapping Black Germany*, ed. Sara Lennox (Amherst: University of Massachusetts Press, 2016), 251.
11 El-Tayeb, "Blackness and its (Queer) Discontents," 252.

and unfixed, and that questions definite categories of ethnicity, language, and nation. In her essay "Age, Race, Class and Sex: Women Redefining Difference," Audre Lorde calls for the acknowledgement of difference both between and within oppressed groups. Lorde posits that it is not difference that leads to oppression but "rather our refusal to recognize those differences, and to examine the distortions which result from our misnaming them and their effects upon human behaviour and expectation."[12] For Black Germans, differences within their minority group are always already conscious. Coming together as a political, cultural, and literary movement is a deliberate decision to use "human difference as a springboard for creative change within our lives."[13]

The editors' foreword to *Farbe Bekennen* describes the way in which Lorde, who traveled to West Berlin in 1984 and gave a series of seminars at the Freie Universität, where she first came into contact with May Ayim and Katharina Oguntoye, was instrumental in developing the vocabulary of the Black German movement, and it highlights the importance of these early self-naming practices to Black Germans' understanding of themselves within the Black diaspora *and* within the German nation:

> Mit Audre Lorde entwickelten wir den Begriff "afro-deutsch" in Anlehnung an afro-amerikanisch, als Ausdruck unserer kulturellen Herkunft. . . . Inzwischen lernten wir Afro-deutsche kennen, deren Eltern beide aus Afrika stammen oder deren einer Elternteil afro-deutsch ist und der andere aus Afrika kommt. Dadurch wurde uns klar, dass unsere wesentliche Gemeinsamkeit kein biologisches, sondern ein soziales Kriterium ist: Das Leben in einer weißen deutschen Gesellschaft.
>
> Mit dem Begriff "afro-deutsch" kann und soll es nicht um Abgrenzung nach Herkunft oder Hautfarbe gehen . . . Vielmehr wollen wir "afro-deutsch" den herkömmlichen Behelfsbezeichnungen wie "Mischling," "Mulatte," oder "Farbige" entgegensetzen, als ein Versuch, uns selbst zu bestimmen, statt bestimmt zu werden.[14]
>
> [Together with Audre Lorde, we developed the term "Afro-German," in reference to Afro-American, as an expression of our cultural heritage. Since then we have met Afro-Germans whose parents both come from Africa or who have one Afro-German and one

---

12   Audre Lorde, "Age, Race, Class and Sex: Women Redefining Difference," in *Your Silence Will Not Protect You* (London: Silver Press, 2017), 95.
13   Lorde, "Age, Race, Class and Sex," 96.
14   May Ayim (Opitz), Katharina Oguntoye, Dagmar Schultz, *Farbe Bekennen: Afro-Deutsche Frauen auf den Spuren ihrer Geschichte* (Berlin: Orlanda Frauenverlag, 2020), 20. (My translation).

African parent. That made it clear to us that our essential similarity is not a biological but a social criterion: life in a white German society.

With the term "Afro-German," cannot and should not be about exclusion because of background or skin color . . . We wanted much more for "Afro-German" to counter conventional terms such as "half-caste," "mulatto," or "colored," as an attempt to define ourselves rather than being defined by others.]

The significance of this collaborative development of the term *afro-deutsch* (Afro-German) is threefold. Firstly, it incorporates the diverse backgrounds and identities inherent in the Black German population, moving away from a monolithic understanding of Black people in Germany as "Africans." Secondly, it encourages Black Germans to "position themselves within and feel themselves to be part of the German nation."[15] Black Germanness is thus established as both specific to the Black experience in Germany and part of a wider global diasporic Blackness, with which it is always in dialogue. Thirdly, this terminology provides an alternative to the racist, negatively connoted language that was all that had previously been available in the German language. This invention went hand in hand with the invention of traditions, the forging of affective bonds and new kinships. Coining the terms "afro-deutsch" and "schwarze Deutsche" in conversation with Lorde arguably facilitated the articulation of a new kind of (Black) German identity, which was dialogic, in communication with the global struggle against racism while remaining rooted in the German nation. May Ayim testifies to this in the poem "soul sister":

1984 prägten schwarze deutsche frauen
gemeinsam mit AUDRE LORDE den begriff
afro-deutsch
da wir viele bezeichnungen hatten
die nicht unsere waren
da wir keinen namen kannten
bei dem wir uns nennen wollten[16]

[In 1984 Black German women coined the term
afro-deutsch
together with Audre Lorde
as we had many labels

---

15   Tiffany Florvil, *Mobilizing Black Germany: Afro German Women and the Making of a Transnational Movement* (Urbana: University of Illinois Press, 2020), 35.

16   May Ayim, *weitergehen* (Berlin: Orlanda Frauenverlag, 2020), 61. Cited in the following as *BSW* with page number. Translations my own unless otherwise cited.

that were not our own
as we didn't know of a name
we wanted to call ourselves]

The transformative power of this self-definition is evident in Ayim's poem. Prior to these collaborative encounters with Lorde, there had simply not been any means by which to discuss race in the German language in a critical, productive, and empowering way; there was no name by which Black Germans *wanted* to call themselves.

Dialogue, then, was central to the formation and assertion of a Black German subjectivity as it took place in the mid-1980s under Audre Lorde's influence. These dialogues were necessary because of the heterogeneity of the Black German population:

> Because of Black Germans' diversity, they did not possess the common narratives of home, belonging, or community that provided other Black communities with foundational resources that they could use as sources of belonging and identity. In this way, Lorde offered them a model for kinship, self-naming, and intellectual activism.[17]

Dialogues enabled Black Germans to reconcile, compare, and conceptualize their disparate experiences and forge a movement and community. Tina M. Campt writes that "memory provides the source of the defining tension of diaspora and diasporic identity."[18] For Black Germans, dialogue is a way of accessing and *creating* the memories and traditions on which to build a diasporic identity.

Dialogue as a means for conceiving and articulating a Black German identity is also central to many works of Black German literature. Their dialogism situates them within the emerging Black German literary tradition, all the while contributing to the foundation of that tradition. It also places Black German literary production within a wider tradition of Black literature. In May Ayim's *blues* and Olivia Wenzel's *Serpentinen*, the authors structure their texts around different forms of dialogue. In the following sections, I will discuss the ways in which Ayim and Wenzel use their dialogic literature to express a transnational, multivalent, and mobile Black subjectivity that is in conversation with itself and with Black literatures across the world.

---

17 Florvil, *Mobilizing Black Germany*, 36.
18 Florvil, *Mobilizing Black Germany*, 36.

blues in schwarz weiß:
May Ayim's Diasporic Dialogues

A central figure of the Black German women's movement in the 1980s and 90s, May Ayim has endured as one of the most prominent and widely read Black German authors. The volume *blues in schwarz weiß*, a collection of works composed between 1984 and 1995, is the only work of poetry by Ayim that was published before her death by suicide in 1996. In this section, I will discuss the ways in which Ayim incorporates different dialogues into her poems. I will begin by engaging with the transcribed dialogues between Black and white Germans that form the structure of many of the poems in *blues*, and then touch on the ways in which Ayim's poetry engages in dialogues with Black diasporic cultural and literary traditions.

In *blues*, Ayim is always in conversation with whiteness, and in particular with white Germanness. In her poems, she uses this dialogue to expose notions of discrete ethnic and national identities as constructed, and in turn to construct a viable hybrid Afro-German identity. Many of her poems are structured as exchanges with a white interlocutor, though it is usually either the Black or the white voice that dominates. Ayim uses these dialogues to draw attention to whiteness and to denaturalize it as the cultural norm.

Karein Goertz suggests that Ayim's poetry "define[s] *ethnicity* as an inclusive, hybrid concept, rather than an exclusive one rooted in a homogenous notion of nation and race" (italics in original).[19] Ayim marks whiteness as a racialized identity itself, and in doing so highlights the misplaced simplification of white conceptions of race and ethnicity. *blues* does not allow the (white) reader to think of ethnicity as something that applies only to Others. Ayim's expansive conception of identity and ethnicity is undoubtedly related to the specific Black German situation, in which Black Germans rely on conscious community-building, embracing difference and solidarity in the face of their shared experiences of racism, rather than any ethnic or national homogeneity, for their sense of Black German identity. The conception of Black Germans as a collective based on their experiences *in Germany* rather than any common memory or experience of a "home" elsewhere works to dismantle rigid ideas of ethnicity and belonging based on race or nation.

In the poems "afro-deutsch I" and "afro-deutsch II," Ayim critiques the white German understanding of racial identity by staging a dialogue with a white German interlocutor. The poems are constructed as "transcripts"[20] of an encounter between a white German and a

---

19   Karein Goertz, "Borderless and Brazen: Ethnicity Redefined by Afro-German and Turkish German Poets," *Comparatist* 21 (1997): 68.
20   Wright, "Others-from-within from without," 299.

Black German, although only the white German side of the exchange is recorded. Ayim thus engages in dialogue as monologue; the exchange between the two parties is unbalanced; one has the louder voice and the greater possibility for self-expression, while the other remains silenced. The "afro-deutsch" poems are uncompromising in their depictions of German society as one that does not let Black German voices speak to their experiences.

In the opening lines of "afro-deutsch I," Ayim highlights white German incomprehension of the possibility of Afro-Germanness:

> Sie sind afro-deutsch?
> . . . ah, ich verstehe: afrikanisch und deutsch.
> Ist ja 'ne interessante Mischung!
> Wissen Sie, manche, die denken ja immer noch,
>   die Mulatten, die würden's nicht
>   so weit bringen
>   wie die Weißen. (*BSW*, 22)

> [You're Afro-German?
> . . . oh, I see: African and German.
> An interesting mixture, huh?
> You know: there are people that still think
> Mulattos won't get
> as far in life
> as whites.] (*BBW*, 15)

The two identities, "afrikanisch" and "deutsch," are separated, and to the white German they are irreconcilable. The voice labeling Black Germanness as "ne interessante Mischung" [an interesting mixture] also imposes the idea of a biracial identity as exotic and incomplete, a mixture of two things rather than being whole in itself. Further, the white voice also reaches for the outdated and racist signifier "Mulatte" [Mulatto], even after the poem's actual speaker has identified herself as "afro-deutsch." The white voice choosing to ignore that term constitutes an overwriting of Black Germans' chosen terminology, in an "insistent misreading and redefinition that operates in the German imagination."[21] Blackness and Germanness are irreconcilable to the white speaker, reflecting persistent ideas of a homogenous German national identity. In "gegen leberwurstgrau—für eine bunte republik" (no more rotten gray—for a colorful republic) Ayim puts her finger on this insistence on categorizing marginalized or migrantized groups as *in* the nation but not *of* the nation; in the address "liebe ausländische mitbürgerinnen" (*BSW* 67; dear foreign fellow citizens) Ayim also complicates the dialogic dynamic of the

21 Wright, "Others-from-within from without," 299.

poem in having the white voice itself ventriloquize supposed other white opinions. In referring to "manche, die denken ja immer noch" (people that still think), the white voice in the poem attempts to distance itself from the more overt racism that it then expresses, claiming to only relay what others have said. The white voice performatively distances itself from these more starkly racist views and language, but it uses the act of disavowing them as a pretext to express these opinions. The poem "freiheit der kunst" (freedom of art) makes this point even more explicitly. A white German author complains: "einer meiner texte heißt / "ausländer rein" / ich kann also nicht / rassistisch sein . . ." (*BSW*, 80; "one of my texts is called "foreigners in" / so I can't possibly be racist . . ."). Ayim critically exposes whiteness as inherently contributing to a racist society, even—or especially—when white discourses do not self-identity as racist, leading to a displacement of its existence elsewhere, or indeed a complete denial (as is the case in "afro-deutsch II").

Writing about *Serpentinen* and Sharon Dodua Otoo's *Adas Raum*, Sarah Colvin refers to Charles Mills's analysis of Ralph Ellison's *The Invisible Man*, in which the Black narrator finds himself "surrounded by mirrors of hard, distorting glass," which represent "cognitive self-limitation of empowered groups."[22] The poems "afro-deutsch I" and "afro-deutsch II" "reflect white ignorance back on itself, making invisible to white perceivers the possibility of anything that does not serve their interests."[23] Ayim draws attention to the "cognitive self-limitation" of her white interlocutors by ventriloquizing their painstaking self-justification. In labeling this mode of perception as "resolutely non-interactive," Colvin also draws attention to the interactivity of Black discourse. Ayim's act of recognizing and uttering the voice of the white Other contrasts starkly to the white voice, which is chronically limited to its own (pre-)conception of Blackness in Germany as alien and irritant. Ayim's dialogic poetics expose the monologic, single-perspective limitation of the white gaze with which Black Germans are forced to interact daily. In reframing and reclaiming those interactions, in speaking them as a Black German subject, Ayim makes them visible and creates new knowledge through interactivity.

Elsewhere in the collection, Ayim's transnational, diasporic influences emerge even more strongly. Ayim is in conversation with West African and Black American culture in particular, invoking figures such as the multilingual West African trickster deity Afrekete (*BSW*, 44), Audre Lorde (*BSW*, 60), Martin Luther King Jr. (*BSW*, 57), and others. Afrekete is described by Audre Lorde as "an accomplished linguist who both transmits and interprets . . . a prankster, also, a personification of

---

22 Colvin, "Narrative Pilgrimage," 177.
23 Colvin, "Narrative Pilgrimage," 177.

the unpredictable elements in life."[24] Afrekete is often depicted with two mouths to represent her multilingual double-voiced discourse by which she mediates and sometimes misleads.[25] The poem "afrekete," a dialogue between the speaker and this figure, establishes Ayim's connection and mutuality to West African folkloric and oral traditions; it also reinforces her poetic conversation with Lorde, for whom Afrekete is an important figure of multivocality, disruptive language, subversion, and resignification of the status quo. Ayim depicts Afrekete as simultaneously still and in motion, "stehend" and "träumend [sich] bewegend" (*BSW*, 44; standing and moving, dreaming). These seemingly contradictory images situate Afrekete at a crossroads, inhabiting multiple perspectives, and, with her two mouths, as able to speak from multiple positions at once. Ayim presents the Black German speaker-subject as someone who moves between different perspectives, positions, and places.

Ayim's inclusion of West Africa in her poetry is informed and specific. She works against generalized or exoticized notions of a monolithic Africa. Karein Goertz comments on "Ayim's desire to resurrect and validate through her essays and poetry an African heritage that lies behind her. By including the symbolic language of her father's culture within her text, she proposes that it can enrich the German idiom."[26] Goertz's comment points to the dialogic, mutually enriching way that African and German discourses meet and become part of the same entity in Ayim's poetry. Ayim does not rely on tired notions of what "Africa" might mean to white Germany, but inscribes Adinkra symbols and Ghanaian deities with her own Black German experience. In "afrekete," she speaks to the deity, and the deity communicates back: "du hast mich / einmal angelächelt" (*BSW*, 44; you smiled at me once). Ayim is engaging in a dialogic incorporation of African inflections and influences, always on her own terms, and never pandering to white German ideas of what Africa means. In *blues*, Ayim constructs a Black Germanness that rejects Africanness as it is imposed on her by hegemonic white German discourses. Ayim's conception of identity is more radical and expansive; Africa is part of Ayim's history, and her poetry expresses it on her own terms.

Moreover, in poems dedicated to figures of the American civil rights movement and prominent Black American feminists (Martin Luther King and Audre Lorde), Ayim places herself in conversation with Black America. The dedication of the poem "die zeit danach" (the time after)

---

24   Audre Lorde, *The Black Unicorn* (New York: W. W. Norton, 1978), 119–20.
25   Karein Goertz, "Showing her Colors: An Afro-German Woman Writes the Blues in Black and White," *Callaloo* 26, no. 2 (2003): 310.
26   Karein Goertz, "Borderless and Brazen: Ethnicity Redefined by Afro-German and Turkish German Poets," *Comparatist* 21 (1997): 77.

reads: "von einer die noch lebt an einen der schon tot ist. gedicht in erinnerung an Martin Luther King" (*BSW*, 57; from somebody who is still alive to somebody who is already dead. A poem in memory of Martin Luther King). Here, addressing King directly as "Bruder" (*BSW*, 57; Brother), Ayim engages in a dialogue across temporal and spatial boundaries as well as across the boundaries of life and death. In her engagement with King's dream, Ayim consciously inserts herself into a decades- and centuries-long tradition of Black resistance. She echoes the repetitive, rousing structure of King's famous speech, repeating "ich habe einen traum" (I have a dream) while also building on it, alternating with "ich trage meinen traum" (*BSW*, 58; I carry my dream), adding her militancy and radicalism to her calls for a fairer world, her expression of her dream. King's dream, she tells him, has been "konserviert und verkauft, Bruder" (*BSW*, 58; conserved and sold, brother). Ayim carries her dream "hinter / erhobener faust" (*BSW*, 58; behind a raised fist). This is a powerful example of Black diasporic influences being incorporated, adapted, and updated to form Ayim's Black German identity and praxis.

If the spaces left in the dialogue of the "afro-deutsch" poems expose the fault lines in white Germany's conception of itself as an ethnically homogenous nation and of Black Germans as displaced Africans, then Ayim goes further in other poems to represent a Black German subjectivity that is indebted to global diasporic influences and literary and cultural histories but nonetheless maintains its (Black German) specificity.

Call and Response: Olivia Wenzel's *1000 Serpentinen Angst*

In a 2017 interview discussing May Ayim, the Black German poet Mara Sanaga makes the following comment:

> A lot of what [Ayim] wrote feels very much up to date, which is a little bit unfortunate, but for me as a writer it's also a relief, because I feel like she did a lot of the groundwork for us. . . . She did a lot of the work that I don't have to repeat. I feel like there are these great poems like "Afro-German I" and "Afro-German II" for instance, I can rely on these, I have the space that she created.[27]

This statement reveals much about the relationship between Black German writers in the 1980s and those writing more recently, in the 2010s. As Sanaga asserts, contemporary Black German authors still face the same "experiences of everyday racism" but they often choose to

---

27 Katy Derbyshire and Susan Stone, *Dead Ladies Show*, podcast, November 22, 2017, https://deadladiesshow.com/tag/may-ayim/.

engage with these issues in their literature in different ways. The "space" to which Sanaga refers can be more specifically identified as a vocabulary for writing about Blackness and Germanness, an understanding that Black Germanness is a viable and complete identity, as well as the privilege of having access both to established Black German communities and an existing corpus—a literary genealogy of Black German literature to draw on and take departure from.

Sanaga's statement begs the question of how, if they need not repeat the establishing work of writers like Ayim, contemporary Black German authors write Black German identity. Does *Serpentinen* exist in and speak from the space identified by Sanaga, which was created by Ayim and her contemporaries? I will consider the ways in which Wenzel's text has the same properties as the foundational Black German corpus and the ways in which it departs from the conventions established by Black German writing in the 1980s and 90s.

The unnamed narrator is a young Black woman, born in the GDR to a young, rebellious mother and an absent Angolan father. The novel is a nonchronological narrative told in the form of (inner) dialogue, flashback, detailed descriptions of images, photographs, and transcripts from a therapy session. It follows the narrator as she travels to the United States, Vietnam, and East Germany, recounting key episodes from her life.

The dialogue format dominates the novel, with its two longest sections structured around a mysterious entity asking the narrator a series of insistent, often repetitive questions. As will be discussed below, the novel is structured as a conversation, presenting a model of identity formation that, like the testimonials in *Farbe Bekennen*, and like Ayim's poems, is built around exchange. The Black German identity constructed in this novel, then, rejects monologic conceptions of race and nation, deconstructing binaries of ethnicity, sexuality, and nationality, while also dismantling rigid distinctions between self and the Other.

Ein Alternatives Selbstbild: *1000 Serpentinen Angst* as Dialogic Counterdiscourse

Like Ayim, Wenzel incorporates dialogues on the diegetic level and uses her text as a means of integrating Black German narratives into transnational and transhistorical narratives of Blackness, "introducing postcolonial and transnational frames of reference into contemporary German literature."[28] Colvin also notes that *Serpentinen* is "doubly dialogic" following Bakhtin's assertion that modern literary narration is dialogic not

---

28 Dirk Göttsche, "Self-Assertion, Intervention, and Achievement," in *Remapping Black Germany* (Amherst: University of Massachusetts Press, 2016), 67–68.

in its representation of interpersonal dialogue but as a polyphonic discursive mode in which normative beliefs and language are in tension with other points of view.[29] Wenzel's text is therefore doubly dialogic in that the I and the YOU that form the dual narrative voice are in dialogue with each another *and* "their interpersonal exchange puts normative and alternative perspectives in tension with one another."[30] The dialogues on multiple levels open up yet more potential for the representation of multiple perspectives that may be in conflict with one another, creating the possibility for diverse and nonfinal subject formations and expressions of identity. Furthermore, and in addition to the (inner) dialogue that structures the majority of the novel and the dialogues represented within the diegesis, Wenzel also follows Ayim in her situation of the novel as in dialogue with international Black influences, in particular Black feminism in the United States. Where in *blues* the United States remains an implied space, in Wenzel's novel it solidifies into the setting for a significant proportion of the narrative. The narrator's transnational mobility and the periodic inclusion of English-language comments, sayings, and quotations in the text further endorse a transnationally, translationally inflected Black German subjectivity.

By situating the novel in these nascent traditions of Black German writing, Wenzel counteracts the separation and alienation of her protagonist navigating her Blackness in isolation from other Black Germans. According to Wright, "anti-Black German discourse is best countered through a diasporic model of counterdiscourse" in which Black Germanness is constructed as "diasporic rather than national."[31] Wenzel engages in a diasporic and dialogic counterdiscourse, talking back to (white) hegemonic narratives and challenging the white reader through her representation of the interactions between the narrator and her interlocutor which are reminiscent of Ayim's "afro-deutsch I" and "afro-deutsch II." In her construction of a double-voiced counterdiscourse, white expectations and assumptions of what a Black narrative should entail are continually interrogated.

Like many other Black German subjects, the narrator is isolated as a Black woman in Germany. She is compelled to lead a nomadic existence, traveling across the world in search of community and a stable identity. Her international mobility speaks to the fact that she has "mehr Privilegien, als je eine Person in meiner Familie hatte"[32] (I have more

---

29 Colvin, "Narrative Pilgrimage," 180.
30 Colvin, "Narrative Pilgrimage," 180.
31 Wright, "Others-from-within from without," 192, 196.
32 Olivia Wenzel, *1000 Serpentinen Angst* (Frankfurt am Main: S. Fischer Verlag, 2020), 47. Cited in the following as *TSA* with page number.

privileges than anyone in my family ever had).[33] Despite this privilege, she struggles to find the community she seeks; the narrator is "trotzdem . . . am Arsch" (*TSA*, 47; "still fucked," *CF*, 32) as she struggles with grief, trauma, and coming to terms with her racial consciousness. She finds temporary solace in the United States, where, for the first time in her life, she blends in:

> Ich bin immer noch in New York.
> WAS ERLEBST DU?
> Dass ich dazugehöre.
> WEITER, WEITER.
> Dass ich joggen gehe und eine ältere, schwarze Frau ruft mir hinterher: Keep up the good work, baby! Dass ich diesen Satz noch Monate lang mit mir herumtrage. Dass mich Afroamerikanerinnen in der Nachbarschaft grüßen und mir warmherzig einen schönen Tag wünschen. . . . Ständig schwarze Männer in Business-Suits, schwarze jugendliche auf Skateboards, schwarze obdachlose Seniorinnen, die sich in die U-Bahn quetschen—ich bin auf einmal Teil davon. Das kannte ich nicht. (*TSA*, 51)
>
> [I'm still in New York
> WHAT ARE YOU EXPERIENCING
> That I go jogging and an older Black woman calls after me: *Keep up the good work, baby!* That I carry around this sentence with me for months afterward. That African Americans in the neighbourhood greet me and affectionately wish me a nice day. . . . Black men in business suits, Black kids on skateboards, Black homeless seniors who squeeze themselves onto the subway—I'm suddenly part of that. I've never known that.] (*CF*, 35)

Wenzel makes race visible and demonstrates that not seeing color is both a white privilege and the consequence of living in a society (like Germany) that perpetuates a "myth of Germanic ethnic-nationalism."[34] In the United States, the narrator is attuned to Black people to an almost obsessive degree; she notes that "Seit ich in den USA bin, sehe ich zuallererst die Hautfarbe der Menschen" (*TSA*, 13; "Ever since I got to the US, the first thing I notice about people is their skin colour," *CF*, 7). In the United States, the narrator feels relief to exist in an environment in which

---

33   Olivia Wenzel, *1000 Coils of Fear*, trans. Priscilla Layne (London: Dialogue Books, 2022), 32. Cited in the following as *CF* with page number.
34   Helga Emde, "I too Am German—An Afro-German Perspective," in *Who is German? Historical and Modern Perspectives on Africans in Germany*, ed. Leroy Hopkins (Washington, DC: American Institute for Contemporary German Studies, 1999), 37.

the material reality of her Blackness is not systematically denied. When a waitress (specifically identified as a "schwarze Kellnerin" (*TSA*, 12; "Black waitress," *CF*, 6) compliments her hair in a diner, she smiles at her and feels "plötzlich wohl . . . Zugehörig" (*TSA*, 13; "suddenly at ease . . . like I belong," *CF*, 6). The narrator draws her feeling of belonging directly from moments of conversation with other Black women. It is not to be overlooked that in a different context, both these interactions would be interpreted as street harassment or a racist microaggression, encounters with which the narrator is surely all too familiar. However, in the context of an exchange between two Black women, they become acts of solidarity and dialogic utterances of mutual recognition and validation.

The recognition and validation the narrator finds in her exchange with other Black women recalls bell hooks' concept of "talking back."[35] Where the speech of Black women is "audible but not acknowledged as significant speech," hooks emphasizes the empowering potential of "dialogue—the sharing of speech and recognition" that "took place not between mother and child or mother and male authority figure but among black women." It is this dialogue between Black women that compelled hooks to make "speech my birthright—and the right to voice, to authorship."[36] The narrator's dialogues with other Black women similarly empower her and offer a feeling of solidarity and belonging. In the United States, the narrator is liberated by having access to a Black community for the first time. Dialogues with other Black women render her "schwärzer als in Deutschland" (*TSA*, 19; "Blacker than in Germany," *CF*, 12), participating in cultural codes and performances that constitute American Blackness. Just as Black Germans in the 1980s and 1990s spoke their Blackness into being by naming it and entering into dialogue with one another and with transnational Black influences, the narrator seems to come into her Blackness largely through these interactions with and recognition from Black Americans. The narrator can therefore counteract the erasure of her Black identity in Germany by seeking validation among Black people in the United States.

However, it becomes clear over the course of the novel that replacing one ill-fitting identity (an African in Germany) with another (a Black American in the United States), even if it is more comfortable, is not sustainable for the narrator. She gradually realizes, partly through ruthless criticism from her (inner) interlocutor, that acknowledging difference is important; a Black American identity cannot replace her diasporic Black German one. In an episode where the convention of the narrator's voice being rendered in lowercase and the interlocutor in uppercase is reversed,

---

35   hooks, *Talking Back*, 5.
36   hooks, *Talking Back*, 6.

the interlocutor accuses the narrator (or the narrator accuses herself) of appropriating a Black American identity:

> Dort hast du doch auch ein schönes Afroamerikanisches Kostüm übergezogen.
> HÄ?
> Und dir tagelang vorgegaukelt, Teil einer schwarzen Community zu sein. (*TSA*, 310–11)
>
> [There you also wore a pretty African American costume.
> HUH?
> And all day you pretended to be part of the Black community.]
> (*CF*, 246)

By drawing a comparison between the narrator and a white person who is "GEBLACKFACET" (*TSA*, 311; "wore blackface," *CF*, 246), wearing Blackness as a "Kostüm," Wenzel exposes the narrator's deep insecurities about not being (or being perceived as) Black "enough." Elsewhere, the interlocutor accuses her of having a "WEISSES PRIVILEG GESICHT" (*TSA*, 13; "WHITE-PRIVILEGE FACE," *CF*, 7) and reminds her of how, visiting Angola, she was called "KOKOSNUSS ... AUSSEN BRAUN, INNEN WEISS" (*TSA*, 13; "BROWN ON THE OUTSIDE; WHITE ON THE INSIDE," *CF*, 7). The interlocutor insists on essentialist notions of race, that Blackness and whiteness are mutually exclusive, and she implies that despite her appearance, the narrator is "really" white. By highlighting that the narrator cannot ultimately assume a Black American identity in order to (re)claim her Blackness, Wenzel shows that there are, in fact, other ways to be Black. The narrator's realization that her experience in the United States might be more complicated than simply belonging or not belonging is arguably an instance of Wenzel pushing beyond "monologic definitions of race and nation":[37]

> Diese warme Community schwarzer Menschen, hier in den USA, ist nur möglich, weil sie jahrhundertelang zum Überleben nötig war. Die Basis, auf der sich diese Menschen begegnen und bestärken, war und ist blutig, ungerecht, qualvoll. Du kannst dankbar sein, dass du willkommener Gast in dieser Gemeinschaft bist, eine Touristin dieser auf Schmerz gewachsenen Blackness. (*TSA*, 312)
>
> [This warm community of Black people. Here in the USA, is possible only because for centuries it was necessary in order to survive. The basis upon which these people meet and empower one another was and is bloody, unjust, and torturous. You can be thankful that you

---

37 Wright, "Others-from-within-from-without," 197.

are a welcomed guest in this community; a tourist in this Blackness born of pain.] (*CF*, 247)

The narrator will never be able to fully participate in this Blackness born of pain, and in articulating this realization, Wenzel makes space for a Blackness in dialogue with the United States, but separate from it, and particular to the narrator. The novel suggests an understanding of identity in which the narrator can incorporate her experiences in the United States and her validating interactions with Black American women as one aspect of many that constitutes her identity. In the United States, "DIE MÖGLICHKEIT EINES ALTERNATIVEN SELBSTBILDS WIRD ERFAHRBAR" (*TSA*, 312; "THE POSSIBILITY OF EXPERIENCING AN ALTERNATIVE SELF-IMAGE BECOMES TANGIBLE," *CF*, 247).

The narrator's experiences of preliminary belonging and subsequent disillusionment in the United States frustrate the (white) reader's expectations of a teleological move toward a "whole" identity and a sense of belonging. Wenzel destabilizes notions of identity associated with place or any ancestral home for the Black German subject. For Kim, the narrator's girlfriend, is "in Deutschland geboren und aufgewachsen. Sie hat einen vietnamesischen Pass, ihre Eltern stammen aus einem Dorf südlich von Hanoi" (*TSA*, 57; "born in Germany and grew up there. She has a Vietnamese passport. Her parents come from a village south of Hanoi," *CF*, 41); Vietnam is "ihr zweites Zuhause" (*TSA*, 91; "her second home," *CF*, 68). The Black German narrator's sense of self, in contrast, cannot rely on national or familial affiliations:

UND WAS IST DEIN ZWEITES ZUHAUSE?
. . . Ich selbst? (*TSA*, 91)

[AND WHAT'S YOUR SECOND HOME?
. . . Myself?] (*CF*, 68)

The departure from notions of identity and belonging as contingent on nationality or even ethnicity for the Black German subject—who has few familial or community ties to a particular space or time—is thus reinforced in the tentative assertion of the self in the present moment as something that can be considered "home."

Departing from Ayim's "euch" or "ihr" (*BSW*, 65; you), which stands in opposition to a radically new and secure Black German identity that is formed "[am] äussersten rand" (*BSW*, 65; at the outermost edge) of white society, Wenzel collapses the dialogues and conflicts *between* Black and white Germany so that they play out *within* the inner dialogue of an individual. Wenzel constructs a Black protagonist who also benefits from white privilege at certain moments, for whom the white voice also at times comes from within, and who is positioned alternately as an oppressed minority within a Western country and a privileged Western tourist in Morocco and Vietnam. For instance, when she visits Vietnam, she stays in a sterile beach bungalow owned by Lothar, a German property developer, because she *"hatte halt Bock auf deutsche Sauberkeit. / Und Erholung. / Ich weiß. / . . . / . . ."* (*TSA*, 317, italics in original; "I was just looking for German cleanliness. / And relaxation. / I know. / . . . / . . .," *CF*, 251). Kim condemns this as "*Neokolonialismus*" (*TSA*, 317, italics in original; *Neocolonialism*, *CF*, 250). Wenzel's emphatic use of "weiß" here, followed by the ellipsis, recalls Ayim's strategic silence in "afro-deutsch II," in which Ayim includes an ellipsis (". . .") in response to the white voice's invasively asking whether she's glad not to be Turkish, and whether she is affected by "Ausländerhetze" (*BSW*, 29; picking on foreigners, *BBW*, 16). In doing this she establishes a skeptical space with the power to expose racism. In Wenzel's text the silence is turned on the narrator herself. At this moment and others like it, it is the narrator who fleetingly inhabits the position of white privilege. Whereas in *blues* the dialogue between Black and white Germany is carried out as an exchange between two discrete entities, in *Serpentinen* this dialogue plays out largely within the narrator—with herself.

This collapsing of racial categories into one individual (while maintaining the existence and significance of those categories) shows Wenzel's intersectional approach as that approach is articulated by Black feminist scholars like Kimberlé Crenshaw and Patricia Hill Collins. Crenshaw identifies a problematic "tendency to treat race and gender as mutually exclusive categories of experience and analysis,"[38] and I read Wenzel as problematizing Blackness and whiteness as mutually exclusive categories, applying an intersectional perspective not only to axes of experience like race, gender, and sexuality, but also to race itself as hybrid and multidimensional. According to Hill Collins and Sirma Birge, individuals have

> multiple "subjectivities" that they construct from one situation to the next . . . individuals typically express varying combinations of their multiple identities of gender, sexuality, race, ethnicity, and religion across different situations. Social context matters in how people use identity to create space for personal freedom.[39]

---

38 Kimberlé Crenshaw, "Demarginalizing the Intersection of Race and Sex: A Black Feminist Critique of Antidiscrimination Doctrine, Feminist Theory and Antiracist Politics," *University of Chicago Legal Forum*, no. 1 (1989): 139.

39 Patricia Hill Collins and Sirma Birge, *Intersectionality* (Cambridge: Polity Press, 2016), 79.

In *Serpentinen*, we see this when the narrator is asked about her background by a taxi driver while on holiday in Morocco: "Beim Antworten stelle ich fest, dass ich mir angewöhnt habe, anders als in Deutschland, zuerst meinen angolanischen Vater und dann meine deutsche Mutter zu nennen" (*TSA*, 87; "As I answer, I notice that, in contrast to when I was in Germany, here I have become accustomed to mentioning my Angolan father first and then my German mother," *CF*, 65). The narrator feels that her "afrikanischer Vater ist in Marokko mehr wert" (*TSA*, 87; "My African father is worth more in Morocco," *CF*, 65), demonstrating the novel's iconoclastic attitude to (mixed) race identity, which pushes beyond established uses of intersectionality theory, itself a radical resignification of identity.

This acknowledgment of the shifting dynamics of oppressor and oppressed, which are revealed by the novel's (self-)critical dialogism, recalls Lugones's concept of living "across worlds," the ability to remain conscious of shifting positionalities in different environments. Wenzel's protagonist consciously shifts between the positions of oppressed Black German women and privileged Western oppressor with an EU passport while on holiday in Vietnam. She is "act[ing] in accordance with both logics."[40] The epistemic friction created through a heteroglossia consisting of "two voices, two meanings and two expressions"[41] creates space for difference within the individual: a radically diverse Black identity.[42]

Wenzel's dialogic structure, in which the narrator's every utterance is met with a challenge and every thought, action, and memory are questioned, can be read as an instance of what American sociologist, historian, and civil rights activist W. E. B. Du Bois describes as "double consciousness." For Du Bois, this "peculiar sensation," which Black people

---

40   María Lugones, *Pilgrimages, Peregrinajes: Theorizing Coalition against Multiple Oppression* (Lanham, MD: Rowman & Littlefield, 2003), 324.

41   Mikhail Bakhtin, "Discourse in the Novel," in *The Dialogic Imagination: Four Essays*, ed. Michael Holquist, trans. Caryl Emerson and Michael Holquist (Austin: University of Texas Press, 1982), 324.

42   See the introduction to this volume for more detail on the notion of radical diversity, which has "gained particular currency in German cultural discourse since 2016 through the work of writers and artists associated with the Jewish journal *Jalta* and the Maxim Gorki Theater in Berlin." See Leah Carola Czollek and Gudrun Perko "Diversity in außerökonomischen Kontexten: Bedingungen und Möglichkeiten seiner Umsetzung," in *Re-Präsentationen: Dynamiken der Migrationsgesellschaft*, ed. Anne Broden and Paul Mecheril (Oldenburg: IDA, 2007) 161–81; Leah Carola Czollek, Gudrun Perko and Heike Weinbach, "Radical Diversity im Zeichen von Social Justice: Philosophische Grundlagen und praktische Umsetzung von Diversity in Institutionen," in *Soziale (Un)Gerechtigkeit: Kritische Perspektiven auf Diversity, Intersektionalität und Antidiskriminierung*, ed. María do Mar Castro Varela and Nikita Dhawan (Berlin: Lit, 2011), 260–77.

experience, stems from a "sense of always looking at oneself through the eyes of others, of measuring one's soul by the tape of a world that looks on in amused contempt or pity."[43] The presence of the interlocutor ensures that the narrator is always aware (or made aware) of how she is seen by others, of how her actions might be judged or condemned, of what she looks like to the white society she moves through as a queer biracial woman.

Wright contrasts the approach of Du Bois with Ayim's perspective as a Black German poet. For Wright, Du Bois "adhered to concepts of race and nation that, while not as monologic as its [sic] white Western model, nonetheless read the Black subject in the West as a synthesis of these two concepts." May Ayim in her dialogic poetry went "further by mocking the white speaking subject as the one who is sadly misguided by outdated and outmoded concepts based on a binary, nationalist understanding of the subject and Other."[44] Wenzel's novel goes further still in dismantling concepts of race and nation by staging their interaction within one individual who is divided into multiple racial and national subjectivities. The double consciousness of the narrator, a queer, mixed-race Black German woman traveling through the United States, is represented by the shifting interlocutor, whose questions and interjections represent not only the external white gaze but the narrator's own whiteness and privilege, as well as her self-doubt about her legitimacy as a Black subject. These contradictory perspectives and the criticism from within and without echoes Wright's concept of "others-from-within-from-without";[45] the interlocutor's mobility as both an internal and external voice renders the narrator Other both within and without her own body and mind.

When the narrator wonders, "Was soll mir meine weiße Großmutter antworten, auf die Frage, ob sie eine Ahnung hat, was es bedeutet, keinen Ort zu kennen, an dem man selbst die Norm ist?" (*TSA*, 82; "How should my white grandmother answer the question whether she has an idea what it means to know a place in which one is oneself the norm?" *CF*, 60) the interlocutor immediately undercuts her comment, drawing attention to the relative privileges of various other axes of her identity:

DU KANNST DIR DAS ESSEN LEISTEN, DEINE KLEINE EINZIMMERWOHNUNG IN NEUKÖLLN, KLEIDUNG, URLAUB, WENN DIR DANACH IST, FRISEUR, THEATER,

---

43 W. E. B. Du Bois, *The Souls of Black Folk* (Oxford: Oxford University Press, 2007), 3.
44 Wright, "Others-from-within from without," 197.
45 Wright, "Others-from-within from without," 191.

SPRACHKURSE, DIES DAS. WIE VIEL MEHR AN NORM BRAUCHST DU NOCH? (*TSA*, 82)

[YOU CAN AFFORD THE FOOD; YOU CAN AFFORD YOUR LITTLE STUDIO APARTMENT IN A HIP PART OF BERLIN; CLOTHES; A VACATION WHEN YOU WANT; A HAIRCUT; THEATRE TICKETS; LANGUAGE COURSES; THIS AND THAT; HOW MUCH MORE OF A NORM DO YOU NEED?] (*CF*, 60)

The narrator, then, cannot escape the sense, which is both imposed from without but also internalized, of not being Black enough, recalling the comment made by Ayim's white interlocutor in "afro-deutsch II": "und so schwarz bist du ja auch nicht" (*BSW* 29; "And you're not that black anyway, you know," *BBW*, 17). In Ayim's case, the speaker is held to a standard of Blackness defined by the white interlocutor's idea of a Black African. In Wenzel, the narrator is held (and holds herself) to the standards of an American Blackness born of pain.

This negotiation that constitutes a Black German identity that is always in progress is represented in the novel by the contradictions and disagreements between narrator and interlocutor. The interlocutor undermines many of the apparent moments of realization or self-actualization quoted at earlier points in this essay—for example, the bathetic interjection of "Hm. Cuter Gedanke aber nein, so hast du dich nicht gefühlt" ("Hm. Nice idea, but no, that's not how you felt") after the narrator grandiosely declares she has encountered "DIE MÖGLICHKEIT EINES ALTERNATIVEN SELBSTBILDS" (*TSA*, 312; "THE POSSIBILITY OF AN ALTERNATIVE SELF-IMAGE," *CF*, 247). Similarly, after the narrator relates her feelings of belonging in the United States when she sees "schwarze Männer in Business-Suits, schwarze Jugendliche auf Skateboards, schwarze Obdachlose Seniorinnen, die sich in die U-Bahn quetschen" (*TSA*, 51; "Black men in business suits, Black kids on skateboards, Black homeless seniors who squeeze themselves onto the subway," *CF*, 35), the interlocutor remarks, "HM. UND DIE POLITISCHE LAGE?" (*TSA*, 51; "HM: AND WHAT ABOUT THE POLITICAL SITUATION?," *CF*, 35), puncturing the Black narrator's fantasy of an America in which Black people are normalized and in which they can thrive. The narrator is reminded—reminds herself—that although "NUR 13 PROZENT DER GESAMTEN US-BEVÖLKERUNG SCHWARZ SIND" (ONLY 13 PERCENT OF THE ENTIRE UNITED STATES IS BLACK), they represent "KNAPP 40 PROZENT ALLER GEFÄNGNISINSASSEN" (*TSA*, 51; "ABOUT 40 PERCENT OF THE PRISON POPULATION," *CF*, 36). Wenzel's double discourse, in which it is never quite clear which party is more reliable, recalls the trickster

Afrekete's "multi-voiced, outspoken, and disruptive discourse,"[46] which enacts the contradictions of a Black identity and situates Wenzel's text within a diasporic Black literary genealogy.

With its dialogic form, *Serpentinen* interrogates and destabilizes white expectations of what identity should look like. Simon Sahner writes that "in [seiner] dialogischen und chronologischen Zersplitterung ist der Roman auch formal ein Abbild seiner Protagonistin, deren Identität und Persönlichkeit aus ebenso vielen Fragmenten und offenen Enden besteht und gleichzeitig ein individuelles Zentrum besitzt."[47]

In *Serpentinen*, Wenzel asserts a model of Black identity that embraces chaos and contradiction. The nonlinear, nonchronological novel offers no teleological trajectory toward a complete identity. Wenzel uses the cultural and literary references and conventions available to her to create this expansive, chaotic, and contradictory protagonist. The narrator does not find Black German community within the diegesis, but Wenzel's dialogic interactions with the foundational texts, genres, and conventions of the Black German women's movement, as well as her incorporation of dialogues both between narrator and interlocutor and narrator and Black characters as formative and affirmative, show that Wenzel also operates with a dialogic model of Black German identity.

Dialogues on multiple levels are central to Black German subject formation. These dialogues can take the form of conversations represented within the diegesis of Afro-German literature, or they can be the wider dialogues that Wright refers to as "performing diaspora" (196)—that is to say, staging intertextual and intercultural conversations with global Blacknesses. Ayim offers an affirmative model of hybrid Afro-German identity, which breaks new ground in the context of existing German linguistic and cultural racial discourses, using poetry to name Afro-Germanness, and in doing so confirms it as a viable, lived identity and positionality. In *Serpentinen*, on the other hand, Wenzel's narrator's inner dialogue collapses the distinction between the self and the (white) Other. Whereas in *blues*, conflicts occur between a minoritized community of color—either as individuals or a collective—and the oppressive hegemonic voices of white dominant society, *Serpentinen* sees these conflicts play out within one character's consciousness. In illuminating the tension between the narrator's various affiliations—between her privilege and her oppression—Wenzel offers a yet more dialogic subjectivity, which is unstable and ever-shifting in its parameters and its understanding of itself.

---

46   Kara Provost, "The Trickster in the Work of Audre Lorde," *MELUS* 20, no. 4 (1995): 57.

47   Simon Sahner, "'Diskursives Feuerwerk'—Olivia Wenzels *1000 Serpentinen Angst*," 54 Books, accessed May 31, 2021, https://www.54books.de/diskursives-feuerwerk-olivia-wenzels-prosa-debuet/.

Bibliography

Primary Texts

Ayim, May. *Blues in Black and White: A Collection of Essays, Poetry and Conversations*. Translated by Anne V. Adams. Asmara: Africa World Press, 2003.
———. *Grenzenlos und Unverschämt*. Berlin: Orlanda Frauenverlag, 1997.
———. *weitergehen*. Berlin: Orlanda Frauenverlag, 2020.
Wenzel, Olivia. *1000 Coils of Fear*, London: Dialogue Books, 2022.
———. *1000 Serpentinen Angst*. Frankfurt am Main: S. Fischer Verlag, 2020.

Secondary Texts

Adams, Anne V. "Translator's Afterword." In *Showing Our Colors: Afro-German Women Speak Out*, edited by May Ayim (Opitz), Katharina Oguntoye, and Dagmar Schultz, translated by Anne V. Adams. Amherst: University of Massachusetts Press, 1986.
Ayim (Opitz), May, Katharina Oguntoye, and Dagmar Schulz. *Farbe Bekennen: Afro-deutsche Frauen auf den Spuren ihrer Geschichte*. Berlin: Orlanda Frauenverlag, 2020.
Bakhtin, Mikhail. "Discourse in the Novel." In *The Dialogic Imagination: Four Essays*, edited by Michael Holquist, translated by Caryl Emerson and Michael Holquist, 259–422. Austin: University of Texas Press, 1982.
Campt, Tina. *Other Germans: Black Germans and the Politics of Race, Gender and Memory in the Third Reich*. Ann Arbor: University of Michigan Press, 2004.
Colvin, Sarah. "Narrative Pilgrimage and Chiastic Knowledge: Olivia Wenzel's *1000 Coils of Fear* and Sharon Dodua Otoo's *Ada's Room*." In *Epistemic Justice and Creative Agency: Global Perspectives on Literature and Film*, edited by Sarah Colvin and Stephanie Galasso, 176–97. New York: Routledge, 2023.
Crenshaw, Kimberlé. "Demarginalizing the Intersection of Race and Sex: A Black Feminist Critique of Antidiscrimination Doctrine, Feminist Theory and Antiracist Politics." *University of Chicago Legal Forum* 1 (1989): 139–67.
Czollek, Leah Carola, and Gudrun Perko. "Diversity in außerökonomischen Kontexten: Bedingungen und Möglichkeiten seiner Umsetzung." In *Re-Präsentationen: Dynamiken der Migrationsgesellschaft*, edited by Anne Broden and Paul Mecheril, 161–81. Oldenburg: IDA, 2007.
Czollek, Lea Carola, Gudrun Perko, and Heike Weinbach. "Radical Diversity im Zeichen von Social Justice: Philosophische Grundlagen und praktische Umsetzung von Diversity in Institutionen." In *Soziale (Un) Gerechtigkeit: Kritische Perspektiven auf Diversity, Intersektionalität und*

Antidiskriminierung, edited by María do Mar Castro Varela and Nikita Dhawan, 260–77. Berlin: Lit, 2011.
Czollek, Max, Hannah Peaceman, and Leah Wohl von Haselberg. "Allianzen: In die Offensive!" "Allianzen," thematic issue of *Jalta: Positionen zur Jüdischen Gegenwart* 3 (2018): 5–7.
Derbyshire, Katy, and Susan Stone. "May Ayim." *Dead Ladies Show*. Podcast. November 22, 2017. https://deadladiesshow.com/tag/may-ayim/.
Du Bois, W. E. B. *The Souls of Black Folk*. Oxford: Oxford University Press, 2007.
El-Tayeb, Fatima. "Blackness and its (Queer) Discontents." In *Remapping Black Germany*, edited by Sara Lennox. Amherst: University of Massachusetts Press, 2016.
———. *European Others: Queering Ethnicity in Postnational Europe*. Minneapolis: University of Minnesota Press, 2007.
Emde, Helga. "I Too Am German—An Afro-German Perspective." In *Who Is German? Historical and Modern Perspectives on Africans in Germany*, edited by Leroy Hopkins. Washington, DC: American Institute for Contemporary German Studies, 1999.
Florvil, Tiffany N. *Mobilizing Black Germany: Afro German Women and the Making of a Transnational Movement*. Urbana: University of Illinois Press, 2020.
Goertz, Karein K. "Borderless and Brazen: Ethnicity Redefined by Afro-German and Turkish German Poets." *Comparatist* 21 (1997): 68–91.
———. "Showing her Colors: An Afro-German Woman Writes the Blues in Black and White." *Callaloo* 26, no. 2 (2003): 306–19.
Göttsche, Dirk. "Self-Assertion, Intervention, and Achievement." In *Remapping Black Germany*. Amherst: University of Massachusetts Press, 2003.
Hill Collins, Patricia, and Sirma Birge. *Intersectionality*. Cambridge: Polity Press, 2016.
hooks, bell. *Talking Back: Thinking Feminist, Thinking Black*. Abingdon: Routledge, 2015.
Hopkins, Leroy. "Writing Diasporic Identity: Afro-German Literature Since 1985." In *Not So Plain as Black and White*, edited by Patricia Mazon and Reinhild Steingrover. Rochester, NY: University of Rochester Press, 2005.
Layne, Priscilla. "Suspicious Spiral: Autofiction and Black German Subjectivity in Olivia Wenzel's 1000 Serpentinen Angst." Lecture given at Brandeis University, October 26, 2020. https://www.brandeis.edu/cges/news-events/fall-2020/201026_layne_priscilla.html.
Lorde, Audre. *The Black Unicorn*. New York: W. W. Norton, 1978.
———. *Your Silence Will Not Protect You*. London: Silver Press, 2017.
Lugones, María. *Pilgrimages, Peregrinajes: Theorizing Coalition against Multiple Oppression*. Lanham, MD: Rowman & Littlefield, 2003.
Provost, Kara. "The Trickster in the Work of Audre Lorde." *MELUS* 20, no. 4 (1995): 45–59.

Sahner, Simon. "Diskursives Feuerwerk"—Olivia Wenzels "1000 Serpentinen Angst." 54 Books. Accessed May 31, 2022. https://www.54books.de/diskursives-feuerwerk-olivia-wenzels-prosa-debuet/.

Wright, Michelle M. "Others-from-within from without: Afro-German Subject Formation and the Challenge of a Counter-Discourse." *Callaloo* 26, no 2 (2003): 296–305.

5: Black Poetry Matters: A Conversation with Stefanie-Lahya Aukongo

Jeannette Oholi and Nadiye Ünsal

LAHYA (STEFANIE-LAHYA AUKONGO, she, her, they) is a Black intersectional artist, writer, poet, curator, singer, workshop facilitator, photographer, and activist whose social realities are reflected in her artistic work and activism. In 2009, her autobiography *Kalungas Kind* was published and in 2018 Lahya published her first poetry collection, *Buchstabengefühle: Eine poetische Einmischung*. Since 2014, Lahya has curated and hosted the monthly spoken word event One World Poetry Night in Berlin.

As a Black poet, Stefanie-Lahya Aukongo uses poetic language in her texts and performances to make racism in German society visible. The poems are mostly very political, but it is equally the aesthetics of the poems that deserve special attention as well. Identities are reflected in Lahya's work in a multilayered way, as she makes herself visible as a subject through poetry and at the same time denounces the invisibility of German colonial history and a heteronormative social norm that excludes all those who do not conform to it.

Black people in Germany are both hypervisible and invisible. They are always visible in a society that imagines itself as homogeneously white; Black people are made at the same time invisible because they are categorized as strangers and marginalized from society. This is also evident in the literary sphere. The literary canon still excludes Black writers. Lahya challenges these boundaries and shows the plurality of Black identities and the heterogeneity of the Black community. In conversation with the poet, it becomes clear that Black poetry matters—both aesthetically and politically. Lahya talks about her experiences between art and university, about role models, knowledge, rebellion, radicalism, healing, and about the possibilities of decolonizing writing and practices.

The conversation with Stefanie-Lahya Aukongo took place on February 10, 2021, as part of the international conference "Rethinking Postcolonial Europe: Moving Identities, Changing Subjectivities," which was organized as a digital event in cooperation with GAPS (Gesellschaft für Anglophone Postkoloniale Studien) and the GCSC (International Graduate Centre for the Study of Culture). The event was sponsored by the GCSC and the LZG (Literarisches Zentrum Giessen).

Jeannette Oholi: In your introductory comments you dedicated your performance to your ancestors. What influence do your ancestors have on your work?

Stefanie-Lahya Aukongo: For me, what I make, knowledge, is something that already exists. I am not reinventing the wheel. For me, it's important to speak about that. What I do in my texts, in my art, is something that was always in me, it's what I have received. My ancestors are simply present. Nothing I do could have happened without their involvement. It's about old knowledge, about felt knowledge, about traditions, about existing knowledge that seeks to heal. And my ancestors are simply around me. It is almost like a praise of their ways. To imagine what today is, is a part of their imagination, of their possibilities.

A possibility to dream for real. That's why I can't do anything else but keep giving people possibilities to find out about where my grandparents and great-grandparents, my relatives, and sisters were on other continents, what they did, felt, and thought. In the end, we are all bound to each other. And there's no getting around that.

JO: Your poetry is unbelievably powerful. What does poetry mean for you in your life?

SLA: I don't think I can answer this question without describing how I got to art in the first place. I was a very quiet child, a very traumatized [*traumativ*] child. I was a child that observed a lot and had to figure a lot of things out by myself, like how I could navigate this world. At first, I sang and then learned how to speak. For me, singing was a way to communicate in a way in which I could better influence situations. And then at some point came painting and crafts into the picture. I have worked a lot with sound and expressed myself a lot through that. As I started school and learned how to write, I realized, wow, I can write things down and tell stories. I saw that I could fantasize myself into worlds where people like me played the main characters, where people like me really had the power to act. That is a reality that is possible. At the same time, I could also take what I experience in the world and work on it, expressing all the injustices, dreams, and fears in my childlike way. I wrote my first poems when I was about eleven years old and then realized that I could go high, low, and wide. Other forms of art have also made that possible. Writing and poetry were forms that distilled everything; I can express things extremely succinctly that normally need many more words. The words just flow out of me. In three and a half minutes I can describe my world. It doesn't need a lot, and that's why poetry, along with singing and the visual arts, is for me a possibility to find myself. In poetry, there lives an essential urgency to survive—with brilliance. Poetry is also just universal. Even when the language that is being spoken is not understood, there is a rhythm, a mode, a metronome, mimicry, and gestures, all of which can be felt. Even when people say, "I don't write at all" or "I have never written a poem" or "My poems are really bad," I know as a writing instructor that it is possible to express oneself and to share what's inside someone—that which is beyond or behind what is obvious at first. Does that make sense?

JO: Yes, totally. You just said that you are also a writing instructor. Do you work with children and young people? What would you advise children and young people who say that they would like to write but don't know how?

SLA: Just write! I work less with very young people; I'm doing more in adult education. But what is young? A normative idea about age is also a construction. I think it's just about expressing yourself and having fun with playing with words and with what there is to say.

JO: Writing always has something self-reflective, a grappling with one's own relationship to their own identity. What does writing mean regarding healing? In your poems there are often themes about healing. Can you say more about that?

SLA: I think writing means finding expression and the language in which to express yourself, to become visible, to create representation and to occupy space. Even when no one listens, finding expression for something I feel at that moment that I would actually rather hide from myself, like pain, grief, or love—and reading it out to people—for me, that is healing.

Healing also means writing everything down, because it takes up space that the dominant system would rather use for something else. I would like to use this space for something that can contribute to my healing, that I can turn into language. It's about admitting something, taking time to put it down on paper, the thing I don't dare to speak out loud. And I believe that it is a practice. Healing is a practice, just like art. To grapple with something, to deal with that and to consciously decide that I am going to give myself this space, these five minutes, seven minutes, twenty-five minutes, this hour. That is my self-empowerment and my self-love. And that is, I think, something that is healing and that brings us together. When I write and perform, I create spaces and bring people together. Then I realize that means something to people. They felt what is being told, there are connections there and they are healing, and I would like things to be celebrated in those spaces.

JO: We had thought about how we would name the event and then you suggested "Black Poetry Matters: A Decolonial Poetry Performance." What does "decolonial" mean for you?

SLA: For me, decolonial means to question everything as much as possible, ideally over and over again. It's about getting rid of the white construct that is so imbued in everything, like I write in my foreword to *Buchstabengefühle* (Letter feelings). Whether it's economics or love or whether we're speaking about a leaf, water or anything, it always has a colonial origin. And then it's about breaking with origin, grappling with it and looking for answers: what was the actual origin? Who does this knowledge belong to? To whom does the labor belong, to whom does all that belong? It's about dismantling colonial structures in the best and most feasible way. That can happen in different kinds of ways. It can be activist, artful, culinary, scholarly, and/or interpersonal; it can be everything. It's about burying the racist, patriarchal, Eurocentric system in which we live so that we can all take everyone along, so that we are able to live and survive and can grow out of the old and destructive and heal.

For me a decolonial approach means thinking intersectionally, thinking radically, centering healing, and giving as little to this system as I can. That means thinking in new ways, creating in new ways and not just doing something to preserve the old ways. The question is, who do the old ways serve? We have to work this out and ask questions, so that we recognize that phrases like "Yes, but my grandparents did it" or "I didn't mean to" help support the old system. We have to practice that. And it really is an exercise. A continual practice in order to find out what I would like to see in this world and for whom I want it and in which ways it can be done.

With what kind of past do we want to feel right now? How can we act so that the future is colorful, equitable and inclusive for people who have experienced discrimination? How can we show that this world never was or was only ephemeral, if that? What should be better here and for whom?

JO: I find it really beautiful that you brought in the aspect of radicality. You have a poem in *Buchstabengefühle* called "Radikal" (Radical) that I really like. It is set up like a conversation and as you're talking to someone you reframe and redefine the concept of being radical. Radicality is very often negatively defined, in the sense of being an uncomfortable troublemaker. From my point of view there is just so much power in radicality that we must use to bring about change.

SLA: When we see how the Duden defines radicality,[1] we read that it means to change things from the root up. If that is something that bothers people, then I am glad to be radical. Naturally, words have always been seen in context and we must also ask who has brought in what implication for the word in which context. Why has the word "radikal" [or radical in English] become so negatively connoted, practically a swear

---

1   Popular German dictionary.

word? For me, radical is something that means how we can make things different, for the good of humankind and justice, while disregarding the destructive moment that is being propped up right now.

JO: Regarding radicality, change and decolonization, what do you think poetry can achieve?

SLA: First, I think poetry can bear witness to the present and to feelings. In West African cultures or also in old spaces of Color all over the world, singing, poetry and language have always been a part of a community circle. We have always borne witness to what is happening. When I am poetic or artistic, I describe the status quo in which I find myself and what I do. I have a choice to tell what I would like to tell. When I think about Nina Simone's "An Artist's Duty," it is the duty of an artistic person to always describe and give meaning to the era in which they live. Poetry can do this. Poetry can, must, and should always make visible the perspective from which it is narrating. And then if some "white wondering young man" up there in his rooftop apartment writes a poem about the last maple leaf, then he should do that. Ok, I feel you, but I ask myself critically, whom do you write for, where do I recognize the social status quo of your life reality?

We have to speak about feelings and make sure we educate our own communities and listen to them. There is a monthly event in Berlin that I founded in 2014 and have been curating and moderating ever since. It's called One World Poetry Night. Back then I had no idea that so many guests would come and listen. So many people wanted to engage with each other. They listen to people with multiple positionalities who are multiply oppressed—the margins of the margins. They perform texts, tell their stories and share their poetry and realities. There we experience truth telling and storytelling, monologues and poems on the stage, spoken word, singing, sociopolitical themes, the personal, the collective, the individual, the artistic, empowerment, tears, snaps, claps, feeling and encounters. That is something, I think, that academia can't deal with. It could hardly be more filled with feeling, more academic or more political. That's how it should be, we should listen to people and hear what kinds of feelings and experiences are shared.

JO: I find it very important that you make emotions so strong. I often have the impression that feelings aren't given enough value in academia and at universities. I ask myself if poetry could contribute to more feelings coming into institutions. What's your take on it?

SLO: Yes, I think that there should be more movement, more corporeality. If one thing stands out from my many academic years at universities, it is that there are too few places in which we can work with the body. It is seldom about what, where, and how the body is felt. Where do I feel emotions? What does that have to do with my roots? What effect does this seminar have on me? There is no separate, neutral, objective space. Academia and the university are always spaces that describe a certain perspective while also showing that some perspectives are missing there. We all had to learn interpretations of poems and for me that was always like, "huh?" The poems that I learned in school were not the kinds of poems or texts or songs I wrote or heard at home. Quite the opposite—I was not aware that what I was doing at home was also poetry. How can feelings be accommodated? How can we make more space for emotion in the context of the university? How can we create learning and teaching spaces in which people can leave and say, "ok, I feel what I make"? It doesn't matter if it's quantum mechanics, pedagogy, or any other academic subject. There is always an essence of emotionality that can be centralized, because here people are going in and out. I am not the degree that I completed; rather, I am a person with a degree. I am the person with collective marginalization and individual characteristics. I think it's possible to connect those things. I also think that is possible in university contexts.

JO: I would agree with you. I find this strict separation between emotions and knowledge, this understanding that there must always be distance kept between ourselves and what we are studying very difficult. In my case as a scholar of literature, we are talking about literary texts, often poems. I find it difficult to separate those completely, because for me knowledge and emotions don't exclude each other.

Nadiye Ünsal: I would also like to say something about this point and about the topic of emotions and space, particularly that there should be space for emotions. Lahya, we have often met in the context of political and community work. Often, we don't reach anyone with our political pamphlets, but strong, decolonial poetry in our antiracist intersectional movement does this pretty well. I see that again and again when you perform. You know, in our intersectionally marginalized communities we often hardly have any physical space. But there is also no narrative and symbolic room for our demands. The questions about space bother me a lot and it would interest me to know which spaces you think your poetry opens up and which experiences you have in these spaces.

SLA: I don't believe that what you do, what we do, doesn't reach enough people. It reaches a lot of people, and we need all kinds of work, all kinds of different projects that are being done. I am right now here with you all in a very rewarding space where we can exchange ideas. I believe that there are always epochs that define what is on top and how political and activist work should look. I often have the feeling that right now it is about excluding people. If you have done something wrong, you are not allowed to be here. There is a lot of shaming and blaming and I ask myself, how we can create more call-ins and soft spaces, as Sonya Renee Taylor calls them. Soft spaces are spaces in which people can feel safer, in which there is a soft way to deal with each other, in a language, in an encounter, in an awareness. How can we be gentler with each other? How can we be in a space together so that there are enough places for people to go to when harm occurs? How can we do this and what can we learn from marginalized communities of Color?

In the village of my grandparents, people were hugged when something bad happened—for example, when someone lied or stole something. Then the person was given a lot of physical love. What other methods can we learn from? What other possibilities are there for us to bring people along with us as we do this work? We need each and every person and have to ask ourselves, how we can do things so that it is not just about "I want to get to the top!" We have to make sure that we are not just continuing to support the structures that are already there, that those who are marginalized have not yet managed to change.

We support white patriarchal structures when we enter a dynamic of knee-jerk oppositionality for its own sake. That doesn't mean we don't also have to name the injustices that occur. Learning spaces for people are there, also for me. But in situations in which I don't get things right—and in which the person who experiences that harm needs to be recognized—I need a space where I can figure out how to make it good again. And reflecting on that is a point where I realized that in the activist spaces, in which I am involved less and less, are very much divided into good and not good. We are complex, as are the systems that oppress us and the activist spaces, too. We are full of pain, understandably. Mourning, loss, surviving in the most different ways. We need spaces, intersectional, soft spaces. Sometimes they separate us for a while, maybe even permanently, or they have the effect of doing that, even though we have the hope of healing or even finding a path to one another again.

NÜ: Do you think that your poetry also manages to cause something to happen in these spaces, that something breaks through? You are also doing something with our conference space, something extraordinarily beautiful and powerful.

SLA: I believe that poetry creates a space of listening, of being able to empathize. We can't just answer in order to answer. We must listen in order to find our own answer, and that is for me something that poetry can do. Poetry can express things so precious that might be too cerebral in big debates or at a panel discussion. In the rarest of cases, people will bring their texts out on the stage, but mostly they have taken the time to at least write them down, then internalize them in order to be able to recite them from memory. Their texts have to get past a brief, internal, and hopefully self-loving censor. And I believe that is something that decolonial/radical/transformative poetry can achieve: the ones speaking are the ones who should be speaking about it. The listeners are quiet, take breaks, and let it sink in. That is an important aspect.

I want to say the space that we give others, but also ourselves, is empowering. We can witness that another person is on the stage and takes up space. I find that tremendous. It's something that does wonders for activist circles: to listen, to be still, the emerging inner reflections that we share with others, to say that you have hurt me in one way, but you have profoundly touched me in another. Where is the space in which we can say something like that to each other nowadays? It is so beautiful when it's possible to say "thank you, for you and how you live, for how you move yourself and me, for how you perceive the world and in doing so touch me."

NÜ: Thank you, Lahya, those are questions that touch on the themes of our conference and that we will take with us in our academic work. Also, the reflection about the positioning: whom we research, which narratives are confirmed, or which narratives we represent—those are all postcolonial and decolonial questions. And then we see how wonderful it always is to have poetry in scholarly spaces and to reflect, because we all know that academia is not free from power structures and from white supremacy.

JO: Thank you very much for the great conversation.

—Translated by Jennifer Petzen

Part II

Disruptions, Subversions, Interactions

6: Subversive Aesthetics, Embodied Language, and the Politics of Literature: A Conversation with Özlem Özgül Dündar

Joseph Twist

ÖZLEM ÖZGÜL DÜNDAR is an emerging writer who has already won various prestigious awards, including the Retzhofer Drama Prize for the play *Jardin d'Istanbul* in 2015, the Kelag Prize at the forty-second *Tagen der deutschsprachigen Literatur* (Festival of German literature in Klagenfurt) and a fellowship at the Casa Baldi in 2021.[1] The play *türken, feuer* (turks, fire, 2019)[2] is her most celebrated text to date, and the recording made by the WDR (West German broadcasting) was the German Academy of the Performing Arts' Radio Play of the Year in 2020.[3] Dündar was born in Solingen in 1983, and *türken, feuer* draws on her own personal experience in its exploration of different fictionalized perspectives on the arson attack that took place there in 1993, in which Gürsün İnce, Hatice Genç, Gülüstan Öztürk, Hülya Genç, and Saime Genç were murdered by neo-Nazis. This deeply moving text contains monologues from four mothers connected to the attack: a surviving mother; a mother who died leaping out of the window with her child in her arms; a mother who burned to death in the house; and the mother of one of the perpetrators. Whilst the first-person perspective on the violence is harrowing, especially where the dead mothers are concerned, the text also raises hopeful questions of connection and relations beyond linguistic, cultural, and racialized divides.

    1   This interview was conducted in German and has been translated by the author. All other translations from German to English in the text are also by the author.
    2   Özlem Özgül Dündar, *türken, feuer* (Hamburg: Rowohlt Theaterverlag, 2019).
    3   The radio play premiered on WDR on 18th April 2020. For details, see WDR, "türken, feuer," April 18, 2022, https://www1.wdr.de/radio/wdr3/programm/sendungen/wdr3-hoerspiel/tuerken-feuer-solingen-anschlag-100.html.

Human connection is also the central topic of Dündar's debut poetry collection *gedanken zerren* (thoughts wrench, 2018),[4] for which she won the Alfred Müller Felsenburg Prize. On the one hand, the collection thematizes the violence of having one's identity ascribed and fixed by others. On the other, many of the poems are snapshots of seemingly banal interactions (small gestures, touches, and glances) that make visible a prelingual interconnectedness that is felt subconsciously, despite a lack of a shared identity or mutual understanding. Her soon-to-be-released radio play "an grenzen" (at borders)[5] is based on her mother's experience as a so-called "guest worker" in a knife factory, but it broadens out into a tribute to various forms of invisibilized work (especially that done by migrants). Again, rather than language, it is an embodied and affective form of communication, often involving senses such as touch and smell, that comes to the fore. The automatic reactions of the body to these stimuli from other bodies suggest that an empathetic and ethical engagement with the Other is possible, even if the body's initial response is then often quickly overridden. Thus, while Dündar writes neo-Nazi violence and the figure of the "guest worker" into German cultural memory, destabilizing conventional views of Germanness, she also points the way to a more inclusive, alternative understanding of identity and community via the way our bodies respond to one another in their inherent relationality. In the following interview, we discuss the multifaceted role of subversive language in her work, be it linguistic communication, body language, poetic creativity, or multilingualism. We also talk about the depiction of violence and the political nature of her work, which also shapes its reception and her role as a postmigrant public figure. Lastly, we discuss her work as part of artistic collectives and their importance for her development as a writer.

Joseph Twist: Thanks very much, Özlem, for taking the time to speak with me.

Özlem Özgül Dündar: I'm glad to.

JT: I'd like to begin with quite a big question: Why do you write? What meaning does literature have for you?

ÖÖD: I recently wrote a text with the title "Warum ich nicht mehr schreiben will" (Why I don't want to write anymore),[6] but that's about the

---

4   Özlem Özgül Dündar, *gedanken zerren* (Nettetal: Elif, 2018).
5   The radio play will be broadcast by WDR. I am very grateful to Özlem for sharing the unpublished text with me: Özlem Özgül Dündar, "an grenzen" (unpublished manuscript, 2021).
6   Özlem Özgül Dündar, "Warum ich nicht mehr schreiben will," in *Brotjobs & Literatur*, ed. Iuditha Balint, Julia Dathe, Kathrin Schadt, and Christoph

literary scene and how you constantly have to persuade people, which can be a bit tedious at times. I write mostly to show other perspectives and to do something linguistically subversive, to get people to pause for a moment and think about something that they otherwise wouldn't have thought about. And with some perspectives or some stories, such as *türken, feuer*, I think they just have to be told. That was a necessity for me; that had to be told; and if I didn't tell it in this way, then who would? I want to draw attention to certain things by depicting them in a modified language, which possibly can't be achieved through conventional language. That's why I ended up writing poetry very early on.

JT: You said that literature means being able to open new perspectives, and that occurred to me as I read your texts. They show how, through imagination, literature can make other perspectives and new things visible, whether it is the dead speaking to us, or how a thought races through the synapses of the brain. You also said that you want to encourage readers to think about different things. Does that make writing into something political for you?

ÖÖD: A political dimension has come into my writing more and more. I'm not sure, but I'd say that my first poetry collection, *gedanken zerren*, isn't overly political in the usual sense. It's not so obvious. Although, of course, overcoming borders or feeling restricted (things that I write about a lot) are also political. In my other texts, the political aspect has gotten more and more pronounced, because that's also what I look for in literature. I don't just want to be entertained, but also to find out something about the real world, and various topics come to mind, things that preoccupy me—like the "guest workers," for example, in the text "an grenzen." There are things that have always been part of my life and, of course, they then find their way into my writing. My next poetry collection, if what I'm currently writing becomes my next poetry collection, will also be quite political, as it is intended to be about domestic violence and that sort of thing. That is certainly a political topic.

And some things are more explicitly political. *türken, feuer* is about a specific historical event, which has also always been in my thoughts. I come from Solingen, where the arson attack took place, and people tend to write about the things that constantly occupy their thoughts. Literature can also be understood as an escape from the world, but I don't do it like that. I don't view it as escapism; I seize on something that actually exists or has happened and use language to try and make it clearer.

JT: I can see how your writing has changed and become more political, but I also see a lot of links between *gedanken zerren*, *türken, feuer* and

---

Wenzel (Berlin: Verbrecher, 2021), 47–55.

your new text "an grenzen." The body features a lot, and how people encounter one another. *gedanken zerren* is often about very small gestures. Language often fails in these poems. The figures can't make themselves understood—"die worte stolpern" (the words stumble),[7] as it is formulated in the poetry collection. We can't express ourselves in the precise way we'd like to, but bodies seem able to communicate regardless, through reactions like, for example, blushing or shaking, things that perhaps normally go unnoticed but that your poetry makes us more aware of. And also in *türken, feuer*, Mother 2 talks about small gestures, like a nod when you recognize someone or a smile to show you are open for a conversation. Finally, in *an grenzen*, you write: "also so weit sind wir noch nicht mutiert dass wir dann gar keine reaktion zeigen also der körper reagiert schon noch darauf aber nur einen allerkleinsten moment und dann arbeiten beine und arme und füße und was zu dieser körper-weg-geh-bewegung alles dazu gehört" (we have not mutated so much that we don't show any reaction so the body reacts to it but just for the tiniest moment and then legs and arms and feet and everything that goes with this body-leaving-movement works).[8] Here, it is about whether empathy is still possible when you have suffered an act of violence or experienced racism. So, there is a bit of hope in these gestures, that being humane is still possible, at least that is how I read it. What does this understanding of body language have to do with your writing? Why do you write texts, when body language is so important? Why not make films or work with other media?

ÖÖD: I think that we routinely send out a great deal of bodily signals, and we also make gestures, or exchange glances. We think that we supposedly don't pay any attention to such things, or that they aren't that relevant, but they are very important and they really interest me when I'm writing. The reason I don't make films, but write, is because with writing you can extend it indefinitely. You can, for instance, think about a nod in great detail and really unravel every movement for itself and describe it step by step. Something that lasts for perhaps a second goes on for various pages and can be described for ten minutes. I find that interesting. In *gedanken zerren*, for instance, there are sometimes glances that are led by the words or glances of others. A nod, for example, as you mentioned, means something like: I recognize that I walk past you every day. It's about the recognition that a person is there, that you know each other, that you admit all that with a nod. Such small details interest me because they have a really big influence on our lives. We are probably full of such things, but we don't really pay proper attention to them, or they're just

---

7   Dündar, *gedanken zerren*, 17.
8   Dündar, *an grenzen*.

part of our routine. You can't really think about every detail all the time, but literature, or art in general, is perhaps the place where we can keep track of these things and think about them. I also think that's generally why many people want to consume art or read literature, because they want to take time for something that they otherwise wouldn't have time for in their daily lives.

JT: You like to decelerate these small encounters in your writing in order to focus on them more strongly, and that is also the case in the play *türken, feuer*. *türken, feuer* is a harrowing text, perhaps the most harrowing one I have ever read or heard as a radio play. This deceleration, this extension of certain moments belongs to that, since we are then forced to concentrate on them—like, for instance, when Mother 3 recounts her thoughts exactly in the moment when she is falling to her death. We are forced to linger on these moments. You can't look away; you have to look closely, or better yet listen closely.

There are now monuments to the victims of the arson attacks in the nineties in Rostock-Lichtenhagen, Mölln, and Solingen. There are also campaigns, like #SayTheirNames,[9] for example, and you can see them on social media every year. Recently there was also the #Baseballschlägerjahre (Baseball bat years) initiative, where people collected their experiences under this hashtag to try and make the victims of far-right terror visible.[10] What role can literature play here? Is it about commemoration, or something else?

ÖÖD: It is essentially about commemoration, also remembering. It was very important to me when writing *türken, feuer* that people would remember. The characters circle around this event and try to grasp it in language, and it is as though they remember what happened at that moment, or they say: I am there now and am speaking from there. I started to write this text in 2015–16. That's when I wrote the first monologue, and then I left it for a bit and then looked at it again later. There were lots of attacks on refugee hostels in Germany at that time, also in East Germany, where I currently live. Then there were all these Legida demonstrations at the same time. That was very big at the time in East Germany. They demonstrated in Dresden and in Leipzig, sometimes ten thousand people. It's also called Pegida (Patriotische Europäer gegen die Islamisierung des Abendlandes [Patriotic Europeans against

9   Demokratie (er)leben Hanau, "#SayTheirNames: Die Namen der Opfer nie vergessen!," accessed September 16, 2022, https://www.demokratie-leben-hanau.de/projekte/projekte-2021/saytheirnames-projekt.
10   Christian Bangel, "Baseballschlägerjahre," *Die Zeit*, November 7, 2019, https://www.zeit.de/2019/46/neonazis-jugend-nachwendejahre-ostdeutschland-mauerfall.

the Islamization of the West]).[11] There were also counterdemonstrations that I attended and that was the moment when I thought, everything is repeating itself. Even the element of fire, strangely. I don't know if always using fire to express your hatred is a German thing. Using fire as a weapon surely also has a symbolic value for the perpetrators.

I thought, it just keeps on repeating itself. I was really reminded of the nineties and thought that what happened then has already been forgotten. The younger generation, people who are a few years younger than I am, don't know anything about it and I was also pretty shocked that I hadn't thought about it for so long either. People do want to forget, I suppose. You can't think about those kinds of things all the time. That was the moment when I realized that I would like to write about this and that it had also been slightly forgotten. For me, that also opened up the question of why I didn't want to write about it. What was my problem, also wanting to forget about it myself? Then I thought, you can write about refugee hostels being attacked now, but the problem isn't new, and you really have to begin much earlier.

I had this image of mothers in my mind. There was a sort of legend that was told in Solingen, although it actually happened a little differently. Mother 3 talks about what happened two times. One time she jumps out the window with her child, the other time she throws her child, which is actually the correct version. I think she actually threw her child into her mother-in-law's lap. I found it interesting that this legend originated at the time. It's as if people were looking for something positive amidst the trauma. This story is told again and again. I can clearly remember hearing this story often as a ten-year-old. Then I wrote it like that, and I did some research at some point and discovered: hmmm, it wasn't like that at all! And I found the possible reasons behind the legend very interesting. I left it like that—it shouldn't be a documentary, after all—and I thought, "I want to pick up on this version in the text." I'm now also trying to write a novel about it, and that should contain multiple versions—for example, also from Mother 2 and Mother 3, who talk about the same situation. It also has to do with how events are falsified in the course of time as certain people are heard and others aren't, others are heard more, and also because of what the media makes of it, the way in which they also falsify things, including the memory of it too.

I just wanted to tell my version and the victims feature in my version, also the ones who died, as they also experienced something. They might not be able to tell their story anymore, but that is completely irrelevant for my fictional text. When you exploit literature's possibilities, then of course the dead can talk. I have also been asked, is it necessary to tell

---

11 Pegida, and its Leipzig version Legida, is an anti-Islam, antimigrant far-right popular movement.

this story? Yes, because they have experienced it. Who am I protecting if I don't tell this story? There is so much other literature. Just read something else if you don't want to hear that. Nobody is forced to read it.

JT: So there is this dynamic, that certain events repeat themselves constantly, but some people are nevertheless still surprised. Are you familiar with this article by Mely Kiyak in *Die Zeit*? She describes this dynamic and I have a quotation here:

> What is so surprising about Nazis doing what they do? Is it the society in which they do it? . . . Neo-Nazis in tax brackets, that is Germany, that is your people. Ours . . . are stopping to ask, "who is us, who is them?" Them, that is always those with the relatives who have been shot, burned, or beaten to death, whose crying fathers stutter into the microphones of foreign TV stations. Us, that is those who are only frightened by it at a safe distance of ten, twenty, thirty years. Always only when their own institutions and their own integrity are in danger.[12]

Mely Kiyak criticizes mainstream society for forgetting such racist attacks too quickly. And you always hear that it is just "lone wolves," for instance. The idea that there are networks of neo-Nazis in Germany is often played down in some way, or ignored, or repressed.

ÖÖD: That is also my sense of the situation—that people are always so appalled by it, but from a certain distance. I think it's also principally something human, to hope that it is a "lone wolf," because how do you take that kind of thing on? How do you guard against that? It is very difficult. I actually wonder why more educational work isn't done on the topic of antiracism. This article is great. Who are "we" and who are "they"? Clearly "they" means people farther away and affected in some way; "we" means people here who close their eyes, waiting for the problem to go away, but it doesn't.

JT: And there is this "we" and "they," although it is actually a problem for the whole of society. Not only minorities are affected by it.

ÖÖD: It was only in the nineties that politicians admitted that Germany is a country of migration. Forty years passed until somebody said, "These people who came as migrant laborers in the fifties and sixties didn't only come as guests and they aren't going to leave now." A false image is created in the public consciousness, also in a political way, that these people

---

12 Mely Kiyak, "Alufolie drauf und gute Nacht," *Die Zeit*, September 2, 2020, https://www.zeit.de/kultur/2020-09/corona-demo-rechtsextremismus-berlin-verschwoerungstheoretiker-coronavirus/komplettansicht.

are not here to stay and to live with us. That is a fundamental problem and, in my opinion, it takes too long for such things to be recognized and stated by politicians. Then people have totally incorrect ideas in their heads about Turks, and so on, as people who are just here to work and who will go away again in a few years. It would not be human to stay somewhere for ten years without building a life there, but these kinds of things are just not considered.

JT: Yes, and there was a series of events to mark the sixtieth anniversary of the agreement between Germany and Turkey. Would you say that the first generation is finally present in German memory culture, or not? I can hardly remember anything from the fiftieth anniversary. Perhaps it is because there are more Turkish-Germans in the media now, and not only Turkish-Germans but also more people of color.

ÖÖD: I also had the impression that the sixtieth anniversary was very present. Ten years ago, for the fiftieth, which is actually a bigger moment, half a century, I didn't really notice it as much, although I was already quite active on the literary scene then. Now I am more into theater and radio plays than ten years ago und theater and radio plays perhaps react more quickly to political events than prose, and so on. I do think that there were a lot of events this time. There are a lot of associations that organize cultural events. For instance, I did a soundwalk for the theater in Karlsruhe that was about the history of the "guest workers" there.[13] That was a collaborative project. Although I wrote the text, I don't view it as being completely my own since it is based on interviews that the director did and so the material I had to work with was already largely predetermined. I don't know if it's just a lot of hype and everything will quickly calm down again, with nobody doing anything about it again for ten years. Let's see if it was just a lot of hot air that will soon cool down.

JT: I have also read that the SPD politicians Michelle Müntefering and Sevim Aydin are both calling for a monument to the first generation of "guest workers."[14] In your text "an grenzen," you suggest that we already have lots of incentives to commemorate the "guest workers." The text says that every time we get in a German car we should remember that

---

13 Badisches Staatstheater Karlsruhe, "Kent Melodien," accessed September 16, 2022, https://www.staatstheater.karlsruhe.de/programm/extras/kent-melodien/.

14 Carolin Rückl, "Am Berliner Oranienplatz soll ein Denkmal für Gastarbeiter entstehen," *Der Tagesspiegel*, July 15, 2021, https://www.tagesspiegel.de/berlin/vorschlag-von-kreuzberger-bezirkspolitikerin-am-berliner-oranienplatz-soll-ein-denkmal-fuer-gastarbeiter-entstehen/27420920.html.

migrant workers have helped to build it. Why does this work remain invisible? The text reads: "[die Hände] sollten schnell arbeiten eine akkordschicht nach der nächsten machen und dann schnell verschwinden wie nie dagewesen" (their hands should work quickly do one long shift after the next and then quickly disappear like never there). We have already spoken about how racism makes many people and their experiences invisible. But here it is also about capitalism.

ÖÖD: Yes, and about the working class. I think that it isn't only the work of Turks or migrants that isn't seen, but the work of workers in general; or it is taken so much for granted that there are all these things, and we just don't see that they are made. That's perhaps a problem of capitalism. We only want to see the beautiful and shiny products—that's how the world is—but that's all created with effort and work.

Also, workers don't have a strong voice. They aren't really represented much in literature either. Those who write are mostly people with a higher educational qualification. That's how they end up writing. That's why their daily lives are represented more. There have been efforts to bring workers' voices into greater focus—like in the GDR, for example. The Institute for Literature in Leipzig was founded with the aim of supporting workers, who otherwise wouldn't have had the opportunity to write, to give an account of their daily lives, and that's all gone now.

It's really both aspects that interest me, in terms of the extent to which the working classes in general are ignored. You hear a lot that the political center in Germany is falling apart and that this gives parties like the AfD (Alternative für Deutschland [Alternative for Germany]) a boost. I think that workers are in the center and if they don't have any proper political representation, then this leads to new problems that we will need to fight in the future. And with the "guest workers" it is even more intensified, since they are perceived so differently, but what they have done, over decades, is just not valued.

JT: Is it nevertheless easier now to speak about the first generation, as they are all retired and no longer slogging away in factories?

ÖÖD: Well, the very first ones, those who came in '61, are very old or already dead. Maybe it's also the case that more people with a history of migration are journalists and authors and so can write about it anyway. You also have to consider that they were workers who did not come here with educational qualifications and couldn't write about their circumstances. Of course they were able to write in some form, but the majority of those who came had only attended primary school. To some extent, their children also haven't gained any higher qualifications or done any apprenticeships, and only their children now have these kinds of jobs. It's quite significant that so many have now been here for various generations and have received a different type of education from their parents or grandparents, meaning they can now write about it.

JT: I read a text by you in *Die Zeit*, "Die Sätze sind holprig für deine Ohren: ich pflücke mir" (The phrases are jarring to your ears: I pick for myself).[15] It appeared in a series of texts by young authors writing mostly about exclusion in the literary scene, but your contribution was very abstract, very poetic. In the text, you describe how you transform language when writing and that this is also a very embodied experience—how you chew words, and so on. Was that to show that your texts are literary, as there is this expectation that minority writers only write about what it's like being a minority, like nonfiction really? As though people only read books from migrantized or queer authors to learn more about their identities. Was this your intention when writing this text? And also, how has your experience as a Turkish-German writer been up until now?

ÖÖD: What I find important when writing in general, regardless of whether it is political or not, is including subversive moments of language, so that you are looking at something different. In this text, I wanted to describe how language is something very flexible for me because I think bilingually. Language is so very flexible, and I think that many people who can speak two or more languages very well also see that it is, in a way, just a means to an end, allowing you to express something, to be able to communicate with others. And when writing, language is first and foremost material and my entire linguistic knowledge is not only German, but also Turkish, English, and so on, and everything flows into the grammar of the text. That's what I was getting at, that I use all the languages at my disposal as material, taking it to make something new, and we all do that really. Languages are not isolated, but rather are influenced by other languages. That was the meaning behind the text: taking a different look at language. What happens to language when I make use of it?

I also wish that more people would recognize that when deviations from linguistic and grammatical norms appear in texts they are not just to be immediately labeled as "wrong." That happens in some of my texts and at the Institute of Literature a lot is described as wrong, but I just think: rhythmically, that sounds best to me. What is "right" doesn't sound right to me. When I hear how it's actually supposed to be, that also sounds alright, but I want to do something different somehow. It doesn't fit properly into my writing if I do it all totally correctly, so I open it up

---

15   Özlem Özgül Dündar, "Die Sätze sind holprig für deine Ohren: ich pflücke mir," *Die Zeit*, August 8, 2018, https://www.zeit.de/kultur/literatur/2018-08/rassismus-literaturbetrieb-metwo-diskriminierung-autoren-integration/komplettansicht.

and do what I want with it. I sometimes find it difficult when it's seen as wrong, since at that moment it is a question of rhythm for me, and I just bend it to get the best fit. This text was also about how my language isn't always accepted when I deviate from the standard, overwhelmingly by people who are not bilingual.

JT: You don't make it easy for the proofreaders and editors with your texts! Especially in poetry there are lots of examples of people writing multilingually. You normally write in German, so what function does Turkish or English have in your writing if they don't appear concretely?

ÖÖD: My first play for the theater was Turkish-German. There was a lot of Turkish in it, but it was never staged. We'll have to wait and see if it is staged at some point. Here, I was trying very hard to portray daily life in Turkish and German, as using words from two languages is part of how many people with a history of migration speak. After that I didn't write any more texts where this is that relevant. I wrote a short essay, or prose text, "DER ORT" (THE PLACE).[16] I mention a few Turkish words there, but it wasn't really written bilingually. I think, however, that it has a general influence on my language. For example, in some poems I use the phrase "etwas machen" (to do/make something) and people often mistake it for something English. I find it really interesting that people always see the influence of English in my work, and I don't have a clue if it's English or Turkish, since this formulation exists in both languages. That I think in other languages also heavily influences my syntax. German syntax is a mystery to me. If someone tells me what is correct, then I realize: oh yeah, that's right. But why I have to use this version isn't very clear to me.

People often forget how flexible German syntax is. It's also very flexible in Turkish. Turkish is an agglutinative language. Suffixes are added on to express particular things, like the genitive. Everything is then mixed up in my head. These different syntaxes then become my own syntax, whatever I like at that moment in my text.

JT: Your language is certainly very experimental and comes across as strange, even when there are no Turkish words. Especially in your poetry, where words are broken up and some words are replaced with letters in a very minimalistic way. But in your prose texts too and in the play *türken, feuer* there is no punctuation, for example, and everything is written in lower case. Is there a connection between the aesthetic, on the one hand, and the political, on the other? As you said, you write very political texts, but also very aesthetically appealing ones. Do aesthetics and politics go together, do you think?

---

16   Özlem Özgül Dündar, "DER ORT," *die horen* 278 (2020): 42–45.

ÖÖD: Yes, certainly, but it is not necessarily the case that aesthetics and politics always go together. I, of course, always want to write aesthetic texts, in the sense that people should like reading their language. And if the text has a political point, then I think it's important that readers still read the text, even if they are only superficially interested in the political aspect. Let's put it like this, *türken, feuer* has now been quite strongly contextualized through the radio play, but for the first versions I did there was absolutely no context and people still found it very exciting to read. They didn't need the context to read it and to understand what it's about. Now it is very much contextualized through the radio play, and also through interviews I have given, but what it's about isn't explicitly mentioned in the text itself. There is just one part in a short dialogue, where it is said that the town became well known overnight. Yes, Mother 2 says this and then it is picked up again later, but the name of the town is never actually said. My thinking here was to leave it open because it's something that is always repeating itself. It doesn't matter if it's Solingen or Mölln, or if it happened in 2015. It's about the racist attack in itself, and not just about the one event, but also the repetition.

But aesthetics are, of course, always important and the language is part of that, as an interruption of conventional reading habits. I think that the aesthetic aspect is often neglected in texts that are political, where the political message comes so strongly to the fore that you can't read it in a neutral way anymore. For me, it's often important that readers are able to form their own opinion about the subject matter. Especially for a text like *türken, feuer*, I thought for a long time about how I would write it. And I found the idea that a narrator could be between the figures strange. Who is this narrator, then? Is it me, Özlem, who is telling the story, since I'm also from Solingen? I thought, "that's too close to me." It is always difficult when the distance between the narrator and the author isn't big enough. Then people tend to equate them one to one. And in my case that would've happened very quickly.

I also found taking the narrator out very difficult. What kind of narrator is that, then? And how close can she be to the characters when she is telling the story? And then at some point the idea occurred to me to simply let the characters speak; so it's multiperspectival and the figures tell their stories, also telling them a bit differently each time so that there isn't this one truth. It was really important to me that people didn't think Özlem was telling her version and her morality. But the aesthetic dimension was also key to my literary decisions concerning this text. I hope that the text is also interesting for people who aren't explicitly interested in the political side, but in the narrative style or the characters. Like, what does waking up to find your house on fire do to a character? What does it do to a person? And in that regard, in many of the monologues, the question of where the fire came from is, at first, slightly irrelevant, since people don't always know, when they wake up in a burning house, that it is a racist attack.

JT: As you said earlier, it is the fictional nature of the text that allows you to offer these new perspectives.

ÖÖD: Yes, and that is often misconstrued. At one point, in one version, I had a different number of victims. Mother 2 didn't say five members of her family had died, but six or seven. Then it was quoted like that in a newspaper article that six or seven people died in Solingen. And I thought, "Oh my God! What is happening here?" Then I changed it again to five because I thought, "If people are going to quote it, I don't want to be responsible for other people perceive something wrong about the 1993 arson attack." But it must be clear to people that it is fictional when dead people are speaking! Something totally different from what I had intended was made out of it. I ended up keeping these kinds of moments the same, totally accurate, because it is very hard to get people who are in this day-to-day report-reading mode, with newspapers, and so on, to properly listen in.

JT: Yes, and people assume that especially writers with a history of migration just write about what it's like being a migrant, or about their own identity, things that can be proved with facts. I have a funny example: in the novel *Dein Name* (Your name, 2011) by the author Navid Kermani, in which the protagonist is also called Navid Kermani, the protagonist divorces his wife, and I read that after the book was published, his Wikipedia page was soon changed to say that he is divorced, when that isn't the case.

ÖÖD: That's interesting because Michel Houellebecq, the French author, does something similar in his novel *La carte et le territoire* (*The Map and the Territory*, 2010). *La carte et le territoire* is also about an author called Michel Houellebecq, who lived for a period in Cork in Ireland, which he actually did too. Well, the main character is, however, the real Houellebecq. And then the character Houellebecq shows up and is gruesomely murdered. And that's how you know that, yes, it's fiction, or else the book wouldn't exist, in which he is writing about his own death. You have to make it extremely clear to the reader so that they get it.

Autofiction has also been very big in recent years. Texts by people who are affected by something in some way are read like non-fiction to find out about the reality of their lives. It's very fashionable at the moment, I think. In my case, I try to write very generally in my essays, even when they touch on my own personal experiences. There is only one text of mine that I would say is autobiographical. That's an essay called

"Mein Name ist Türke" (My name is Turk, 2021).[17] That is certainly autobiographical, but otherwise I try to keep things separate from me. The text *türken, feuer*, the first text of mine that attracted a lot of attention, is also linked to my biography, as it happens, owing to the fact that I come from Solingen. The more texts of mine that there are, eventually—and I hope there will be more—the clearer it will perhaps become that a lot of what I write is fiction.

I don't really know how my experience in the literary scene has been. I'm being invited to a lot of things at the moment, for readings and that kind of thing. And I don't know how it would be received if I wrote a text about something completely different that has nothing to do with my biography, because a lot of people want something "authentic." I heard this once from a playwright. Her family comes from Bosnia, but she herself doesn't, it's her grandparents' generation—and she said that she has problems getting texts published when they are not about war, since they apparently don't have this "authenticity." Although she doesn't have this wartime experience, she is expected to write about it because it is projected onto her. Other texts where she writes about very German topics are rejected. It's like that in theater. You write a play and then give it to the publisher and then they can decide if they want it or not. Even if the publisher has featured five of your plays, it can still mean that they have rejected various others. For instance, *Jardin d'Istanbul*, this Turkish-German play of mine, was rejected by my theatrical publisher. Presumably it didn't contain enough conflict, who knows?

JT: And when the expectation that authors with a history of migration write about conflicts, or the cliché of living between two cultures is constantly repeated, you get a vicious circle.

ÖÖD: Yes, that's right. It's repeated through the publishers' choices. When she does write plays that don't have anything to do with her family's experiences in the war, but they are rejected, of course the impression of her that is given is that she only writes about war and what it means to be Bosnian, which she doesn't do. I think that's very sad, but we can also think about how autofiction is, in part, produced by the publisher. Yeah, so let's see, I'm curious. I also, of course, plan to write texts that have little or nothing to do with me. Will they attract the same attention as the texts with a stronger link to my biography?

Jardin d'Istanbul is about Turkish-Kurdish people who work in a restaurant. At the time, it was nominated for the Retzhofer Drama Prize, which it won, but it was still never performed, which is very strange. It

---

17   Özlem Özgül Dündar, "Mein Name ist Türke," *Cope*, accessed September 16, 2022, https://www.cope-mag.com/texte/oezlem-oezguel-duendar/index.html.

is, however, not a play with loads and loads of conflict, and during one of the discussions with actors someone asked: "Yes, but this Turkish-Kurdish constellation, that is full of conflict and so why does nothing happen there?" And I said, "Hmmm, but Turkish-Kurdish daily life in Germany isn't like that, and neither is it in Turkey." If these people were always in conflict with one another, as is seemingly expected, that would be absolutely terrible. I mean, how could you live like that at all? But it isn't like that. A majority, whatever nationality they are, live very peacefully with one another.

Here in Germany, you are also sort of in the same boat. You're abroad and here you have completely different problems, which can also be a strong unifying force. I used to work in a restaurant like this and there was no conflictual relationship, but that is what is expected; and because this is lacking in the play people don't understand it. I also didn't know how I could make it clear, in a literary way, that it's normal that they aren't in conflict. I guess, as long as I don't have this solution, it won't appeal to a German-speaking audience. That's my assumption, anyway.

JT: Here perhaps one last question: Are collectives, such as Kanak Attak[18] and Kaltsignal, or the Gorki Theater, for example, where all this is perhaps a bit more self-evident, all the more important then? What role do such groups play in your creative work?

ÖÖD: In collectives, you can do some things that are difficult to achieve on your own. I'm unfortunately no longer active in the collectives Kanak Attak Leipzig and Kaltsignal. Kaltsignal also doesn't exist anymore. Kanak Attak has changed its name—they have changed their name so often in recent years that I have lost track of what the current name is! I was a cofounder and what happened was really great, as really distinct projects came out of it. The writers' collective Postmigrantische Störung (Postmigrant disturbance) came out of it. They call themselves PMS, like the phase for women during menstruation—it's a women's collective and that's why they play with this term. There is also a radio show for the community radio in Leipzig, and other projects.

What I also think is good about work as part of a collective is that, because so many people are involved, there is a very intensive group discussion before you make what you have created public. I've also been a member of the collective Ministerium für Mitgefühl (Ministry of Empathy) since 2018 and of the collective flexen, which came about after the book *FLEXEN: Flâneusen* schreiben Städte* (FLEXEN: Flâneuses

---

18 The term "Kanake" is a racist slur that has been reappropriated by different writers and musicians since the 1990s. See, for example, Kanak Attak, "Manifesto (English)," accessed September 16, 2022, https://www.kanak-attak.de/ka/about/manif_eng.html.

write cities, 2019),[19] which was mostly about urban space from the perspectives of people of color, queer people, and women. The aim was to bring the flâneuse into being, describe who or what she is, and to do that you have to produce texts to show different facets of the flâneuse. An individual person can't do that.

It's similar with Ministerium für Mitgefühl. The initial idea was to do something against right-wing politics, but with literary, linguistic means that we know how to use. How could we contribute to the political narrative without becoming politicians or activists? And then we founded this collective to do something with our skills as authors. Texts have also come out of this. This year [2021] we ran a slogan campaign during the general election. The minister for empathy asked, for example: "Is my equality too expensive?" In the sense that, if we want to be a fair society, so that everyone gets enough of the pie, then for many that will mean giving up some of their share. These are the sorts of things that the minister asks. For instance, she asked, "Who made my decision?," because as a woman you are often not considered. I couldn't do that as an individual, and I also couldn't be so loud.

And what I also really like about collectives is that everything is very well thought out. Everyone is an artist or a journalist and in a collective a very vigorous exchange can take place, with lots of influences, which are also present in society. People who are anxious about certain topics, or who aren't so loud themselves, or don't feel comfortable with something, all that is thrashed out in a collective until you find a good solution, or until the people who aren't sure are persuaded and then participate. A collective is also intrinsically polyphonic. It isn't just that I, Özlem, am saying it. Ten people are saying it and that naturally has a different force, a different weight. There are also collectives that aren't political, but I think that working in a collective lends itself to political topics. I hope I have answered that now?

JT: Yes, brilliantly answered! I don't have any other questions. Thank you so much for our conversation and I wish you every success with your writing and with the collectives, and I'm excited to see what you do next!

ÖÖD: I'm also excited. Thanks for your questions.

---

19   Özlem Özgül Dündar, Ronya Othmann, Mia Göhring, and Lea Sauer, ed., *FLEXEN: Flâneusen* schreiben Städte* (Berlin: Verbrecher, 2019).

Bibliography

Badisches Staatstheater Karlsruhe. "Kent Melodien." Accessed September 16, 2022. https://www.staatstheater.karlsruhe.de/programm/extras/kent-melodien/.

Bangel, Christian. "Baseballschlägerjahre." *Die Zeit*, November 7, 2019. https://www.zeit.de/2019/46/neonazis-jugend-nachwendejahre-ostdeutschland-mauerfall.

Demokratie (er)leben Hanau. "#SayTheirNames: Die Namen der Opfer nie vergessen!" Accessed September 16, 2022. https://www.demokratie-leben-hanau.de/projekte/projekte-2021/saytheirnames-projekt.

Dündar, Özlem Özgül. "an grenzen." Unpublished manuscript, 2021.

———. "DER ORT." *die horen* 278 (2020): 42–45.

———. "Die Sätze sind holprig für deine Ohren: ich pflücke mir." *Die Zeit*, August 8, 2018. https://www.zeit.de/kultur/literatur/2018-08/rassismus-literaturbetrieb-metwo-diskriminierung-autoren-integration/komplettansicht.

———. *gedanken zerren*. Nettetal: Elif, 2018.

———. "Mein Name ist Türke." *Cope*, 2021. Accessed September 16, 2022. https://www.cope-mag.com/texte/oezlem-oezguel-duendar/index.html.

———. *türken, feuer*. Hamburg: Rowohlt Theaterverlag, 2019.

———. "Warum ich nicht mehr schreiben will." In *Brotjobs & Literatur*, edited by Iuditha Balint, Julia Dathe, Kathrin Schadt, and Christoph Wenzel, 47–55. Berlin: Verbrecher, 2021.

Dündar, Özlem Özgül, Ronya Othmann, Mia Göhring, and Lea Sauer, eds. *FLEXEN: Flâneusen* schreiben Städte*. Berlin: Verbrecher, 2019.

Kanak Attak. "Manifesto (English)." Accessed September 16, 2022. https://www.kanak-attak.de/ka/about/manif_eng.html.

Kiyak, Mely. "Alufolie drauf und gute Nacht." *Die Zeit*, September 2, 2020. Accessed September 16, 2022. https://www.zeit.de/kultur/2020-09/corona-demo-rechtsextremismus-berlin-verschwoerungstheoretiker-coronavirus/komplettansicht.

Rückl, Carolin. "Am Berliner Oranienplatz soll ein Denkmal für Gastarbeiter entstehen." *Der Tagesspiegel*, July 15, 2021. Accessed September 16, 2022. https://www.tagesspiegel.de/berlin/vorschlag-von-kreuzberger-bezirkspolitikerin-am-berliner-oranienplatz-soll-ein-denkmal-fuer-gastarbeiter-entstehen/27420920.html.

WDR. "türken, feuer." April 18, 2022. https://www1.wdr.de/radio/wdr3/programm/sendungen/wdr3-hoerspiel/tuerken-feuer-solingen-anschlag-100.html.

7: Deintegrative Rewriting of the Bildungsroman: Social Criticism from a Postmigrant Perspective in Fatma Aydemir's *Ellbogen* (2017)

Lea Laura Heim

THIS CHAPTER ENGAGES WITH Fatma Aydemir's debut novel *Ellbogen* (Elbows, 2017) and the literary means it employs to voice social criticism. The main argument is that Aydemir rewrites the genre of the Bildungsroman to challenge mechanisms and structures of discrimination and marginalization. Bringing together literary and historical scholarship on the Bildungsroman and employing the analytical perspective of postmigration, I will explore how, as a deintegrative rewriting of the genre, *Ellbogen* poses a critical intervention into contemporary German society.

Ellbogen's protagonist, Hazal Akgündüz, is born and raised in Germany as a child of Kurdish immigrants. Many commentators have picked up on the protagonist's anger,[1] which plays a significant role in the text as it steers toward the central event: on the night of her eighteenth birthday, Hazal pushes a young man onto the train tracks, where he dies as a consequence of her actions. To escape punishment, Hazal flees to Istanbul and attempts to start a new life in an unknown environment.

Regarding *Ellbogen*, Claudia Breger argues that the "affective reflexivity" evoked in the reading process holds the potential to "contribute to a reconfiguring . . . of public norms as grounded in structures of perception and experience."[2] I agree with Breger regarding the potency of the text to intervene in public discourse and I will

---

1 See, for instance, Philipp Bovermann, "Diese Wut gehört ihr," *Süddeutsche Zeitung*, February 3, 2017, https://www.sueddeutsche.de/kultur/deutsche-gegenwartsliteratur-diese-wut-gehoert-ihr-1.3362316; Moritz Herrmann, "'Ellbogen': Gewaltige Wut," ZEIT ONLINE, April 16, 2018, https://www.zeit.de/2018/16/ellbogen-fatma-aydemir-junges-schauspielhaus.

2 Claudia Breger, "Affect(ive) Assemblages. Literary Worldmaking in Fatma Aydemir's *Ellbogen*," in *Public Spheres of Resonance: Constellations of Affect and Language*, ed. Anne Fleig and Christian von Scheve (London: Routledge, 2020), 206.

demonstrate this potential in relation to the notion of deintegration, brought into conversation recently via Max Czollek's polemic *Desintegriert Euch!*,[3] together with Kobena Mercer's thoughts on the burden of representation.[4]

Debates about diversity in Germany as a country of immigration are significantly shaped around the idea of integration. The demand for integration is based on the idea of a cultural and political center—in recent debates often referred to as *Leitkultur*—into which all those who are perceived as different are supposed to integrate. The targets of this one-sided demand to integrate are mostly immigrants but also their descendants who did not immigrate to but grew up in Germany, like Hazal. The understanding of integration is based on a distinction between *us* and *them*, whereby this construction of difference serves to stabilize the dominant culture.[5] Czollek elaborates on this in reference to the function of Jews regarding the self-conceptualization of Germans, especially in connection with memory culture. He also mentions how stereotypical images of Muslims serve as a counterimage to the self-image of tolerant and enlightened Germans.[6]

Critical of the integration paradigm, Czollek proposes the term *deintegration* to challenge the expectation of minorities to integrate into an allegedly homogeneous center that does not conform to the present social reality.[7] Deintegration is understood by Czollek as a strategy to resist exclusion and ascribed role expectations that marginalized minorities face from the hegemonial parts of society. Czollek finds the strategy of deintegration applied in the realm of arts and culture and sees the respective artworks as offering self-empowerment and self-determination. According to Czollek, the overall aim of deintegration is to aesthetically enforce the recognition and appreciation of radical diversity as the basis of German society.[8]

Timo Sestu identifies the deintegrative potential of *Ellbogen* in its ironic narrative style[9] and considers Hazal's act of violence to be

3   Max Czollek, *Desintegriert euch!* (Munich: Carl Hanser Verlag, 2018).
4   Kobena Mercer, "Black Art and the Burden of Representation," *Third Text* 4, no. 10 (1990).
5   Czollek, *Desintegriert euch!*, 65.
6   Czollek, *Desintegriert euch!*, 10.
7   Czollek, *Desintegriert euch!*, 16.
8   Czollek, *Desintegriert euch!*, 133.
9   Timo Sestu, "Verlangen ohne Liebe, Rand ohne Mitte. Literarische Figurationen von Desintegration," in *Fremdheit, Integration, Vielfalt? Interdisziplinäre Perspektiven auf Migration und Gesellschaft*, ed. Christine Lubkoll, Eva Forrester, and Timo Sestu (Leiden: Brill Fink, 2021), 231.

deintegrative.[10] Expanding on this, I aim to demonstrate how Hazal's subsequent behavior, even more than the act of violence itself, embodies a deintegrative strategy that effectively rejects the burden of representation.

When delving into the origins of Hazal's anger, it becomes essential to consider her position within a classed society that perceives her as an outsider—a migrant seen as not fully belonging. To investigate these complex circumstances, I employ what I term a *postmigrant perspective*.[11] While critics of postmigration have indicated that the term lacks clarity, other scholars argue that "the absence of consensus is exactly what has made the term so effective" and that "it is more important . . . what it can do as a *strategic term*. . . ."[12]

In this chapter, postmigration is understood as a—potentially temporary—strategic term that is utilized to negotiate and reflect on Germany's societal structures as a country of immigration. To avoid "perpetuating migrant identity ascriptions and thereby reproducing the discursive separation of certain population groups from society as a whole . . . ,"[13] I employ postmigration as an analytical perspective rather than as a descriptor for individual subjectivities.[14] Such an analytical lens draws attention to a pivotal societal conflict that is often portrayed as unfolding around immigration but actually evolves around equality as the key promise in a pluralist democratic society, as Naika Foroutan states.[15] The promise of equal opportunity for all motivates immigrants and their descendants, as well as their allies, to demand equal social participation, while other parts of society are increasingly denying them these rights.[16] Dominant debates around migration hide the fact that the societal conflicts are indeed sociostructural issues. According to Foroutan, migration has become a

---

10   Sestu, "Verlangen ohne Liebe," 226.

11   For a thorough overview of the origin of the term postmigration, see Anne Ring Petersen, Moritz Schramm, and Frauke Wiegand, "Postmigration as a Concept (Reception, Histories, Criticism)," in *Reframing Migration, Diversity and the Arts: The Postmigrant Condition*, ed. Moritz Schramm, Sten Pultz Moslund, and Anne Ring Peterson (New York: Routledge, 2019), 1–64.

12   Anne Ring Petersen, Moritz Schramm, and Frauke Wiegand, "Postmigration as a Concept," 3.

13   Anne Ring Petersen, Moritz Schramm, and Frauke Wiegand, "Postmigration as a Concept," 13.

14   For further insights into postmigration as an analytical perspective in literary studies, see Moritz Schramm, "Jenseits der binären Logik: Postmigrantische Perspektiven für die Literatur- und Kulturwissenschaft," in *Postmigrantische Perspektiven: Ordnungssysteme, Repräsentationen, Kritik*, ed. Naika Foroutan, Juliane Karakayali, and Riem Spielhaus (Bonn: Campus Verlag, 2018).

15   Naika Foroutan, *Die postmigrantische Gesellschaft: Ein Versprechen der pluralen Demokratie* (Bielefeld: transcript, 2019), 71.

16   Foroutan, *Die Postmigrantische Gesellschaft*, 71.

metanarrative that is used to explain complex social problems such as educational and gender inequality, crime, antisemitism, and housing shortages.[17] This narrative is used to legitimize unequal treatment of immigrants and migrantized people, such that Germany's promise of equal social participation for all is not realized.[18]

A postmigrant analytical perspective allows us to pay attention to the dominant parts of society and to render visible their usually unmarked social positions, which are assumed to be normative. When considering the prevalent discourse on integration, the role of the dominant part of society is generally not considered. For example, white people in Germany are not used to having their whiteness addressed in the same way that male gender identities have been set as the norm and are rarely named as such in comparison to female or nonbinary gender identities.[19] The postmigrant perspective, therefore, encompasses the understanding that the ramifications of migration and the consequent conflicts and struggles affect not only those who have immigrated but every member of a society shaped by immigration.[20]

When applying a postmigrant analytical perspective to a literary text, one should pay attention to its depiction of the ways plurality is dealt with in a country of immigration.[21] In keeping with its roots as a term of empowerment and as a tool to protest and critique the exclusion of immigrants and their descendants, a postmigrant perspective engages with artistic interventions into hegemonic societal structures and representational expectations. This ties in with Czollek's notion of deintegration, which helps to identify and describe such interventions.

Almost all studies that engage with *Ellbogen* also mention postmigration, albeit in different ways. Jon Cho-Polizzi argues that narratives of return are deconstructed and transcended in the novel and uses postmigration to describe a generation and places like Europe and Berlin, as well

---

17 Foroutan, *Die Postmigrantische Gesellschaft*, 12f.
18 Foroutan, *Die Postmigrantische Gesellschaft*, 81f.
19 See, for instance, Richard Dyer, "The Matter of Whiteness," in *White Privilege: Essential Readings on the Other Side of Racism*, ed. Paula S. Rothenberg (New York: Worth, 2008); bell hooks, "Representations of Whiteness in the Black Imagination," in *Black Looks: Race and Representation* (New York: Routledge, 2015); Peggy McIntosh, "White Privilege: Unpacking the Invisible Knapsack," accessed April 4, 2023, https://psychology.umbc.edu/wp-content/uploads/sites/57/2016/10/White-Privilege_McIntosh-1989.pdf.
20 Anna Meera Gaonkar et al., "Introduction," in *Postmigration: Art, Culture, and Politics in Contemporary Europe*, ed. Anna Meera Gaonkar et al. (Bielefeld: transcript, 2021), 25.
21 Plurality here is to be understood as diversity regarding race, gender, class, sexuality, disability, and religion.

as Hazal's "postmigrant fantasies of Istanbul."[22] Anna Hampel explores the political in *Ellbogen* and uses the notion of a postmigrant society to describe a specific group, on the one hand, and as a term that aims to overcome the divide between migrant and nonmigrant perspectives, on the other.[23] Examining the lack of effective dialogue in the text, Hampel determines that a postmigrant society fails in the narrated world of the novel. While Hampel mainly concentrates on migration and its social implications for Hazal's biography, my analysis here additionally considers the conditions of social class as highly significant in determining her chances in life. As Foroutan notes, the concept of postmigration is not limited to questions of migration but rather functions as a "cipher for plurality including how questions of gender, religion, sexual autonomy, racism, and class are dealt with."[24]

Alvaro Luna and Kyung-Ho Cha have explored postmigration in relation to the Bildungsroman. Luna interprets two texts from Chicana/o and Franco-Maghrebi literature as "the postmigrant variant of the *Bildungsroman*."[25] He examines how the hierarchization of language influences subject formation and how multilingualism challenges the strong connection between the protagonist and the nation-state. Differing from the approach to postmigration in this article, Luna primarily utilizes postmigration as a generational marker. Cha reads Deniz Ohde's novel *Streulicht* (2020) as a postmigrant critique of the Bildungsroman, stating that Ohde imitates the form "in order to show that this traditional genre belongs to a hegemonic knowledge system called *Bildung*, from which the postmigrant subject is excluded."[26] Similarly to Luna, Cha uses postmigration as a descriptor for a specific subject position—namely, that "of

---

22 Jon Cho-Polizzi, "'Almanya: A [Different] Future is Possible' Defying Narratives of Return in Fatma Aydemir's *Ellbogen*," *TRANSIT* 13, no. 2 (2021): 100.

23 Anna Hampel, *Literarische Reflexionsräume des Politischen: Neuausrichtungen in Erzähltexten der Gegenwart* (Berlin: de Gruyter, 2021), 154–55.

24 Naika Foroutan, "Die postmigrantische Perspektive: Aushandlungsprozesse in pluralen Gesellschaften," in *Postmigrantische Visionen: Erfahrungen—Ideen—Reflexionen*, ed. Marc Hill and Erol Yıldız (Bielefeld: transcript, 2018), 18 (my translation).

25 Alvaro Luna, "The Way of the Majority's World: Language as a *Bildung* Lesson in Tomás Rivera's . . . *y no se lo tragó la tierra* and Azouz Begag's *Le Gone du Chaâba*," *Symposium* 73, no. 3 (2019): 176.

26 Kyung-Ho Cha, "The Postmigrant Critique of the Bildungsroman and the Epistemic Injustice of the Educational System in Deniz Ohde's *Scattered Light*," in *Epistemic Justice and Creative Agency: Global Perspectives on Literature and Film*, ed. Sarah Colvin and Stephanie Galasso (New York: Routledge, 2022), 135.

a young postmigrant woman" and describes Ohde's novel as a "recent example of postmigrant literature."[27]

In the following, I will briefly outline historical aspects and discussions around the Bildungsroman to clarify why it is productive to read *Ellbogen* as a rewriting of this genre. The reception history illustrates the Bildungsroman's importance in the emergence of a German national literature in the late eighteenth and nineteenth centuries. Regional particularism and political fragmentation yielded a desire for national unity. To strengthen a German cultural tradition, the Bildungsroman was retrospectively advanced to a genre, which allegedly "expresses the mysterious essence of the German soul. . . ."[28] Historically, the Bildungsroman is therefore profoundly linked to the imagination of a German national identity.

While Goethe's *Wilhelm Meisters Lehrjahre* (*Wilhelm Meister's Apprenticeship*, 1795–96) is still widely considered to be the founding text of the genre, to date there has been little agreement on characteristics of the Bildungsroman. Some consider it to be solely a historical form;[29] others interpret it as an "unfulfilled genre,"[30] still others question the existence of the Bildungsroman altogether, deeming it to be a "phantom genre" or "formation," respectively.[31] Despite being highly contested, the Bildungsroman proves to be a subject that countless scholars engage with.

Of interest for this study is Joseph R. Slaughter's exploration of the "intersection of the conceptual vocabularies of human rights and narrative theory."[32] Calling them "enabling fictions," Slaughter states that "*Bildung* and modern human rights were both technologies of incorporation,"[33] reinforcing ideological constructs that underpin the inclusion of the bourgeois subject in the nation-state. Proceeding from this insight, Slaughter analyzes postcolonial novels and argues that "the

---

27   Cha, "The Postmigrant Critique of the Bildungsroman," 132.

28   Todd Kontje, "The German Tradition of the Bildungsroman," in *A History of the Bildungsroman*, ed. Sarah Graham (Cambridge: Cambridge University Press, 2019), 10.

29   Rolf Selbmann, "Der Bildungsroman ist tot—es lebe der Bildungsroman? Überlegungen zur Begriffsbestimmung einer bedrohten Gattung," *Prospero: Rivista di letterature e culture straniere*, no. 26 (2021).

30   Jürgen Jacobs, *Wilhelm Meister und seine Brüder: Untersuchungen zum deutschen Bildungsroman* (Munich: Wilhelm Fink Verlag, 1972), 271–78.

31   Jeffrey L. Sammons, "The Mystery of the Missing Bildungsroman, or What Happened to Wilhelm Meister's Legacy?," *Genre* 14, no. 2 (1981); Marc Redfield, *Phantom Formations: Aesthetic Ideology and the Bildungsroman* (Ithaca, NY: Cornell University Press, 1996).

32   Joseph R. Slaughter, *Human Rights, Inc.: The World Novel, Narrative Form, and International Law* (New York: Fordham University Press, 2007), 87.

33   Slaughter, *Human Rights, Inc.*, 114.

affirmative *Bildungsroman* has consistently served as a genre of demarginalization. . . ."[34] The substantive body of research on adaptations of the Bildungsroman that employ a marginalized protagonist supports this argument, as has also been emphasized by Tobias Boes, who states that the genre is highly adaptive and "continues to thrive in post-colonial, minority, multi-cultural, and immigrant literatures worldwide."[35] In this chapter, *Ellbogen* is interpreted as one such adaptation, one that transforms traditional motifs of the Bildungsroman and represents a deintegrative rewriting of the genre.

Historically, the Bildungsroman was significantly shaped by the emancipative ideals of the Enlightenment, lending a humanistic *Bildungsideal* (cultural or educational ideal) to the form. The optimistic mentality of the rising bourgeoisie cultivated the idea that success should not be granted by an authority but deserved through personal efforts, centering the individual's responsibility in shaping one's own life.[36] This journey toward maturity and social conformity takes place through confrontation with society, implying a reciprocal relationship between the individual and their environment. As Slaughter notes, "the *Bildungsroman* has its own double subjects—the individual and society—that need to be reconciled in the plot through dialectical interaction."[37] This inherent duality of the Bildungsroman, coupled with its historical importance in the development of a German national identity, renders contemporary rewritings of the genre especially effective for offering critical perspectives on current German society.

While the historical hero, a young, bourgeois white man, is altered by Aydemir, an exponentiation of the humanistic Bildungsideal can be observed. Current sociological analyses emphasize how contemporary capitalist societies of the Global North like Germany are significantly affected by social competition, economic growth, and an acceleration affecting almost all areas of life.[38] Hence the economic logic of optimization has expanded to all aspects of everyday life, and constant self-improvement has become imperative. Ideally, one strives for permanent self-optimization in both the professional and the private sphere, shifting any blame for failure onto the individual. The imperative of self-optimization hides any biographical as well as structural and institutionalized advantages and disadvantages, respectively, and thus also

---

34 Slaughter, *Human Rights, Inc.*, 134.

35 Tobias Boes, "Modernist Studies and the *Bildungsroman*: A Historical Survey of Critical Trends," *Literature Compass* 3, no. 2 (2006): 239.

36 Jacobs, *Wilhelm Meister und seine Brüder*, 274.

37 Slaughter, *Human Rights, Inc.*, 100.

38 Niels Uhlendorf, *Optimierungsdruck im Kontext von Migration: Eine diskurs- und biographieanalytische Untersuchung zu Subjektivationsprozessen* (Wiesbaden: Springer Fachmedien, 2018), 9.

functions as a strategy that legitimizes social inequalities by implying that those considered unsuccessful simply did not try hard enough.[39]

In the following, I will illustrate how Aydemir's novel *Ellbogen* offers a critical commentary on and intervention into these contemporary societal dynamics. In the first section, the focus will be on Hazal's social position, highlighting her experiences of violence and heteronomy. The following section explores how the text exposes the false promise of equal opportunity for all and analyzes how Hazal liberates herself through an act of violence. The final section attempts to interpret *Ellbogen* as a deintegrative rewriting of the Bildungsroman, culminating in a discussion of the ways in which this reinterpretation intersects with the concept of the burden of representation.

Hazal's Social Position in Society

Ellbogen's first-person narrator Hazal Akgündüz gives an account of her everyday life in Germany as the seventeen-year-old daughter of Kurdish immigrants from Turkey with a working-class background.

Hazal's father has been working as a taxi driver for twenty years. Her mother does not speak fluent German and, like Hazal herself, works in her uncle's bakery: "Einen anderen Job würde sie nie finden, sie kann ja nicht mal richtig lesen und schreiben" (She would never find another job; she can't even read and write properly).[40] Her parents' class background and German language skills make it difficult for them to support her at school and in daily life.

Despite writing nearly sixty applications, Hazal finds herself struggling to secure either a job or an apprenticeship; she consequently takes part in a prevocational education scheme offered by the job center. However, even with her secondary school education, Hazal departs from the school system at a disadvantage, soon realizing that her diploma does not readily convert into employment opportunities. Sociologist Aladin El-Mafaalani points to "educational inflation" owing to the reform and expansion of the German educational system in the last sixty years. Keeping people in school for longer and increasing the level of education of the general population ultimately leads to a devaluation of secondary school diplomas. Since opportunities increase for everyone, already privileged groups benefit more than disadvantaged ones, minimizing the positive effects for

---

39 Uhlendorf, *Optimierungsdruck*, 18.
40 Fatma Aydemir, *Ellbogen* (Munich: Hanser, 2017), 44f. Subsequent references to this source will be indicated by the abbreviation *EL* and page numbers in the text, followed by an English translation of the German original. All translations are my own.

deprived groups.[41] Hence, other qualifications, such as foreign language skills, gain significance with rising competition.

Such language skills and multilingualism are ambivalent forms of cultural capital in contemporary Germany. Olga Grjasnowa points to the hierarchization of languages within Germany, linking, for example, English and French to higher education and prestige while devaluing languages like Turkish or Arabic.[42] The perception of certain language skills crucially depends on the person who is speaking. While children with Turkish or Arabic roots are penalized for speaking their respective languages on German schoolyards, white Germans are praised for speaking "unusual" languages like Turkish, Arabic, or Chinese and further profit from it.[43] Since she does not benefit from the white privilege Grjasnowa refers to, Hazal's second language, Turkish, does not present an extra qualification in the eyes of potential employers.

A further hurdle for Hazal is the racism she is confronted with. Despite having been born and raised in Germany, occurrences like never being invited to her German friend's apartment (*EL*, 8) or being subjected to racial profiling (*EL*, 12) repeatedly remind her that many do not really perceive her as part of German society. When her Facebook friend Mehmet talks about how racist his teachers were, Hazal's internal reaction is "Standard" (*EL*, 148, standard). Children and young people of color experience various structural obstacles and discrimination on an institutional level. These mechanisms of unequal treatment can be identified especially with regard to school, where students of color performing equally well as white students do not get recommended for high-ranking schools.[44]

While Hazal is interrogated because she has forgotten to pay for mascara, the shop detective threatens to deport her to Turkey after checking her passport (*EL*, 14). Although she was born and raised in Germany, only spending summer holidays in Turkey, Hazal does not possess a German passport (*EL*, 27).[45] This denial of belonging on a structural level, paired with the enforced separation of Hazal and her cohort through spatial

---

41   Aladin El-Mafaalani, *Mythos Bildung: Die ungerechte Gesellschaft, ihr Bildungssystem und seine Zukunft* (Cologne: Kiepenheuer & Witsch, 2020), chap. 14.

42   Olga Grjasnowa, *Die Macht der Mehrsprachigkeit: Über Herkunft und Vielfalt* (Berlin: Duden Verlag, 2021), 65.

43   Grjasnowa, *Die Macht der Mehrsprachigkeit*, 92–93.

44   Tupoka Ogette, *exit RACISM: rassismuskritisch denken lernen* (Münster: Unrast Verlag, 2018), 109.

45   Hazal is born shortly before the reform of the citizenship law in the year 2000, which allowed children born in Germany to non-German parents to hold dual citizenship until they are obliged to decide on either one of them in their early twenties.

segregation, expressed through Hazal's frustration toward German girls who attended better schools than she did (*EL*, 164), all point to the structural racism permeating German society.

A scene in which Hazal tells her friend Elma how she is learning to write résumés at the job center draws attention to the racist discrimination on the job market. Through her reappropriation of the racist slur "Kanake,"[46] Elma asks, "Und was ist mit deiner Kanakenfresse? Gibt es auch irgendwelche Tricks für das Foto?" (*EL*, 54, What about your Kanakvisage? Are there any tricks for the photo?), to which Hazal replies: "Klar, das kann man photoshoppen" (*EL*, 54, Of course, you can photoshop it).[47] Both are aware that racist assumptions based on their appearance significantly lower their chances of finding employment in comparison with their white German competitors. *Ellbogen* illustrates that racism and discrimination not only reveal themselves in the form of intentional acts of individuals but must be understood as a system; that is, racism is not only expressed in direct hatred or violence, but also in the form of privileges and access.[48]

So far, it has become apparent that Hazal's position in a society that is permeated by misogyny, racism, white privilege, and class privilege is a disadvantaged one. In her daily life Hazal is subjected to what Pierre Bourdieu calls symbolic violence and power. The repressive effect of the symbolic violence does not present itself consciously or openly but lies in its self-evidence, which contributes to its general unrecognized acknowledgement necessary for the reproduction of social orders.[49] As Bourdieu puts it, "symbolic violence is violence wielded with tacit complicity

---

46 "Kanake" is a racist slur used in Germany for people with roots in Southeast Europe, the Middle East, and North Africa. The term has been reclaimed as a self-description and is being used in an empowered way by various communities. In 1995, Feridun Zaimoğlu published a book that drew public attention to the word. See Feridun Zaimoğlu, *Kanak Sprak—24 Mißtöne vom Rande der Gesellschaft* (Hamburg: Rotbuch, 2004).

47 Lucas Riddle analyzes how in *Ellbogen* the shared experiences of discrimination are reappropriated to "create laughter communities based on shared ... experiences of oppression, xenophobia, sexism, classism, and racism." See Lucas Riddle, "Constructing an 'Inside': Transcultural Laughter Communities in Fatma Aydemir's *Ellbogen* (2017) and Olga Grjasnowa's *Der Russe ist einer, der Birken liebt* (2012)," in *Germany from the Outside: Rethinking German Cultural History in an Age of Displacement*, ed. Laurie Ruth Johnson (New York: Bloomsbury Academic, 2022), 278.

48 Ogette, *exit RACISM*, 88, 108.

49 Pierre Bourdieu, *Masculine Domination* (Cambridge: Polity Press, 2001), 35. Bourdieu points out that the term of the symbolic is often misunderstood as downplaying physical violence. He reiterates that the symbolic is not to be understood as the opposite of the real and actual and that the real effects of symbolic violence should be recognized. See Bourdieu, *Masculine Domination*, 34.

between its victims and its agents, insofar as both remain unconscious of submitting or wielding to it."[50] Thus, a key element in maintaining symbolic violence is unconscious participation, which is the "personal contribution" of the dominated to their domination.

Regarding *Ellbogen*, Breger argues that "media images have an affective impact and contribute in piecemeal fashion to the performative configuration of experiences into individual and collective identifications."[51] How vital representation is for the development of a self-confident individual becomes apparent when Hazal recalls watching Fatih Akın's 2004 film *Gegen die Wand* (*Head-On*), stating that "[ich] zum ersten Mal das Gefühl hatte, dass ich nicht unsichtbar bin" (*EL*, 78; for the first time, I felt as if I'm not invisible). Bourdieu indicates that symbolic domination can also be exercised through a lack of visibility of certain subject positions, as it translates into "a refusal of legitimate, public existence."[52]

Exclusion from society is symbolized by closed doors throughout the novel. Hazal is not invited to her friend's apartment; she does not get access to the job market or to a nightclub; and, in reverse, she also encounters closed doors from within the patriarchal realm of her family, who forbid her to go out as she wishes. Throughout the novel, Hazal's subtle yet growing awareness of her disadvantaged social position, both in Germany and Turkey, is threaded between the lines. Aydemir's creation of a character like Hazal challenges the integration paradigm, presenting it as paradox. The narrative highlights the inherent contradiction of expecting Hazal to integrate into a societal structure that actively excludes her, thereby questioning the feasibility and fairness of such demands.

Rewriting Class in the Bildungsroman

Historically, the Bildungsroman served as a means of self-expression and profiling for the rising bourgeoisie in a period of sociohistorical change induced by the Enlightenment. The traditionally bourgeois heroes of the Bildungsroman therefore "venture out into the world to encounter experiences, often with members of different social classes, which leave a lasting mark on their evolving sense of self."[53] Aydemir alters this specific class position of the protagonist to a working-class background. Furthermore, the striving for a higher social status in the traditional form of the genre is not fulfilled. In Istanbul, Hazal meets the student Gözde, whose apparent higher social status, expressed through her disposition,

50 Pierre Bourdieu, *On Television*, trans. Priscilla Parkhurst Ferguson (New York: New Press, 1998), 17.
51 Breger, "Affect(ive) Assemblages," 201.
52 Bourdieu, *Masculine Domination*, 119.
53 Kontje, "The German Tradition of the Bildungsroman," 11.

appearance, and taste, upset Hazal. She thinks: "Gözdes gesamtes Leben ist wie eine Schablone, an der ich millimetergenau abmessen kann, was in meinem alles schiefläuft" (*EL*, 199; Gözde's entire life is like a template against which I can measure to the millimeter what is going wrong in mine). After lending Hazal her health insurance card, Gözde says, "Wow, da haben wir echt Glück gehabt, Hazal, Denn du siehst mir wirklich überhaupt nicht ähnlich. . . . Nebeneinander wirken wir wie . . . schwarz und weiß" (*EL*, 198; Wow, we got lucky there, Hazal, because you really don't look like me at all. . . . Next to each other we seem like . . . black and white).

This binary opposition of black and white evokes the terms *beyaz* and *siyah türkler*, meaning "white" and "black" Turks and referring to two contrasting social groups in Turkey. Class differences are commonly referred to by these attributes, whereby the term "white" Turks relates to the politically and economically dominant urban elite and "black" Turks stands for those from the rural areas of Anatolia. These are "figurative expressions that reflect a dualism in society, not based on skin color but on culture, lifestyle and social class."[54] Hazal's class position evidently does not change in Turkey but is rather reaffirmed by Gözde's distinction.

Rewriting the crucial plotline of upward social mobility, *Ellbogen* takes a critical stance toward the above established contemporary Bildungsideal of permanent self-optimization. The text demonstrates Hazal's limited opportunities and subtly points to the symbolically violent power and domination dynamics and discriminatory structures based on racism and sexism ingrained into a classed society. The resulting exclusion and oppression significantly restrict Hazal's chances in life, and they are worsened by the lack of recognition and support from her family. "Egal, was ist, für sie bin ich immer an allem selbst schuld. Wenn Lehrer mich scheiße behandelten, dann hatte ich mich 'nicht genug angestrengt'" (*EL*, 26, No matter what, in their eyes everything is always my fault. When teachers treat me like shit, I "didn't try hard enough").[55]

Aydemir's text implicitly critiques the mantras of a society entrenched in neoliberal, meritocratic, and capitalist ideologies. By exposing the harsh realities of social inequalities, the novel questions the validity of the pervasive belief that hard work alone leads to success, and it challenges the notion that failures are purely personal and self-inflicted. Considering not only the negatives for respective individuals but also the positives for dominant groups, it becomes evident that the principle of meritocracy is based on the systemic and structural discrimination of certain groups,

---

54 Seda Demiralp, "White Turks, Black Turks? Faultlines Beyond Islamism Versus Secularism," *Third World Quarterly* 33, no. 3 (2012): 514.
55 See also *EL* 249.

which in return implies privileges for others. In Aydemir's novel, the promise of equal opportunity for all is therefore exposed as false.

Countering Stereotypical Victimization

The difficult external conditions influencing Hazal's development are reinforced in the realm of the family. Previous research on Bildungsromane featuring marginalized protagonists often highlights the strong bond between the individual and their community.[56] However, Hazal's experience diverges from this pattern. Her family is characterized by violent conflicts, restrictions, and rejection. Hazal has hardly spoken to her father since he violently cut off her waist-length hair at the age of fourteen in response to her forgetting her keys and spending the afternoon at her friend Gül's house. Hazal's father holds prejudices against Gül's family because they are Alevi, a group that has been persecuted since the Ottoman Empire and continues to be in the Turkish Republic, as the pogroms of Kahramanmaraş (1978), Çorum (1980), and Sivas (1993) showed. Hazal's parents deploy a centuries-old stereotype of Alevi pursuing incestuous relationships (*EL*, 204).[57] Here, Aydemir complicates the stereotypical perception of the Turkish community in Germany as a homogeneous group.

In response to the violence from her father and the apparent indifference of her mother, Hazal reaches a point of desperation. Mirroring Sibel's actions in Akın's *Gegen die Wand*, she attempts suicide (*EL*, 205). The severity of her situation is further underscored when her mother, upon discovering Hazal's self-harm, coldly remarks that she would quickly move on and eventually forget her if Hazal were to die (*EL*, 186). It is therefore not surprising that Hazal feels despised by her mother and, conversely, looks down on her too (*EL*, 44). Her mother openly expresses her disdain for Hazal: "Ich war ehrlich zu Pelin. Ich habe gesagt: Hazal ist nicht die klügste. Aber putzen und Haare waschen, das kriegt sie gerade noch so hin" (*EL*, 41; I was honest with Pelin. I said: Hazal is not the smartest. But she will just about manage to clean and wash hair [in the salon]).

Hazal experiences her family primarily as a patriarchal place of heteronomy that grants her younger brother Onur significantly more freedom and where her future seems to be predetermined. She anticipates that she is supposed to get married (*EL*, 49) and have children—"was sollen wir

---

56 Stella Bolaki, *Unsettling the Bildungsroman: Reading Contemporary Ethnic American Women's Fiction* (Amsterdam: Rodopi, 2011), 91.

57 Severin Weiland, "Aleviten demonstrieren gegen 'Inzest'-Tatort," *Der Spiegel*, December 27, 2007, https://www.spiegel.de/kultur/gesellschaft/ard-buero-berlinaleviten-demonstrieren-gegen-inzest-tatort-a-525505.html.

denn sonst tun?" (*EL*, 116, what else are we supposed to do?)—and has little hope for a different or better future, which is only increased by her mother's lack of confidence in her. Therefore, Hazal experiences a doubled devaluation of herself. On the one hand, from the dominant part of society and additionally through the reinforcement of this marginalized position by her family's lack of appreciation and support.

Ellbogen shares notable similarities with *Gegen die Wand* not only in the portrayal of Hazal's and Sibel's attempted suicides but also in its depiction of patriarchal and misogynist violence, as well as the protagonists' yearning to break free from their constrained lives. Moreover, Hazal and Sibel both reject the stereotype of the Muslim woman as a victim while using it to their advantage at the same time.[58] To avoid a police complaint, Hazal performs the role of "das arme, arme türkische Mädchen, fehlt nur noch das Kopftuch" (*EL*, 17, the poor, poor Turkish girl, only missing the headscarf). Anticipating the detective's perception of Turkish women to be biased and based on the stereotype of the oppressed Turkish woman in need of rescue, she successfully garners his sympathy and avoids prosecution by embodying the cliché.[59] Both Akın and Aydemir offer counter narratives to the conventional portrayal of Muslim women solely as victims. While Sibel and Hazal *are* victims of symbolic and physical male violence, they also challenge the notion of victimhood by themselves becoming agents of violence.[60]

Liberation through Violence

In the novel, there is a dramatic turning point at which Hazal conclusively breaks ties with her community as well as German society. On the night of her eighteenth birthday, Hazal and her friends are rejected at the door of a nightclub on racist and classist grounds (*EL*, 114). When Hazal is later asked if only Germans were allowed in, she replies: "Nein, aber auch keine Kanaken. Nur so . . . Ausländer, die Kohle haben und keinen Ärger machen. Und so dreckige Turnschuhe tragen" (*EL*, 240; No, but no

---

58   For the literary motif of Turkish women as victims, see Tom Cheesman, *Novels of Turkish German Settlement: Cosmopolite Fictions* (Rochester, NY: Camden House, 2007), 113–22.

59   Timo Sestu interprets Hazal's use of a cliché as a strategy of doubled irony as reality and illusion coincide. See Sestu, "Verlangen ohne Liebe," 227. See the following for the way Sibel uses clichés to her advantage: Jochen Neubauer, *Türkische Deutsche, Kanakster und Deutschländer: Identität und Fremdwahrnehmung in Film und Literatur; Fatih Akın, Thomas Arslan, Emine Sevgi Özdamar, Zafer Şenocak und Feridun Zaimoğlu* (Würzburg: Königshausen & Neumann, 2011), 235.

60   Even though Sibel does not commit homicide, she does stand up for herself and physically attacks a man after being verbally harassed.

Kanaks either. Just like foreigners who have money and don't cause trouble and wear dirty sneakers). Dressed up in high heels and wearing a lot of makeup and perfume (*EL*, 95), the friends do not match the style and the appearance required by the nightclub.[61] Classism and Islamophobia intersect, and the symbolic violence that Hazal and her friends have been subjected to for their entire lives culminates in this rejection. Their social exclusion is once again epitomized by a closed door, symbolized by the "Wand aus Beton" (*EL*, 109; wall of concrete) the doorman builds up by refusing them entry. The friends go home, "nicht, weil wir nach Hause wollen, sondern, weil wir immer nach Hause müssen" (*EL*, 116; not because we want to go home, but because we always have to go home). The accumulated anger about their marginalization and exclusion leads to a violent outbreak in an underground station, where Hazal pushes a man onto the train tracks killing him.

Even if it can be argued that it happened impulsively and was not intended, the homicide is preceded by the intangible yet pervasive experiences of symbolic violence, discrimination, and exclusion that Hazal has endured. This underlying turmoil is encapsulated in Hazal's own words: "Aber das war nicht nur wegen der Nacht oder wegen dem Studenten, ich war schon vorher wütend, die ganze Zeit" (*EL*, 245; But it wasn't just because of the night or because of the student, I was angry before, all the time). The young man, whom Hazal kills with a grin on her face (*EL*, 210), becomes an allegory for the three cornerstones of her oppression. His masculinity, which is exaggerated when he threatens to show them his genitals (*EL*, 121), represents the gendered discrimination Hazal experiences. Her projection of him being a student epitomizes the systemic educational inequities affecting Hazal's prospects. Being a white German (*EL*, 121), he further represents the dominant part of society that Hazal is excluded from. He therefore symbolizes all the microaggressions, all the "Ellbogen, die uns das Leben reingerammt hat, immer wieder, und immer noch. Überall nur Ellbogen von denen, die stärker sind als wir" (*EL*, 237, Elbows that life has rammed into us, again and again, and still. Everywhere just elbows from those who are stronger than us). There is a temporary reversal of power when the metaphorical elbows materialize in the moment Hazal uses her elbow to attack the young man (*EL*, 122).

By killing the figurative white, educationally privileged, male center, Hazal temporarily liberates herself from being symbolically dominated, which is reiterated when she describes how the push feels like "ein Stoß an der richtigen, passenden Stelle" (*EL*, 123, a push at the right, appropriate place). The destructive moment paradoxically presents an opportunity and a way out for Hazal: "Und nach der Nacht war alles plötzlich

---

61 Being able to wear dirty and worn-out sneakers as a distinctive style without being stigmatized is matter of a privileged class position.

anders. . . . [E]s hat sich so angefühlt, als sei nicht schon jeder Stein auf meinem Weg vorherbestimmt. Als gäbe es da einfach noch eine andere Möglichkeit vor mir" (*EL*, 245, And after this night, everything was suddenly different. . . . [I]t felt as if not every stone on my path was predetermined. As if there was just another possibility in front of me). Even though Hazal's escape entails fleeing to Istanbul to avoid persecution, her flight represents more than just a physical departure. It symbolizes an escape from the confining and unpromising life that seemed predestined for her in Germany. In the context of *Ellbogen*, Hazal's act of violence thus acquires a liberatory connotation. Moreover, I agree with Timo Sestu's interpretation of the violent act as deintegrative.[62] However, in the following I want to extend this interpretation by paying attention to Hazal's behavior *after* the homicide and how it relates back to Aydemir's deintegrative rewriting of the Bildungsroman.

A Deintegrative Rewriting of the Bildungsroman

In a key scene, Hazal talks to Aunt Semra, who initially appears to assume a mentor role, which is a typical figure in the Bildungsroman.[63] Semra follows Hazal to Istanbul to convince her to return to Germany, and it briefly seems like the Bildungsroman will hold true to its traditional form, in which the protagonist eventually integrates into their original society. However, after the conversation with Semra, Hazal's integration into German society seems highly unlikely, since Aydemir's text denies both Aunt Semra and the reader any anticipated catharsis. This is epitomized in Hazal's declaration: "Wir sind nicht auf ihn losgegangen, weil es ein schlechter Abend war. Sondern weil er es verdient hat!" (*EL*, 243, We didn't attack him because we had a bad night. But because he deserved it!). In expressing her lack of remorse for having killed a person, Hazal breaks with the rules and unquestioned beliefs that underpin social coexistence. Typically, in cases where a homicide is unplanned and impulsive, there is an expectation for the perpetrator to express regret for their actions. Hazal's defiance of this expectation marks a significant break from conventional responses. It becomes apparent that Hazal does not feel guilty about what she has done because she despises the entitlement and the unearned privileges of the dominant part of society, epitomized by the young man she has killed (*EL*, 244).

The disruption that lies in the liberatory connotation of Hazal's violence is enhanced by her lack of remorse, which leaves the reader with

---

62 Sestu, "Verlangen ohne Liebe," 226.
63 Ortrud Gutjahr, *Einführung in den Bildungsroman* (Darmstadt: WGB, 2007), 46.

unanswered questions. The novel's extratextual effects are thus twofold. On the one hand, it holds the possibility for a partial identification for German Turks and people of color who have similar experiences of racism and discrimination, just like Fatih Akın's film does for Hazal. By writing about marginalized social positions and pointing to relations of power and domination on the other hand, it addresses an implicit white German readership and demands self-reflection about one's own privileges and social position. Here, Aydemir's text intersects with the traditional Bildungsroman, which was known for its didactic function, extending its educational scope to the reader's self-reflection.[64]

Unlike the conventional Bildungsroman, which often offers clear answers or role models, *Ellbogen* challenges readers with open questions, inviting them to reflect and take initiative to pursue one's own *Bildung* on how a peaceful coexistence could look like in contemporary German society. This aspect relates back to the notion of deintegration, which shifts the focus from how individual groups integrate into society to recognizing society itself as a space of radical diversity.[65]

Hazal dismisses Semra's attempts to persuade her to return and instead abandons her and her life in Germany. In contrast to the traditional Bildungsroman, there is no return or successful integration of the protagonist into society. In the rewriting of a genre, the modification of a traditional element often points to its original function and in its subversion assigns it with new meaning.[66] In the traditional Bildungsroman, the successful return and integration of the protagonist functions as an affirmation and confirmation of the values and structures of society.[67] By modifying it, *Ellbogen* illustrates that the plot structure of integration does not suffice for protagonists like Hazal, because racist, sexist, patriarchal and classed society excludes her in the first place. This rejection of the traditional plot structure highlights the societal circumstances that prevent a successful *Bildung* in the classical sense of the genre. Furthermore, by challenging this particular part of the form of the Bildungsroman, Aydemir, by extension, criticizes the integration paradigm prevalent in German society.

Hazal leaves the country she grew up in behind but finds herself in a similar situation in Istanbul. Her social position is reaffirmed during encounters with people like Gözde and her relationship with Facebook

---

64 Rolf Selbmann, *Der deutsche Bildungsroman*, 2nd rev. ed. (Stuttgart: Metzler, 1994), 8. See also Slaughter, *Human Rights, Inc.*, 117.

65 Czollek, *Desintegriert euch!*, 73–74.

66 Petra Fachinger, *Rewriting Germany from the Margins: "Other" German Literature of the 1980s and 1990s* (Montreal: McGill-Queen's University Press, 2001), 21.

67 Slaughter, *Human Rights, Inc.*, 124.

friend Mehmet turns out to be full of emotional and sexual violence in real life. Briefly attempting to connect with her Kurdish roots, which are curiously absent in the novel and never discussed within the family, she quickly concludes: "Ich gehöre nirgendwo hin" (*EL*, 214; I don't belong anywhere). Hazal withdraws into her own world, into "Hazalia," where all her traumatic experiences lie but where it is also warm and familiar (*EL*, 270). This retreat into her innermost self, points to total individuality, which corresponds to the individualistic form of the Bildungsroman. However, individualism is not constructed as something worth striving for in the sense of successful formation of the self through a process of emancipation, but as a necessity to escape the repressive and discriminatory societal structures. "Mir kann sowieso keiner helfen, nur ich selbst" (*EL*, 251; No one can help me, except me, anyway).

By presenting individualism as a chance for unhindered development but reframing it as a necessary shield against oppression, and by fundamentally challenging the key plot structure of integration, *Ellbogen* reads as an antagonistic rewriting of the genre. Crucially, Hazal's withdrawal represents a stark departure from the duality typically seen in the Bildungsroman, as discussed above. The classic reconciliation between the protagonist and society becomes unattainable in the novel, given the one-sided nature of the integration demands that inherently exclude the individual from the outset. Consequently, Slaughter's claim that the Bildungsroman is a "demarginalizing genre" seems ill-fitted in the context of *Ellbogen*.[68] Instead, Aydemir rewrites the Bildungsroman as a genre of deintegration, since it challenges the idea of a dominant societal center, which demands integration from those it perceives as outsiders, questioning whether this is a viable approach to ensuring equal participation in a radically diverse society.[69]

From a postmigrant perspective, the deintegrative rewriting of the Bildungsroman proves to be an effective literary strategy to articulate social criticism about how plurality is managed in a nation of immigration. It underscores "the societal negotiations linked to migration" and does not solely center migrated or migrantized individuals but rather "focus[es] on the power relationships and struggles unfolding in society as a whole."[70]

Although *Ellbogen* is a deintegrative rewriting of the Bildungsroman and hence does not fulfill the expectations of the traditional form in terms of moral growth and maturity, or an integration into and an acceptance of society's values, its main character Hazal does realize something crucial:

---

68 Slaughter, *Human Rights, Inc.*, 134.
69 Czollek, *Desintegriert euch!*, 15.
70 Gaonkar et al., "Introduction," 21.

Ich soll Reue zeigen, na klar. Dabei müsste Semra doch wirklich wissen, wie der Scheiß läuft. . . . Irgendwelche Leute haben das Sagen und versuchen, die anderen fertigzumachen und mit dem Finger auf sie zu zeigen. . . . Und ja, hier in Istanbul werde ich auch nie etwas zu melden haben, aber darum geht es nicht. Ich verstehe nur endlich, wie die Sache läuft, ich verstehe, dass die Welt scheißungerecht ist und dass sie anders besser wäre, aber anders wird sie nie werden. Doch das liegt nicht an mir. Und dass ich das weiß, wird mir vielleicht nicht helfen so im praktischen Leben. Aber es hilft meinem Herz. (*EL*, 249–50)

[I'm supposed to show remorse, of course. But Semra should really know how this shit works. . . . Random people are in charge and try to screw others over and point their finger at them. . . . And yes, I will never have a say here in Istanbul either, but that's not the point. I just finally understand how things work, I understand, that the world is fucking unfair and that it would be better if it was different, but it will never be any different. But that's not my fault. And knowing that might not practically help me in life. But it helps my heart.]

Hazal's growing awareness of symbolic violence and domination—even if it occurs unconsciously—is critical to her sense of well-being. While she may be powerless to alter the overarching social conditions in which she finds herself, this realization itself embodies a form of resistance. Crucially, the symbolic violence is being met with the realization of its arbitrariness, which deprives it of its power.[71] Hazal at least partially withdraws her "personal contribution" to and her "tacit complicity" in being symbolically dominated, which gives her a level of inner peace and agency and a different perspective on her life. Hence, even though she does not achieve *Bildung* in the classical sense of the word, she does arguably undergo a process of formation and liberation, which is paradoxically induced through an act of violence.

Concluding Remarks: Rejecting the Burden of Representation

With the Bildungsroman, Aydemir rewrites a genre historically seen as a quintessentially German form of the novel that was instrumentalized in establishing a German national literature and to advance the idea of a shared national identity. In order to analyze *Ellbogen*, I adopted a postmigrant perspective, focusing on the negotiation and struggle for equal

---

71 Pierre Bourdieu and Richard Nice, *The Logic of Practice* (Cambridge: Polity Press, 1990), 303.

participation in a society characterized by immigration. This perspective reveals the Bildungsroman, with its inherent duality of the individual and society, as an especially effective tool for critically examining and reflecting on the fabric of contemporary German society.

The text exemplifies how descendants of immigrants—even if they are born and raised in Germany—are still Othered and discriminated against; it therefore challenges Germany's understanding of itself as a country of immigration and an open society.[72] Furthermore, Hazal's limited chances in life are not only related to her ascribed Turkishness being perceived as problematic by the dominant society, but crucially also to her working-class background. By rewriting the dimension of class in the Bildungsroman and altering the plotline of social mobility, *Ellbogen* exposes the promise of equal opportunity for everyone as false and thereby explicitly critiques one of the main pillars of Germany's current understanding of itself. Hazal's personal failure, which is only partly rooted in her upbringing, thus points to society's failure to accept and appreciate its own diversity in terms of cultural, ethnic, *and* class backgrounds.

The liberatory connotation of Hazal's violent act and especially her lack of remorse afterward, leave open questions and confront white readers and members of the dominant part of society with uncomfortable questions regarding their privileges and their supremacy. *Ellbogen* is an invitation to reflect and think about how equal coexistence can be realized in a society marked by profound diversity. Simultaneously, it acts as a cautionary tale urging us not to limit our attention to marginalized groups only during times of crisis, a fact that is underlined by the following quotation: "Wenn wir einen Thorsten vor die U-Bahn schmeißen, wollen sie auf einmal wissen, wer wir sind" (*EL*, 249; When we throw a Thorsten in front of the train, they suddenly want to know who we are).

In *Ellbogen*, the traditional plot structure of the Bildungsroman—which typically culminates in the protagonist's successful integration into society—is rewritten and ascribed with new meaning. Through the homicide, Hazal kills the figurative dominant center that demands her integration rather than affirming and accepting its condition and values. Her failed integration therefore points to the social inequality and to the exclusion she experiences from that center, preventing her integration in the first place. Therefore, *Ellbogen* can be seen as a deintegrative rewriting of the canonical genre of the Bildungsroman. This approach emerges as a potent literary strategy for voicing social criticism, illuminating the realities of subject positions that have been commonly marginalized both in

---

72 It should be added here that Black people and people of color without a history of immigration can also experience said discrimination.

German society and its literature,[73] as well as the role the dominant part of society plays in this.

Furthermore, the concept of deintegration holds additional significance in the interpretation of *Ellbogen*, particularly in how Aydemir addresses the burden of representation. It is often minorities that are exposed to the burden of representation, a notion that Kobena Mercer uses in reference to Black art.[74] The burden of representation implies that the work of an individual artist or author who is associated with a minority or a marginalized group is often thought of as representing and speaking on behalf of the entire community.[75] Therefore, the dominant part of society evaluates such art and literature based on certain expectations, often foregrounding a supposed documentary over an aesthetic value of the work. Additionally, the community wants to or rather does not want to be represented in a certain way. Therefore, there exists a "hunger for minority success stories,"[76] putting a doubled burden of representation on minority groups.

With Fatih Akın, Aydemir references a filmmaker who himself was confronted with the burden of representation, as he states in an interview with the author.[77] Within the novel this becomes apparent through the comment of Hazal's mother after having watched the film: "Aber Mama hat nur mit der Zunge geschnalzt und 'Allah Allah' gemurmelt, und dann behauptet, die hätten den Film nur gemacht, damit wir Türken schlecht Dastehen" (*EL*, 78f; But mom just clucked her tongue and muttered "Allah Allah" and then claimed that they only made the film to make us Turks look bad). *Gegen die Wand* is a reference to an important work in the struggle of authors and filmmakers experiencing migrantization or

---

73   For a historic overview on the exclusion and ghettoization of writers with a family history of immigration, see Wiebke Sievers and Sandra Vlasta, "From the Exclusion of Individual Authors to the Transnationalisation of the Literary Field: Immigrant and Ethnic-Minority Writing in Germany," in *Immigrant and Ethnic-Minority Writers since 1945: Fourteen National Contexts in Europe and Beyond*, ed. Wiebke Sievers and Sandra Vlasta (Leiden: Brill Rodopi, 2018).

74   It was Mark Stein who used this concept in relation to Black British novels of formation, which he calls *novels of transformation*. See Mark Stein, *Black British Literature: Novels of Transformation* (Columbus: Ohio State University Press, 2004).

75   Mercer, "Black Art and the Burden of Representation," 65.

76   Kobena Mercer, "Iconography after Identity," in *Shades of Black: Assembling Black Arts in 1980s Britain*, ed. David A. Bailey, Ian Baucom, and Sonia Boyce (Durham, NC: Duke University Press, 2005), 51.

77   Fatih Akin, "Rache ist nichts Ethnisches," interview by Fatma Aydemir, *taz*, November 19, 2017, https://taz.de/Fatih-Akin-zum-Film-Aus-dem-Nichts/!5460666/.

Othering in general, to having their work perceived solely as art in its own right, rather than as a representation of a heterogeneous group of people.

By creating an antiheroine like Hazal and connecting her intertextually with Sibel, Aydemir deliberately follows in Akın's footsteps. Through Hazal's complex character, *Ellbogen* resists feeding the hunger for success stories and rejects the doubled burden of representation while at the same time drawing its transformative potential from the tension created by such an antagonistic protagonist. This rejection of the burden of representation can be circled back to Czollek's notion of deintegration: the narrative neither caters to expectations of positive community representation nor fears misappropriation by right-wing groups. Just as the act of violence in the story liberates Hazal, it frees the author from the extratextual burden of representation. Consequently, this approach can be seen as a twofold application of deintegration as a literary strategy.

Bibliography

Akin, Fatih. "Rache ist nichts Ethnisches." Interview by Fatma Aydemir. *Taz*, November 19, 2017. https://taz.de/Fatih-Akin-zum-Film-Aus-dem-Nichts/!5460666/.

Aydemir, Fatma. *Ellbogen*. Munich: Hanser, 2017.

Boes, Tobias. "Modernist Studies and the *Bildungsroman*: A Historical Survey of Critical Trends." *Literature Compass* 3, no. 2 (2006): 230–43.

Bolaki, Stella. *Unsettling the Bildungsroman: Reading Contemporary Ethnic American Women's Fiction*. Amsterdam: Rodopi, 2011.

Bourdieu, Pierre. *Masculine Domination*. Cambridge: Polity Press, 2001.

———. *On Television*. Translated by Priscilla Parkhurst Ferguson. New York: New Press, 1998.

Bourdieu, Pierre, and Richard Nice. *The Logic of Practice*. Cambridge: Polity Press, 1990.

Bovermann, Philipp. "Diese Wut Gehört Ihr." *Süddeutsche Zeitung*, February 3, 2017. https://www.sueddeutsche.de/kultur/deutsche-gegenwartsliteratur-diese-wut-gehoert-ihr-1.3362316.

Breger, Claudia. "Affect(ive) Assemblages. Literary Worldmaking in Fatma Aydemir's *Ellbogen*." In *Public Spheres of Resonance: Constellations of Affect and Language*, edited by Anne Fleig and Christian von Scheve, 189–209. London: Routledge, 2020.

Cha, Kyung-Ho. "The Postmigrant Critique of the Bildungsroman and the Epistemic Injustice of the Educational System in Deniz Ohde's *Scattered Light*." In *Epistemic Justice and Creative Agency: Global Perspectives on Literature and Film*, edited by Sarah Colvin and Stephanie Galasso, 131–47. New York: Routledge, 2022.

Cheesman, Tom. *Novels of Turkish German Settlement: Cosmopolite Fictions*. Rochester, NY: Camden House, 2007.

Cho-Polizzi, Jon. "'Almanya: A [Different] Future Is Possible' Defying Narratives of Return in Fatma Aydemir's Ellbogen." *TRANSIT* 13, no. 2 (2021): 98–110.
Czollek, Max. *Desintegriert Euch!* Munich: Carl Hanser Verlag, 2018.
Demiralp, Seda. "White Turks, Black Turks? Faultlines Beyond Islamism Versus Secularism." *Third World Quarterly* 33, no. 3 (2012): 511–24. https://doi.org/10.1080/01436597.2012.657487.
Dyer, Richard. "The Matter of Whiteness." In *White Privilege: Essential Readings on the Other Side of Racism*, edited by Paula S. Rothenberg, 9–14. New York: Worth, 2008.
El-Mafaalani, Aladin. *Mythos Bildung: Die ungerechte Gesellschaft, ihr Bildungssystem und seine Zukunft*. Cologne: Kiepenheuer & Witsch, 2020.
Fachinger, Petra. *Rewriting Germany from the Margins: "Other" German Literature of the 1980s and 1990s*. Montreal: McGill-Queen's University Press, 2001. https://www.jstor.org/stable/j.ctt80rcq.1.
Foroutan, Naika. *Die postmigrantische Gesellschaft: Ein Versprechen der pluralen Demokratie*. Bielefeld: transcript Verlag, 2019.
———. "Die Postmigrantische Perspektive: Aushandlungsprozesse in Pluralen Gesellschaften." In *Postmigrantische Visionen: Erfahrungen—Ideen—Reflexionen*, edited by Marc Hill and Erol Yıldız, 15–27. Bielefeld: transcript, 2018.
Gaonkar, Anna Meera, Astrid Sophie Øst Hansen, Hans Christian Post, and Moritz Schramm. "Introduction." In *Postmigration: Art, Culture, and Politics in Contemporary Europe*, edited by Anna Meera Gaonkar, Astrid Sophie Øst Hansen, Hans Christian Post, and Moritz Schramm, 11–42. Bielefeld: transcript, 2021.
Grjasnowa, Olga. *Die Macht der Mehrsprachigkeit: Über Herkunft und Vielfalt*. Berlin: Duden Verlag, 2021.
Gutjahr, Ortrud. *Einführung in den Bildungsroman*. Darmstadt: WGB, 2007.
Hampel, Anna. *Literarische Reflexionsräume des Politischen: Neuausrichtungen in Erzähltexten der Gegenwart*. Berlin: de Gruyter, 2021.
Herrmann, Moritz. "'Ellbogen': Gewaltige Wut." ZEIT ONLINE, April 16, 2018. https://www.zeit.de/2018/16/ellbogen-fatma-aydemir-junges-schauspielhaus.
hooks, bell. "Representations of Whiteness in the Black Imagination." In *Black Looks: Race and Representation*, 165–78. New York: Routledge, 2015.
Jacobs, Jürgen. *Wilhelm Meister und seine Brüder: Untersuchungen zum deutschen Bildungsroman*. Munich: Wilhelm Fink Verlag, 1972.
Kontje, Todd. "The German Tradition of the Bildungsroman." In *A History of the Bildungsroman*, edited by Sarah Graham, 10–32. Cambridge: Cambridge University Press, 2019.
Luna, Alvaro. "The Way of the Majority's World: Language as a *Bildung* Lesson in Tomás Rivera's . . . *Y No Se Lo Tragó La Tierra* and Azouz Begag's *Le Gone Du Chaâba*." *Symposium* 73, no. 3 (2019): 172–84.

McIntosh, Peggy. "White Privilege: Unpacking the Invisible Knapsack." Accessed April 4, 2023. https://psychology.umbc.edu/wp-content/uploads/sites/57/2016/10/White-Privilege_McIntosh-1989.pdf.
Mercer, Kobena. "Black Art and the Burden of Representation." *Third Text* 4, no. 10 (1990): 61–78.
———. "Iconography after Identity." In *Shades of Black: Assembling Black Arts in 1980s Britain*, edited by David A. Bailey, Ian Baucom, and Sonia Boyce. Durham, NC: Duke University Press, 2005. https://ebookcentral-proquest-com.manchester.idm.oclc.org/lib/manchester/detail.action?docID=3007876.
Neubauer, Jochen. *Türkische Deutsche, Kanakster und Deutschländer: Identität und Fremdwahrnehmung in Film und Literatur; Fatih Akın, Thomas Arslan, Emine Sevgi Özdamar, Zafer Şenocak und Feridun Zaimoğlu*. Würzburg: Königshaus & Neumann, 2011.
Ogette, Tupoka. *exit RACISM: rassismuskritisch denken lernen*. Münster: Unrast Verlag, 2018.
Petersen, Anne Ring, Moritz Schramm, and Frauke Wiegand. "Postmigration as a Concept (Reception, Histories, Criticism)." In *Reframing Migration, Diversity and the Arts: The Postmigrant Condition*, edited by Moritz Schramm, Sten Pultz Moslund, and Anne Ring Petersen, 1–64. New York: Routledge, 2019.
Redfield, Marc. *Phantom Formations: Aesthetic Ideology and the Bildungsroman*. Ithaca, NY: Cornell University Press, 1996.
Riddle, Lucas. "Constructing an 'Inside': Transcultural Laughter Communities in Fatma Aydemir's *Ellbogen* (2017) and Olga Grjasnowa's *Der Russe ist einer, der Birken liebt* (2012)." In *Germany from the Outside: Rethinking German Cultural History in an Age of Displacement*, edited by Laurie Ruth Johnson, 261–80. New York: Bloomsbury Academic, 2022.
Sammons, Jeffrey L. "The Mystery of the Missing Bildungsroman, or What Happened to Wilhelm Meister's Legacy?" *Genre* 14, no. 2 (1981): 229–46.
Schramm, Moritz. "Jenseits der binären Logik: Postmigrantische Perspektiven für die Literatur- und Kulturwissenschaft." In *Postmigrantische Perspektiven: Ordnungssysteme, Repräsentationen, Kritik*, edited by Naika Foroutan, Juliane Karakayali, and Riem Spielhaus, 83–94. Bonn: Campus Verlag, 2018.
Selbmann, Rolf. "Der Bildungsroman ist tot—Es lebe der Bildungsroman? Überlegungen zur Begriffsbestimmung einer bedrohten Gattung." *Prospero: Rivista di letterature e culture straniere*, no. 26 (2021): 31–52. https://doi.org/10.13137/2283-6438/33288.
———. *Der Deutsche Bildungsroman*. 2nd rev. ed. Stuttgart: Metzler, 1994.
Sestu, Timo. "Verlangen ohne Liebe, Rand ohne Mitte. Literarische Figurationen von Desintegration." In *Fremdheit, Integration, Vielfalt? Interdisziplinäre Perspektiven auf Migration und Gesellschaft*, edited by Christine Lubkoll, Eva Forrester, and Timo Sestu. Ethik—Text—Kultur, 215–35. Leiden: Brill Fink, 2021.

Sievers, Wiebke, and Sandra Vlasta. "From the Exclusion of Individual Authors to the Transnationalisation of the Literary Field: Immigrant and Ethnic-Minority Writing in Germany." In *Immigrant and Ethnic-Minority Writers since 1945: Fourteen National Contexts in Europe and Beyond*, edited by Wiebke Sievers and Sandra Vlasta, 219–58. Leiden: Brill Rodopi, 2018.

Slaughter, Joseph R. *Human Rights, Inc.: The World Novel, Narrative Form, and International Law*. New York: Fordham University Press, 2007.

Stein, Mark. *Black British Literature: Novels of Transformation*. Columbus: Ohio State University Press, 2004.

Uhlendorf, Niels. *Optimierungsdruck im Kontext von Migration: Eine Diskurs- und Biographieanalytische Untersuchung zu Subjektivationsprozessen*. Wiesbaden: Springer Fachmedien, 2018.

Weiland, Severin. "Aleviten demonstrieren gegen 'Inzest'-Tatort." *Der Spiegel*, December 27, 2007. https://www.spiegel.de/kultur/gesellschaft/ard-buero-berlinaleviten-demonstrieren-gegen-inzest-tatort-a-525505.html.

Zaimoğlu, Feridun. *Kanak Sprak—24 Mißtöne vom Rande der Gesellschaft*. Hamburg: Rotbuch, 2004.

8: Reorienting Knowledge of Structural Systems of Violence in Sharon Dodua Otoo's *Adas Raum* and Antje Rávik Strubel's *Blaue Frau*

Alrik Daldrup[1]

In Need of Just Representations

THE REPRESENTATION OF violence in literature or on screen raises ethical problems in the context of power relations. To want more disturbing images that depict death and annihilation risks reinforcing voyeuristic addiction. To do so may even reproduce the act of violence by portraying it in way that silences the victims. Sharon Dodua Otoo, a British-German writer of Ghanaian descent, has made the observation that most marginalized characters in German literary history have either been killed off or simply described in terms of "the bad things that happen to them, how poor they are."[2] She wants to tell stories of resistance, in search of representations that do not ridicule, violate, or retraumatize real-life marginalized readers. Antje Rávik Strubel, a long-established author who is still largely unrecognized in German studies even within Germany,[3] intervenes in the debate over who has the authority to determine who we can be and what kind of names and appellations we can adopt. In her acceptance speech for the German Book Prize 2021, Strubel stated that her

---

1   I would like to thank the editors Selma Rezgui, Laura Marie Sturtz, and Tara Talwar Windsor for their support and patience. My thanks also go out to Jeannette Oholi and Kendal Karaduman for reading an earlier version of this article.

2   "Afropolitanism and 'Ada's Realm': A Conversation with Sharon Dodua Otoo," Jesus College, Cambridge, October 16, 2023, YouTube video, 1:14:45, https://www.youtube.com/watch?v=FXBcO1MpAvI.

3   Simone Pfleger notes that it is mainly American Germanists who have published on Strubel's writing. See Simone Pfleger, "Temporal and Corporeal Re-Imaginings in Antje Rávic Strubel's *Kältere Schichten der Luft* (2007)," in *Protest und Verweigerung/Protest and Refusal*, ed. Hans Adler and Sonja Klocke (Leiden: Brill, 2018), 179.

characters resist common sense.[4] Both writers reflect, in their works of fiction, on political discourses regarding intersectionality, rape, human rights, and European politics of memory.

By comparing Otoo's *Adas Raum* (Ada's Room, 2021)[5] and Strubel's *Blaue Frau* (Blue Woman, 2021),[6] I argue that both texts represent violence against those outside the social norm in nonvoyeuristic ways. For my analysis, I combine Sara Ahmed's discussion of structural violence and trigger warnings[7] with James Odhiambo Ogone's notion of "representational epistemic injustice."[8] I use these theories to analyze the violent processes of Othering that declare marginalized subjects legitimate targets of racist and sexist practices, and I consider how these processes are counteracted by the literary texts. In this way, both novels stand against systemic structures of violence without themselves being agents of harm in entangled apparatuses of domination.

Although different in scope and scale, the forms of violence juxtaposed in *Adas Raum* and *Blaue Frau* are multiple: linguistic harassment, physical captivity, enslavement, torture, rape, forced abortion, femicide, and genocide. Across four temporal strands, Otoo's *Adas Raum* narrates the multiple lives of Ada, an African and a European woman who wanders on a *Bildungsweg* through space and time. All of Otoo's Adas share the traumatic experience of violence and carry a history of femicides with them; only the fourth survives as a young IT student in Berlin in 2019. In each of her incarnations, the same man, known variously as Guilherme, William, or Wilhelm, is on the hunt for a golden bracelet that belongs to Ada and that, according to African spiritual knowledge, promotes fertility, serving as a connecting story device. As Áine McMurtry points out, the narrative establishes connections and parallels between repeating power struggles that transcend their particular social settings, as violent

---

4   Antje Rávik Strubel, "Dankesrede zum Deutschen Buchpreis," in *Es hört nie auf, dass man etwas sagen muss: Essays* (Frankfurt am Main: S. Fischer Verlag, 2022), 11–13.

5   Sharon Dodua Otoo, *Adas Raum* (Frankfurt am Main: S. Fischer Verlag, 2021), cited in the text as *AR* with page number. All translations are from Sharon Dodua Otoo, *Ada's Room*, translated by Jon Cho-Polizzi (New York: Riverhead Books, 2023), cited in the text as *ART* with page number.

6   Antje Rávik Strubel, *Blaue Frau* (Frankfurt am Main: S. Fischer Verlag, 2021), cited in the text as *BF* with page number. All translations are my own.

7   Sara Ahmed, *The Feminist Killjoy Handbook* (London: Penguin House, 2023).

8   James Odhiambo Ogone, "Representational Epistemic Injustice. Disavowing the 'Other' Africa in the Imaginative Geographies of Western Animation Films," in *Epistemic Justice and Creative Agency: Global Perspectives on Literature and Film*, ed. Sarah Colvin and Stephanie Galasso (New York: Routledge, 2023), 88.

Eurocentric interests consistently impose gendered, capitalist, and racial hierarchies on bodies that deviate from white masculine norms.[9]

It seems as if the life of Ada is paralleled in Strubel's protagonist Adina Schejbal, who makes her way to Germany from her village in the Giant Mountains of the Czech Republic, ending up in Finland after she is raped by the German cultural ambassador Johann Manfred Bengel during an internship in the Uckermark region, where West and East meet. At the heart of both novels lie instances of literary self-reflection in the form of the eponymous blue woman in *Blaue Frau* and a shape-shifting being in *Adas Raum*. Both elusive figures complicate the narrative structure of the novels by enabling multiple perspectives, disrupting the unity of a singular narrative voice. Strubel has been called a "master of uncertainty,"[10] a term that could be extended to Otoo, whose fiction features abrupt shifts in focalization and temporality and subverts conventional modes of seeing in order to challenge preexisting categorizations.

While brute force is often acknowledged as violence, linguistic and structural acts of violence have not been adequately reflected in public discourse and political theory. In her work on institutional violence, *Complaint!*, Sara Ahmed thinks about inequalities from the perspective of those who raise complaints against abuses of power in universities. According to Ahmed, violence as a relation of force and harm is rarely perpetrated by single individuals but maintained through systems and patterns that are in place to keep those who are marginalized quiet and alone. Those who benefit from dominating these Others are protected by societal factors so that the violence remains unreal: "It might be that some people are protected because of how violence is not seen."[11] Power, in this sense, can be understood as the right to suspend what is supposed to be binding.[12] As a strategy to counter the violence of a system, Ahmed suggests insisting on naming and making visible the harm caused by systemic abuses of power. The aim behind this strategy must be to change how violent acts are understood, how they are made sense of, and how they are valued.

Ultimately, this "reorienting"[13] of normalized knowledge about violence is a question relevant to literary representation and cultural production. Making violence visible solely in spectacular and sensationalist

9   Áine McMurtry, "Othertongues. Multilingualism, Natality and Empowerment in Sharon Dodua Otoo's *Adas Raum*," *German Life and Letters* 77, no. 1 (2024): 112.
10   Beret Norman, "Antje Rávic Strubel's Ambiguities of Identity as Social Disruption," *Women in German Yearbook* 28 (2012): 65 (my translation).
11   Sara Ahmed, *Complaint!* (Durham, NC: Duke University Press, 2021), 189.
12   Ahmed, *Complaint!*, 48.
13   Ahmed, *Complaint!*, 264.

images of explicit physical damage often collides with the stories and feelings of survivors.[14] It gives the epistemically dangerous impression that violence has an extraordinary character and can therefore be isolated as a pathological anomaly. In the context of discussions over the use of trigger warnings, indicators that alert recipients to potentially distressing content, Ahmed remarks that the insistence on showing graphic rape scenes can expose traumatized people to their pain again. This ethical judgment of art as distressing is perceived by right-wingers as an attempt to "get in the way of our freedom, of our freedom to show what we do, to do what we show."[15] Inherent in this vision of freedom is the accusation that minorities feel too easily offended. However, as I will argue, the desire for the most haunting images literally does not do justice to the true, more insidious nature of violence. Ogone has coined the term *representational epistemic injustice* to describe a type of injustice that occurs in such fictional representations, which are based on fantasies, desires, and perceptions by members of dominant groups.[16] By focusing on a queer feminist and a Black feminist German writer, I argue that their novels stage the resistance of the imagined other(s), who talk and imagine back to their misrepresenters.[17]

Temporalities of Violence

As Otoo notes, violence is part of our lives and shapes the world we live in; literature can't simply write it away.[18] The communities of those who resist hegemonic norms are frequently the target of epistemic, linguistic, or physical violence. Thus, to portray this violence without giving it center stage or making it the only defining story of those who suffer from it can also be powerful. It can give the community the momentum of a shared suffering that empowers and enables the formation of bonds that go beyond time and space. Both novels imagine oppressive and hurtful pasts and present-day events without retraumatizing, ridiculing, or insulting their own characters. For instance, like many other Black writers, instead

---

14 See, for an analytical approach that takes these concerns into account, Shoshana Schwebel, "Lulu's Smile: An Archive of Trauma in *Die Büchse der Pandora* (1929)," *German Quarterly* 95, no. 2 (2022): 149–66.

15 Sara Ahmed, "Feminist Hurt/Feminism Hurts," in *The Power of Vulnerability*, ed. Anu Koivunen, Katariina Kyrölä, and Ingrid Ryberg (Manchester: Manchester University Press, 2018), 64.

16 Ogone, "Representational Epistemic Injustice," 201.

17 bell hooks, *Talking Back: Thinking Feminist, Thinking Black* (Boston: South End Press, 1999). See also Mihaela Mihai, "Epistemic Marginalisation and the Seductive Power of Art," *Contemporary Political Theory* 17 (2018): 395–416.

18 Otoo mentioned this during an online reading at Kiel University on May 31, 2022. Sadly, there is no recording of the event available.

of using the N-word, Otoo decidedly takes the stand of "avoid[ing] unnecessary and excessive (re)production of racist language"[19] in order to reclaim art as the space of resistance. In the parts of her novel that deal with power relations in a predominantly white society, she actively avoids any trace of the racist slur. Grada Kilomba points out the retraumatizing effect of the N-word for Black people: it reactualizes the colonial order in the present.[20] By refusing to incorporate the term into the language of her novel, Otoo establishes her fiction as a space that is inimical to hierarchies or division. This careful use of language *empowers*, because it signals that it is the Black—not the dominant white—perspective that matters. It *enables* the usage of less offensive vocabulary.[21] The choice of language already indicates the disruptive potential of Otoo's fiction. Contrary to the right-wingers Strubel mentions in her acceptance speech, who see in sensitive language an instrument of oppression of free speech, *Adas Raum* ensures that those with a traumatic history feel represented and encouraged to participate in conversations about violence, while the affective politics of exposure, with its insistence on linguistic violence as a right and a freedom, would cause minoritized readers to feel bad.[22]

Since, as Otoo points out, discrimination has existed for centuries and will likely continue to exist for a long time, the first way to implement nonvoyeuristic representation in storytelling is to acknowledge and recognize the marks left on the bodies of nonnormative Others by the dominant system. To call out violence and "bring things to the surface,"[23] it is necessary to take Others' embodied knowledge seriously. Audre Lorde finds unambiguous terms: "looking on the bright side of things is a euphemism used for obscuring certain realities of life, the open consideration of which might prove threatening to the status quo."[24] An excessively optimistic outlook would fail to address the painful traces of violence the system leaves in individual and collective histories.

Both narratives revolve around the questions of who is seen, heard, and allowed to speak—that is, who counts as human. In *Adas Raum*'s four time strands, the narrating being, which takes the form of various

---

19   Sharon Dodua Otoo, "'The Speaker is using the N-Word': A Transnational Comparison of Resistance to Racism in Everyday Language," in *Rassismuskritik und Widerstandsformen*, ed. Karim Fereidooni and Meral El (Wiesbaden: Springer, 2017), 294.

20   Grada Kilomba, *Plantation Memories: Episodes of Everyday Racism* (Münster: Unrast, 2007), 95.

21   Otoo, "The Speaker is using the N-Word," 294.

22   Ahmed, *The Feminist Killjoy Handbook*, 27.

23   Sara Ahmed, *Living a Feminist Life* (Durham, NC: Duke University Press, 2017), 246.

24   Audre Lorde, *The Cancer Journals* (San Francisco: Aunt Lute Books, 1997), 76.

inanimate objects, proves to be a witnessing observer of the attempted violent assimilation of minoritized subjects' knowledges, cultures, traditions, and lifeworlds, inviting us to consider many different lifeworlds and often stopping narrative time to inform the reader about the paths and feelings of the characters. Starting with the arrival of the Portuguese colonial merchants led by Guilherme Zarcos and Diogo Gomes de Sintra in the West African seaside town of Totope in 1459, the first Ada experiences the theft of resources and people. Although Guilherme embarks on the sea voyage to pay off debts, he nevertheless belongs to a group of self-proclaimed *explorers*—and to explore here means greedy appropriation by white Europeans. The men rename the island in honor of Saint Thomas, and Ada's little brother Damfo becomes Afonso, a name that originates from the Christian tradition of the Portuguese men. Instead of showing distressing scenes of enslavement, the novel focuses more on its epistemic effects. The "exploration" of the African continent eradicates diversity and replaces it with a whitewashed hierarchy of difference.[25] Although Totope is Damfo's place of origin, Europe seems to be a much more familiar point of reference: "Hier war Afonso: Ein Junge, der in Lissabon ein kleines Pferd auf seinen bloßen Händen hatte tragen können" (*AR*, 84; "there Afonso stood: a young man who could have carried a small horse through the streets of Lisbon," *ART*, 82).

The arrival of Guilherme brings Damfo back to his former village, where he coincidentally meets Naa-Lamiley, a close friend of Ada. This scene is marked by his internalized European understanding of the world. Not only is it no longer possible for him to speak his original language; he has been expelled from his own knowledge of the world and of himself: he thinks he is a white person. To him, his master Guilherme is all-knowing (*AR*, 81). He is the one whose knowledge counts, while the identity "Damfo" is rendered an unreal nonbeing. The gaze of Guilherme and his men establishes whiteness "as a violent and voracious ideology that will extract, consume, and call the 'other' its own."[26] As Naa-Lamiley asks Damfo about the whereabouts of Ada, Damfo is reminded of the potentially violent effect of white words that imprison subjects in dissociative states: "Mitnehmen. Das Wort klang . . . nein. Das Wort *war* Gewalt" (*AR*, 86, emphasis in original; "Take her. These words sounded . . . no. These words *were* violent," *ART*, 64, emphasis in original). Here, what Sara Ahmed calls the "net of language"[27] repeats the act of capture by dis-

---

25 Claudia Brunner, *Epistemische Gewalt: Wissen und Herrschaft in der kolonialen Moderne* (Bielefeld: transcript, 2020), 134.
26 kara lynch and Henriette Gunkel, "Lift Off . . . an Introduction," in *We Travel the Space Ways: Black Imagination, Fragments, and Diffractions*, ed. kara lynch and Henriette Gunkel (Bielefeld: transcript, 2019), 27.
27 Ahmed, *The Feminist Killjoy Handbook*, 209.

tressing Damfo and bringing up a whole history of shattering experience. By using a topos of unspeakability, the narrating being shows awareness of the ethical potential of linguistic carefulness: "'Betrüger!,' nannten sie [die Versklaver] ihn. Und einiges Schlimmeres, was ich hier nicht wiederholen mag" (*AR*, 81; "'Swindler, impostor!' they [the enslavers] had called him. And something worse, which I do not care to repeat here," *ART*, 79). Furthermore, the narrator recounts Damfo's memory of his capture by his enslavers:

> Es wurde weiter gelacht und gejauchzt, als Afonso am Arm gepackt wurde. Wurde er auch geschlagen? Vielleicht hatte die Person ihn getreten? Auf jeden Fall spürte er, wie die Haut über seiner linken Augenbraue platzte. (*AR*, 86–87)

> [They had only whooped and hooted as they dragged Afonso by the arm. Had they beaten him, too? Perhaps he had been kicked? In any case, he remembered when the skin above his left eyebrow had burst open.] (*ART*, 85)

Although horrific violence is at work, the narrative voice seems less interested in the acts themselves, which are not explicitly depicted but only vaguely implied in the form of questions, thus appearing to be interchangeable and senseless. *Schlagen* (to beat) and *treten* (to kick) have clear denotations, but these acts are not further showcased. Instead of foregrounding the power of white sovereignty in sensationalist ways, the only thing the narrator conveys with certainty is that the wounds inflicted on Damfo's Black body, and the fear that he experiences, matter, thereby also affirming his humanity. Following Ahmed, the empathetic narrative voice in *Adas Raum* asserts that Damfo's "body is vulnerable; we are vulnerable. A body tells us the time; bodies carry traces of where we have been."[28] Instead of looking at Damfo as an object, the recipients are rather encouraged to look *with* him, as more bad memories come up:

> Und da war das Mädchen. Zwischen all den Beinen hindurch. Ganz oben in einer Palme. Er wusste noch, wie er nach dem Mädchen geschrien hatte, trotz des ausgeschabten Halses, über die Weite des Strandes, gegen das Rauschen des Meeres: "Nalamle! Naalamle!" (*AR*, 86)

> [And the girl had been there. Between the many legs. High up in a palm tree. He still remembered how he had screamed for the girl, despite his ragged throat, across the stretch of beach, over the din of the sea: "Nalamle! Naalamle!"] (*ART*, 84–85)

28 Ahmed, *Living a Feminist Life*, 247.

Despite the literal silencing, Damfo's screams are a refusal against the violence, marking his connection to Naa-Lamiley as a guiding point. Similar to Ahmed, the text evokes, in an intertextual allusion to Chinua Achebe's *Things Fall Apart*, the lived reality of being traumatized by oppression as a form of "weather"[29] that presses and pounds against the surface of the body: "Der Wind heulte um die Bäume und ärgerte die Palmblätter und lachte ihm ins Gesicht und alles, alles drohte auseinanderzufliegen" (*AR*, 87; "Wind howled over the trees, enraging the palm fronds and laughing in his face while everything, everything threatened to fall apart," *ART*, 85). These scenes are certainly not characterized by voyeurism that would insist on graphic provocations and offense. Damfo isn't helplessly alone as a victim, which would allow readers to take pleasure in his suffering. White supremacy still prevails in Euro-Atlantic societies. Portraying the victims of this pernicious ideology and putting the reader in a position of empathic identification with those who suffer from it can ignite epistemic and social change. For that purpose, readers don't need to fully see the enslavers' brutality. They know what they have inflicted by apprehending the visible and invisible traces of enslavement on Damfo's body.

In the end, Damfo's story is not the story of his captivity, which we only see glimpses of, but the story of his reunion with Naa-Lamiley, who addresses him with his original name so that he regains the courage to remember. While the touch of the colonizers causes pain and bloodshed, Naa-Lamiley's touch embodies care and is able to break the stasis of Damfo's mind through warm affection. Her hug seems to revitalize him: "Eine Wärme breitete sich in ihm aus, von der Stelle, an der ihr Kopf seine Haut berührte" (*AR*, 83; "A warmth began to spread across him from the place where her head rested on his skin," *ART*, 81). With the act of remembering—and this is something Strubel's protagonist Adina knows too well—a process of resistance begins. Even though Damfo cannot recall everything and still struggles to access his native Ghanaian language while being haunted by images of brutality, the possibility of his healing is affirmed. He has determined for himself that he wants to speak in no other language than his mother tongue. Damfo's story confirms Ahmed's point that the unwanted feelings of violent pain can be the origin of a political resource for transformation.[30]

In Otoo's novel's 2019 temporal loop, the golden bracelet appears in a catalogue from an exhibition at a German museum that Ada Lamptey and her sister Elle find during an apartment tour given by the Berlin hipster Alfons Müller. Ada is pregnant, searching for a new apartment. Named Alfons and Afonso (Damfo), the two figures appear to be the same character, like Ada. As Sarah Colvin notes, different social structures

---

29   Ahmed, *Living a Feminist Life*, 185.
30   Ahmed, "Feminist Hurt/Feminism Hurts," 65.

in the novel's time strands lead to different identities:[31] the privileged Alfons does not have much in common with the fifteenth-century victim of colonialism. During the tour, his monodirectional, awkwardly smiling gaze at Ada and Elle sees in them some exotic curiosity. Elle, mirroring the 1459 character Naa-Lamiley, loses her temper after the flat tour—an emotional reaction in which a seemingly distant past is manifested. The afterlife of slavery and the colonial past forms a "memory trace,"[32] embodied information that reactivates and perpetuates power relations but may also be the starting point for a change in these relations. Such a memory trace is a bodily haunting, insofar as it is felt in reactions to what is personally experienced in the present. Although Elle hasn't experienced slavery herself, its historical impact can be felt viscerally in everyday situations. The transgenerational power relation is inscribed into the body. This becomes particularly clear when Elle discovers the bracelet in the German museum catalogue and learns of Damfo's fate there. As she put it, "Sie spielen mit uns" (*AR*, 218; "They toy with us," *ART*, 226). The present tense and the inclusive usage of *uns* (us) indicate that the violence of slavery persists in today's racism and gives Black people the feeling of being transported back in time. "These histories are alive, they are not over. Racism and colonialism are the present we are in."[33] How these histories are brought into the discourse is a political act.

Finally, the memory trace culminates in the fact that the bracelet was given to the museum in exchange for money by the elderly Mr. Wilhelm, the son of SS-Obersturmbahnführer Helmut Wilhelm, after he found it in an old box in the cellar. Otoo uses the figure of Mr. Wilhelm to paint the picture of a white, ignorant Nazi descendant who consciously decides against taking responsibility for history, despite ongoing rightwing extremism in Germany. The narrator comments as follows: "2019 redeten auffällig viele, die in Deutschland lebten, immer wieder von der Vergangenheit, auch nach dem Anschlag in Halle, als wäre es etwas, das schnellstmöglich bewältigt werden könnte" (*AR*, 283; "In 2019, there were many people living in Germany who spoke always of the past—particularly after the terror attack in Halle—discussing it as though this history was something that could be overcome as quickly as possible," *ART*, 296). Mr. Wilhelm's white ignorance "proceeds through the carefully

---

31   Sarah Colvin, "Freedom Time. Temporal Insurrections in Olivia Wenzel's *1000 Serpentinen Angst* und Sharon Dodua Otoo's *Adas Raum*," *German Life and Letters* 75, no. 1 (2022): 156.
32   Brigitte Bargetz, "Jenseits emotionaler Eindeutigkeiten. Überlegungen zu einer politischen Grammatik der Gefühle," in *Affekt und Geschlecht: Eine einführende Anthologie*, ed. Angelika Baier et al. (Vienna: Zaglossus, 2014), 109 (my translation).
33   Ahmed, "Feminist Hurt/Feminism Hurts," 63.

cultivated refusal to see and acknowledge certain things."[34] Mr. Wilhelm refuses to do his "Hausaufgaben" (*AR*, 282; "homework," *ART*, 195): he is unwilling to look further into the historical origins of the bracelet and does not want to know anything about whose property the bracelet might be, thus preventing him from becoming aware of the trauma his actions trigger in the present: "Er war der Schurke, der nicht die Bedeutung seines irdischen Auftrages verstanden haben wollte" (*AR*, 282; "He was the rascal who was determined to misunderstand the meaning of his earthly mission," *ART*, 295). His *earthly mission* would be to live up to the novel's epigraph, the Ghanaian Sankofa proverb: a person can develop further if they remember what they have forgotten. If he followed the idea of Sankofa, Mr. Wilhelm would realize that the bracelet does not belong to him, and that the diasporic community should decide about the object's fate instead of it going to a German museum. But he does not take these voices into consideration.

The white gaze at the bracelet exposes how violence involves a collision of different temporalities. Thus, the novel reorients common knowledge about histories of injustice by emphasizing their fundamental and omnipresent nature, overlaying the time of physical damage. On the one hand, there is the personal time of experiencing an act of harm, which may be swift and immediate. On the other hand, there is a structural time, characterized by its slow and resistant nature, creating obstacles for those seeking progress or change: all three historical Adas die at the hands of white male imperialists armed with guns. The first is shot by Guilherme after he steals the bracelet from the corpse of her newborn son. In the nineteenth-century timeline of the novel, Sir William King, escalating domestic violence in his relationship with his wife, the mathematician Ada King, kills her so he can call the bracelet his own. In 1945, forced to be a prostitute at the concentration camp Ravensbrück, the Pole Ada Marianska runs toward the electric fence of the camp in order to save her friend Linde, after Helmut Wilhelm, the Obersturmbahnführer, sees the shiny bracelet. Her suicidal run is stopped by the gunfire of the Nazi guards, yet still causes a moment of surprising disruption for the Kapo, Walde: "Zu Waldes großem Erstaunen schaffte sie es sogar bis kurz vor den elektrischen Zaun, ihre Fingerspitzen nur Millimeter von dem Strom" (*AR*, 96; "To Walde's great astonishment, she almost made it to the electric fence, the tips of her fingers were mere millimeters from the wires," *ART*, 95). Each time the characters try to move forward, the system resists these movements with speed. In the slow time of violence, the genocidal atrocities perpetrated by the National Socialism do not appear

---

34 José Medina, "Epistemic Injustice and Epistemologies of Ignorance," in *The Routledge Companion to the Philosophy of Race*, ed. Paul C. Taylor, Linda Alcoff, and Luvell Anderson (New York: Routledge, 2018), 248.

as an exceptional aberration but as "part of a historical continuum of racialized violence."[35]

Strubel reminds her readers of the "stability of violence"[36] too. Soviet crimes against those European states that are located at the periphery, such as Estonia, may be added to Otoo's historical continuum. Adina has often helped her mother, who owns a wellness hotel near the Czech mountains, at work. After the collapse of the Soviet Union, many of the guests at the hotel were Russians: "Sie trugen knielange Boxershorts, die sie nach dem Schwimmen nicht auszogen. Klatschnass fläzten sie damit auf den trockenen Holzbänken der Sauna und hinterließen dunkle Wasserflecken" (*BF*, 149; They wore knee-length boxer shorts that they didn't take off after swimming. Soaking wet, they flattened themselves on the dry wooden benches of the sauna, leaving dark water stains behind). They bought themselves expensive oils, "die die Russinnen nach der Massage sofort in die Dusche trugen, wo eine schlierige Schicht auf den Kacheln zurückblieb" (*BF*, 149; which the Russian women immediately carried into the shower after the massage, where a greasy layer remained on the tiles). The dark water stains introduce the novel's leitmotif of dark spots of history. Moreover, according to the jargon of the KGB, the expression *wet things* referred to an intelligence operation that was carried out on the direct orders of the Central Committee of the Soviet Union and involved bloodshed—for example, murder, torture, or execution.[37] Through this metaphorical interpretation in connection with the semantic area of dark spots, the stains, liquids, and oily streaks evoke associations with the present day. In the text, it is no longer the Soviets, but modern-day Russians who wear *nasse Sachen* (wet things). This can be understood as an allusion to today's murders by the Russian secret service, which repeatedly—for example, in the Salisbury poisonings[38]—left behind certain substances at the crime scene in the form of neurotoxins or other dangerous substances that were difficult to remove and required thorough cleaning work: "Wenn die Russen kamen, musste Adina danach jedes Mal saubermachen" (*BF*, 149; Every time the Russians came, Adina

---

35   McMurtry, "Othertongues," 123.

36   Ahmed, *Complaint!*, 268. Drawing on Anthony Reed's notion of freedom time, Colvin argues that Otoo's aesthetics undermine this stability and reveal "power in its impermanence." See Colvin, "Freedom Time," 162.

37   Faye Stewart notes about *wet things* as a leitmotif in Strubel's fiction: "The symbolic value of 'wet things' in Strubel's book links fiction with history, raising compelling questions about the relationship between present-day Germany and the twentieth-century vestiges of totalitarianism and violence." See Faye Stewart, "Queer Elements: The Poetics and Politics of Antje Rávic Strubel's Literary Style," *Women in German Yearbook* 30 (2014): 64.

38   "Salisbury Declared Decontaminated after Novichok Poisoning," BBC, March 1, 2019, https://www.bbc.com/news/uk-england-wiltshire-47412390.

had to clean up afterward). In that respect, violence has a persistent pace in both novels.

Adina's personal story of abuse is also one of looping memory traces: most parts of the *histoire* are narrated by a heterodiegetic voice, which moves between external and internal observations, while fragments of memory sometimes abruptly haunt the narrative, instead of merely showcasing the rape in a longer flashback scene. The novel's structure mirrors the struggle to reaccess the past, starting in Helsinki, where Adina finds refuge after the rape at the residence of her lover Leonides Siilmann, an Estonian member of the European parliament. Through flashbacks, the narrative occasionally jumps to scenes from her youth in Harrachov. The middle part of the novel concerns Adina's path to Germany, where her fateful encounter with Bengel takes place, while the final section centers on the aftermath of the assault. This main theme of coming to terms with the past is interwoven with Leonides's political fight for a European day of remembrance for the crimes of the Soviet Union and National Socialist Germany. Although on a political level he advocates that both were times of horror, he leaves out references to the present day in his belief in human rights, which prevents him from seeing Adina's suffering. Adina remembers various abuses of power that are part of more general structural misogyny and racism against Eastern European women. Although Strubel mentions in public statements that in the process of the "Verwestlichung des Ostens" (Westernization of the East)[39] some ideas of collectivity were lost, her novel is not indicative of any romanticization of the Eastern European past.

Far away from home in Berlin, Adina remembers the Neptunfest, which was part of Eastern European youth culture and widely practiced in holiday camps. The process of coming to terms with the histories of *schwarze Pädagogik* (poisonous pedagogy) in these camps has just recently begun.[40] During the festival, an adult man disguises himself as the god Neptune: "Auf seinem Kopf saß eine mit Algen und Tang bestückte Krone, in der Hand hielt er einen Dreizack aus Pappe. Ein grüner Tischtennisball steckte in seinem Mund, weshalb er nicht zu verstehen war" (*BF*, 185; On his head sat a crown covered with algae and seaweed; in his hand he held a cardboard trident. A green ping-pong ball was stuck in his mouth, which is why he could not be understood). The artificiality

---

39 Faye Stewart, "Das Politische und Sozialkritische in den Romanen Antje Ravic Strubels," in *Antje Ravic Strubel: Schlupfloch: Literatur*, ed. Andreas Erb and Anna Beughold (Bielefeld: Aisthesis Verlag, 2016), 79. All translations of the secondary literature are my own.

40 Susanne Donner, "DDR-Heimkinder: Seelisch und körperlich misshandelt," *Tagesspiegel*, January 21, 2021, https://www.tagesspiegel.de/wissen/seelisch-und-korperlich-misshandelt-4223887.html.

of the appearance makes it seem as if this Neptune comes from another, dark dimension. Neptune has *Häscher* (pursuers) at his service, catching the children, who are to be baptized and must drink a disgusting cocktail of "Milch, Salz, Essig und Senf" (*BF*, 186; milk, salt, vinegar, and mustard). What at first glance seems to be a harmless, fun ritual is narrated using the language of flight, force, and physical overpowering: Adina "war ... um ihr Leben gerannt" (was running for her life); the pursuers "warfen sie ins scharfkantige Schilf, packten sie an Hand- und Fußgelenken und schleppten sie ans Ufer zurück" (*BF*, 185; threw her into the sharp-edged reeds, grabbed her by the wrists and ankles and dragged her back to shore). All the children vomit. There is a shocking effect here because the reader does not know at first that this is supposed to be a festival game for children. What the reader perceives is an act of coercion taking place. The other children laugh as the camp leader slaps Adina in the face with some algae after she tries to shake off his foot from her neck, as he forces her to kneel. With reference to Laura Moisi's research on narrative alliances between stories of abuse, Strubel's strategy can be described as a phenomenology of violence.[41] The text does not use obvious words such as *violence* or *coercion*, but it evokes an uneasy gut feeling and associations with sexualized violence. The fact that both the other children happily participate in the spectacle and that there is a system behind the violence (a group leader translates Neptune's unintelligible shouting) points to the discrepancy between the reality of experiences (of child abuse) and the structural context that determines whether these experiences can and may be called experiences of violence at all.[42]

This challenge in common patterns of perception (the *Neptunfest* as a funny game in culture) reorients cultural and social knowledge about how abusive situations are understood. As with every outdated tradition of the past, fierce defenses of the *Neptunfest* have been mounted by those who call it an initiation to the "Ernst des Lebens" (serious side of life).[43] Strubel undermines this insensitive "'Jetzt habe dich nicht so,' 'stell dich nicht so an'[-Haltung]" (let's-not-exaggerate attitude)[44] by exposing the *Neptunfest* as a painful event and providing a counterlanguage of unambiguous vocabulary. A young teenage girl is forced to be a mermaid of Neptune, "ob sie wollte oder nicht" (*BF*, 186; whether she wanted or not), foreclosing any possibility of consent. The assaults were

---

41 Laura Moisi, "Etwas stimmte nicht. Narrative Allianzen und retrospektive Zeug*innenschaft," *Femina Politica* 28, no. 2 (Autumn 2019): 112.

42 Moisi, "Narrative Allianzen," 111.

43 Ulrich Seidler, "Das Neptunfest: Kindesmisshandlung oder Initiationserlebnis?," *Berliner Zeitung*, July 26, 2022, https://www.berliner-zeitung.de/kultur-vergnuegen/das-neptunfest-in-der-ddr-kindesmisshandlung-oder-initiationserlebnis-li.249955.

44 Strubel, "Dankesrede," 12.

perceived by Adina as life-threatening in retrospect, but they are socially considered consensual.

Looking back at the past helps make it possible to recognize instances of violence for what they are and to explicitly label them as such. The collective sharing of Adina's (fictitious) individual memories through literature makes it possible for others to bring up the effects of silent injustices that have gone unacknowledged in their own biography so far.[45] Returning to my original idea of a nonvoyeuristic approach to violence, it can be noted that Strubel pays attention to acts of abuse that are not visible to everybody and are obscured by nostalgia, as the public discourse about the *Neptunfest* above shows, or are hidden within a deeply patriarchal culture in which children are drilled to honor Neptune. Violence is often reproduced by not being made manifest.[46] With Moisi, it can be asserted that Strubel's phenomenology of violence demonstrates how the perception of abuse *as* abuse requires a preceding affective willingness to engage with and listen to a narrative that explores violence in all its dimensions.[47]

Otoo and Strubel both recognize that much of the system's power plays out in everyday life, which can quickly become one of the most dangerous places for those who are outside the white masculine norm. Kara Keeling defines quotidian violence as "the violence that the reproduction, reinscription, and survival of what exists relies upon and enacts in order to manage . . . 'the only lasting truth.' In other words, quotidian violence names the violence that maintains a temporality and a spatial logic hostile to the change and chance immanent in each now."[48] Quotidian violence does not include spectacles such as arson, mass murder, or torture, but manifests itself in everyday microaggressions, which often go unnoticed und unaddressed in common theories of violence.

The aptronym of the West German cultural ambassador Johann Manfred Bengel already alludes to the *Narrenfreiheit* (fool's license) of a badly behaved boy. It's a trope of masculine power. Arriving at the big mansion on the Oder owned by the entrepreneur Razvan Stein, he meets Adina, who is doing an internship there, for the first time. Bengel violates a physical boundary, unable to suppress his fetish for Eastern European women:

> In der Eingangshalle griff Johann Manfred Bengel zur Begrüßung nach Adinas Hand. Mit einem Lächeln seines zerklüfteten Gesichts

---

45 Moisi, "Narrative Allianzen," 111.
46 Ahmed, *Living a Feminist Life*, 256.
47 Moisi, "Narrative Allianzen," 112.
48 Kara Keeling, *Queer Times, Black Futures* (New York: New York University Press, 2019), 17.

hielt er sie fest, und während sein Mittelfinger in ihrem Handteller zu flappen begann wie ein nervöser Schmetterling, murmelte er: "Nur mal anfassen. So nett, so nett." (*BF*, 251)

[In the entrance hall, Johann Manfred Bengel reached for Adina's hand to greet her. With a smile on his craggy face, he held it tightly, and while his middle finger began to flutter in her palm like a nervous butterfly, he murmured: "Just one touch. So nice, so nice."]

Bengel seems to think of his "freedom to be offensive" as unassailable.[49] The deformation of the usually romantic image of the butterfly, which often appears in love poetry, signals how microaggressions are a disturbing experience. By showing that Bengel thinks he can do as he pleases with women and the "wild" land of the East, Strubel, like Otoo, refuses to look on the bright side of things. Quotidian powerplays are not the sites of violent brutalities, but they imprison marginalized individuals in the logic of larger systems. In Strubel's case, this is the temporal-spatial logic of the still-divided continent (geteilter Kontinent) of Europe enacted on Adina's body. Similar to the Wilhelm character in *Adas Raum*, Bengel relies on violence as a means to secure *the only lasting truth*. This violence is protected by societal and cultural perceptions of rape as a mere misunderstanding. "Sind solche Anschuldigungen im Moment nicht sehr in Mode?" (*BF*, 264; Aren't such accusations very common at the moment?) asks a Swiss businesswoman who is a colleague of Bengel's after Adina tries to speak to her about what has happened. Pacifying gestures downplay the true nature of abuse. Yet they prevail in public discourse on sexualized assaults, often supporting a logic of victim blaming.[50] By highlighting structures of silencing, the novel refers to but also changes the unjust knowledge of violent judgments that rely on gaslighting tactics to estrange victims from themselves.

Strubel has stated that she was not interested in providing yet another literary depiction of rape, which would—in terms of representational justice—aggrandize the violent act.[51] Readers first meet Adina in a state of acute dissociation and numbness. In an apartment in Helsinki, Adina synesthetically tries to regain a sense of herself and the world, while at the same time keeping her inner feelings at bay. The narrative voice (in Adina's internal focalization) gives no contextual information, but instead scatters hints from the very first pages of the novel that an act

---

49 Ahmed, *Living a Feminist Life*, 262.
50 Moisi, "Narrative Allianzen," 111.
51 Antje Rávik Strubel in conversation with Jagoda Marinić, *Freiheit Deluxe*, podcast, December 2, 2021, https://www.ardaudiothek.de/episode/freiheit-deluxe-mit-jagoda-marinic/antje-ravik-strubel-blaue-frau-und-der-ewige-tanz-um-den-maulbeerbaum/hr/95435442/.

of literally unspeakable violence must have happened. The most striking stylistic device Strubel uses to show that something isn't right with Adina is a series of declarative sentences in the novel: "Im Flur liegt ein abgewetzter Läufer. Walkingstöcke stehen an der Garderobe. Das sind die Gegenstände" (*BF*, 10; A well-used carpet lies in the hallway. Walking sticks lean against the coat check. Those are the objects). Throughout the whole novel, Adina uses declarative sentences or constatives, claims about the here and now, to take stock of what is there. Adina undertakes a careful survey of her immediate surroundings, a first attempt to gain mastery over the sensory world, but her exact inner state remains elusive. The fact that she needs to recollect not only things but also emotions, movements, or names of the people around her through these constatives reveals her deeply damaged lifeworld, as she tries to stabilize herself and piece her life back together to counteract the overwhelming experience of sexual assault.[52] Thus, the lived experience of violence is transformed into a nonvoyeuristic literary form that does justice to the nuances of this experience. With these aesthetic choices the author Strubel engages in a direct politics of refusal, rejecting the obsession with describing traumatic events in minute detail.

How to Deal with Violence?

The representational politics of Otoo and Strubel prove that it's necessary to *show* the perpetrators to a certain extent. However, as Kyung-Ho Cha remarks, *Adas Raum* is not solely a novel about the violence that individuals inflict on each other against the backdrop of historical disasters. It also centers on a narrative about the kinds of solidarity that can emerge among victims of violence.[53] The same can be said about *Blaue Frau*, because both novels present various ways of dealing with violence.

The diegetic worlds constructed by Otoo and Strubel have in common that official institutions such as courtrooms, parliaments, museums, or prize committees put a lot of effort into things staying the same. In 2019 Berlin, Ada Lamptey meets Mr. Wilhelm at the third apartment viewing where he suffers from a heart attack, living through all his former selves of Guilherme, William, and Helmut Wilhelm. He offers an all-too-easy solution to the fate of the golden bracelet, disguising himself in the role of the ignorant white savior: "Ich schenke es dir!" (*AR*, 309; "I'll give it to you," *ART*, 323). Turning the bracelet into a gift for the Black

---

52   Antje Rávik Strubel, *Nah genug weit weg* (Göttingen: Schönstatt, 2023), 44.

53   Kyung-Ho Cha, "Ghanaian Folk Thought, Akan Religion and an Ethic of Care in Sharon Dodua Otoo's *Adas Raum*," *German Life and Letters* 77, no. 1 (2024): 100.

community would position Mr. Wilhelm in charge of discourse and give him narrative control, making him the center of attention. The debate about cultural heritage would be all about him and his noble actions, without offering an honest apology that involves responsibility and accountability. He demands that Ada understand that his goodwill means historical progression: "Ohne mich bekommst du das Armband doch gar nicht!" (*AR*, 310; "Without me, you won't get the bracelet!," *ART*, 324). Nonetheless, Ada defends herself with patience as a virtue of resistance: "Wir finden einen Weg . . ." (*AR*, 310; "We'll find a way," *ART*, 324). In that respect, Otoo's novel criticizes how projects of reconciliation do not adequately deal with past atrocities. For the bracelet to be displayed in a German museum, where it would be gazed on by the public, would be a failure to address the bloody history of this object properly. By displaying it, the institution of the museum would make itself an accomplice with white supremacy. Merely giving the object back like a gift for which the Black community should be grateful, as Mr. Wilhelm suggests, does not address the contemporary forms of racism and the persistent inequality on which the system of white supremacy is predicated. Otoo exposes restitution as a dishonest method that claims to repair historical wrongs but ultimately only makes empty promises of alleged goodwill and insufficient solidarity.[54]

In *Blaue Frau*, there is a similar critique made by the text regarding how institutions exacerbate the stability of violence. As the narrative progresses in the fourth part of the novel, after Adina remembers the events in Germany she speaks to the activist and member of Finnish parliament Kristiina, a friend of Leonides. In contrast to the Swiss businesswoman, Kristiina listens to Adina and uses the time and space she has owing to her political position to take on the struggle against Johann Manfred Bengel. At the end of *Blaue Frau*, the jury of a prestigious international award for human rights and freedom of speech, the Eeva-Liisa-Manner award, holds its meeting to nominate Adina's rapist because of his commitment to help exiled scientists and artists and for fostering European networking in the cultural sector. Leonides and Kristiina are part of the jury, and both express their outrage at Bengel's nomination during the jury's meeting. But their attempts fail. The other members of the jury refuse to recognize the rape as real. To an older female professor, it's entirely unclear why they are even discussing the accusations against Bengel: "Wenn dieses Mädchen mit dem Leben nicht klarkommt, sollte sie zu Hause bleiben" (*BF*, 416; If this girl can't cope with life,

---

54 See, for a thorough discussion of the restitution debate and its representation in the novel, Maureen O. Gallagher, "Decolonial Gazing and Hermeneutic Resistance. Black German Challenges to White German Cultural Hegemony in the Museum," *Forum for Modern Language Studies* 59, no. 4 (2023): 545–64.

she should stay at home). Ahmed would probably comment on the professor's acceptance of abuse as an inevitable and permissible part of life: "Oh, the violence and the smugness of this sentence, this sentencing."[55] In the end, the only change the jury undertakes is to highlight the values of democracy, nonviolence, and equality in their official statement. The supposedly progressive but meaningless rhetoric is used to cement a perception of Bengel that allows him to get away with what he has done, neutralizing the critical potential of these terms. Strubel makes visible what Ahmed describes in her analysis of complaints in institutions: sexism and racism "can be reproduced in the spaces where [they are] supposedly being questioned."[56] By opening the closed doors of a jury meeting and emphasizing how difficult it is to bring about actual social change, Strubel doesn't simply reveal the occurrence of problematic decision-making. She offers her readers the epistemic possibility to make sense of institutional complicity as an influential factor that enables, repeats, and intensifies violence.

However, one other member of the jury, a young doctoral student, who comes from the north, resigns in protest during the meeting after reminding the jury that every act of slavery should be condemned. Kristiina notices that his resignation is an attention-grabbing gesture intended to shake things up:

> Die Unbeirrbarkeit dieses jungen Mannes hatte [Kristiina] beeindruckt. Oben im Norden, schlussfolgerte sie, hatten die Menschen Erfahrung mit Kolonialherrengehabe. Von ihrer Radikalität, mit der sie sich seit Jahrzehnten gegen die feindliche Übernahme ihrer Rentierweiden, ihrer Lieder und Körper wehrten, ließ sich noch einiges lernen. (*BF*, 418)

> [The imperturbability of this young man impressed Kristiina. Up north, she concluded, the people had experience with colonial attitudes. There was still a lot to learn from their radicalism, with which they had resisted the hostile takeover of their reindeer pastures, their songs, and their bodies for decades.]

Kristiina and the unnamed young man from the north share a readiness to dispute, to not give in, to make a scene, and to fight for the right of others to have rights, whatever it takes. Although they don't know each other, both of them have seen the violence in the meeting room. During her Schröder Lecture at the University of Cambridge in March 2022, Otoo remarked on the genealogies of resistance, which resonate with Strubel's conceptualization of the indigenous regions of Scandinavia

---

55 Ahmed, *Living a Feminist Life*, S. 238.
56 Ahmed, *Complaint!*, 158.

as a space of radicality: "Centuries before me, people were enslaved and somehow still managed to hold on to their humanity and still managed to keep hold of the languages they brought from Africa, the stories, the songs, the dances, the recipes. They kept hold of all of that and passed it to their children and grandchildren in an effort to stay alive."[57] The struggle of others can be an inspiration for one's own struggle. Similar to Otoo, who foregrounds an ethics of care in many of her characters, Damfo and Naa-Lamiley among them,[58] Strubel affirms that those who suffer under power inequalities are not alone. Staying connected to others is required for withstanding the harshness of dominant systems.

Literary Resistance

Read together, the novels of Sharon Dodua Otoo and Antje Rávik Strubel discussed here offer a panorama of the stability of racialized, gendered, and imperialist forms of violence, and in doing so they interrupt the powers that be. The nonlinear storytelling of both novelists intertwines various memory traces as political and personal *Dunkelstellen* (dark spots), underscoring that the histories of colonialism, Nazi Germany, and Stalinism are still alive and well. *Adas Raum* and *Blaue Frau* both transform the understanding, interpretation, and valuation of violence by offering other modes of referential, linguistic, and creative engagement with it. They engage in a broader political struggle to change normalized attitudes toward racism and sexism, aiming to shift the understanding from acceptance or neutral objectivity to a stance that views inequality as not inevitable. Both novels focus on bad memories, feelings, scars, and wounds as effects of violence, but do not exercise a voyeuristic gaze as an exploitative spectacle. Otoo and Strubel follow Audre Lorde by not looking on the bright side of things, but recognize multiple forms of systemic harm, even if they are small and quotidian. However, the temporality of violence is constantly unsettled by a simultaneity with structures of solidarity. Ada, Adina, the young man from the North, the fierce activist Kristiina, the former slave Damfo, and Naa-Lamiley—all of them share a commitment to nonhierarchical modes of collectivity, bonding, and kinship to withstand the system. *Adas Raum* and *Blaue Frau* claim literature

57 Sharon Dodua Otoo, Schröder Lecture 2022, MMLL, University of Cambridge, March 14, 2022, YouTube video, 1:28:13, https://www.youtube.com/watch?v=p3wlTykhzq4.
58 I have argued elsewhere that the various acts of resistance in *Adas Raum* can be seen as echoes of radical democratic activism. See Alrik Daldrup, "Von der 'Macht, Welt zu machen': Radikale Demokratie in Sharon Dodua Otoos *Adas Raum*," *German Life and Letters* 77, no. 1 (2024): 125–45. See also Cha, "Ghanaian Folk Thought," 100–101.

as a space of bearing witness to painful injustices that have been denied by the dominant cultures and thus have been written out of conventional histories and stories. As such, the novels perform literary resistance in the best sense of that term.

Bibliography

Ahmed, Sara. *Complaint!* Durham, NC: Duke University Press, 2021.
———. "Feminist Hurt/Feminism Hurts." In *The Power of Vulnerability*, edited by Anu Koivunen, Katariina Kyrölä, and Ingrid Ryberg, 59–67. Manchester: Manchester University Press, 2018.
———. *The Feminist Killjoy Handbook*. London: Penguin House, 2023.
———. *Living a Feminist Life*. Durham, NC: Duke University Press, 2017.
Bargetz, Brigitte. "Jenseits emotionaler Eindeutigkeiten. Überlegungen zu einer politischen Grammatik der Gefühle." In *Affekt und Geschlecht: Eine einführende Anthologie*, edited by Angelika Baier, Christina Binswanger, Yv Eveline Nay, Jana Häberlein, and Andrea Zimmermann, 117–36. Vienna: Zaglossus, 2014.
Brunner, Claudia. *Epistemische Gewalt: Wissen und Herrschaft in der kolonialen Moderne*. Bielefeld: transcript, 2020.
Cha, Kyung-Ho. "Ghanaian Folk Thought, Akan Religion and an Ethic of Care in Sharon Dodua Otoo's *Adas Raum*." *German Life and Letters* 77, no. 1 (2024): 88–101.
Colvin, Sarah. "Freedom Time. Temporal Insurrections in Olivia Wenzel's *1000 Serpentinen Angst* and Sharon Dodua Otoo's *Adas Raum*." *German Life and Letters* 75, no. 1 (2022): 138–65.
Daldrup, Alrik. "Von der 'Macht, Welt zu machen': Radikale Demokratie in Sharon Dodua Otoos *Adas Raum*." *German Life and Letters* 77, no. 1 (2024): 125–45.
Donner, Susanne. "DDR-Heimkinder: Seelisch und körperlich misshandelt." *Tagesspiegel*, January 21, 2021. https://www.tagesspiegel.de/wissen/seelisch-und-korperlich-misshandelt-4223887.html.
Gallagher, Maureen O. "Decolonial Gazing and Hermeneutic Resistance. Black German Challenges to White German Cultural Hegemony in the Museum." *Forum for Modern Language Studies* 59, no. 4 (2023): 545–64.
hooks, bell. *Talking Back: Thinking Feminist, Thinking Black*. Boston: South End Press, 1999.
Keeling, Kara. *Queer Times, Black Futures*. New York: New York University Press, 2019.
Kilomba, Grada. *Plantation Memories: Episodes of Everyday Racism*. Münster: Unrast, 2007.
Lorde, Audre. *The Cancer Journals*. San Francisco: Aunt Lute Books, 1997.
lynch, kara, and Henriette Gunkel. "Lift Off . . . an Introduction." In *We Travel the Space Ways: Black Imagination, Fragments, and Diffractions*,

edited by kara lynch and Henriette Gunkel, 21–44. Bielefeld: transcript, 2019.

McMurtry, Áine. "Othertongues. Multilingualism, Natality and Empowerment in Sharon Dodua Otoo's *Adas Raum*." *German Life and Letters* 77, no. 1 (2024): 102–24.

Medina, José. "Epistemic Injustice and Epistemologies of Ignorance." In *The Routledge Companion to the Philosophy of Race*, edited by Paul C. Taylor, Linda Alcoff, and Luvell Anderson, 247–60. New York: Routledge, 2018.

Mihai, Mihaela. "Epistemic Marginalisation and the Seductive Power of Art." *Contemporary Political Theory* 17 (2018): 395–416.

Moisi, Laura. "Etwas stimmte nicht. Narrative Allianzen und retrospektive Zeug*innenschaft." *Femina Politica* 28, no. 2 (Autumn 2019): 107–20.

Ogone, James Odhiambo. "Representational Epistemic Injustice. Disavowing the 'Other' Africa in the Imaginative Geographies of Western Animation Films." In *Epistemic Justice and Creative Agency: Global Perspectives on Literature and Film*, edited by Sarah Colvin and Stephanie Galasso, 83–105. New York: Routledge, 2023.

Otoo, Sharon Dodua. *Adas Raum*. Frankfurt am Main: S. Fischer Verlag, 2021.

———. *Ada's Room*. Translated by Jon Cho-Polizzi. New York: Riverhead Books, 2023.

———. "Afropolitanism and 'Ada's Realm': A Conversation with Sharon Dodua Otoo." Jesus College, Cambridge. October 16, 2023. YouTube video, 1:14:45, https://www.youtube.com/watch?v=FXBcO1MpAvI.

———. Schröder Lecture 2022. MMLL, University of Cambridge. March 14, 2022. YouTube video, 1:28:13. https://www.youtube.com/watch?v=p3wlTykhzq4.

———. "'The Speaker is using the N-Word': A Transnational Comparison of Resistance to Racism in Everyday Language." In *Rassismuskritik und Widerstandsformen*, edited by Karim Fereidooni and Meral El, 291–305. Wiesbaden: Springer, 2017.

Pfleger, Simone. "Temporal and Corporeal Re-Imaginings in Antje Rávic Strubel's *Kältere Schichten der Luft* (2007)." In *Protest und Verweigerung/ Protest and Refusal*, edited by Hans Adler and Sonja Klocke, 179–204. Leiden: Brill, 2018.

"Salisbury Declared Decontaminated after Novichok Poisoning." BBC, March 1, 2019. https://www.bbc.com/news/uk-england-wiltshire-47412390.

Schwebel, Shoshana. "Lulu's Smile. An Archive of Trauma in *Die Büchse der Pandora* (1929)." *German Quarterly* 95, no. 2 (2022): 149–66.

Seidler, Ulrich. "Das Neptunfest: Kindesmisshandlung oder Initiationserlebnis?" *Berliner Zeitung*, July 26, 2022. https://www.berliner-zeitung.de/kultur-vergnuegen/das-neptunfest-in-der-ddr-kindesmishandlung-oder-initiationserlebnis-li.249955.

Stewart, Faye. "Das Politische und Sozialkritische in den Romanen Antje Ravic Strubels." In *Antje Ravic Strubel: Schlupfloch; Literatur*, edited by Andreas Erb and Anna Beughold, 63–84. Bielefeld: Aisthesis Verlag, 2016.

———. "Queer Elements: The Poetics and Politics of Antje Rávic Strubel's Literary Style." *Women in German Yearbook* 30 (2014): 44–73.

Strubel, Antje Rávik. *Blaue Frau*. Frankfurt am Main: S. Fischer Verlag, 2021.

———. "Dankesrede zum Deutschen Buchpreis." In *Es hört nie auf, dass man etwas sagen muss: Essays*, 11–13. Frankfurt am Main: S. Fischer Verlag, 2022.

———. *Nah genug weit weg*. Göttingen: Schönstatt, 2023.

Strubel, Antje Rávik in conversation with Jagoda Marinic. Freiheit Deluxe. Podcast. December 2, 2021. https://www.ardaudiothek.de/episode/freiheit-deluxe-mit-jagoda-marinic/antje-ravik-strubel-blaue-frau-und-der-ewige-tanz-um-den-maulbeerbaum/hr/95435442/.

9: Epistolary Interventions, Epistemic Insurrections: Creative Writers, Open Letters, and Solidarity with the "Womxn, Life, Freedom" Movement in Contemporary Postmigrant Germany

Tara Talwar Windsor

IN OCTOBER 2022, German Book Prize winner Kim de l'Horizon caused a stir during their acceptance speech at the award ceremony in Frankfurt's historic townhall. Having retrieved an electric shaver from their bag, de l'Horizon proceeded to shave their hair in solidarity with Iranian women protesting against the repressive clerical regime of the Islamic Republic. The author suggested that the jury's decision to honor *Blutbuch*, a novel with a nonbinary protagonist, had set an example "gegen den Hass, für die Liebe, für den Kampf aller Menschen, die wegen ihres Körpers unterdrückt werden" (against hatred, for love, for the struggle of all people who are oppressed because of their bodies). The prize was therefore also dedicated, de l'Horizon continued, to the womxn in Iran: "Zu denen wir alle schauen . . . Wir schauen alle nach Iran bewundernd für diesen Mut, diese Kraft. Es zeigt uns wie dumm unser Weltbild war, dass wir dachten, Weiblichkeit ist nur im Westen emanzipiert." (To whom we are all looking . . . We're all looking to Iran admiring this courage, this strength. It shows us how stupid our worldview was that we thought femininity was only emancipated in the West.)[1]

Kim de l'Horizon's striking political statement in Frankfurt was just one of many public interventions that emanated from the European cultural sphere in response to the latest wave of protests against the Iranian government, which was sparked by the murder of the twenty-two-year-old Kurdish-Iranian woman, Jina Mahsa Amini, on September 16, 2022,

---

1 ZEIT ONLINE, "Kim de l'Horizon rasiert sich bei Dankesrede die Haare in Solidarität mit iranischen Frauen," October 18, 2022, YouTube video, 1:16, https://www.youtube.com/watch?v=Lad9WyHoEbA&t=1s. Translations are mine unless otherwise stated.

following her arrest by the Islamic regime's so-called morality police. The notional "wir" constructed by de l'Horizon in the improvised speech that accompanied their symbolic head shaving thus gave expression to the global solidarity and resonance the Iranian protesters had found as symbols of resistance to patriarchal and misogynistic structures that oppress womxn and other gender minorities around the world. De l'Horizon's speech nonetheless conjured a conspicuously Western-centric "wir" in relation to a hitherto Orientalized Other—in this case, the figure of the oppressed Iranian or "Eastern" woman waiting to be liberated by "the West"—exposing the epistemic injustice imposed by the historical, yet enduring Western tendency to homogenize, distort, and/or erase (feminist) perspectives rooted in non-Western contexts.[2] At the same time, de l'Horizon's candid admission of a deficit in knowledge about non-Western feminisms points, in turn, to the emergence of what the philosopher José Medina calls "beneficial epistemic friction"—the continual interaction between alternative standpoints and ways of knowing—triggered, in this case, by de l'Horizon's engagement with those antiregime protests in Iran. More particularly, the apparently revelatory confrontation with the "subjugated knowledge" produced by emancipated femininity in that non-Western context had exerted a kind of productive resistance to the dominant Western epistemology "by forcing oneself to be self-critical, to confront one's limitations and to become attentive to internalized patterns of ignorance."[3] As such, the issues raised by de l'Horizon's speech and wider expressions of European solidarity with the Iranian protesters were not only political in nature but also epistemological.

This chapter takes up these issues with reference to a different form of literary intervention—the open letter—which has a long tradition in Western intellectual history and has experienced a further boom in the age of the internet. My main focus is on two letters that originated in the German literary sphere in response to Amini's murder and the subsequent eruption of protests, in Iran and worldwide, under the Kurdish feminist slogan "Jin, Jiyan, Azadî" (Womxn, Life, Freedom). The first of these was written by the novelist Shida Bazyar and addressed directly to Amini, while the second was co-instigated by the essayist Asal Dardan and signed by more than six hundred artists and intellectuals who addressed their letter to the protesters in Iran. Although the notions of individual

---

2 On epistemic injustice and orientalism, see Andrea J. Pitts, "Decolonial Praxis and Epistemic Injustice," in *The Routledge Handbook of Epistemic Injustice*, ed. Ian James Kidd, José Medina, and Gaile Pohlhaus, Jr. (New York: Routledge, 2017), 151–52; Edward W. Said, *Orientalism* (New York: Vintage Books, 1978).

3 José Medina, "Epistemic Injustices and Epistemologies of Ignorance," in *The Routledge Companion to the Philosophy of Race*, ed. Paul Taylor, Linda Alcoff, and Luvell Anderson (New York: Routledge, 2017), 252.

and collective authorship behind them differ, both of these letters shine a light on transnational feminist alliances forged in solidarity with the Iranian protesters, while simultaneously addressing and redressing the kind of epistemological limitations alluded to in Kim de l'Horizon's speech. Through these examples, the chapter interrogates the role of open letters as instruments of intellectual intervention in a German public sphere that is both inextricably linked with and disrupted by global events and discourses.

I shall argue that these variants of epistolary nonfiction enable a form of public intervention, which illustrates and advances the transformative potential of what has become known as the "postmigrant perspective" in Germany, and thus exert resistance to dominant Western epistemologies. Writing about open letters in the US context, Emily Lordi observes that "amid and despite their blogospheric ubiquity, open letters have become powerful forms of literary activism for writers who have used them to protest anti-black violence and the rise of U.S. neofascism, as well as to build community."[4] In addition to highlighting the community-building potential of collective open letters, Lordi examines other personal-political letter-essays by authors of color, which "take shape amid the Internet's open letter boom," and views these as a part of a "network" across time and space that reveals "such common themes as the psychic effects of racial oppression."[5] Lordi's understanding of the political functions of epistolary writing dovetails with Jeannette Oholi's explanation of the postmigrant paradigm, which she argues is both resistant and generative: "Es macht nicht nur hegemoniale Strukturen und die Auswirkungen auf Individuen wie auch Gesellschaften sichtbar, sondern kann eben Neues schaffen. . . . Ich sehe es als etwas Verbindendes, das neue—auch transnationale—Allianzen zwischen marginalisierten Communitys schaffen kann." (It not only makes hegemonic structures and their effects on individuals and societies visible, but can also create something new. . . . I see it as something unifying that can create new—including transnational—alliances between marginalized communities.)[6] Developing this further with Medina's framework of epistemic resistance, the letters under discussion can be seen as "critical and subversive interventions" that not only

---

4   Emily J. Lordi, "Between the World and the Addressee: Epistolary Nonfiction by Ta-Nehisi Coates and His Peers," *College Language Association Journal* 60, no. 4 (2017), 435.
5   Lordi, "Between the World and the Addressee," 435.
6   Jeannette Oholi in Jeannette Oholi, Maha El Hissy, Kyung-Ho Cha, and Maryam Aras, "Postmigration Reloaded," *PS Politisch Schreiben* 7 (2022): 64, https://www.politischschreiben.net/ps-7/postmigration-reloaded-ein-schreibgesprch.

have the potential to make "oppressive structures collapse but also put something (or contribute to the building of something) in their place."[7]

In order to illustrate how my central examples stage and enact such interventions and alliances, I begin by exploring recent debates in Germany about the inflationary use of open letters—particularly in response to the Russian invasion of Ukraine in 2022—in a digital public sphere that is governed by a so-called attention economy. In a second step, I turn to arguments forwarded by Asal Dardan in defense of the open letter as a means of critiquing power and amplifying marginalized voices, illustrating how Dardan's quest to rehabilitate the genre is situated in a genealogy of critical intellectuals, which she extends into the digital age, and is related to a notion of exile as a practice of resistance. Against this backdrop, I offer close readings of Bazyar's letter to Amini and the letter signed by six hundred intellectuals addressed to the protesters in Iran, and I highlight strategies employed by their authors and signatories to adopt, adapt, and subvert the genre. I suggest that these letters generate "epistemic friction" in a number of overlapping ways—for example, by reengaging and reconfiguring longer-standing traditions to redistribute cultural and emotional capital at a moment when the genre's usefulness had been called into question in a saturated public sphere; by privileging marginalized perspectives and exposing ambivalent positionalities, not only thematically but also through their strategic use of personal and collective pronouns; and by making creative use of the genre's dual mode of address to (imagined) named recipients as primary addressees and to wider reading publics as the secondary audience. As well as exploring these formal and textual strategies, I trace the methods and media used to circulate these letters, which thereby activate networks of solidarity across time and space. Overall, I argue that these epistolary interventions instigate what Medina (drawing on Foucault) terms "epistemic insurrections"—"pointed critical incursions,"[8] which mobilize invisible "subjugated knowledges" to continually "disrupt and interrogate epistemic hegemonies and mainstream perspectives"[9]—and go some way to facilitating a form of "multiperspectivalism" and "network solidarity"[10] that reflects the radical diversity of contemporary German society.

---

7   José Medina, *The Epistemology of Resistance: Gender and Racial Oppression, Epistemic Injustice, and Resistant Imaginations* (Oxford: Oxford University Press, 2013), 199.

8   José Medina, "Toward a Foucaultian Epistemology of Resistance: Counter-Memory, Epistemic Friction and Guerilla Pluralism," *Foucault Studies* 12 (2011): 11.

9   Medina, "Toward a Foucaultian Epistemology of Resistance," 33.

10 Medina, *Epistemology of Resistance*, 21–26.

Open Letters, Cultural Capital, and the Attention Economy

On April 29, 2022, twenty-eight writers, filmmakers, and actors—including Alice Schwarzer, Robert Seethaler, Martin Walser, Juli Zeh, Alexander Kluge, Harald Welzer, Andreas Dresen, and Lars Eidinger—published an open letter addressed to Chancellor Olaf Scholz on the online platform *EMMA*. Their letter praised Scholz for his "Besonnenheit" (level-headedness or moderation), warning of the danger of a Third World War, and questioning the desirability of sending armaments to Ukraine in support of its war of defense against Putin's Russia.[11] A counterletter followed five days later in *Die Zeit*, signed by fifty-seven intellectuals, including Maxim Biller, Olga and Wladimir Kaminer, Dmitrij Kapitelman, Daniel Kehlmann, Jagoda Marinić, Eva Menasse, Herta Müller, Ronya Othmann, Antje Rávik Strubel, and Deniz Yücel. This time, the authors and signatories praised Scholz for an impassioned speech he had given at a May Day event, where he expressed his willingness, not yet affirmed by a Bundestag vote, to provide Ukraine not just with financial and humanitarian aid but also with military support.[12] Blurring the boundaries between conventional open letters and political petitions, both letters have since been endorsed by members of the public via the online platform change.org.[13]

These letters addressed to Scholz were among the earliest and most controversial contributions to what was soon described as an "Inflation offener Briefe" (inflation of open letters),[14] which has ignited a metadiscussion on the function of open letters and the role of intellectuals as arbiters of public opinion and morality in contemporary Germany. In an

---

[11] "Der Offene Brief an Kanzler Scholz," *EMMA*, April 29, 2022, https://www.emma.de/artikel/offener-brief-bundeskanzler-scholz-339463.

[12] "Waffenlieferung an die Ukraine: Offener Brief," *Die Zeit*, May 4, 2022, https://www.zeit.de/2022/19/waffenlieferung-ukraine-offener-brief-olaf-scholz; for Scholz's May Day speech, see *tagesschau*, "Tag der Arbeit: Bundeskanzler Scholz spricht auf DGB-Kundgebung in Düsseldorf," May 1, 2022, YouTube video, 9:08, https://www.youtube.com/watch?v=-3CApjm14-0.

[13] "Offener Brief an Bundeskanzler Scholz," change.org, accessed March 13, 2024, https://www.change.org/p/offener-brief-an-bundeskanzler-scholz; "Die Sache der Ukraine ist auch unsere Sache!" change.org, accessed March 13, 2024, https://www.change.org/p/die-sache-der-ukraine-ist-auch-unsere-sache?utm_source=share_petition&utm_medium=custom_url&recruited_by_id=835568b0-caa5-11ec-a137-77c2dc6ca625. When last accessed, the number of signatories stood at 512,153 and 96,869 respectively.

[14] Ocke Bandixen, "Kommentar: Mehr offene Briefe an Olaf Scholz!" NDR Kultur, July 1, 2022, accessed May 13, 2023, https://www.ndr.de/kultur/kulturdebatte/Kommentar-Mehr-offene-Briefe-an-Olaf-Scholz,offenebriefe100.html.

"Offener Brief über offene Briefe" (Open letter about open letters) published in July 2022—misleadingly titled since it has neither an addressee nor a signatory—the writer Leander Steinkopf noted:

> Nicht nur die Themen der Briefe sind in die Diskussion gekommen, sondern auch das Medium "offener Brief" an sich. Dieses identitätsstiftende Instrument der Intellektuellen unterliegt einer Inflation, die Intellektuelle dessen Wert hinterfragen lassen. Warum gibt es sie überhaupt noch, die offenen Briefe, wird da gefragt. Und es klingt, als wäre es die stellvertretende Erörterung der Frage, warum es sie überhaupt noch gibt: die Intellektuellen.[15]
>
> [Not only have the themes of the letters come under discussion, but also the medium of the "open letter" per se. This identity-generating instrument used by intellectuals is prone to inflation, which makes intellectuals question its value. People ask why they still exist at all, these open letters. Which sounds like a substitute question for asking why they, the intellectuals, still exist at all.]

The recent revival of open letters in Germany has attracted a mixture of fascination, perplexity, and ridicule, not least because the genre is often considered to be "überholt und aus der Zeit gefallen" (obsolete and anachronistic), particularly in the age of social media.[16] Such virulent reactions to contemporary open letters arguably result precisely from their continuation of and/or deviation from the long tradition of the genre. Literary historian Anne Lorenz situates the recent trend of open letters "ganz am Ende einer neuzeitlichen Reihe" (right at the end of a modern series) of epistolary interventions,[17] ranging from Émile Zola's *J'accuse* in the Dreyfus affair to Thomas Mann's public renunciation of Nazi Germany in 1936, and the declaration by thirteen GDR artists protesting Wolf Biermann's expulsion from East Germany forty years later. Lorenz traces the origins of the genre further back in relation to the development of Western democracy and emphasizes its historical importance as a mode of courageously voicing uncomfortable truths in the interests of the common good. In this light, she concludes

---

15 Leander Steinkopf, "Ein offener Brief über offene Briefe: Wozu dienen sie eigentlich? Woher kommt die Mode?" *Berliner Zeitung*, July 9, 2022, https://www.berliner-zeitung.de/open-source/ein-offener-brief-ueber-offene-briefe-wozu-dienen-sie-eigentlich-woher-kommt-die-mode-li.244791.

16 Anne Lorenz, "Die ungefährliche Rückkehr eines unzeitgemäßen Genres. Der offene Brief online," geschichte der gegenwart, May 29, 2022, https://geschichtedergegenwart.ch/die-ungefaehrliche-rueckkehr-eines-unzeitgemaessen-genres-der-offene-brief-online/.

17 Lorenz, "Die ungefährliche Rückkehr."

that Germany's recent wave of open letters highlights "wie mächtig *die Geste* der freimütigen Rede noch immer ist" (how powerful the *gesture* of speaking out candidly remains).[18] In contrast to the restrictive public sphere in Putin's Russia, for instance, or during other periods in German history, the political freedoms enjoyed by contemporary German intellectuals mean that such gestures might justifiably attract "der Vorwurf des bloßen Lippenbekenntnisses" (accusations of paying mere lip service).[19] Similarly, literary scholar Johannes Franzen has written sardonically of German intellectuals' apparent "Unterzeichneritis" (signaturitis).[20] This results in a cycle of borrowing and lending cultural capital to particular causes and, more significantly, to each other, for which they are rewarded with ever more attention (and in some cases given the opportunity to make hypocritical claims that public criticism of their positions is akin to having their own right to free speech "cancelled"). In this reading, open letters seem less about the causes and more about doing "ein gutes Geschäft am Markt der Aufmerksamkeitsökonomie" (good business in the market of an attention economy).[21]

One striking contribution to this public discussion was an "Offener Brief an den offenen Brief" (Open letter to the open letter)—in this case aptly titled—published by the journalist and actress Samira El Ouassil on the critical media platform übermedien. In this, El Ouassil reflects on the paradoxical status of the epistolary protest in the changed attention economy of the digital era. On the one hand, she acknowledges the historical weight of the genre and the potential for more letter writers to reach greater audiences through digitization: "Du warst der Outcall, lange bevor es das Internet gab. Als ein Hybrid zwischen Individual- und Massenkommunikation, bist du heutzutage vielleicht sogar das Kampagneninstrument schlechthin einer digitalisierten Gesellschaft" (You were public outcry, long before the internet existed. As a hybrid of individual and mass communication, you may well even be the quintessential campaign instrument in today's digital society).[22] On the other hand, she points out that this (digital) proliferation can dilute the effectiveness of such letters. The fact that letters addressing "Gedanken, Kritik und Wünsche ... an die Welt" (thoughts, critique, and desires to the world) appear almost daily as Tweets, Instagram slides, Facebook posts, and other digital forms prompts El Ouassil to ask: "Wirkst du deswegen

18   Lorenz, "Die ungefährliche Rückkehr." (Emphasis mine.)
19   Lorenz, "Die ungefährliche Rückkehr."
20   Johannes Franzen, "Nach offenem Brief an Olaf Scholz in der '*EMMA*': Von der Unterzeichneritis," *Frankfurter Rundschau*, May 13, 2022, https://www.fr.de/kultur/gesellschaft/unterzeichneritis-von-der-91538514.html.
21   Steinkopf, "Ein offener Brief über offene Briefe."
22   Samira El Ouassil, "Offener Brief an den offenen Brief," übermedien, May 4, 2022, https://uebermedien.de/71165/offener-brief-an-den-offenen-brief/.

nicht nur anachronistisch, sondern in Anbetracht der komplexen, globalen Probleme, die du zumeist adressierst, in deiner Form nicht auch ein wenig hilflos?" (Does that not only make you seem anachronistic but also a little helpless in your form given the complex global problems that you mostly address?).

El Ouassil's personification of the open letter as the primary addressee appears to afford it a life, agency, and power of its own, albeit one structured and altered by the dynamics of the digital sphere. Indeed, her letter also indicates that it is the genre itself, rather than the specific issues and indeed real lives at stake, that now attracts the most attention in a saturated economy where attention is a scarce commodity: "Du stehst im Mittelpunkt, die Medienöffentlichkeit arbeitet sich an Dir ab." (You take center stage, the media is obsessed with you.)[23] In the case of the notorious *EMMA* open letter discussed above, this fixation overshadows the experiences and agency of Ukrainians fighting for their sovereignty or fleeing for their lives; instead of talking about Ukrainian "Angst vor einer angekündigten Auslöschung" (fear of their preannounced obliteration), the German public sphere was consumed with "eurozentristische Angst vor einer möglichen Eskalation" (Eurocentric fear of a possible escalation). Yet El Ouassil's rhetorical strategy of adopting, addressing, and satirizing the genre also exposes to the reader—the secondary, but real-life audience—the simultaneous absence and presence of the human actors behind such letters, as well as those human actors who drive the media hype these letters attract in their wake. Given the fictional nature of her letter's ostensible recipient, it is that secondary audience—most specifically El Ouassil's colleagues in the (digital) media industry—to whom her parting message and collective "wir" is directed: "Wir schenken dir einfach zu viel Aufmerksamkeit" (we're simply paying you too much attention). El Ouassil's seemingly ironic use of this very genre to thematize its apparent obsolescence can therefore be seen as a strategic formal choice, which elicits critical reflection from her readers both on her own piece and on the public skepticism about open letters more generally. It also points to the possibility that the digital sphere might both necessitate and offer creative strategies to reinvigorate the beleaguered genre.

Critiquing Power: Open Letters and Intellectual Exile from Zola to Dardan

The recent explosion of open letters has not only registered skepticism about the contemporary usefulness of the genre but also prompted calls to rehabilitate the format. In response to the open letter on *EMMA*

---

23 El Ouassil, "Offener Brief an den offenen Brief."

discussed above and, still more, to the outcry and mockery it provoked, the essayist Asal Dardan took to the social media platform formerly known as Twitter (now X) to redirect public attention to the genre's historical roots and ongoing potential as a method of critiquing power. Dardan's use of a three-part Twitter thread to offer a counterpoint to wider public reactions in the wake of the *EMMA* letter is instructive. Often reduced to a site of political polemic and personalized belligerence (if not outright abuse), Twitter is arguably yet another medium that draws more attention to itself than to the matters at hand. However, Dardan's interjection here not only makes a case for open letters but also exploits the concentrated brevity of the Twitter thread as means of dissecting public discourse and pushing back against (mis-)appropriations of both of those genres for hegemonic rather than counterhegemonic ends, without dismissing them entirely as methods of intellectual intervention:

> Tweet 1: Bequemlichkeit, gegen das Format des offenen Briefs zu wettern. Zola hat vorgemacht, wie wichtig sie sein können—sie sollten Macht kritisieren, Machtmissbrauch entgegenwirken, das Licht auf Ungerechtigkeit lenken. Machthabern Honig um den Bart schmieren ist was anderes.[24]

> [Too convenient to rail against the format of the open letter. Zola showed how important they can be—they should criticize power, counter abuses of power, shine a light on injustice. Buttering up the people in power is something else.]

The implication here is that the *EMMA* letter was a misuse of the genre—not least because of its signatories' praise for Chancellor Scholz—and distorted the genre's original purpose, co-opting it in a manner that affirmed top-down power structures instead of "critiqu[ing] figures of authority and call[ing] for reform."[25]

Like El Ouassil's open letter discussed above, Dardan's Twitter thread recentered attention on the positionality of various people involved in and affected by the issuing of open letters:

> Tweet 2: Politische Gefangene etwa brauchen Menschen, die sich dieses zur peinlichen Form erklärten Mittels bedienen. Wenn

---

24 Asal Dardan (@asallime), "Bequemlichkeit, gegen das Format des offenen Briefs zu wettern. Zola hat vorgemacht, wie wichtig sie sein können—sie sollten Macht kritisieren, Machtmissbrauch entgegenwirken, das Licht auf Ungerechtigkeit lenken. Machthabern Honig um den Bart schmieren ist was anderes," Twitter, April 29, 2022, 8:21 a.m., https://twitter.com/asallime/status/1520030523313303555.

25 Lordi, "Between the World and the Addressee," 436.

Privilegierte sich dessen bedienen, nur um für sich selbst zu sprechen, macht das dieses Werkzeug nicht nutzlos.[26]

[Political prisoners, for example, need people to use this medium, which has been declared embarrassing. If the privileged use it just to speak for themselves, that doesn't render it useless as a tool.]

The importance of having a voice versus being voiceless—of public audibility and inaudibility—is underscored here. Oppressed groups, such as political prisoners, are often or entirely dependent on other people to speak on their behalf, precisely because their freedom is curtailed. Dardan juxtaposes this with privileged groups whose freedom, material comfort, and societal status mean they can afford to use their voices as dominantly positioned speakers to defend their own interests (which they assume, in turn, to be the interests of the majority). While she is undoubtedly critical of this latter group, her intervention highlights the similarly privileged position of comfort ("Bequemlichkeit") from which otherwise well-meaning commentators focus on critiquing the circular exchange of cultural capital among self-interested intellectuals, which diverts attention away from and thus risks perpetuating the marginalization of oppressed groups. Her thread therefore turns the public debate on its head; instead of writing it off as an overused and misused genre, critical intellectuals must confront the limitations of their own reactions and reclaim the open letter in the name of social justice.

Dardan's commentary gets to the heart of the history and sociology of public intellectuals, highlighting their position at the intersection of intellectual labor (she describes open letters as a "Werkzeug" [tool] in the second tweet, for instance) and cultural affluence and prestige. Rather than continuing to devalue the open letter, and instead of abandoning it as an inflationary intellectual and political currency, she calls for a collective pooling and reinvestment of cultural and emotional capital into the genre. This would recover the value of open letters not as a method of self-proliferation and self-enrichment in the aforementioned "attention economy," but as a means of redistributing those resources to increase the attention paid to the causes of groups who most need it:

Tweet 3: Vergebt mir das Pathos, aber sein kulturelles Kapital ggf. mit anderen zu verbinden in einem Appell für andere Menschen

---

26 Asal Dardan (@asallime), "Politische Gefangene etwa brauchen Menschen, die sich dieses zur peinlichen Form erklärten Mittels bedienen. Wenn Privilegierte sich dessen bedienen, nur um für sich selbst zu sprechen, macht das dieses Werkzeug nicht nutzlos," Twitter, April 29, 2022, 8:24 a.m., https://twitter.com/asallime/status/1520031321850011649.

oder gegen Ungerechtigkeiten—das ist ein wichtiges politisches Mittel, das mir (als Exilantin) unglaublich wichtig erscheint.[27]

[Forgive my pathos, but the possibility of combining one's cultural capital with others in an appeal for other people or against injustice— that's an important political tool that I (as an exile) find incredibly important.]

By grounding her defense of the genre in the European history of critical intellectuals (with the reference to Zola's *J'accuse* in the first tweet), Dardan assumes a role as a kind of guardian and carrier of Zola's legacy.[28] At the same time, her self-identification as an exile in the third and final tweet—as someone who was forced (as a child) to flee Iran during the 1979 revolution and establishment of the Islamic Republic—not only aligns her sympathies with those affected by ongoing political oppression but also gestures toward the historical relationship between intellectuals, open letters, and the experience of exile. Zola, for instance, went into self-imposed exile in England after he was found guilty of libel in *J'accuse*.[29] Thomas Mann's (delayed) public renunciation of Nazi Germany and commitment to the exile cause in an open letter to the Swiss literary critic, Eduard Korrodi, meanwhile, is just one (albeit probably the most famous) in a wide catalogue of open letters issued by exiled opponents and persecutees of Nazism in the 1930s and 1940s to criticize the regime and address its intellectual supporters—many of whom also made use of open letters to affirm rather than challenge the Nazis' power.[30]

By referring to herself as an exile while making use of Twitter to defend the open letter, Dardan situates herself within that historical lineage and extends it into the contemporary digital age. Yet her place in the genealogy of critical intellectuals is not one of simple continuation, but an ongoing, self-reflexive reckoning with intellectual politics in general and different meanings of exile more particularly. The parentheses in that

---

27   Asal Dardan (@asallime), "April 29, 2022, "Vergebt mir das Pathos, aber sein kulturelles Kapital ggf. mit anderen zu verbinden in einem Appell für andere Menschen oder gegen Ungerechtigkeiten—das ist ein wichtiges politisches Mittel, das mir (als Exilantin) unglaublich wichtig erscheint," Twitter, April 29, 2022, 8:32 a.m., https://twitter.com/asallime/status/1520033272901816320.

28   On Zola's role in the Dreyfus affair and the social history of critical intellectuals, see Christophe Charle, *Birth of the Intellectuals, 1880–1900*, trans. David Fernbach and G. M. Goshgarian (Cambridge: Polity, 2015).

29   Émile Zola, *Notes from Exile*, trans. Dorothy E. Speirs (Toronto: University of Toronto Press, 2003); Rolf-Bernhard Essig, *Der Offene Brief. Geschichte und Funktion einer publizistischen Form von Isokrates bis Günter Grass* (Würzburg: Königshausen & Neuman, 2000), 173–94.

30   Essig, *Der Offene Brief*, 245–47.

final tweet—"mir (als Exilantin)"—simultaneously mark out and moderate the significance of exile as an ambivalent facet of her intellectual identity. This ambivalence is a recurring theme and a key device in her writings and public engagement. In her autobiographical essay "Neue Jahre" (New Years), for instance, she asks "Bin ich überhaupt im Exil, wenn ich das Land, aus dem ich komme, nie gesehen habe?" (Am I even in exile if I've never seen the country I come from?)[31] More recently, when she gave the inaugural Erika Mann Lecture in Munich on the ninetieth anniversary of the book burnings in Nazi Germany in May 2023, she reflected openly on the tentative and sometimes performative nature of her exilic identity: "Seit dem brutalen Mord an der Kurdin Jina Amini, seit der neuen revolutionären Bewegung im Iran, frage ich mich, ob ich überhaupt ein Anrecht habe, mich mit dem Land meiner Geburt und seinen Menschen in Verbindung zu bringen, indem ich die Rolle einer iranischen Exilantin spiele." (Since the brutal murder of the Kurdish woman Jina Amini, I've been asking myself if I have any right at all to link myself to the land of my birth and the people of that country by playing the role of an Iranian exile.)[32]

Such reflections are often bound up with Dardan's discussion of the historical and contemporary connotations of exile in Germany: "[Das Land, in dem ich aufwuchs] kennt das Exil sehr gut, hat es zum Teil seiner Kultur gemacht" ([The country I grew up in] is very familiar with exile, has made it part of its culture).[33] Noting that Erika Mann never returned from exile and was never invited back to the city of her birth, Dardan confesses in her lecture to feeling "etwas unwohl damit, hier zu stehen und daran beteiligt zu sein, dass man sie nun posthum zurückholt und für sich beansprucht" (a little uncomfortable standing here and taking part in this effort to bring her back posthumously and claim her for ourselves).[34] These pointed statements highlight an uncomfortable paradox. While fascist Germany once created the conditions that forced thousands of intellectuals (and others) into exile, and although the work of those exiled individuals was not immediately accepted as German after 1945,[35] the cultural and intellectual production of twentieth-century émigrés has since been elevated and, in many cases, canonized as quintessentially German. Indeed, in the contemporary context, the categories "exile"

---

31   Asal Dardan, *Betrachtungen einer Barbarin* (Hamburg: Hoffmann und Campe, 2021), 23.
32   Asal Dardan, "Vor dem Dunkel, ausgerechnet Wir" (Erika Mann Lecture, Ludwig-Maximilian University, May 10, 2023), https://erika-mann-lecture.de/lecture-2023/.
33   Dardan, *Betrachtungen*, 24.
34   Dardan, "Vor dem Dunkel, ausgerechnet Wir."
35   Mónica Jato and John Klapper, *The Exile Writing of Nazi Germany and Francoist Spain* (Rochester, NY: Camden House, 2020), 1–2.

and "exile literature" carry considerable cultural prestige, particularly when compared with the standing of labels like "migrant" or "migrant literature."[36] On the one hand, this has the effect of masking elements of "Asyl, Flucht und Exil" (asylum, flight, and exile) in the experiences of those deemed to be economic or labor migrants—for example, in the case of Emine Sevgi Özdamar, as Maha El Hissy has pointed out.[37] On the other hand, it risks co-opting previously marginalized, persecuted, and often resistant figures like Erika Mann into mainstream discourses, a danger of which Dardan is all too aware and that she endeavors to avoid: "Ich möchte Erika Mann . . . den Gefallen tun, das Nachdenken über sie und das Denken mit ihr nicht glatter und geschmeidiger zu machen als es ihr und anderen Exilant*innen gebührt." (I want to do Erika Mann the favor of not making my reflections on her and my thinking with her smoother and slicker than she and other exiles deserve.) It was, after all, Erika Mann's courage that pushed her father to finally shed his hesitation as an "unpolitische[r] Künstler" (unpolitical artist)[38] and to position himself openly against the Nazis in his aforementioned open letter.[39]

In this light, Dardan's use of the marker "exile" in that Twitter thread (and more generally) is neither merely biographical, nor is it about garnering cultural prestige to self-serving ends. Rather, it can be understood as a reminder and reinvigoration of exile, in its historical and contemporary iterations, as an intellectual, ethical, and political practice of resistance; to borrow from Edward Said, it is an unwillingness to accommodate dominant power relations and a preference "to remain outside the mainstream, unaccommodated, uncoopted, resistant."[40] Such resistance to top-down co-optation is also integral to the subversive origins of the postmigrant perspective[41] and an essential feature of Medina's (Foucaultian) understanding of the "insurrection of subjugated knowledges" as a "critical battle against the monopolization of knowledge-producing practices."[42]

---

36 Christian Palm, "Migrant versus Exilant: Zur Konzeptualisierung und Positionierung einer 'deutschsprachigen Literatur exilierter Autoren.'" In *Zukunftsfragen der Germanistik: Beiträge der DAAD-Germanistentagung 2011 mit den Partnerländern Frankreich, Belgien, Niederlande, Luxemburg*, ed. Deutscher Akademischer Austauschdienst (Göttingen: Wallstein, 2012), 283–95.
37 Maha El Hissy in Oholi et al., "Postmigration Reloaded," 66.
38 Dardan, "Vor dem Dunkel, ausgerechnet Wir."
39 See also Essig, *Der offene Brief*, 251n173.
40 Edward W. Said, "Intellectual Exile: Expatriates and Marginals," *Grand Street* 47 (Autumn, 1993): 116.
41 See Jeannette Oholi in Oholi et al., "Postmigration Reloaded," 63–64.
42 Medina, "Toward a Foucaultian Epistemology," 13.

"Diese Fantasielosigkeit ist ein Privileg": Shida Bazyar's Open Letter to Jina Amini

If Dardan's Twitter defense of the open letter was, in the first instance, a direct response to the fallout of the letter published by the twenty-eight intellectuals on *EMMA* regarding the war in Ukraine, it would take on additional relevance with the eruption of new antiregime protests in Iran a few months later. A week after Jina Amini's death, Shida Bazyar—a prize-winning novelist and the daughter of Iranian political activists who fled the Islamic Republic in 1987, a year before her birth—published an open letter in the *Süddeutsche Zeitung* that she addressed directly to the murdered young woman. The letter is at once a poignant tribute to Amini and the courage of the women who have resisted and protested the Islamic regime for many years as well as a scathing critique of the murderous Iranian state apparatus and what Bazyar refers to as the West's "Fantasielosigkeit" (lack of imagination) and ignorance.[43] While all of this might have been achieved in a standard journalistic article or literary essay, it is the epistolary form that challenges Western readers to question the kinds of "standard interpretations"[44] that structure dominant perceptions of Amini's death and the Iranian protest movement.

With its personal form of address to Amini, Bazyar's letter can be seen as a variation on the kind of "intimate open letter" or personal-political letter-essay popularized by James Baldwin with the letter he addressed to his fifteen-year-old nephew that was first published in the white liberal magazine the *Progressive* in 1962 and later as part of his book *The Fire Next Time*.[45] My purpose here is not to compare or equate the oppression faced by Iranian women today and Black Americans in the 1960s, but to explore the literary style and devices of the epistolary form. Whereas more conventional forms of open letter are addressed to figures of authority—such as Olaf Scholz in the examples mentioned above or white liberal clergymen in Martin Luther King's "Letter from a Birmingham Jail"—Baldwin's "letter-essay rhetorically privileged his nephew and namesake (with whom black readers were invited to identify)" while "elegantly nudging white readers to the margin, making them the 'they' to a centered black 'you.'"[46] At the same time, according to Lordi, Baldwin's letter stages a "rhetorical closing of the ranks" and "models the literary

---

43 Shida Bazyar, "Frau. Leben. Freiheit. Ein offener Brief an die in Iran umgekommene Jina Amini," *Süddeutsche Zeitung*, September 23, 2022, https://www.sueddeutsche.de/kultur/jina-amini-iran-proteste-1.5662685?reduced=true.
44 Medina, "Toward a Foucaultian Epistemology," 11.
45 Lordi, "Between the World and the Addressee," 434–36.
46 Lordi, "Between the World and the Addressee," 436–37.

creation of a defiant in-group intimacy, whereby one expects to be 'overheard' but refuses to be silenced."[47]

Unlike Baldwin's nephew, Bazyar's primary addressee was neither a biological relative nor alive at the time of writing. Nonetheless, Bazyar's rhetorical privileging of Amini similarly nudges German readers to the margin and cultivates a kind of "defiant in-group intimacy" that exposes the epistemological limits of Western perspectives. As a Kurdish woman, Amini not only represents an oppressed Other in the context of the Islamic Republic's misogyny and "staatlich organisierter Rassismus gegen Kurd:innen" (state organized racism against Kurds*). She is also symbolic of a marginal, distant Other in dominant Western discourse:

> Im sogenannten Westen kann man sich dein Leben nicht vorstellen. Ist überrascht, dass Menschen wie du ganz selbstverständlich das Internet für Memes, Musik und zur Selbstdarstellung nutzen, ist überrascht darüber, dass du glücklich sein kannst, trotz der systematischen Unterdrückung. Diese Fantasielosigkeit ist ein Privileg. Denn Menschen können unter den widrigsten Umständen leben. Das relativiert nicht die Umstände, das entlarvt lediglich den Außenblick.[48]

> [In the so-called West, people can't imagine your life. They're surprised that people like you use the internet as a matter of course for memes, music, and self-expression, they're surprised that you can be happy, despite the systematic oppression. That lack of imagination is a privilege. Because people can live under the most appalling circumstances. That doesn't relativize those circumstances; it just exposes the outside gaze.]

Bazyar's own detailed depiction of Amini's everyday life and surroundings in the letter creates a sense of familiarity, even kinship, and affords Amini an agency and individuality that contrasts with those processes of Othering and a state of unknowing that correlates with what Medina (drawing on Lorraine Code) calls the "white epistemic gaze."[49] The letter's familiarity is reinforced by Bazyar's use of the informal second person "du" to refer to Amini, which stands in stark contrast to the abstract "man" used to refer to the Iranian regime and the West at various points in the letter. While Western readers are staged as a subordinate secondary audience, and even placed explicitly on the outside, they are given

---

47 Lordi, "Between the World and the Addressee," 437.
48 Bazyar, "Frau. Leben. Freiheit."
49 Medina, "Toward a Foucaultian Epistemology," 31. Medina refers here to Lorraine Code, "The Power of Ignorance," in *Race and Epistemologies of Ignorance*, ed. Shannon Sullivan and Nancy Tuana (Albany: State University of New York Press, 2007), 213–29.

access to and expected to "overhear"—to return to Lordi's terminology—Bazyar's rhetorical intimacy and knowledge of her imagined recipient. Her narrative strategy is not simply an act "of 'enlightening' the dominant culture";[50] it opens an opportunity for those readers to confront their own assumptions, positionality, and the possible limits of their privileged "Fantasielosigkeit."

Bazyar's language here is consistent with Medina's claim that "our inability to even register certain forms of exclusion and stigmatization and to become sensitive to them involves a failure of the imagination."[51] As an extension of this, Bazyar's letter unearths a failure to imagine, understand, and become sensitive to forms of agency and resistance. This failure is even—or perhaps especially—evident among left-wing and liberal Germans who might consider themselves to be champions of female emancipation but who continue to overlook the complex reality of Iranian feminism: "Diese Fantasielosigkeit ist es, die dazu führt, dass linke deutsche Tageszeitungen sich erdreisten, den Kampf iranischer Frauen auf den Wunsch nach 'dem bisschen Wind im Haar' zu reduzieren. Diese Fantasielosigkeit ist es, die dazu führt, dass sich nichts an einer deutschen Außenpolitik zu ändern scheint, auch wenn sie sich als feministisch bezeichnet." (It is this lack of imagination that leads left-wing German daily newspapers to have the audacity to reduce the struggle of Iranian women to the desire for "a little wind in their hair." It is this lack of imagination that means nothing seems to change in German foreign policy, even if it describes itself as feminist.)[52] In addition to gesturing

---

50   Lordi, "Between the World and the Addressee," 435.

51   Medina, *The Epistemology of Resistance*, 309. See also Sarah Colvin and Stephanie Galasso, "Introduction: Changing the Story? Epistemic Shifts and Creative Agency," in *Epistemic Justice and Creative Agency: Global Perspectives on Literature and Film*, ed. Sarah Colvin and Stephanie Galasso (New York: Routledge: 2022), 7.

52   Bazyar, "Frau. Leben. Freiheit." Bazyar's first reference here is to an article published in the left-wing *taz* (before Amini's death), which presents a reductive view of Iranian exile activism and the politics of headscarves in Iran. See Julia Neumann, "Frauenrechte im Nahen Osten: Das bisschen Wind im Haar," *taz*, August 11, 2022, https://taz.de/Frauenrechte-im-Nahen-Osten/!5870604/. For a further critique of that article, which questions but also carries the same headline, see Petra Klug, "Frauenrechte im Nahen Osten: Das bisschen Wind im Haar . . ." *taz*, August 20, 2022, https://taz.de/Frauenrechte-im-Nahen-Osten/!5874586/. Her second reference is to the self-styled feminist foreign policy (FFP) associated with the Green Party and minister of foreign affairs, Annalena Baerbock. For a critical panel discussion of FFP in relation to Iran, including Baerbock as a participant, see "In Solidarity with the Women on the Streets: Feminist Foreign Policy Demands towards Iran," Centre for Feminist Foreign Policy, October 20, 2022, https://centreforfeministforeignpolicy.org/event/in-solidarity-with-the-women-on-the-streets-feminist-foreign-policy-demands-towards-iran/.

toward the ignorance and hypocrisy of contemporary Western feminisms, Bazyar's letter anticipates and, in doing so, counteracts a form of historiographical epistemic injustice whereby decades of Iranian feminist resistance to the regime's "systemloses System" (systemless system) is likely to be misinterpreted or written out of history:

> Niemand wird es den Frauen Irans jemals explizit danken, die Geschichte wird sie nachträglich nicht dafür honorieren, es wartet kein kollektiver Friedensnobelpreis auf sie, aber: jede Frau, die das Kopftuch durch das lockere Tragen im Alltag, beim Einkauf, auf dem Weg zur Arbeit, in seinen Grenzen verschoben hat, hat einen Teil eines radikalen Kampfes gekämpft, ein Stück Geschichte geschrieben.[53]

> [No one will thank the women of Iran explicitly, history won't honor them retrospectively, there's no collective Nobel Peace Prize waiting for them. But: every woman who pushed the boundaries by wearing the headscarf loose on an everyday basis, when they went shopping, on their way to work, was part of a radical struggle, has written a piece of history.]

By explaining the contested symbolism of the headscarf in the Iranian context and by acknowledging how Iranian women have gradually but continually turned an object of oppression into one of self-assertion, Bazyar's letter provides space for the kind of "epistemic friction" that ensures that "eccentric voices and perspectives are heard and can interact with mainstream ones."[54] It makes transparent the process by which dominant histories and narratives are produced and offers a preemptive countermemory that, according to Medina (this time drawing on the philosopher Charles Mills), is needed to "resist and subvert the epistemic oppression that condemns the lives of marginalized people to silence or oblivion."[55]

Although Bazyar does not refer to herself as an exile as such, her own epistemological advantage and ability to offer correctives to existing and emerging narratives are arguably a reflection of what Edward Said

---

53 Bazyar, "Frau. Leben. Freiheit."
54 Medina, "Toward a Foucaultian Epistemology," 21. On German public debates about headscarves, see Beverly M. Weber, "Hijab Martyrdom, Headscarf Debates: Rethinking Violence, Secularism, and Islam in Germany," *Comparative Studies of South Asia, Africa and the Middle East* 32, no. 1 (2012): 102–15; Reyhan Şahin, *Die Bedeutung des muslimischen Kopftuchs: Eine kleidungssemiotische Untersuchung Kopftuch tragender Musliminnen in der Bundesrepublik Deutschland* (Münster: LIT Verlag, 2014).
55 Medina, "Toward a Foucaultian Epistemology," 31–32.

called a "double or exile perspective," which "impels a Western intellectual to see what is usually thought of as a simple issue of judgement . . . as part of a much wider picture."[56] This double perspective impels her, for instance, to underscore the historical and political importance of the headscarf while also complicating a reductive discourse centered on that very object: "Jina, du bist tot, aber du bist nicht wegen des Kopftuches gestorben. Das Kopftuch war der Anlass, nicht der Grund." (Jina, you're dead, but you didn't die because of the headscarf. The headscarf was the pretext, not the reason.)[57] While the author's epistemic authority vis à vis white Western readers derives from her understanding and privileging of Iranian women's perspectives, the "defiant in-group intimacy"[58] and diasporic identity conjured in Bazyar's letter is self-consciously ambivalent, precisely because of her own position as someone who lives and writes in the West:

> Ich könnte die vergangenen Jahre auch anders interpretieren. Ich könnte auch der Lethargie verfallen, die mich immer wieder einholt und sagen: Auch diese Proteste werden Tote bringen und niedergeschlagen werden, auch diesmal wird sich nichts ändern . . . Aber das tue ich nicht. Denn das, was wir im Westen als verwackelte Handybilder sehen und als Randnotiz, als immer wiederkehrende Proteste abtun, sind Menschen, die mehr Mut aufbringen, als Menschen wie ich in ihrem Leben jemals zu tun imstande wären.[59]

> [I could also interpret the years gone past differently. I could also succumb to the lethargy that keeps catching me up and say: these protests will bring deaths and will be crushed, too, nothing will change this time round either . . . But I'm not going to do that. Because what we in the West see as shaky cell phone pictures and dismiss as a side note, as eternally recurring protests, are human beings who summon up more courage than people like me will ever be able to.]

Here, Bazyar aligns herself with Western readers using the first-person plural and underscores both her geographical and existential distance from the ground-level reality faced by protesters in Iran. At the same time, her use of the first-person singular demonstrates the choice she faces between accepting or challenging lazy or inadequate perspectives ("Ich könnte . . . Aber das tue ich nicht"). This personal defiance is also encapsulated in her rejection of the euphemistic language frequently

56   Said, "Intellectual Exile," 121–22.
57   Bazyar, "Frau. Leben. Freiheit."
58   Lordi, "Between the World and the Addressee," 437.
59   Bazyar, "Frau. Leben. Freiheit."

used in connection with Amini's death: "man gibt sich Mühe, nicht von Mord zu sprechen, ich gebe mir diese Mühe nicht" (people are making every effort not to talk of murder—I'm making no such effort). Bazyar performs and opens a model of defiance and cross-border solidarity that, ultimately, does not even demand greater imagination of Western readers, but only a more empathetic perspective "um sich gegen die Lethargie zu entscheiden und in tiefsten Respekt vor den Menschen Irans zu verfallen" (decide against lethargy and to be beholden in deep respect for the people of Iran).

While Bazyar posted images of her letter in its print edition on Instagram,[60] others—including Asal Dardan—shared the online version on Twitter. Dardan's endorsement of Bazyar's "beeindruckend klaren, durchdringenden Brief" (impressively clear and penetrating letter)[61] is imbued with a sense of common exilic identity that—despite the very different nature and circumstances of their families' exile from Iran—appears to coalesce around the recent revolutionary protests: "Ich bin froh, dass es diesen Brief von Shida Bazyar gibt, denn er fängt viele der Gefühle ein, für die man sich im Exil leise schämt und die man doch ausdrücken möchte." (I'm glad that this letter by Shida Bazyar exists, because it captures many of the feelings you're quietly ashamed of in exile but would still like to express.)[62] In this framing, Bazyar acquires the role of spokesperson who is able to transform a helpless or passive notion of exile into the resistant stance advocated by Said and Dardan, as discussed in the previous section of this chapter. Bazyar's letter found further resonance when it was read aloud by the actress Jasmin Tabatabai as part of a solidarity event she organized with her colleagues Melika Foroutan and Sarah Sandeh at the Berliner Ensemble theater in late November 2022, an event that also featured other high-profile figures, including

---

60 Shida Bazyar (@shida.baz), "Man gibt sich Mühe, nicht von Mord zu sprechen, ich gebe mir diese Mühe nicht," Instagram, September 24, 2022, https://www.instagram.com/p/Ci4jX0oshKU/?img_index=1.

61 Asal Dardan (@asallime), "Shida Bazyar hat einen beeindruckend klaren, durchdringenden Brief geschrieben, dem die Überschrift nicht gerecht wird. Denn Jina Amini ist nicht im Iran umgekommen, sie wurde von der islamischen Diktatur ermordet. Shida selbst findet die richtigen Worte," Twitter, September 23, 2022, 3:13 p.m., https://twitter.com/asallime/status/1573405281459093505.

62 Asal Dardan (@asallime), "Sie schreibt sogar selbst '... man gibt sich Mühe, nicht von Mord zu sprechen, ich gebe mir diese Mühe nicht.' Ich bin froh, dass es diesen Brief von Shida Bazyar gibt, denn er fängt viele der Gefühle ein, für die man sich im Exil leise schämt und die man doch ausdrücken möchte," Twitter, September 23, 2022, 3:17 p.m., https://twitter.com/asallime/status/1573406159947669505.

Meret Becker, Iris Berben, and Katja Riemann.[63] In a related Instagram post, Tabatabai described the letter as "kraftvoll, wütend, auf den Punkt" (powerful, raging, to the point).[64] Through this public performance, Bazyar's letter was not only mobilized as part of ongoing (diasporic) initiatives to support the protesters in Iran, making the individually authored text part of a wider collaborative network; it was also embedded in a longer, now canonical tradition of political literature associated with the Berliner Ensemble and its founders Helene Weigel and Bertolt Brecht. At the same time, a recording of the event made Tabatabai's reading widely available through the ARD Mediathek, expanding its reach and locating the letter at the heart of a mainstream, multimedia outlet. These various venues and media of publication, performance, and circulation enhance the significance and potential efficacy of this open letter as a method of literary intervention and epistemological disruption in contemporary German discourse.

"Aufmerksamkeit ist ihr Schutzschild!": An Open Letter to the Protesters in Iran

Both Shida Bazyar's letter and Asal Dardan's Twitter interventions discussed above provide important context for a further letter that Dardan co-instigated in support of the protesters who took to the streets following Amini's death. The letter was circulated online and in the German media on October 4–5, 2022, and issued in four languages: German, English, Farsi, and the Kurdish dialect Sorani. It was signed by almost 650 writers, musicians, actors, and other cultural figures from the German-speaking world, including Nobel Prize winner Elfriede Jelinek.[65] Collectively, the

63   "FRAU LEBEN FREIHEIT—ZAN ZENDEGI AZADI—زن زندگی آزادی: Solidarität mit den Protestierenden in Iran," Berliner Ensemble, accessed April 24, 2024, https://www.berliner-ensemble.de/frau-leben-freiheit.

64   Jasmin Tabatabai (@jazmatab), "Shida Bazyar's 'Brief an die nach der Verhaftung durch die iranische Polizei um's Leben gekommene Jina Mahsa Amini' ist kraftvoll, wütend, auf den Punkt," Instagram, December 6, 2022, https://www.instagram.com/p/Cl0xrQrIcYi/.

65   The press release that accompanied the letter included the following names: Elfriede Jelinek, Feo Aladag, Aleida Assmann, Fatma Aydemir, Iris Berben, Teresa Bücker, Thelma Buabeng, Carolin Emcke, Theresia Enzensberger, Alexandra Maria Lara, Samira El Ouassil, Julia von Heinz, Dmitrij Kapitelman, Ulrich Matthes, Sharon Dodua Otoo, Robert Stadlober, Jasmin Tabatabai, Josef Winkler, and David Wagner, as well as institutions such as the Bildungsstätte Anne Frank: "Pressemitteilung: Knapp 650 namhafte Kulturschaffende richten sich an Protestierende im Iran," CryptPad, accessed April 23, 2024, https://cryptpad.fr/file/#/2/file/o-bIQjnbh65J-9h2lGgmbvCD/. Other literary intellectuals who signed the letter included the novelists Lin Hierse, Kim de l'Horizon,

signatories are referred to as "Kulturschaffende," translated as "cultural workers" in the English version, which casts them as laborers and creators—in an echo of Dardan's earlier Twitter thread—who make use of the open letter as a tool in their public efforts.[66] In addition to those who lent their names and therefore their cultural capital to increase the impact of the letter, other signatories were compelled, somewhat paradoxically, to remain anonymous—signing with only their initials, for example—to avoid putting their own families in Iran in danger.[67] In these partly veiled cases, participation in such public declarations carries a degree of risk and courage associated with earlier forms of open letters (when speaking out openly might have entailed political consequences or even a threat to life). This, in turn, enhances the weight of the letter; as Anne Lorenz explains, "je größer . . . das Risiko für den freimütigen Sprecher, desto glaubwürdiger, wahrhaftiger und authentischer wirkt seine kritische Stimme" (the greater the risk for the outspoken speaker, the more believable, truthful, and authentic their critical voice appears).[68] The named and the unnamed—the prominent and the concealed—thus come together in this instance to offer mutual legitimation and authority to each other, their letter, and its causes.

In the accompanying press release, the letter's instigators made a point of highlighting what they saw as their unconventional approach to the genre: rather than addressing the German government or international political institutions "wie bei ähnlichen Formaten üblich" (as is usual in similar formats),[69] this open letter was addressed directly "An die Protestierenden im Iran" (to the protesters in Iran). As co-instigator, Dardan explained the reason for this approach: "Diese Bewegung [im

---

Sasha Marianna Salzmann, Mithu Sanyal, Senthuran Varatharajah, Deniz Utlu, and Hengameh Yaghoobifarah, along with poets such as Max Czollek and Ozan Zakariya Keskinkılıç. See "Brief Kulturschaffender an die Protestierenden im Iran," Frauen Leben Freiheit, October 4, 2022, accessed April 24, 2024, https://frauenlebenfreiheit.wordpress.com/.

66 "Letter from Cultural Workers to the Protesters in Iran," Frauen Leben Freiheit, October 4, 2022, accessed April 24, 2024, https://frauenlebenfreiheit.wordpress.com/. All English translations from this letter are taken from this original English version.

67 Asal Dardan (@asallime), "Ich danke allen, die unterzeichnet haben. ALLEN! Jeder einzelnen Person. Manche können es nur anonym, weil ihre Familien im Land sind. Andere stehen solidarisch neben ihnen mit ihrem Namen, etwa 650: Von Feo Aladag über Elfriede Jelinek bis hin zu Mirjam Zadoff," Twitter, October 4, 2022, 11:52 a.m., https://twitter.com/asallime/status/1577340800865898496.

68 Lorenz, "Die ungefährliche Rückkehr."

69 "Pressemitteilung," CryptPad, accessed April 23, 2024, https://cryptpad.fr/file/#/2/file/o-bIQjnbh65J-9h2lGgmbvCD/.

Iran] geht von den Menschen aus, dezentral und feministisch. Deshalb war es uns wichtig, uns direkt an sie zu richten. Ihnen gilt die Solidarität, weil die nichts haben als ihre Körper und ihre Stimmen." (This movement [in Iran] emanates from the people, decentralized and feminist. That's why it was important for us to address them directly. They deserve solidarity because they have nothing but their bodies and their voices.)[70] Mirroring this, she also framed the letter itself as an outcome and expression of decentralized queer feminism in the German-speaking context when she posted it on Twitter and Instagram: "Manchen kann ich nicht öffentlich danken, aber wir sind ein starkes Netzwerk von Frauen und nicht-binären Menschen, mit Verbindung zum Iran." (Some people can't be thanked publicly, but we are a strong network of women and non-binary people with connections to Iran.)[71] The letter itself expresses admiration for the intersectional diversity of the people engaged in the struggle in Iran despite harsh restrictions and the real threat of violence from the regime: "alle Altergruppen, alle Klassen, alle Geschlechter [sind] vereint in diesem Befreiungskampf" (people regardless of age, class, and gender are united in this struggle for liberation).[72]

Both the origins and the content of the letter demonstrate that the significance of this struggle is not limited to Iran, highlighting common causes and sympathies across borders, despite, and in full acknowledgment of, vast differences in political contexts. In addition to the thousands of people marching on the streets of Iran and Eastern Kurdistan, the letter noted that thousands more had taken to the street around the world—"Vereint rufen sie: Jin, Jiyan, Azadi!" (In unity they call: Jin, Jiyan, Azadi!).[73] The use of that Kurdish phrase and the reference to Eastern Kurdistan add an additional layer that points to the emancipatory impulses of this oppressed ethnic group. At the same time, the protestors' resistance to the Iranian regime demonstrates, according to the letter, "dass die Befreiung von Frauen und queeren Menschen der Weg zur

---

70 "Pressemitteilung," CryptPad, accessed April 23, 2024, https://cryptpad.fr/file/#/2/file/o-bIQjnbh65J-9h2lGgmbvCD/.

71 Asal Dardan (@asallime), "Manchen kann ich nicht öffentlich danken, aber wir sind ein starkes Netzwerk von Frauen und nicht-binären Menschen, mit Verbindungen zum Iran. Andere haben die letzten Tage unglaublich geholfen," October 4, 2022, 11:54 a.m., https://twitter.com/asallime/status/1577341495014789121; Asal Dardan (@asaldardan), "Wie stark Solidarität wirken kann, zeigt dieser Brief Kulturschaffender an die Protestierenden im Iran, so hoffe ich. Er ist auf Deutsch, Farsi, Sorani und Englisch verfügbar," Instagram, October 4, 2022, https://www.instagram.com/p/CjTRLQAsAQ7/.

72 "Brief Kulturschaffender" / "Letter from Cultural Workers," Frauen Leben Freiheit, accessed April 24, 2024, https://frauenlebenfreiheit.wordpress.com/.

73 "Brief Kulturschaffender" / "Letter from Cultural Workers," Frauen Leben Freiheit, accessed April 24, 2024, https://frauenlebenfreiheit.wordpress.com/.

Befreiung aller ist" (that the liberation of women and queer people is the path to the liberation of all of us).[74] This sense of cross-border intersectional unity evoked in the letter was further strengthened by images circulated together with the letter on social media depicting a demonstration that had taken place in Berlin a few days earlier: in addition to displaying throngs of people, these images show placards with messages, such as "It's about having choice" (Fig. 9.1).[75] The letter not only addresses the grassroots movement in Iran, then, but simultaneously conjures and speaks to a transnational community of grassroots and intellectual activism: "Wir danken euch für euren Widerstand und euren Mut. Wir werden euren Kampf begleiten" (We will support [sic] your resistance and courageous struggle, and walk with you on the road to freedom).[76] The first-person plural voice "wir" (we) addressing the familiar plural "ihr/euch" (you) connects the "community of cosignatories"[77] with the Iranian protesters and their supporters in Germany, Europe, and around the world, illustrating the local and global relevance of (and threats to) queer and feminist rights movements.

By privileging the protesters as the primary addressees, the letter's signatories relocate the center of political power to those people on the streets (and, by extension, their international supporters), rather than situating it in the hands of an individual "politisch einflussreiche Person" (politically influential person)[78] or in the corridors of governmental institutions. Yet the genre's scope for reaching multiple audiences means it has additional informative and appellative dimensions that are addressed indirectly both to policymakers and to mainstream German and/or international publics who may not know much about or immediately identify with the issues at stake in both the protests and the letter. This was once again alluded to in the press release. The journalist Gilda Sahebi, for example, noted an inability or unwillingness in the German public sphere to acknowledge or fully understand the significance of the protests following Amini's death, which Sahebi described as "eine historische Zäsur in der iranischen Geschichte" (a historical caesura in Iran's history); "Und doch schauen viele deutsche Medien nicht hin, oder

---

74   "Brief Kulturschaffender" / "Letter from Cultural Workers," Frauen Leben Freiheit, accessed April 24, 2024, https://frauenlebenfreiheit.wordpress.com/.

75   "Title option C, poster with 'It's about having a choice,'" CryptPad, accessed April 24, 2024, https://cryptpad.fr/pad/#/2/pad/view/i1O2ePQaNJb43tI12xfkLsIFB3FplGa+pZAlCvIBP-0/. Image by @anne_vlpx.

76   "Brief Kulturschaffender" / "Letter from Cultural Workers," Frauen Leben Freiheit, accessed April 24, 2024, https://frauenlebenfreiheit.wordpress.com/. This is the official English translation, which does not quite capture the element of thanks and indebtedness in the same way that the German verb "danken" does.

77   Lordi, "Between the World and the Addressee," 435.

78   Lorenz, "Die ungefährliche Rückkehr."

Figure 9.1. Letter of Solidarity 'Sharepic' #IranProtests2022 #JinJiyanAzadî: "Title option C, poster with 'It's about having a choice,'" © Copyright @anne_vlpx.

berichten falsch." (And yet much of the German media isn't paying attention or is reporting incorrectly.)[79] Inadequate reporting means that the protesters' experiences are doubly marginalized or even erased: violently by the Iranian regime, on the one hand, and discursively by an inattentive and ill-informed West, on the other. The letter therefore spells out clearly what is at stake in the Iranian protests: the rejection of laws that restrict bodily autonomy and freedom of expression; the desire to make independent decisions without fear; and the demand for an end to forty-three years of dictatorial rule.[80] With this in mind, and building on Sahebi's critique of the German media in the press release, the author and

---

79 "Pressemitteilung," CryptPad, accessed April 23, 2024, https://cryptpad.fr/file/#/2/file/o-bIQjnbh65J-9h2lGgmbvCD/.

80 "Brief Kulturschaffender" / "Letter from Cultural Workers," Frauen Leben Freiheit, accessed April 24, 2024, https://frauenlebenfreiheit.wordpress.com/.

political activist Sanaz Azimipour underscored the importance of "internationale Solidarität und mediale Aufmerksamkeit. Sie [die demonstrierenden und streikenden Menschen im Iran] brauchen vor allem politische Unterstützung, damit ihre Stimmen gehört werden. Sie haben sehr konkrete Anliegen. Aufmerksamkeit ist ihr Schutzschild!" (international solidarity and media attention. Above all, they [the people demonstrating and striking in Iran] need political support so that their voices are heard. They have very concrete objectives. Attention is their protective shield!)[81] In line with this statement and Dardan's defense of the open letter discussed above, the letter therefore mobilizes the very thing about open letters that has garnered criticism in other contexts—namely, attention.

In this case, however, the attention generated by the open letter's prominent signatories is redistributed as an invaluable commodity to those who need it most.[82] To this end, the language of visibility and audibility is used conspicuously both in the press release and the text of the letter: "Wir sehen euren couragierten Widerstand, wir hören eure entschlossene Stimmen. . . . Wir sehen, was ihr riskiert. Wir sehen die Opfer, die ihr bringt." (We see your courageous resistance. We hear your determined voices. . . . We see the risks you are taking. We see the sacrifices you make.)[83] In its direct mode of address to the protesters, this language of seeing and hearing is empowering and encourages them to persist. As a form of indirect address to secondary audiences of German and/or international leaders and readers, by contrast, it can be read as an invitation to reflect on a possible or probable deficit of attentiveness—a lack of seeing and hearing—of the kind that Sahebi referred to in the press release. In the penultimate line, the signatories make a hopeful yet shaky assertion on behalf of their governments and institutions: "Wir sehen euren Kampf und sind überzeugt, dass auch unsere Regierungen und unsere Institutionen euch sehen und unterstützen" (We see your struggle and are certain [*sic*] that our governments and institutions will also see and support you).[84] On one level, this rhetorical tactic puts pressure on those political actors to step up and take notice. At the same time, the claim can be read against the grain as a signal that the letter's authors and signatories are in fact anything but convinced about the reliability and efficacy of

81 "Pressemitteilung," CryptPad, accessed April 23, 2024, https://cryptpad.fr/file/#/2/file/o-bIQjnbh65J-9h2lGgmbvCD/.

82 On the importance of attention as a key resource for social movements and the role of social media, especially in repressive regimes, see Zeynep Tufekci, "'Not This One': Social Movements, the Attention Economy, and Microcelebrity Networked Activism," *American Behavioral Scientist* 57 (2013): 848–70.

83 "Brief Kulturschaffender" / "Letter from Cultural Workers," Frauen Leben Freiheit, accessed 24, 2024, https://frauenlebenfreiheit.wordpress.com/.

84 "Brief Kulturschaffender" / "Letter from Cultural Workers," Frauen Leben Freiheit, accessed April 24, 2024, https://frauenlebenfreiheit.wordpress.com/.

official politics and diplomacy in this situation. This doubt is subtly and perhaps serendipitously backed up by one of the images of the solidarity protests in Berlin, which shows a second placard in the background with the phrase "Mullahs Diplomaten Raus!" (Mullahs' diplomats get out!), indicating that no official measures had been taken to expel representatives of the repressive regime (Fig. 9.1).[85] Two weeks later, moreover, the original open letter was supplemented on the same "frauenlebenfreiheit" website with a template for individual letters to be addressed directly to Chancellor Scholz, Foreign Minister Annalena Baerbock, Interior Minister Nancy Faeser, Economic Minister Robert Habeck, and members of the federal government and parliament.[86] This letter uses the formal "Sie" (you) and reads more like a conventional open letter to political leaders, presenting thirteen demands to effect a radical change in Germany's foreign and economic policy toward Iran. Yet its publication as a template for individual letters, rather than a fully fledged and collectively endorsed open letter, further accentuates the unconventional nature and rhetorical power of the original open letter addressed to the protesters and underscores a lack of effective solidarity from the German government, who are seen to be complicit in upholding the Iranian regime.

As well as shining a spotlight on the political activity of global protest movements and the apparent inactivity of established political actors, the collective open letter to the protesters of October 4 creates additional space for political agency on the part of its wider readership. Precisely because it speaks to them indirectly as secondary addressees, readers are required to work out for themselves that this letter is also appealing to them as a call to action, and that they too are in positions of power. The collective "Wir" constructed by the open letter is ambivalent, but open and extendable. Nonsignatory readers are able to decide for themselves if they (want to) belong to the letter's inclusive and empowering "Wir," and to ask themselves what they might do to enhance the international visibility and audibility of the protesters' queer feminist causes. This action might simply take the form of sharing social media posts by signatories (or, later on, using the aforementioned template to address an individual letter to the German government). But the potential for further interactive participation in this open letter initiative was also evident in the creation of a so-called "CryptPad," an open-source collaborative suite, to make materials freely

85   "Title option C, poster with 'It's about having a choice,'" CryptPad, accessed April 24, 2024, https://cryptpad.fr/pad/#/2/pad/view/i1O2ePQaNJ b43tI12xfkLsIFB3FplGa+pZAlCvIBP-0. Image by @anne_vlpx.

86   Asal Dardan, "Briefvorlage für ein individuelles Schreiben an die Bundesregierung: Keine Wirtschaftsdeals ohne Menschenrechte: Forderung nach einem neuen Kurs in der deutschen Iranpolitik," October 22, 2022, accessed April 24, 2024, https://frauenlebenfreiheit.wordpress.com/2022/10/22/ briefvorlage-fur-ein-indivuelles-schreiben-an-die-bundesregierung/.

available so they can be shared on social media. These materials included the full press release, the various translations of the letter text, and images with captions as well as ALT-text descriptions, which are used to make pictures accessible to people with visual impairments (an indication of the thought given to all-round inclusivity). Although Dardan's announcement of the open letter on Twitter suggested that the materials were meant for signatories to share,[87] the CryptPad was accessible in a read-only version with downloadable content by anyone who clicked on the link. The use of the CryptPad was a further sign of the detailed planning process behind this particular letter, and its digital, decentral, and democratizing character, which reflects its contemporary adaptation and update of the historical function of open letters.

Such transparency and openness to wider participation also propagates a broad and arguably egalitarian understanding of the societal role and position of intellectuals. By instigating, conceptualizing, and distributing the letter in this way, Dardan and her associates go some way to challenging an image of aloof and detached intellectuals whose moral authority derives from a perceived "vernünftige Distanz zum politischen Geschehen" (reasonable distance from political events).[88] Sharing the CryptPad link, Dardan declared: "Wir sind alle keine Profis, ich hoffe dennoch, dass dieser Brief weit und breit gelesen und geteilt wird. Damit die Richtigen ihn finden und sich gegenseitig stützen—auf Veränderung hoffend: [link to CryptPad]" (none of us are pros, but I nevertheless hope that this letter will be read and shared far and wide. So that the right people find it and support each other—in the hope of change: [link to CryptPad]).[89] As this section has demonstrated, Dardan's reference here to "die Richtigen" can be understood in multiple senses and directions since the letter has the potential to engage numerous audiences and participants.

87 Asal Dardan (@asallime), "Unterzeichnende können hier Materialien zum Teilen finden. Wir sind alle keine Profis, ich hoffe dennoch, dass dieser Brief weit und breit gelesen und geteilt wird. Damit die Richtigen ihn finden und sich gegenseitig stützen—auf Veränderung hoffend: https://cryptpad.fr/pad/#/2/pad/view/i1O2ePQaNJb43tI12xfkLsIFB3FplGa+pZAlCvIBP-0/," Twitter, October 4, 2022, 1:20 p.m., https://twitter.com/asallime/status/1577363032472256514.
88 Lorenz, "Die ungefährliche Rückkehr."
89 Asal Dardan (@asallime), "Unterzeichnende können hier Materialien zum Teilen finden. Wir sind alle keine Profis, ich hoffe dennoch, dass dieser Brief weit und breit gelesen und geteilt wird. Damit die Richtigen ihn finden und sich gegenseitig stützen—auf Veränderung hoffend: https://cryptpad.fr/pad/#/2/pad/view/i1O2ePQaNJb43tI12xfkLsIFB3FplGa+pZAlCvIBP-0/," Twitter, October 4, 2022, 1:20 p.m, https://twitter.com/asallime/status/1577363032472256514.

Concluding Remarks

In his "Offener Brief über offene Briefe," Leander Steinkopf lamented a "Mangel an Sprache und Inhalt" (deficiency in language and content) in a genre that had become, in his eyes, "eine inflationierte Institution des Geisteslebens" (an inflated institution of intellectual life).[90] Steinkopf's skepticism is based on an assumption that the "Nachrichtenwert" (news value) of open letters derives from their signatories' fame rather than any form of creative argumentation. Conventional open letters issued by intellectuals are, in his words, "Eindeutigkeitsinterventionen" (interventions of unambiguity). Questioning the desirability of such clear-cut interventions, Steinkopf instead expresses a quiet plea for "Texte, die verhärtete Gegenpositionen verbinden, neue Ideen und Konzepte einbringen, Zweifel und Unwissen offenlegen, das Überraschende, Provozierende, eben das bisher Undiskutierte ausführen oder sich schlicht der Komplexität einer Angelegenheit widmen" (texts that combine hardened opposing positions, introduce new ideas and concepts, reveal doubts and ignorance, elaborate on the surprising, the provocative, the previously undiscussed, or simply devote themselves to the complexity of a matter). In this form, Steinkopf suggests, the open letter would enrich debate, yield better insights, and, moreover, avoid "der Verdacht der Anmaßung, Selbstgewissheit und PR in eigener Sache" (the suspicion of hubris, self-assurance, and PR on one's own behalf).

Steinkopf's piece was written before Shida Bazyar's letter to Jina Amini and the "Letter from cultural workers to the protesters in Iran" were issued. Nonetheless, this chapter has shown that both of those letters display a stylistic and substantive complexity which corresponds with—and in fact extends well beyond—the benchmarks that Steinkopf lays out for a potential redemption and reinvigoration of the genre as a method of intellectual intervention. While their solidarity for the Iranian protesters is unambiguous, the implications of these letters as critical interventions in mainstream German and Western discourses lie in their rhetorical complication and reconfiguration of hierarchies of power and knowledge. At precisely the moment when the value of both the open letter and the figure of the public intellectual appears to be dwindling and undermined as self-serving sideshows in an attention-driven economy, the letters discussed here have reengaged the genre and history of critical intellectuals to advance a form of postmigrant literary activism that enriches political debate by foregrounding marginalized perspectives and exposing epistemological gaps and imbalances. Furthermore, these examples of epistolary nonfiction cultivate diverse networks of authors, signatories, recipients, and readers that generate "resistance and friction of

---

90 Steinkopf, "Ein offener Brief über offene Briefe."

heterogeneous perspectives" and thereby foster "epistemic and political solidarity"[91] across communities and borders. They reflect and enact the kind of solidarity that Asal Dardan has referred to as "ein nicht endendes Projekt, das ohne andere nicht funktioniert, das ebenso Selbstdiziplin wie Zusammenarbeit erfordert" (a never-ending project that does not work without others, that requires self-discipline as well as cooperation).[92] Emerging in response to a specific historical moment of revolutionary activity in Iran, these letters can be seen as creative acts of intellectual rebellion that serve to pluralize public debate in the contemporary German context.

Bibliography

Bandixen, Ocke. "Kommentar: Mehr offene Briefe an Olaf Scholz!" NDR Kultur, July 1, 2022. Accessed May 13, 2023. https://www.ndr.de/kultur/kulturdebatte/Kommentar-Mehr-offene-Briefe-an-Olaf-Scholz,offenebriefe100.html.

Bazyar, Shida. "Frau. Leben. Freiheit. Ein offener Brief an die in Iran umgekommene Jina Amini," *Süddeutsche Zeitung*, September 23, 2022. https://www.sueddeutsche.de/kultur/jina-amini-iran-proteste-1.5662685?reduced=true.

"Brief Kulturschaffender an die Protestierenden im Iran" / "Letter from Cultural Workers to the Protesters in Iran." October 4, 2022. Accessed April 24, 2024. https://frauenlebenfreiheit.wordpress.com/.

"Briefvorlage für ein individuelles Schreiben an die Bundesregierung: Keine Wirtschaftsdeals ohne Menschenrechte: Forderung nach einem neuen Kurs in der deutschen Iranpolitik." Frauen Leben Freiheit. October 22, 2022. Accessed April 24, 2024. https://frauenlebenfreiheit.wordpress.com/2022/10/22/briefvorlage-fur-ein-indivuelles-schreiben-an-die-bundesregierung/.

Charle, Christophe. *Birth of the Intellectuals, 1880–1900*. Translated by David Fernbach and G. M. Goshgarian. Cambridge: Polity, 2015.

Code, Lorraine. "The Power of Ignorance." In *Race and Epistemologies of Ignorance*, edited by Shannon Sullivan and Nancy Tuana, 213–29. New York: State University of New York Press, 2007.

Colvin, Sarah, and Stephanie Galasso. "Introduction: Changing the Story? Epistemic Shifts and Creative Agency." In *Epistemic Justice and Creative Agency: Global Perspectives on Literature and Film*, edited by Sarah Colvin and Stephanie Galasso, 1–20. New York/London: Routledge: 2022.

Dardan, Asal. *Betrachtungen einer Barbarin*. Hamburg: Hoffmann and Campe, 2021.

———. "Vor dem Dunkel, ausgerechnet Wir." Erika Mann Lecture, Ludwig-Maximilian-Universität, May 10, 2023. https://erika-mann-lecture.de/lecture-2023/.

---

91 Medina, *The Epistemology of Resistance*, 309.
92 Dardan, "Vor dem Dunkel, ausgerechnet Wir."

El Ouassil, Samira. "Offener Brief an den offenen Brief." übermedien. May 4, 2022. https://uebermedien.de/71165/offener-brief-an-den-offenen-brief/.

Essig, Rolf-Bernhard. *Der Offene Brief: Geschichte und Funktion einer publizistischen Form von Isokrates bis Günter Grass*. Würzburg: Königshausen & Neuman, 2000.

Franzen, Johannes. "Nach offenem Brief an Olaf Scholz in der '*EMMA*': Von der Unterzeichneritis." *Frankfurter Rundschau*, May 13, 2022. https://www.fr.de/kultur/gesellschaft/unterzeichneritis-von-der-91538514.html.

"FRAU LEBEN FREIHEIT—ZAN ZENDEGI AZADI—زندگی آزادی‌ زن: Solidarität mit den Protestierenden in Iran." Berliner Ensemble. Accessed April 24, 2024. https://www.berliner-ensemble.de/frau-leben-freiheit.

"In Solidarity with the Women on the Streets: Feminist Foreign Policy Demands towards Iran." Centre for Feminist Foreign Policy. October 20, 2022. https://centreforfeministforeignpolicy.org/event/in-solidarity-with-the-women-on-the-streets-feminist-foreign-policy-demands-towards-iran/.

Jato, Mónica, and John Klapper. *Fractured Frontiers: The Exile Writing of Nazi Germany and Francoist Spain*. Rochester, NY: Camden House, 2020.

Klug, Petra. "Frauenrechte im Nahen Osten: Das bisschen Wind im Haar . . ." *taz*, August 20, 2022. https://taz.de/Frauenrechte-im-Nahen-Osten/!5874586/.

Lordi, Emily J. "Between the World and the Addressee: Epistolary Nonfiction by Ta-Nehisi Coates and His Peers." *College Language Association Journal* 60, no. 4 (2017): 434–47.

Lorenz, Anne. "Die ungefährliche Rückkehr eines unzeitgemäßen Genres. Der offene Brief online." geschichte der gegenwart. May 29, 2022. https://geschichtedergegenwart.ch/die-ungefaehrliche-rueckkehr-eines-unzeitgemaessen-genres-der-offene-brief-online/.

Medina, José. "Epistemic Injustices and Epistemologies of Ignorance." In *The Routledge Companion to the Philosophy of Race*, edited by Paul Taylor, Linda Alcoff, and Luvell Anderson, 247–60. New York: Routledge, 2017.

———. *The Epistemology of Resistance: Gender and Racial Oppression, Epistemic Injustice, and Resistant Imaginations*. Oxford: Oxford University Press, 2013.

———. "Toward a Foucaultian Epistemology of Resistance: Counter-Memory, Epistemic Friction and Guerilla Pluralism." *Foucault Studies* 12 (2011): 9–35.

Neumann, Julia. "Frauenrechte im Nahen Osten: Das bisschen Wind im Haar." *taz*, August 11, 2022. https://taz.de/Frauenrechte-im-Nahen-Osten/!5870604/.

"Der Offene Brief an Kanzler Scholz." *EMMA*. April 29, 2022. https://www.emma.de/artikel/offener-brief-bundeskanzler-scholz-339463.

"Offener Brief an Bundeskanzler Scholz." change.org. Accessed March 13, 2024. https://www.change.org/p/offener-brief-an-bundeskanzler-scholz.

Oholi, Jeannette, Maha El Hissy, Kyung-Ho Cha, and Maryam Aras. "Postmigration Reloaded." *PS Politisch Schreiben* 7 (2022): 62–73, https://www.politischschreiben.net/ps-7/postmigration-reloaded-ein-schreibgesprch.

Palm, Christian. "Migrant verus Exilant: Zur Konzeptualisierung und Positionierung einer 'deutschsprachigen Literatur exilierter Autoren.'" In *Zukunftsfragen der Germanistik: Beiträge der DAAD-Germanistentagung 2011 mit den Partnerländern Frankreich, Belgien, Niederlande, Luxemburg*, edited by Deutscher Akademischer Austauschdienst, 283–95. Göttingen: Wallstein, 2012.

Pitts, Andrea J. "Decolonial Praxis and Epistemic Injustice." In *The Routledge Handbook of Epistemic Injustice*, edited by Ian James Kidd, José Medina, and Gaile Pohlhaus Jr., 149–57. New York: Routledge, 2017.

"Pressemitteilung: Knapp 650 namhafte Kulturschaffende richten sich an Protestierende im Iran." CryptPad. Accessed April 23, 2024. https://cryptpad.fr/file/#/2/file/o-bIQjnbh65J-9h2lGgmbvCD/.

"Die Sache der Ukraine ist auch unsere Sache!" change.org. Accessed March 13, 2024. https://www.change.org/p/die-sache-der-ukraine-ist-auch-unsere-sache?utm_source=share_petition&utm_medium=custom_url&recruited_by_id=835568b0-caa5-11ec-a137-77c2dc6ca625.

Şahin, Reyhan. *Die Bedeutung des muslimischen Kopftuchs: Eine kleidungssemiotische Untersuchung Kopftuch tragender Musliminnen in der Bundesrepublik Deutschland*. Münster: LIT Verlag, 2014.

Said, Edward W. "Intellectual Exile: Expatriates and Marginals." *Grand Street* 47 (Autumn, 1993): 112–24.

———. *Orientalism*. New York: Vintage Books, 1978.

Steinkopf, Leander. "Ein offener Brief über offene Briefe: Wozu dienen sie eigentlich? Woher kommt die Mode?" *Berliner Zeitung*, July 9, 2022. https://www.berliner-zeitung.de/open-source/ein-offener-brief-ueber-offene-briefe-wozu-dienen-sie-eigentlich-woher-kommt-die-mode-li.244791.

tageschau. "Tag der Arbeit: Bundeskanzler Scholz spricht auf DGB-Kundgebung in Düsseldorf." May 1, 2022. YouTube video, 9:08. https://www.youtube.com/watch?v=-3CApjm14-0.

"Title option C, poster with 'It's about having a choice.'" CryptPad. Accessed April 24, 2024. https://cryptpad.fr/pad/#/2/pad/view/i1O2ePQaNJb43tI12xfkLsIFB3FplGa+pZAlCvIBP-0/. Image by @anne_vlpx.

Tufekci, Zeynep. "'Not This One': Social Movements, the Attention Economy, and Microcelebrity Networked Activism." *American Behavioral Scientist* 57 (2013): 848–70.

"Waffenlieferung an die Ukraine: Offener Brief." *Die Zeit*, May 4, 2022. https://www.zeit.de/2022/19/waffenlieferung-ukraine-offener-brief-olaf-scholz.

Weber, Beverly M. "Hijab Martyrdom, Headscarf Debates: Rethinking Violence, Secularism, and Islam in Germany." *Comparative Studies of South Asia, Africa and the Middle East* 32, no. 1 (2012): 102–15.

ZEIT ONLINE. "Kim de l'Horizon rasiert sich bei Dankesrede die Haare in Solidarität mit iranischen Frauen." October 22, 2022. YouTube video, 1:16. https://www.youtube.com/watch?v=Lad9WyHoEbA&t=1s.

Zola, Émile. *Notes from Exile*. Translated by Dorothy E. Speirs. Toronto: University of Toronto Press, 2003.

10: Seen as Friendly, Seen as Frightening? A Conversation on Visibilities, Kinship, and the Right Words with Mithu Sanyal

Leila Essa[1]

THE ACT OF REWRITING IDENTITIES is at the heart of Mithu Sanyal's debut novel *Identitti* (2021), in which Saraswati, a celebrated and supposedly Indian professor, turns out to be a white German woman who considers herself transracial. While her questionable case presents the most obvious changed identity in the text, it functions as a narrative springboard for examining the ever-ongoing identity reformations of its other characters.[2] In particular Nivedita, the novel's protagonist and one of the students of color previously awed by their professor, interrogates her own difficult path toward identity claims as a person of mixed heritage—and Saraswati's crucial role in this process. Set in motion through the latter's identity scandal, the dialogue-driven plot accompanies the characters up until the moment each one finds their form of moving forward from it.

All this unfolds in Oberbilk, the Düsseldorf neighborhood where both Sanyal and I grew up and where we also met for this conversation in January 2023. Overlooking its rooftops, much like the characters in *Identitti*, we discussed ways of being seen (and heard!), writing in community and degrees of marginalization, anticipated audiences and living characters, her next novel, uneasy labels, and shared challenges.

Leila Essa: Recording! We're officially talking. And *have* been talking about our work on various occasions in the past, so you already know

---

1 This research was funded by the Dutch Research Council (NWO): VI.Veni.211C.012. I have obtained approval for the interview from the Faculty Ethics Assessment Committee Humanities at Utrecht University (reference number 22-181-01) and edited it for length and clarity.

2 Mithu Sanyal, *Identitti* (Munich: Hanser, 2021). I analyze how the novel formally reflects the continuous change described above in "Die Wir-Identität," ZEIT ONLINE, March 23, 2021, https://www.zeit.de/kultur/2021-03/mithu-sanyal-asal-dardan-cancel-culture-rassismus-identitaet-marginalisierte-gruppen.

that my current research project focuses on authorial strategies against exclusionary discourses, particularly in Germany and Britain. I'm interested in the decisions authors from marginalized communities take inside and around their fiction when facing exclusionary cultural scenes, but also exclusionary societies. How do artistic interventions in public discourses, individual and collective ones, aim to reach and possibly even teach wide audiences? Questioning that, I want to rethink the significance of authorial intention for literary studies more widely. And I'd also like to begin our conversation today by thinking through intention—or through what you have once called your core work ethos: "Literatur muss freundlich sein" (literature must be friendly)! That's how Ronald Düker cites you in a portrait for *Die Zeit*, in its very title actually.[3] I was wondering if you could unpack that today. Friendly in what way? And friendly to what end? And *must* it really always be friendly?

Mithu Sanyal: I don't think I ever said that! [*Both laugh.*] It's one of those instances: that's what was understood. What *I* want when I'm writing is that my literature has a warm view of the characters. They belong to groups that haven't been written about much in Germany—or that have too often been written about with a dehumanizing gaze. Writing is always a conversation with everything that's been written beforehand—and what I'd like to bring to that is this warm gaze. I have a sneaking suspicion that I, as an author, would make myself invulnerable if I were very caustic and ironic instead: then nobody would be able to pinpoint me. I want to make myself—yes, vulnerable. That's when things kick off in literature! "Friendly" sounds like I don't want to hurt anyone, be inoffensive. I think you can work with hurt, though, get quite close to it, as long as you're warm. It's not a formula, and I will make mistakes, but this warmth is very important to me.

LE: Düker paraphrases you on the ideal relationship between your characters and your readers: that you neither want anyone to look down on your characters, nor to feel small themselves.

MS: What I'm aiming for is that the characters speak to you directly. Not me saying, "Oh dear reader, this is my index finger!" [*raises said index finger educationally*] or "Aw, these poor characters!" I don't want to look down on or up to my readers from my perspective as author, either. You know, this interview for the *Zeit* portrait: it was a lovely conversation—probably the first one about the book!—but I didn't recognize myself in the finished piece. That's something I experienced a lot after the publication if *Identitti*.

---

3 Ronald Düker, "Literatur muss freundlich sein," *Die Zeit*, February 11, 2021, 52.

LE: Rereading that particular piece, I was struck by a line that also resonates with a wider response to your novel: it suggests the label of "*Love-and-Peace* Roman" for *Identitti*.

MS: And there *is* a love-and-peace ending in it, but also a whole journey to get there! People often jump the parts beforehand.

LE: Yes, the reception really highlighted the aspect of forgiveness: indeed often skipping how hard-won it is for the characters, but also what happens *after* the moment of reconciliation between protagonist and professor. Something I've barely seen mentioned is the final revelation that Saraswati has planted the scandal as a strategic career move.

MS: Absolutely! There are alternative endings, in a way. You offer people different readings and they're all right readings. But from an academic viewpoint, at least, it's important to account for *all* these endings.

LE: And the way they're in interplay with each other! What you say about different readings brings me back to the notion of literature's "friendliness." You have now clarified this to be an approach to your characters rather than your readers. At the same time, your novel also displays an active openness to readers joining its discussions from all sorts of perspectives.

MS: That is definitely true for the novel's theory aspects, but when I first constructed *Identitti*, it was my priority to center Nivedita, to position her view of the world as norm. The novel is very open to different viewpoints, but you still have to get into her skin. Toni Morrison said that she's not writing for white readers, but for Black readers. Which doesn't mean that white readers aren't allowed to read her books, but that the books' reality is that of Black readers. The reality in mine is that of "post-migrational subjects" [*she speaks the quotation marks*], uncompromisingly. Others are invited, too, but they do not get explanations for my "weird" reality. Intellectually, all kinds of readings are possible, but emotionally every reader has to make their way toward the novel first.

LE: Anticipated audiences: let's talk about this more. One idea I grapple with in my research is that of *didactic* art. That, of course, has a bad reputation—very much in line with that raised finger! If a reviewer calls a novel didactic, they are usually decrying an aesthetic failure. I see some parallels to the way German-language media employ "activist" as a derogatory adjective for art engaging with marginalization.

MS: Even "political" is often used in that derogatory way, automatically meaning "didactic."

LE: Yes! And the necessary pushback to this "it's activism, not art" criticism then all too often insists that the supposedly didactic or activist work is not on *this* side of the suggested binary, but, in fact, on the correct one: art. It's a frustrating dynamic because closely reading a text *as text* and paying attention to its aesthetics does not, in fact, preclude attention to its didactic and/or activist potential. To me even your process of centering—or refusing to center—specific experiences could be called didactic, especially in the context of your novel being so directly set in spaces of learning, demonstrating its high stakes, its possible pitfalls. Saraswati is the goddess of learning and knowledge after all—and, in your character's case, an imperfect goddess. Your novel really questions what we *can* teach, what we *can* learn, everything that can go wrong in the process. Which, to me, shows that "didacticism" does not deserve its trite, one-dimensional image! Since you're both a writer and a critic of literature, I wondered how you'd respond to the idea of literature, in general, or of your novel, in particular, being didactic?

MS: I have so many thoughts now! First of all, I believe that all literature is political. If I write a love story about a heterosexual couple, that might go unnoticed, but if I write one about people who don't have passports, it's obvious to everyone. Which stories do I want to tell? How do I want to tell them? These are all political *and* aesthetic decisions. Only when the political aspect becomes *more* important, there can be issues. I understand the "didactic" criticism in the case of novels that seem to take their message more seriously than their story. In my works, I always want the story to be more important: even if you're not interested in the message, I want you to follow the characters emotionally. Right now I feel convinced that I've achieved this, but I might read over my work again in ten years and see it differently.

LE: I haven't come across texts that criticize *Identitti* as the bad kind of didactic, by the way, but I've seen a couple praising it precisely for *not* being didactic . . .

MS: Which is also weird! What matters to me is that my writing isn't only important because it's about an "important theme." That seems to be an easy strategy in reviewing at the moment: spotting the important theme. Ideally, a book should have an emotional impact on us readers and also offer us all these other levels to engage with it: politically, psychologically. The wonderful thing about writing stories is being able to work with time: showing a conflict and asking what it looks like nine months later or ten years later. How do people develop? In *Identitti*, all the characters are upset about what Saraswati has done, but their reasons are all different and connected to their own past, to what made them the people they are now. So when I see a reviewer dismiss it as "just about politics," that just doesn't strike me as accurate.

LE: There seems to be so little acknowledgment of the fact that the political and artistic dimensions of a work cannot be neatly separated. Political impulses—or didactic ones, in my positive use of the term—don't come at the expense of being formally inventive either, quite the opposite. One way of playing with the conventional boundaries of the novel comes to the fore in your choice to invite a whole host of other writers to contribute the tweets or blog posts they *would* write if the Saraswati scandal was real. The resulting multivoiced nature of *Identitti* already questions the authority of a single person imparting knowledge to others just as much as its plot does.

MS: I write reviews myself, so I know: you only have so much time, you only get paid so much. My recent nonfiction book about *Wuthering Heights* was the first time I got to write about a text after thinking about it for thirty-five years—a luxury![4] Of course you can't expect that level of engagement regularly, but I still think literary criticism has a lot to answer for. I'm part of the Ingeborg Bachmann Prize jury now and I have huge respect for that responsibility: talking about people's work while they are sitting there! I've always been preaching that juries need to be more diverse and now I've been asked to join quite a few. I said yes to that of the Bachmann and the Friedenspreis des Deutschen Buchhandels. I'm very grateful to be part of them, but it also makes me nervous!

LE: This issue of juries often being homogeneous of course also points to the wider literary field.

MS: And the juries are still homogenous! The fact that I've been asked to be on so many of them makes me think that I'm seen as less frightening than others—whether rightly or wrongly so. I've been inside the literary system for a long time as a journalist; I know the codes. So whenever people want to diversify anything, they turn to me because they feel I won't rock the boat.

LE: Can you spell out what you mean by frightening a bit more?

MS: There are quite a few potential invitees who'd be a lot angrier, who'd say "this isn't working, we need to change the entire thing." Many who invite me focus on the aspect of forgiveness and resolution in my writing—and that's incredibly important to me, but I'm also fifty-one! I have been *very* angry for a long time and if they'd asked me in an earlier phase

---

4 Mithu Sanyal, *Über Emily Brontë* (Cologne: Kiepenheuer & Witsch, 2022).

of my life I'd have interacted quite differently. And it's not just generational. I've been to university, I have a PhD. And I've been in a translating role all my life. Between older and younger feminists, between all these different camps, between my father and bureaucracy. It would be interesting to invite someone to join these juries who doesn't translate. It's brilliant that the system is rethinking itself. Yet every time it does, it opens up to people who might have made it in the system anyway, or who *have* made it. I've said yes to those juries to which I can genuinely add something—bringing the authorial perspective to the Bachmann jury, for instance. My previous work aligns with the work of these juries. That's not the case for all invitations that I receive in the name of diversity, and I can't diversify anything by simply being there! Overall, it's an odd experience to become part of the establishment because my emotions and my brain need to catch up. I can't really say I'm marginalized, but I do still encounter people who are simultaneously quite patronizing toward my literature and really frightened of me: "Am I allowed to ask this question, Mithu?"

LE: This simultaneity in how you're seen says so much: not as frightening as others; not *not* frightening either. I often use the phrasing "authors from marginalized communities"—which is quite a mouthful—because I want to account for different forms of marginalization but avoid "marginalized authors." For, exactly, it isn't necessarily the individual author who is marginalized in the literary scene. And yet, as your answer also highlights, BIPOC authors, for example, are constantly perceived in contrast with each other, and too often pitted against each other. Can you say more about this process of becoming more visible in the establishment? And about the push toward further change?

MS: I don't really use the word *visibility* as much as *becoming a voice*. To me it's more about being audible, being listened to. I always felt visible in a way. You can't do anything about that, but in the past, I couldn't speak with my own voice and had others speak about me. Of course this dynamic also fueled my literature. So, I really hope becoming established won't make it impossible for me to write! [*Both laugh.*] That's a real identity crisis in the best possible way and I wouldn't want it any other way. With increased audibility or visibility—or whatever you call it—comes responsibility. Noticing that your position has changed means opening doors for other people. I think the next big issues to address in the literary scene are class and health. Intersectionally: they aren't white issues.

LE: Yes, holding doors open for each other, working together: these are much more joyful reasons to group authors from marginalized communities together. Authors actively grouping *themselves* together, rather than being weighed up against each other from a hegemonic perspective. Thinking through such networks is also central to my research and there's so much happening right now! You were part of *Eure Heimat ist unser Albtraum*,[5] freshly translated as *Your Homeland Is Our Nightmare*.[6] Its editors, Fatma Aydemir and Hengameh Yaghoobifarah, appear in *Identitti* through the tweets they wrote for you. Your fellow contributor to their anthology, Simone Dede Ayivi, is currently preparing a theater production of your novel and its reception for the Schauspielhaus Graz. Authorial intention—when it is taken into account—is so often discussed in terms of an author's individual decisions, but I'm fascinated by collective choices, collective intentions. Could you talk about the role of collaboration and solidarity in your work? Is there such a thing as shared strategizing, both artistically and beyond?

MS: I think so because it's an amazing moment: there is a community. And we've been connecting since before we were perceived as connected from the outside. I was incredibly lucky that so many other books came out when mine did and am still figuring out what our common denominator is. There is this feeling of kinship and I almost don't want to question it too much because there could be an identitarian idea in that kinship. But maybe there isn't! It's like mutual recognition. And it's not just being the only other non-white face in the room, either: we don't share all our strategies, but we're all storytellers. If I may be very generalizing, there's been a lot of walking-around-literature and looking-at-things-literature in German. It's not that ours can't be experimental, just look at Olivia Wenzel's *1000 Serpentinen Angst* and its collage approach.[7] Rather, the novels that come to mind all *also* tell stories about specific characters and communities, like Fatma Aydemir's, Shida Bazyar's, Sasha Salzmann's... What I loved about the discourse around Fatma's *Dschinns*,[8] for instance, were comments in the vein of "I don't like her politics, but I like the novel." It's impressive that it gets through these filters. And I think it does because it tells its story well.

LE: On this worry about creating an exclusionary countercommunity: I like how Nikesh Shukla tackles that in *The Good Immigrant*.[9] As you

---

5 Fatma Aydemir and Hengameh Yaghoobifarah, eds., *Eure Heimat ist unser Albtraum* (Berlin: Ullstein, 2019).
6 Fatma Aydemir, Jon Cho-Polizzi, and Hengameh Yaghoobifarah, eds., *Your Homeland Is Our Nightmare: An Antifascist Essay Collection* (Berlin: Literarische Diverse, 2022).
7 Olivia Wenzel, *1000 Serpentinen Angst* (Frankfurt am Main: S. Fischer Verlag, 2020).
8 Fatma Aydemir, *Dschinns* (Munich: Hanser, 2022).
9 Nikesh Shukla, ed., *The Good Immigrant* (London: Unbound, 2016).

know, I'm thinking about *Eure Heimat* in comparison to this British essay collection a lot. Back in 2019, you and I even had a wonderful event on both anthologies and the politics of storytelling together with Vinay Patel, one of its contributors. While *Eure Heimat* directly announces itself as a response to the "Heimatministerium,"[10] *The Good Immigrant* really started being perceived as a political intervention in relation to the Brexit vote shortly after its publication.[11] Originally, it had mainly taken aim at UK publishing and at this sentiment of "Oh, we wish we could diversify, but alas!"

MS: "So difficult!"

LE: "We just don't know how to find the writers!"

MS: "There *are* no writers!"

LE: Exactly. The idea was to offer an answer to this supposed conundrum in book form, showcasing twenty-one BIPOC writers.[12] Shukla even goes so far to playfully say that he's happy to admit nepotism, that he presents "a brand-new old boys' network"[13]—which of course doesn't actually consist of old Eton boys or even "boys" at all. I don't see any issues with forming specific networks that aim to invite others in.

MS: Of course there are always people missing, too. Even in our own circles, some positions are marginalized.

LE: For sure. While such collections only offer a selective snapshot, I find it encouraging that they also tend to inspire further ones, and new networks.

MS: Speaking of: so looking forward to *anders bleiben*![14]

LE: Thank you, it's very exciting to be part of an anthology myself now. Let's zoom in from collective publishing to the supposedly individual creative process, though. In *Identitti*, you include a highly detailed

---

10   See Aydemir and Yaghoobifarah, "Vorwort," in *Eure Heimat*, 9.
11   As Shukla and his coeditor Chimene Suleyman state in their introductory words to a follow-up collection focused on the United States. See Nikesh Shukla and Chimene Suleyman, "Editor's Note," in *The Good Immigrant USA: 26 Writers Reflect on America* (London: Dialogue Books, 2019), xii.
12   See Shukla and Suleyman, *The Good Immigrant USA*, xi.
13   Shukla, "Editor's Note" to the initial, UK-focused *The Good Immigrant* (2016).
14   Selma Wels, ed., *anders bleiben: Briefe der Hoffnung in verhärteten Zeiten* (Hamburg: Rowohlt, 2023).

afterword—a gift to the curious!—in which you list all those who have actively contributed their words or otherwise influenced you, alongside a long bibliography. In a previous interview for my piece on Asal Dardan's and your writing, you mentioned that conversations with colleagues had caused you to make changes to the already published novel.[15] And you even went on to make another one afterward: adding the tweet on Saraswati that Dardan sent me for that same text. All of this strikes me as an extraordinary openness to—and about—other people's input.

MS: Where theory is concerned, I'm incredibly open; less so on an aesthetic level. I'm in very close conversation with my partner when I write, though, and recently he said, "No, of *course* not, she wouldn't do that" about one of my characters. It's excellent having someone who really knows the characters, too. They are like living entities, so people can suggest things, and if it's in the character's nature, I might put it in. But if not, I just can't—because I can't make the character inconsistent. Well, human beings *are* inconsistent, but the characters can't be . . . inconsistently inconsistent. [*She laughs.*]

LE: Now I'm thinking of Toni Morrison's introduction to *Song of Solomon*. She begins it by stating that she used to scoff at other authors' talk about "voices" that determine their creative process until her father's death, until that novel, when she just followed this absolutely assured voice.[16] Was there a particular point where this certainty about the characters changed for you, too?

MS: For me it changed when I started going as far away from myself as possible, when I said: "all of this is fiction." Back when I started out writing, twenty-five years ago, it was much more autofiction and the characters didn't speak to me because they *were* also me. Once I decided that I can just tell a story, it felt like the characters had the freedom to talk to me. Only when I started writing, though. You start doing it, start making them out of mud and then they react to you. It's very interesting to think about the writing process changing for Toni Morrison after her father's death now. Death and its aftermath are such important aspects in my new novel.

LE: That *I* cannot wait to read.

---

15   See Essa, "Die Wir-Identität."
16   See Toni Morrison, "Foreword," in *Song of Solomon* (New York: Vintage International, 2004), xi–xii.

MS: Writing with the certainty that people will read it this time around is amazing. It gives your characters more power. At the same time your internal sensor starts being louder than before.

LE: You're more aware of your audience while writing this second one?

MS: I'm afraid that I am. It's very different to *Identitti*, but suddenly I look at it and think: could it be construed as being similar on this aspect or that? Of course, on some levels it's *me*: I can only write about things I'm interested in because it takes so long. [*She laughs.*] I'm also spending a lot of time thinking through one big challenge in this one: it centrally features Savarkar as a character.[17]

LE: Yes, I can only imagine fictionalizing him to be a tough task.

MS: I'm writing about him as a very young man, in his early twenties. So that's a different character from the person he becomes later in his life. My protagonist, however, travels through time from the present day. That means she knows about his impact and that'll color the way she sees him.

LE: And that main character has grown up in Germany and brings all the knowledge about fascism there with her, right?

MS: Yes, that's in there, too!

LE: So you've set yourself a real double-challenge in terms of audience: besides the question of how it's received, there's the question of how much context to provide. For *Identitti*, you already figured out how to write for readers that know its core debates intimately, while also making sure that those who have never heard about any of it can follow. And now Indian and British colonial history: there isn't nearly enough knowledge about it in the United Kingdom, let alone in Germany.

MS: Exactly! These are my main conversations with my editor right now: why is this story important for Germany? Not because *he* doesn't believe it is, but to tease it out, clarify it. Colonial history and the fight against British colonial power are central to the novel. If I were writing it in England, it would be self-evident that all this matters for the way people live now. But even apart from the fact that India wasn't among the German colonies, postcolonialism has been discussed very unproductively here in the last few years.

---

17 Vinayak Damodar Savarkar (1883–1966) was an Indian political thinker and the founder of Hindutva (Hindu nationalist) ideology.

LE: "Postcolonial" as the new pejoratively used adjective to join "political" and "activist"?

MS: There were even statements like "postcolonialism is fascism"—which is just shocking and antihistorical.

LE: My final point of discussion for today actually relates to the usage of "postcolonial"—and that of another "post-". One word that doesn't appear in your novel but *does* appear in its reception is "postmigrantisch."

MS: Oh! Not even in the afterword?

LE: Not according to my computer search at least—I'll double-check![18] But this past autumn you've curated a panel discussion with Professor Riem Spielhaus and author Deniz Utlu at the Wuppertaler Literaturbiennale to dissect the positive potential and downsides of the term, particularly of labeling *literature* as postmigrational.[19] Around the same time "Postmigration Reloaded" was published in *PS Politisch Schreiben*: a written conversation between the literary scholars and critics Jeannette Oholi, Maha El Hissy, Maryam Aras, and Kyung-Ho Cha.[20] While completely independent of your event, the four of them talk about very similar dynamics—and actually mention the three of you: Utlu's and your literary writing, Spielhaus's research.

MS: I want to read that! The discussion in Wuppertal was so important. We need a label, but labels always have problems. I want to be able to talk about being in the world as a postmigrational subject, to talk about postmigrational stories. About different kinds of belonging and not belonging—and their effects on creating literature, creating art. But how exactly do we define postmigrational literature? In Deniz's second novel, *Gegen Morgen*, it doesn't matter whether the characters are postmigrational or not.[21] So is it supposed to be a postmigrational novel just because he's postmigrational? It was great having him and Riem at the same table, him commenting on the aesthetic aspects more and her on issues of reception.

---

18   No mention detected.
19   For a write-up of the discussion, see "Labeln oder nicht labeln? Die Wuppertaler Literatur Biennale diskutiert über "postmigrantische Literatur,'" *Auf der Höhe*, September 17, 2022, https://aufderhoehemagazin.com/2022/09/17/labeln-oder-nicht-labeln-die-wuppertaler-literatur-biennale-diskutiert-uber-postmigrantische-literatur/.
20   Jeannette Oholi, Maha El Hissy, Kyung-Ho Cha, and Maryam Aras, "Postmigration Reloaded," *PS Politisch Schreiben* 7 (2022): 62–73, https://www.politischschreiben.net/ps-7/postmigration-reloaded-ein-schreibgesprch.
21   Deniz Utlu, *Gegen Morgen* (Berlin: Suhrkamp, 2019).

I'd love to hold a whole conference because there's so much more to think through!

LE: Please do! Regarding definitions: in "Postmigration Reloaded" the discussants very much position themselves against the idea of postmigrational literature as a *genre* and define it rather via its destabilizing perspective. They especially talk about the subversive origins—and possible futures—of the concept, with Jeannette Oholi tracing it from Shermin Langhoff's emancipatory approach in the theater of the early 2000s to the "weichgespülte," softened version now circulating in white cultural criticism.[22]

MS: As a box that you can put people in.

LE: Yes or, sometimes, a box so wide that everything and anything seems to fit in. What's particularly interesting for me as a comparatist is how specific *any* usage of the term now is to the German cultural scene or its study. On the one hand, that makes sense, given how much it was shaped by cultural practitioners themselves here. On the other, it actually first appeared in academic scholarship outside Germany, in UK anthropology and political science, and with a comparative angle.[23] Yet it doesn't hold much sway in contemporary discourses around British literature, for instance. So one thing that's on my mind a lot and that I'd love to hear your thoughts on is Maha El Hissy's argument in the "Schreibgespräch" that the term and category of *postmigration* has become so urgent in Germany precisely *because* of the strong reluctance to engage with postcolonial theory here.[24] "Das Postmigrantische als die bravere, deutsche Antwort auf das Postkoloniale"—that's how Maryam Aras sums up El Hissy's line of thought there: postmigrant approaches as the tamer, German answer to postcolonial ones.[25] How would you respond to this? Especially as someone who's written a novel that directly incorporates postcolonial theory and that bridges discursive gaps between English-language and German-language contexts.

MS: That's *really* interesting. I fully get this argument and think I'd ultimately agree, but there are also issues that "postmigrational" helps to make visible in a way that "postcolonial" doesn't. I can definitely see the danger of the term being watered down—maybe all the more so because

---

22 See Oholi et al., "Postmigration Reloaded," 63–65.
23 See Anna Meera Gaonkar, Astrid Sophie Øst Hansen, Hans Christian Post, and Moritz Schramm, "Introduction," in *Postmigration: Art, Culture and Politics in Contemporary* Europe (Bielefeld: transcript, 2021), 14–16.
24 See Oholi et al., "Postmigration Reloaded," 68.
25 Oholi et al., "Postmigration Reloaded," 68.

it's not vilified as much. People can use "postmigrational" to gloss over differences between visible and invisible backgrounds of migration, when postmigrational subjects are not, in fact, racialized equally. Nevertheless, I want to be able to talk about what *is* similar about their experience, too. So I think that both terms can still be used productively: with a clear focus, but also inclusively. For there are quite a lot of people whose experience falls through all the cracks—and that's something I'm always interested in.

LE: Like your characters in *Identitti*! Yet they do find the tools they need to understand their individual experiences in postcolonial theory, right?

MS: Absolutely. Though when it comes to understanding one's experience, another thing that is very important to me is holding both the specific and the universal in balance. I remember a phase in my journey as a feminist, in which it felt really powerful to me to emphasize that men had not had the same experiences, that we're not the same. But in one form or another we will all experience being an outsider—at the very latest when we're old. Whenever I feel that I veer too much in one direction, that I focus too much on specific experiences or too much on universal ones, I try to correct it.

LE: When I wrote out my questions to you, I noticed that we start at the question of literature being friendly and arrive at that of literary discourses becoming too tame. That made me think of a different kind of tension, or aspiration: being friendly without being tame. Just like approaches to postmigration don't have to be tame and can still be subversive, friendliness or rather warmth, as you put it, can definitely be radical in its impact.

MS: I often struggle with this question of being too tame, too friendly—because that's a problem. At the same time, friendliness *is* part of my political program. And maybe I'm even more worried about being too hard, about being excluding, being hard in our own circles. The way we're living our politics should correspond to our aims and it doesn't always. My research into love politics is related to that. How can we achieve such politics without pretending that everything's fine? I do criticize, but I'll err on the side of being too friendly.

LE: The great thing about being in kinship with others is that it also applies to such shared challenges, right? Am I too hard, am I too friendly, does my behavior align with my politics? It's a relief not to be alone with one's own approach, that a community can bring together different ones. Even us two sitting here and having this conversation, as researchers and writers and just people in the world. And talking about your conversation in Wuppertal, and the written one in *Politisch Schreiben*, ours being printed in a joint volume that contains further conversations. It strikes me as a hopeful approach to the work of literature and literary criticism. And I'm sure we could continue much longer, but . . .

MS: Oh, we could talk for hours more!

LE: . . . it's ten to four!

MS: I've got to be there at five! [*Recording stops.*]

Bibliography

Aydemir, Fatma. *Dschinns*. Munich: Hanser, 2022.

Aydemir, Fatma, and Hengameh Yaghoobifarah, eds. *Eure Heimat ist unser Albtraum*. Berlin: Ullstein, 2019.

Aydemir, Fatma, Jon Cho-Polizzi, and Hengameh Yaghoobifarah, eds. *Your Homeland Is Our Nightmare: An Antifascist Essay Collection*. Berlin: Literarische Diverse, 2022.

Düker, Ronald. "Literatur muss freundlich sein." *Die Zeit*, February 11, 2021.

Essa, Leila. "Die Wir-Identität." ZEIT ONLINE, March 23, 2021. https://www.zeit.de/kultur/2021-03/mithu-sanyal-asal-dardan-cancel-culture-rassismus-identitaet-marginalisierte-gruppen.

Gaonkar, Anna Meera, Astrid Sophie Øst Hansen, Hans Christian Post, and Moritz Schramm, eds. *Postmigration: Art, Culture and Politics in Contemporary* Europe. Bielefeld: transcript, 2021.

"Labeln oder nicht labeln? Die Wuppertaler Literatur Biennale diskutiert über "postmigrantische Literatur."" *Auf der Höhe*, September 17, 2022. https://aufderhoehemagazin.com/2022/09/17/labeln-oder-nicht-labeln-die-wuppertaler-literatur-biennale-diskutiert-uber-postmigrantische-literatur/.

Morrison, Toni. *Song of Solomon*. New York: Vintage International, 2004.

Oholi, Jeannette, Maha El Hissy, Kyung-Ho Cha, and Maryam Aras. "Postmigration Reloaded." *PS Politisch Schreiben* 7 (2022): 62–73. https://www.politischschreiben.net/ps-7/postmigration-reloaded-ein-schreibgesprch.

Sanyal, Mithu. *Identitti*. Munich: Hanser, 2021.

———. *Über Emily Brontë*. Cologne: Kiepenheuer & Witsch, 2022.

Shukla, Nikesh, ed. *The Good Immigrant*. London: Unbound, 2016.

Shukla, Nikesh, and Chimene Suleyman, eds. *The Good Immigrant USA: 26 Writers Reflect on America*. London: Dialogue Books, 2019.

Utlu, Deniz, *Gegen Morgen*. Berlin: Suhrkamp, 2019.

Wels, Selma, ed. *anders bleiben: Briefe der Hoffnung in verhärteten Zeiten*. Hamburg: Rowohlt, 2023.

Wenzel, Olivia, *1000 Serpentinen Angst*. Frankfurt am Main: S. Fischer Verlag, 2020.

Afterword: Rewriting Identities: Conversations about What Might Be

Sarah Colvin

THE EDITORS EXPLAIN in their introduction that this volume is conceived of as a conversation, or as part of multiple and ongoing conversations. For me the conversation began when, in 2021, Selma Rezgui and Laura Sturtz invited me to give a keynote paper at a conference in Oxford about marginalized identities in contemporary German literature and culture. I was excited partly because the topic spoke directly to research I was already engaged in; but also because two emerging scholars in German Studies wanted to make the event happen, and that said something about a direction of travel in German studies that fired optimism in me.

I was also daunted. As an idea, the keynote implies privileged knowledge and authority, and as a white British person I had no experiential knowledge of some of the lifeworlds the Black German writing I discussed in my keynote spoke to and about. That discomfort is an effect of interactivity, in the sense María Lugones uses the word, which for a white feminist like me means acknowledging a self that lacks authority and insight, a self that is "not quite consistent with [my] image of [my]self" and imbued with difficult ambiguity.[1] The paper, on practices of possibility in novels by Sharon Dodua Otoo and Olivia Wenzel, was already promised elsewhere for publication, so couldn't appear in this volume. That makes me particularly grateful to be asked to write this afterword—and again I'm daunted, having read the insightful, stimulating, and important essays and interviews that are collected here. This afterword is written in a spirit of deep appreciation of this work and gratitude at being allowed to be part of it.

New voices have joined the conversation as it is continued here. This collection is driven by a question that seems fundamentally important in a Germany that (with much of Europe) is now facing a choice: either to take a historical opportunity to rethink itself, or to struggle against that opportunity (as my own country of citizenship, the United

---

1   María Lugones, *Pilgrimages/Peregrinajes: Theorizing Coalition against Multiple Oppressions* (Lanham, MD: Rowman & Littlefield, 2003), 72 and 74.

Kingdom, is currently struggling) and face the personal, social, and economic consequences. The question is, what can art do at these moments of possible change?

In *Provoking Democracy: Why We Need the Arts* (2007), Caroline Levine distinguishes between the democratic and the (avant-garde) aesthetic, positing that one reflects what *is*, while the other tests what might be: "Democracy claims to reflect the will of the people—to bear witness to its current values and desires—while the avant-garde [is] . . . willing to challenge the public into the future."[2] That resonates with Prathama Banerjee's more recent distinction, in *Elementary Aspects of the Political* (2020), between culture and aesthetics, where in her argument the former is about the identity of the community, the latter about the potential transformation of the community:

> I think of the distinction between culture and aesthetics in the following terms: if culture is about what the people are, habitually and organically, aesthetics is about what the people can become, consciously and politically; if culture is about community and identity, aesthetics is about the reorientation of experience and sense perception in ways that transform community and identity.[3]

Culture (also in the form of democracy) reflects the already there; aesthetics produces what isn't (or isn't yet) there,[4] and is "capable of summoning the future."[5] Borrowing from Saidiya Hartmann, one could see the aesthetic as wayward, "a practice of possibility . . . an ongoing experiment of what might be."[6]

---

2   Caroline Levine, *Provoking Democracy: Why We Need the Arts* (Malden, MA: Blackwell 2007), 63.

3   Prathama Banerjee, *Elementary Aspects of the Political: Histories from the Global South* (Durham, NC: Duke University Press, 2020), 190.

4   This discussion of politics and aesthetics derives from another conversation, with Melina Mandelbaum, Chalo Waya, Tara Talwar Windsor, and Charlotte Woodford—the Cambridge research team for the Horizon/UKRI-funded project Cartography of the Political Novel in Europe, https://cordis.europa.eu/project/id/101094658)—all of whom I would therefore like to acknowledge as coauthors of this section.

5   Levine, *Provoking Democracy*, 5.

6   Saidiya Hartman, *Wayward Lives, Beautiful Experiments: Intimate Histories of Social Upheaval* (New York: W. W. Norton, 2019), 228. I am indebted for this reference to Dionne Brand, whose wonderful lecture "A Short Entry on Time: Capitalism, Time, Blackness and Writing" (Jackman Humanities Institute, Toronto, March 3, 2021) I heard while I was writing my keynote for the conference. (The lecture was not recorded, so is sadly not available online.) See also Sarah Colvin, "Beautiful Experiments. Praxen des Möglichen bei Sharon Dodua Otoo und Olivia Wenzel," *Neue Rundschau* 132, no. 3 (2021): 19–32.

Aesthetics, then, can be understood to be about movement in its various senses (as well as the movement *of* various senses). bell hooks once described love as "a verb, not a noun,"[7] and Sharon Dodua Otoo has more recently suggested that Black literature ("Schwarze Literatur") is "eher ein Verb" (rather a verb).[8] It is, she continues, "eine Suche, eine Bewegung" (a search, a movement); it is about movement, not the stasis or fixity we associate with nouns. The aesthetic more broadly might similarly be understood as more like a verb. Art (in Anthony Reed's words) "exceeds the ideological confines of its moment,"[9] and so has a politics that is about movement. Politics more broadly, however, only sometimes exceeds the ideological confines of its moment; at other times it tries to enforce them. One might, then, envisage politics as poised between art and culture as read by Banerjee. Like culture, the political is about community and identity, and a temporally bound what is; but like aesthetics, politics is also (sometimes) about transformation, and can imagine what might be. It therefore both overlaps with and is distinct from the aesthetic. The political, one might say, can be a noun or a verb. When it is a noun it tends to be deadening, where death is the ultimate hinderer of movement; when it is a verb it tends (like aesthetics) to be enlivening. As the former it is in Achille Mbembe's terms *necropolitical*; as the latter it could (like the aesthetic) be termed *animapolitical*,[10] as an antonym for Mbembe's descriptor of lethal control. Art can and has been used in the service of necropolitics, but art is not in itself necropolitical: I would argue that art becomes art (ergo distinct from other forms of technically accomplished cultural production) in that its aesthetic tendency is animapolitical or geared to enlivenment or renewal.[11] Memorable works of art, argue Izabella Penier and Anna Suwalska-Kolecka, challenge "our moral imagination," offering "a new outlook on the world";[12] literature, sug-

---

7   "A Chat with the Author of All About Love: New Visions," CNN, February 17, 2000, http://edition.cnn.com/chat/transcripts/2000/2/hooks/index.html.
8   Sharon Dodua Otoo, "Schwarze Literatur ist eher ein Verb." Conversation with René Aguigah, Deutschlandfunk Kultur, May 23, 2022. https://www.deutschlandfunkkultur.de/schwarzes-literaturfestival-recklinghausen-100.html.
9   Anthony Reed, *Freedom Time: The Poetics and Politics of Black Experimental Writing* (Baltimore: Johns Hopkins University Press, 2014), 209.
10 I use *anima* as prefix to connote life or enlivenment in the more metaphysical sense, where *vitapolitics* now refers to attempts to enforce reproductive control and *biopolitics* is long established as the Foucauldian term for government of the body.
11 My distinction does not solve the problem of who gets to say what is art and what is "merely" cultural production.
12 Izabella Penier and Anna Suwalska-Kolecka, "Art, Ethics, and Provocation," in *Art, Ethics and Provocation* (New York: Peter Lang, 2016), 11.

gests Reed, "articulates new aesthetic communities, addresses itself to an encounter with audiences not yet known or imaginable."[13]

Literary writing is a particular kind of "productive thought experiment."[14] It can, as the editors explain in their introduction to this volume, push back against the cultural violence that (in Johan Galtung's terms) "makes direct and structural violence look, even feel, right."[15] It can unsettle stereotypical or normative imaginaries and offer aesthetic renewal. It can produce, as Alrik Daldrup argues in his essay for this volume on Otoo's *Adas Raum* and Antje Rávik Strubel's *Die blaue Frau*, an "aesthetic interruption." However: in interrupting or challenging a contemporary imaginary, art also challenges dominant aesthetic expectations.[16] In situations where culture and politics are inclined to resist movement, therefore, writing that looks for movement ("eine Suche, eine Bewegung" [a search, a movement]) always risks being denied aesthetic value. Mithu Sanyal and Leila Essa in their conversation in this volume touch on the perception of political "didacticism" in literary writing as an aesthetic problem. As Levine contends, most people agree that art is challenging—the "fundamental disagreement . . . centers on the value of critical outsiders and difficult challenges."[17] When Salman Rushdie wrote that "it is untrue that politics ruins literature" he was clearly responding to those who claimed that it did.[18] When art imagines or invokes the transformation of a contemporary what-is, aesthetic value (in general or particular terms) is likely to be denied or ignored by those who have an interest in avoiding that transformation.

This volume is also a conversation about *what might be* in literary scholarship. In her essay on May Ayim and Olivia Wenzel, Selma Rezgui describes Black German cultural production as "notably dialogic"; and this collection of essays and interviews is also notably dialogic. The approach, as the introduction explains, is to talk *with* rather than just about contemporary authors. That moves away from the assertion of a monolithic scholarly authority and toward epistemic interactivity. Understood in this way as an interaction of the knowledges of the reader with the knowledges of the writer, literary criticism has the potential to avoid what Elizabeth Spelman called "boomerang perception": a mode

13   Reed, *Freedom Time*, 9.
14   Caroline Levine, *Forms: Whole, Rhythm, Hierarchy, Network* (Princeton, NJ: Princeton University Press, 2015), 19.
15   Johan Galtung, "Cultural Violence," *Journal of Peace Research* 27 (1990): 291.
16   Penier and Suwalska-Kolecka, *Art, Ethics*, 11.
17   Levine, *Provoking Democracy*, 10.
18   Salman Rushdie, "Outside the Whale," *Granta* 11, March 1, 1984, https://granta.com/outside-the-whale/.

where the gaze barely skims the other as it continually comes back to the self ("I look at you and come right back to myself").[19] An interactive conversation avoids producing that "universal voice" that erases others from the discourse.[20] Rezgui highlights "the creation of a hybrid Black German identity that is multivalent"; "each character's trials and tribulations are about race, but they are also about gender, citizenship, sexuality and any number of additional identity categories," adds Priscilla Layne of the literature of new Black German Subjectivity she examines. Multivalent identity, Rezgui explains, is "polyphonic, and always in conversation with itself." There is potentially much to be said for a dialogic literary critical scholarly praxis that is multivalent, polyphonic, and always in conversation with itself.

Dialogue builds networks, and networks (also as rhizomes) recur as an idea in this volume. Networks as forms are both productive and subversive, as Levine argues when describing them as one of her key topics in *Forms* (2015): "networks usefully confound containing forms."[21] For José Medina, networks are what really enable epistemic change. Emphasizing the danger of singling out "epistemic heroes" whose deeds are "(mis)remembered as isolated and individualized acts of heroism," Medina argues that "the transformative influence of performance that we consider heroic is crucially dependent on social networks"; for even the insights of exceptional individuals can only be effective if they are accompanied or followed by networked actions which lead to movement and sometimes to movements.[22]

In conversation with Jeannette Oholi and Nadiye Ünsal in this volume, Stefanie-Lahya Aukongo observes that "writing means finding expression and the language in which to express yourself, to become visible, to create representation and to occupy space." Taking up space—particularly when certain kinds of bodies do it[23]—is regularly received as provocation; but the view from that space offers the *what-is* perspective on *what might be*. This volume does the same.

---

19 Elizabeth Spelman, *Inessential Woman: Problems of Exclusion in Feminist Thought* (Boston: Beacon, 1988), 12. Cited in Lugones, *Pilgrimages*, 71.
20 Lugones, *Pilgrimages*, 70.
21 Levine, *Forms*, 112.
22 José Medina, *The Epistemology of Resistance: Gender and Racial Oppression, Epistemic Injustice, and Resistant Imaginations* (New York: Oxford University Press, 2013), 186–229.
23 See, e.g., Nirmal Puwar, *Space Invaders: Race, Gender, and Bodies Out of Place* (Oxford: Oxford University Press, 2004); see also Chelsea Kwakye and Ore Ogunbiyi, *Taking Up Space: The Black Girl's Manifesto for Change* (London: Merky Books, 2019).

Bibliography

Banerjee, Prathama. Elementary Aspects of the Political: Histories from the Global South. Durham, NC: Duke University Press, 2020.

"A Chat with the Author of All About Love: New Visions." CNN, February 17, 2000. http://edition.cnn.com/chat/transcripts/2000/2/hooks/index.html.

Colvin, Sarah. "Beautiful Experiments. Praxen des Möglichen bei Sharon Dodua Otoo und Olivia Wenzel." Neue Rundschau 132, no. 3 (2021): 19–32.

Galtung, Johan. "Cultural Violence." Journal of Peace Research 27 (1990).

Hartman, Saidiya. Wayward Lives, Beautiful Experiments: Intimate Histories of Social Upheaval. New York: W. W. Norton, 2019.

Kwakye, Chelsea, and Ore Ogunbiyi. *Taking Up Space: The Black Girl's Manifesto for Change.* London: Merky Books, 2019.

Levine, Caroline. Forms: Whole, Rhythm, Hierarchy, Network. Princeton, NJ: Princeton University Press, 2015.

———. Provoking Democracy: Why We Need the Arts. Malden, MA: Blackwell 2007.

Lugones, Maria. *Pilgrimages/Peregrinajes: Theorizing Coalition against Multiple Oppressions.* Lanham, MD: Rowman & Littlefield, 2003.

Medina, José. The Epistemology of Resistance: Gender and Racial Oppression, Epistemic Injustice, and Resistant Imaginations. New York: Oxford University Press, 2013.

Otoo, Sharon Dodua. "Schwarze Literatur ist eher ein Verb." Conversation with René Aguigah. Deutschlandfunk Kultur. May 23, 2022. https://www.deutschlandfunkkultur.de/schwarzes-literaturfestival-recklinghausen-100.html.

Penier, Izabella, and Anna Suwalska-Kolecka. "Art, Ethics, and Provocation." In Art, Ethics and Provocation. New York: Peter Lang, 2016.

Puwar, Nirmal. *Space Invaders: Race, Gender, and Bodies Out of Place.* Oxford: Oxford University Press, 2004.

Reed, Anthony. Freedom Time: The Poetics and Politics of Black Experimental Writing. Baltimore: Johns Hopkins University Press, 2014.

Rushdie, Salman. "Outside the Whale." *Granta* 11, March 1, 1984. https://granta.com/outside-the-whale/.

Spelman, Elizabeth. Inessential Woman: Problems of Exclusion in Feminist Thought. Boston: Beacon, 1988.

Contributors

SARAH COLVIN is the Schröder Professor of German at the University of Cambridge, UK. She has a DPhil, MA, and BA in German from the University of Oxford and held chairs at the universities of Edinburgh, Birmingham, and Warwick before moving to Cambridge. Her current research focuses on alternative epistemologies and literary aesthetics. Her recent publications include *Shadowland: The Story of Germany Told by Its Prisoners* (2022), *Epistemic Justice and Creative Agency: Global Perspectives on Literatures and Film* (editor, with Stephanie Galasso, 2023), and a special issue of *German Life and Letters* on "Sharon Dodua Otoo—Literature, Politics, Possibility" (editor, with Tara Talwar Windsor, 2024). She is a consortium member of the EU Horizon/UKRI project "The Cartography of the Political Novel in Europe" and codirects the collaborative research group "Cultural Production and Social Justice" with Melina Mandelbaum, Tara Talwar Windsor, and Charlotte Woodford.

ALRIK DALDRUP is a Schröder PhD candidate in German at the University of Cambridge. He has an MA and a BA in German and political science from the University of Kiel, Germany. His PhD project centers on the practical use of literary fiction as companion texts that "catalogue" knowledge about violence from the perspective of those who protest against structures of power. His broader research interests include politics and literature, theories of violence and resistance, and ecocriticism.

LEILA ESSA is Assistant Professor in Comparative Literature at Utrecht University, where she currently leads a Dutch Research Council project on authorial strategies against exclusionary discourses in Germany and Britain. Leila regularly writes and talks about literature and its politics on public platforms—for example, for ZEIT ONLINE, *Berlin Review*, or the Goethe Institute. She is one of the authors of the anthology *anders bleiben* and, as of 2023, a judge for the Kurt-Tucholsky-Preis for politically engaged writing in German. Her academic work has appeared in journals like *Comparative Literature Studies* and the book project building on her PhD thesis "Partitioned Nations, Shared Narratives: Contemporary Novels on India and Germany" won the Women in German Studies Book Prize 2021.

LEA LAURA HEIM is a PhD candidate at the European University Viadrina's Chiellino Research Unit for Literature and Migration in Frankfurt (Oder) and was a Sylvia Naish Visiting Scholar at the ILCS at the University of London. Addressing contemporary themes in the German literary field, such as experiences of social and structural marginalization due to attributed origin, gender, and class, her research delves into the literary strategies writers use to counter these exclusions on an artistic-aesthetic level. Her PhD project investigates the aesthetic practices in novels by Fatma Aydemir, Deniz Ohde, Sasha Marianna Salzmann, and Olivia Wenzel, focusing on how they express social criticism, challenge common reception habits, and resist the burden of representation while demanding discursive participation.

PRISCILLA LAYNE is Professor of German and Adjunct Associate Professor of African, African American, and Diaspora Studies at the University of North Carolina at Chapel Hill. She received her PhD from the University of California at Berkeley. Her research and teaching draw on postcolonial studies, gender studies, and critical race theory to address topics like representations of Blackness in literature and film, rebellion, and the concept of the Other in science fiction / fantasy. In addition to her work on representations of Blackness in German culture, she has also published essays on Turkish German culture, translation, punk, and film. She is the author of *White Rebels in Black: German Appropriation of African American Culture* (2018), and her current book project is on Afro-German Afrofuturism.

JEANNETTE OHOLI is a postdoctoral fellow at Dartmouth College. She received her PhD from Justus-Liebig-University Giessen, Germany, in 2023. She is the author of *Afropäische Ästhetiken: Plurale Schwarze Identitätsentwürfe in literarischen Texten des 21. Jahrhunderts* (transcript 2024) and editor of *Schwarze deutsche Literatur: Ästhetische und politische Interventionen von den 1980er Jahren bis heute* (transcript, forthcoming 2025). In her research she focuses on Black German and European literature with a special interest in poetry. She is currently working on her second book project focusing on the intersections of antiracism and literature from the nineteenth century to the present.

SELMA REZGUI is an editor, translator, and project organizer at the Berlin-based TOLEDO-Program. She has an MSt in German Literature from the University of Oxford and her research interests are Black German literature, and postmigrant and dialogic literature in German. Outside academia, she organizes and moderates literary events in Berlin. Her translations have been published in the LCB-Diplomatique journal, TOLEDO, *DELPHI_RATIONALE* by Philipp Lachenmann (Distanz

Verlag, 2023), *Zeichnung/Drawing* by Beate Terfloth (Kehrer Verlag, 2022) and others.

LAURA MARIE STURTZ is a PhD candidate and research assistant in the research group "Literature and the Public Sphere in Differentiated Contemporary Cultures" at the Friedrich-Alexander-University Erlangen-Nuremberg. She holds an MA in European literatures and cultures from the Albert-Ludwig-University Freiburg and an MSt in German from the University of Oxford. Her work engages with substantial shifts in the representation and visibility of minoritized authors in the contemporary German cultural sphere and the increasing number of literary interventions that foreground the complexity and radical diversity of German identities.

JOSEPH TWIST is Assistant Professor in German Studies at University College Dublin. He holds a PhD, an MA, and a BA from the University of Manchester. His research concerns the ways in which literature can transform our understanding of religion, the subject, and community. He is the author of *Mystical Islam and Cosmopolitanism in Contemporary German Literature: Openness to Alterity* (Camden House, 2018) and has coedited, with Rey Conquer, a special issue of *German Life and Letters* titled *Imagining the Beliefs of Others in German Literature from the Enlightenment to the Present* (2023), as well as a special issue of *Oxford German Studies* titled *Rethinking Community and Subjectivity in Contemporary German Culture and Thought* (2020) with Maria Roca Lizarazu.

NADIYE ÜNSAL is a doctoral candidate at the Justus-Liebig-University in Giessen and works on the topics of coloniality and migration, intersectionality and human rights. She has been active for many years in self-organized political initiatives fighting against racism, discrimination, and for the freedom of movement for everyone. She is codirector and coproducer of the documentary *Without Community, There Is No Liberation* by the Activistar Film and Video Productions Collective. The film documents the BIPOC self-organized antiracist movements and struggles since the fall of the Wall in Germany. She currently works as a communication officer for the Anti-Discrimination Association Germany and has been teaching at the Evangelical University of Berlin since 2019.

TARA TALWAR WINDSOR is Research Associate and Affiliated Lecturer in the Faculty of Modern and Medieval Languages and Linguistics at the University of Cambridge. Her research focuses on the role played by creative writers as public intellectuals from the early twentieth century to the present. She is a consortium member of the EU Horizon/UKRI project "The Cartography of the Political Novel in Europe" and coleads the collaborative research group "Cultural Production and Social Justice" with Sarah Colvin, Melina Mandelbaum, and Charlotte Woodford. From 2021 to 2023, she was Schröder Research Associate at Cambridge with a special remit for Equality and Diversity in German Studies and previously held research and teaching positions in Birmingham, Liverpool, Dublin, and Wuppertal. She is coeditor, with Sarah Colvin, of a special issue of *German Life and Letters* titled "Sharon Dodua Otoo—Literature, Politics, Possibility" (2024).

Index

academia, 139–40, 142
activism, 16–17, 21, 26, 28, 53, 83, 85, 97, 115, 128, 135, 138, 140–42, 160, 203, 205, 211, 222, 224n52, 231, 233, 236, 243–44, 251
Adams, Anne V., 111
ADEFRA, 16
Adelson, Leslie, 19–20, 93
aesthetics, 14, 18, 22, 27, 59, 79, 109, 135, 145, 163, 182, 197n36, 243–44, 249, 251, 256–58; aesthetic approach, 2, 24, 53, 202; aesthetics and culture, 256; aesthetic intervention, 25, 79; aesthetics and politics, 155–56, 244, 257; subversive aesthetics, 25, 27, 145–61; queer aesthetics, 79
Afghanistan, 47
Afrekete, 118–19, 130
Africa, 83n1, 112–13, 119, 188n8, 205; North Africa, 171n46; West Africa, 119
African American identity, 91, 101–2, 123, 125, 129
African American literature, 90, 110–11
African identity, 16, 91, 99, 111–14, 119, 124, 128, 188
Afro-German identity, 21, 27, 111–14, 116–17, 124, 130–31
Afro-German literature, 90, 96, 120, 131
Ahmed, Sara, 28, 188–94, 195n33, 197n36, 200n46, 201n49, 204
Akın, Fatih, 172, 174–75, 178, 182–83
Aladag, Feo, 228n65, 229n67
alienation, 23, 68, 94–95, 110, 122
Alternative für Deutschland (AfD), 3, 153

Amini, Jina Mahsa, 209–10, 212, 220, 222–24, 227–28, 231, 236
Amjahid, Mohamed, 7
Amo, Anton Wilhelm, 83
Anderson, Benedict, 58n9
Angelou, Maya, 90
Angola, 66, 121, 125, 128
anti-Blackness, 94, 99–101
antisemitism, 6, 7, 10, 13, 62
Arabic, 7n22, 97, 170
Asfaha, Nouria N., 17n63
assimilation, 9, 61, 63, 112, 192
Assmann, Aleida, 228n65
asylum, 3, 11, 104, 221
Aras, Maryam, 18–19, 23, 251–52
Arendt, Hannah, 44, 48
attention economy, 212–13, 215, 218, 233n82, 236
audibility, 13–15, 17, 29, 60, 124, 218, 233–34, 246
Aukongo, Stefanie-Lahya, 1, 15, 27, 135–42, 259
Aukongo, Stefanie-Lahya, works by: *Buchstabengefühle,* 109, 135, 138; *Kalungas Kind,* 135
autofiction, 41, 69, 100, 157–58, 249
Aydemir, Fatma, 1, 13n45; open letter Iran, 228n65
Aydemir, Fatma, works by: *Dschinns,* 4n10, 247; *Ellbogen,* 28, 162–83; *Eure Heimat ist unser Albtraum,* 2, 247–48
Ayim, May, 18, 24, 27, 92, 100n40, 109–10, 113–22, 126–27, 129–31, 258
Ayim, May, works by: *blues in schwarz weiss,* 109–10, 115–20, 122, 126–27, 130–31; *Farbe bekennen,* 83, 90, 111, 113, 121; *weitergehen,* 114n16

Ayivi, Simone Dede, 85n3, 247
Azimipour, Sanaz, 233

Baerbock, Annalena, 224n52, 234
Bakhtin, Mikhail, 121, 128n41
Baldwin, James, 222–23
Balibar, Etiénne, 10
Banerjee, Prathama, 256–57
Bargetz, Brigitte, 195n32
Baumann, Gerd, 22, 60n17
Bazyar, Shida, 1, 4, 24, 28, 247; open letter Iran 210, 212, 222–28, 236
Bazyar, Shida, works by: *Drei Kameradinnen*, 4n10, 12n43
Becker, Meret, 228
belonging, 22, 26, 40, 45, 49, 56–57, 67–68, 75–77, 95, 112, 124–26, 130, 170; Black German belonging, 97, 115–16; cultural belonging, 60; familial belonging, 37, 76, 79; identity and belonging, 2, 25–27, 59–60, 62, 110, 115, 126; linguistic belonging, 58; Muslim belonging, 6n18; narrative belonging, 65; national belonging, 58, 95–96; postmigrant belonging, 8n25, 58n8, 60n19, 164, 251
Berben, Iris, 228
Beutin, Wolfgang, 93, 94n27
Biendarra, Anke, 84
Biermann, Wolf, 214
Bildungsroman, 24n102, 28, 162, 166–69, 172, 174, 177–81
Biller, Maxim, 213
Birge, Sirma, 127
Black America, 95, 119
Black British literature, 182n74
Black German literature, 16, 27, 83–87, 90–93, 105–6, 109–10, 112, 115, 121–22, 255
Black German studies, 16, 21, 89
Black literature, 16, 27, 83n1, 90, 92, 115, 257
Blackness, 14, 87–88, 95, 102, 109–12, 114, 117–18, 121–22, 124–26, 131, 256n6
Black studies, 89–90
Boes, Tobias, 168

Bolaki, Stella, 174n56
Bourdieu, Pierre, 28, 171–72, 180
Brand, Dionne, 256n6
Brecht, Bertolt, 228
Breger, Claudia, 162, 172
Brexit, 248
British literature, 252
Brumlik, Micha, 9n27
Brunner, Claudia, 192n25
Buabeng, Thelma, 228n65
Bücker, Teresa, 228n65
Bühler-Dietrich, Annette, 64–65.
burden of representation, 28, 43–44, 163–64, 169, 180, 182–83
Burnley, Clementine Ewokolo, 84
Butler, Judith, 63

Campt, Tina M., 115
Cha, Kyung-Ho, 23–24, 166, 202, 205n58, 251
CDU, 3, 10, 97
Charle, Christophe, 219n28
Cheesman, Tom, 175n58
Chernivsky, Marina, 4, 6, 9n27
Chiellino, Carmine, 20n73
Chimakonam, Jonathan O., 25
Cho-Polizzi, Jon, 2n2, 165–66, 247n6
citizenship, 93, 98, 104, 106, 112, 170n45, 255, 259
civil rights movement, 119, 128
classism, 171n47, 175
Code, Lorraine, 223
Coffey, Judith, 13
colonialism, 20, 27, 83n1, 102, 111, 135, 138, 191–92, 195, 204–5, 250
Colvin, Sarah, 13n45, 24–25, 64, 74n41, 110n2, 118, 121–22, 194–95, 197n36, 224n51, 255–59
community, 2, 4, 7, 18–20, 25–26, 43, 45, 47, 52, 56–59, 64, 74–75, 79, 86, 90, 102, 111, 135, 140, 146, 171n46–47, 182–83, 190, 196, 211, 231, 237, 241, 247, 253, 256–58; community of color, 131, 141; Black community, 86, 90, 96, 109, 112, 115–16, 121–26,

131, 135, 139, 202–3; Jewish community, 8; lesbian community, 50; marginalized community, 15, 43, 140–41, 211, 242, 246; queer community, 96; Turkish community, 174–75
Crenshaw, Kimberlé, 127
critical intellectual, 212, 218–19, 236
critical race theory, 13, 24
Czollek, Leah Carola, 128n42
Czollek, Max, 8, 9n27, 11–12, 28, 38, 42n1, 60n18, 163, 165, 178n65, 179n69, 183; open letter Iran, 228n65

Daldrup, Alrik, 28, 187–206, 258
Dardan, Asal, 1, 249; open letter Iran, 28, 210, 212, 216–20, 227–30, 233–35, 237; Twitter (X), 217–19, 221–22, 227–30, 233, 235, 249
Dardan, Asal, works by: *Betrachtungen einer Barbarin* 4n10, 220; "Vor dem Dunkel, ausgerechnet Wir" lecture, 220–21, 237n92
Davis, Angela, 45
decolonization, 135, 137–40, 142, 203n54, 210n2
deintegration, 8–9, 11, 28, 42, 162–65, 168–69, 177–79, 181–83
Deleuze, Gilles and Felix Guattari, 26, 56n3, 57–59, 61, 75, 79
de l'Horizon, Kim, 209–11, 228n65
Demiralp, Seda, 173n54
democracy, 4, 164, 204, 214, 235, 256
diaspora, 27, 91, 96n31, 106, 109, 111–16, 118, 120, 122, 131, 196, 226, 228
didacticism, 178, 243–45, 258
discourse, 2, 6–8, 21, 25–26, 29, 37, 40–42, 66, 109, 111, 118–19, 128n40–41, 130–31, 162, 165, 188–89, 195, 200–201, 203, 211, 217, 221, 223, 226, 228, 236, 242, 247, 252–53, 259; counterdiscourse, 121–22
demarginalization, 127n38, 168, 179

DeMeritt, Linda C., 94, 95n30
disability, 14, 25; disability studies, 13
discrimination, 62, 75, 79, 86, 102, 138, 176, 178, 181, 191; gendered discrimination, 176; racist discrimination, 171; structural discrimination, 5, 28, 162, 170, 173
diversity, 8–9, 11–12, 17, 19, 22, 48, 87, 115, 163, 165n21, 181, 192, 230, 246; radical diversity, 2, 8–9, 11, 13, 21, 25, 37–38, 60, 109n1, 128n42, 163, 178, 212
Doll, Georgia, 40
Dominanzkultur, 11–12, 15, 28
Donbas, 53
Donner, Susanne, 198n40
Dotan-Dreyfus, Tomer, 7
double consciousness, 65–66, 70, 87, 128–29
Dresen, Andreas, 213
Dreyfus affair, 214, 219
Du Bois, W.E.B., 66, 128–29
Düker, Ronald, 242
Dündar, Özlem Özgül, 1, 15, 27, 145–60
Dündar, Özlem Özgül, works by: "an grenzen", 146–48, 152–53; *gedanken zerren*, 146–48; *türken, feuer*, 145, 147–49, 155–56, 158
Dyer, Richard, 165n19

Eastern Kurdistan, 230
East German identity, 67, 86–87, 100
Eckermann, Patricia, 16
Eidinger, Lars, 213
El Bulbeisi, Sarah, 6n18
El Hissy, Maha, 4, 22n94, 23–24, 221, 251–52
Ellison, Ralph, 118
El-Mafaalani, Aladin, 169–70
El-Tayeb, Fatima, 10–11, 20, 23n97, 90, 112
El Ouassil, Samira, 215–17, 228n65
Emcke, Carolin, 228n65
EMMA, 213, 216–17, 222
Enzensberger, Theresia, 228n65

epistemics, 14–15, 19n70, 22, 24–25, 192, 194, 204, 209–37, 258–59; epistemic friction, 25, 28, 128, 210, 212, 225; epistemic injustice, 17n65, 24, 28, 166n26, 188, 190, 196n34, 210, 225; epistemic insurrection, 28, 209, 212; epistemic resistance, 25, 211
erasure, 14, 16, 124
Essa, Leila, 29, 241–54, 258
Essig, Rolf-Bernhard, 219n29, 221n39
ethnicity, 9–11, 24, 26, 109, 113, 116, 121, 126–27
Eurocentrism, 23, 103, 138, 189, 216
exclusion, 2, 10–11, 14, 20, 43, 59, 95, 114, 140, 154, 163, 165, 172–73, 176, 181, 182n73, 224, 242, 247

Fachinger, Petra, 178n66
Faeser, Nancy, 234
Farsi, 228, 230n70
Federal Republic of Germany, 3, 100
feminism, 24, 28, 210, 231, 246, 253, 255; Black feminism, 16, 28, 96n31, 116, 119, 122, 127, 190; feminist foreign policy, 224; Iranian feminism, 224–25, 230; Kurdish feminism, 210; Western feminism, 225; queer feminism, 28, 190, 230–31; transnational feminism, 211
Florvil, Tiffany N., 16n62, 114n15, 115n17, 115n18
Foroutan, Melika, 227
Foroutan, Naika, 22n88, 164–66
Foucault, 19, 212, 221, 257n10
Franzen, Johannes, 215
Fricker, Miranda, 24

Galasso, Stephanie, 24–25, 224n51
Gallagher, Maureen O., 203n54
Galtung, Johan, 258
Gaonkar, Anna Meera, 165n20, 179n70, 252n23
gaslighting, 201
Gastarbeiter, 19, 146–47, 151–53

Gaza, 6
GDR, 57, 65–67, 87, 100–101, 121, 149, 153, 214
Genç, Hatice, 145; Genç, Hülya, 145; Genç, Saima, 145
German-Jewish literature, 7n22, 37–38, 57–58
German Jewish studies, 21
German Jews, 6–8, 42n1
Germanness, 1–2, 9, 12, 14, 19–21, 25–26, 57, 59–62, 110–22, 131, 146
German studies, 21, 24, 187, 255
German-Turkish literature, 19–20
Gezen, Ela, 21n81–86
Ghanaian culture, 119, 196, 202n53
Ghanaian descent, 85, 187
Ghanaian language, 194
Goertz, Karein, 116, 119
Götting, Michael, 84, 86
Gorelik, Lena, 4n10
Gorki Theater, 7n21, 8, 11, 37, 42n1, 128n42, 159
Grjasnowa, Olga, 170, 171n47
Gunkel, Henriette, 192n26
Gutjahr, Ortrud, 177n63

Habeck, Robert, 234
Hagen, Zoe, 86
Halle, 4–5, 195
Hall, Stuart, 11n37, 12n42, 23, 86–87, 91–92, 95
Hamas, 6, 8
Hampel, Anna, 166
Hanau, 4
Handke, Peter, 52
Hartmann, Saidiya, 256
Heim, Lea Laura, 28, 162–83
Heimat, 2, 96–97, 247–48
Heinz, Julia von, 228n65
heteronormativity, 42–43, 49, 76, 78–79, 96n31, 135
Hetzl, Sandra, 7
Hierse, Lin, 228n65
Hill Collins, Patricia, 96n31, 127
Hillgärtner, Jule, 83
hooks, bell, 110n4, 124, 165n19, 190n17, 257

Hopkins, Leroy, 90
Houellebecq, Michel, 157
Hügel-Marshall, Ika, 92
human rights, 167, 188, 198, 203
hybridity, 20, 78n51

identity, 2, 9, 25–27, 59–62, 65, 67, 70, 75–76, 79, 88–94, 105–6, 109–31, 137, 146, 157, 189n10, 214, 246, 256–57, 259; Black identity, 27, 124, 128, 131, 135; Black American identity, 111, 124–25; Black German identity, 86–94, 97–100, 105, 109–17, 119–22, 124–26, 130–31, 259; diasporic identity, 115, 226; exilic identity, 220, 227; gender identity, 37, 70, 76, 165; German identity, 6, 21, 48–49, 60, 90, 97, 105, 109, 111–12, 114–16, 120–21, 126, 130–31, 259; Jewish identity, 8, 13, 26, 42n1, 44, 46, 56–57, 163; national identity, 10, 117, 167–68, 180; political identity, 93; racial identity, 88–89, 116–17, 128, 241; racialized identity, 92, 116; queer identity, 13, 48–49
ignorance, 15, 25, 210, 222, 225, 236; racial ignorance, 15, 96, 98; white ignorance, 15n55, 118, 195
immigration, 28, 94, 98, 163–65, 181
inaudibility, 15, 18, 218
İnce, Gürsün, 145
inclusivity, 1n1, 17, 21, 37, 51–52, 116, 138, 146, 195, 234–35, 253
Indian history, 250
integration, 3, 8–11, 28, 42, 97–98, 162–65, 168–69, 172, 177–79, 181–83
intersectionality, 20–21, 23, 67, 79, 87–88, 101, 105, 127–28, 135, 138, 140–41, 188, 230–31
invisibility, 12–15, 17–18, 23, 27, 61, 83, 88, 92, 112, 118, 135, 146, 153, 172, 194, 212, 253
Iran, 6, 209–12, 219–20, 222–37
Islam, 10n32, 17, 173n54, 225n54

Islamic Republic, 209–10, 219, 222–23, 227n61
Islamic terror, 68–69, 97
Islamophobia, 6n18, 149–50, 176
Israel, 6, 8
Istanbul, 41, 56, 62, 64, 71, 76, 145, 158, 162, 166, 172, 177–78, 180

Jacobs, Jürgen, 167n30, 168n36
Jalta journal, 5, 8, 9n27, 128n42
Jato, Mónica, 220n35
Jelinek, Elfriede, 228
Jewish identity, 8, 13, 26, 42n1, 44, 46, 56–57, 163
Jewish-Muslim alliance, 11–12

Kaczmarek, Nele, 83
Kafka, Franz, 58
Kaminer, Olga and Wladimir, 213
Kapitelman, Dmitrij, 213, 228n65
kebe-nguema, joseph, 13–14
Keeling, Kara, 200
Kehlmann, Daniel, 213
Kermani, Navid, 20n76, 157
Keskinkılıç, Ozan Zakariya, 10n32, 17, 228n65
Kilomba, Grada, 191
Kinder, Katja, 16
kinship, 20, 29, 77, 79, 114–15, 205, 223, 241, 247, 253
Kinsky, Esther, 52
Kiyak, Mely, 151
Klapper, John, 220n35
Kluge, Alexander, 213
Koepsell, Phillip Khabo, 24, 83–84
Kontje, Todd, 167n28, 172n53
Korrodi, Eduard, 219
Kosofsky Sedgwick, Eve, 96n31
Kuhnke, Jasmina, 84–85
Kuloğlu, Tuncay, 40
Kurdish, 162, 169, 179, 210, 220, 223, 228, 230; Kurdish-Iranian, 209; Turkish-Kurdish, 158–59
Kwakye, Chelsea, 259n23

Langhoff, Shermin, 22, 60, 252
Lara, Alexandra Maria, 228n65

Laumann, Vivien, 13
Layne, Priscilla, 21n81–6, 27, 56n1, 69, 73n40, 83–106, 110, 259
Legida, 149
Leitkultur, 9–12, 15, 17, 163
Lennox, Sara, 90
lesbian, 38, 47–50
Levine, Caroline, 256, 258–59
Littler, Margaret, 58n12, 59, 61n23
Lorde, Audre, 26n110, 44, 48, 57, 61–62, 79n54, 89–90, 113–15, 118–19, 131n46, 191, 205
Lordi, Emily J., 211, 217n25, 222–24, 226n58, 231n77
Lorenz, Anne, 214–15, 229, 231n78, 235n88
Lugones, María, 128, 255, 259n20
Luna, Alvaro, 166
Luther King, Martin, 118–20, 222
lynch, kara, 192n26

Makeba, Miriam, 99
Maizière, Thomas de, 9n31
Mandelbaum, Melina, 256n4
Mann, Erika, 220–21
Mann, Thomas, 214, 219
marginalization, 2, 4, 7, 9, 13, 15–16, 18, 23, 25–26, 28–29, 38–39, 41–43, 45–46, 59, 66, 86, 90, 94, 98–99, 110, 117, 127n38, 135, 139–41, 162–63, 168, 174–76, 178–79, 181–82, 187–90, 201, 211–12, 218, 221–23, 225, 232, 236, 241–43, 246, 248, 255
Marinić, Jagoda, 213, 201n51
Massaquoi, Hans-Jürgen, 92
Matthes, Ulrich, 228n65
Mbembe, Achille, 257
McIntosh, Peggy, 165n19
McKittrick, Katherine, 89
McMurtry, Áine, 188, 197n35
Mecklenburg, Norbert, 20n73
Menasse, Eva, 213
Mercer, Kobena, 28, 163, 182
Medina, José, 15, 17n65, 19, 24–25, 28, 196n34, 210–12, 221–25, 237n91, 259

memory, 84, 109, 112, 115–16, 120, 128, 142, 150, 195, 198, 205;
memory culture, 5, 27, 146, 152, 163, 188
Mican, Hakan Savaş, 40
microaggression, 124, 176, 200–201
migrant literature, 18–20, 221
migration, 3, 10, 19, 22, 24, 37, 58, 62, 85, 151, 153, 155, 157–58, 164–66, 179, 182n73, 253
Mihai, Mihaela, 190n17
Mills, Charles W., 15, 25n107, 118, 225
minoritarian, 59
minoritization, 2, 4, 6, 9, 11, 13, 17–21, 25, 27–28, 39, 59, 100, 131, 191–92
minority, 5, 7–8, 20–21, 48, 58, 61, 100, 112–13, 127, 151, 154, 163, 168, 182, 190, 210
minor literature, 26, 57–61, 75, 79
Misipo, Dualla, 83
multilingualism, 21, 27, 40–41, 58, 118–19, 146, 155, 166, 170
Mölln, 4, 149, 156
Moisi, Laura, 199–201
Morrison, Toni, 44, 48, 90, 243, 249
Morocco, 66, 92, 102, 127–28
Müller, Herta, 213
Muslim, 6, 10–11, 17–18, 47, 175

narrative, 2, 11–12, 18, 22, 24, 28, 37, 57, 60, 62, 64–67, 69, 75, 79–80, 83, 85, 87, 90, 96, 104, 109, 110n2, 115, 121–22, 140, 142, 156, 160, 163, 165–67, 172, 175, 183, 188–89, 191–93, 198–203, 224–25, 241, 261
Nationalsozialistischer Untergrund (NSU), 4
Nazi, 52, 68–69, 151, 195–96, 221; Nazi Germany, 92n21, 205, 214, 219, 220; Nazism, 4, 219
Ndikung, Bonaventure Soh Bejeng, 83
neocolonialism, 103, 127
neo-Nazi, 2–3, 145–46, 151

network, 44–45, 75–78, 151, 203, 211–12, 228, 230, 233n82, 236, 247–48, 259
Neubauer, Jochen, 175n59
New Subjectivity, 27, 87, 92–95, 105–6
Nice, Richard, 180n71
nonbinary identity, 13, 26, 45, 56, 57n4, 63, 86n7, 165, 209, 230
Norman, Beret, 189n10

Ören, Aras, 18
Özdamar, Emine Sevgi, 4n10, 18, 221
Öztürk, Gülüstan, 145
Özyürek, Esra, 6n18
Ogette, Tupoka, 170n44, 171n48
Ogone, James Odhiambo, 28, 188, 190
Ogunbiyi, Ore, 259n23
Oguntoye, Katharina, 113, 90n16
Ohde, Deniz, 24, 166–67
Oholi, Jeannette, 16, 23, 27, 135–42, 211, 221n41, 251–52, 259
open letter, 28, 210–19, 221–22, 228–29, 233–36
oppression, 15, 24, 89, 94, 101, 113, 131, 171n47, 173, 176, 179, 191, 194, 211, 219, 222–23, 225
orientalism, 210n2
Øst Hansen, Astrid Sophie, 252n23
Otherness, 10, 12, 14, 18, 20, 22, 26, 28, 43, 46, 56–59, 61, 65, 67–70, 72, 75, 79, 112, 116, 118, 121, 129, 131, 146, 181, 183, 188–92, 210, 223, 259
Othmann, Ronya, 213, 160n19
Otoo, Sharon Dodua, 1, 15–16, 17n63, 24, 42, 88, 92, 189–90, 201–2, 255–57; Ingeborg Bachmann Prize, 85; open letter Iran, 228n65; Schröder Lecture, 204–5
Otoo, Sharon Dodua, works by: *Adas Raum*, 24n101, 28, 64n29, 84–85, 109, 110n2,118, 187–88, 194–97, 201–5, 258; "Dürfen Schwarze Blumen malen?", 86–89; *Herr Gröttrup setzt sich hin*, 24n101; *Synchronicity*, 13–14, 84; "The Speaker is using N-Word", 191; *the things i'm thinking about while smiling politely*, 84; "Vor der Grenze", 91; *Winter Shorts*, 84

Palestine, 6, 8
Palm, Christian, 221n36
Patel, Vinay, 248
patriarchy, 45, 75–76, 138, 141, 172, 174–75, 178, 200, 210
Peaceman, Hannah, 5–6
Pegida, 149
Penier, Izabella, 257, 258n16
people of color, 68, 152, 160, 170, 178, 181n72, 211, 241
perestroika, 37, 43, 50
Perko, Gudrun, 128n42
Pfleger, Simone, 187n3
Pitts, Andrea J., 210n2
Plumly, Vanessa, 96, 97n34
poetry, 8,17, 27, 38, 53–54, 61–62, 83–84, 92, 109, 111, 116, 118–20, 129, 131, 135–42, 146–48, 154–55, 201
Poikane-Daumke, Aija, 90
Popoola, Olumide, 84
positionality, 67, 75, 87, 92, 100–101, 131, 217, 224
positioning, 9, 68, 106, 142
Post, Hans Christian, 252n23
postcolonialism, 22–24, 29, 60n17, 121, 135, 142, 167–68, 250–53
postmigration, 21–23, 26, 28–29, 146, 159, 166–67, 209, 236, 251–53; postmigrant identity, 40, 59–61, 79–80, 60, 164; postmigrant perspective, 23, 28, 162, 164–65, 179–80, 211, 221; postmigrant storytelling, 57, 60–61; postmigrant writing, 37, 58, 159, 166–67
public intellectual, 42, 218, 236
public sphere, 4, 6, 26, 28, 44, 211–12, 215–16, 231; digital public sphere, 212

Putin, 213, 215
Puwar, Nirmal, 259n23

queerness, 13, 26, 28, 38, 42–44, 50–51, 56–57, 63–64, 74–76, 78–79, 86, 96, 100, 129, 154, 160, 190, 230–31, 234
quota refugee, 44

racialization, 11, 15, 20, 23, 85, 91–95, 98, 101, 104, 106, 116, 145, 197, 205, 253
racism, 2, 17, 20, 27, 57, 72–75, 99, 110, 138, 148, 153, 166, 175, 178, 195, 203–5; anti-Arab racism, 6; anti-Black racism, 57, 65–70, 85n3, 86–93, 97–99, 101–2, 104–6, 110, 116–18, 120, 127, 135; anti-Eastern European racism, 198; anti-Kurdish racism, 223; anti-Muslim racism, 6; everyday racism, 120; racist language, 48, 114, 118, 159n18, 171, 191; racist violence, 4, 65–66, 73, 68–69, 102, 151, 156–57, 171, 195; structural racism, 15, 97–98, 170–71, 173, 178
radicalism, 120, 135, 204
radicality, 138–39, 205
Red Army Faction, 93
Redfield, Marc, 167n31
Reed, Anthony, 197n36, 257–58
refugee, 10, 92, 97, 104, 149–50
Reich-Ranicki, Marcel, 93
resistance, 11, 17, 24, 28, 69, 180, 187, 190–91, 194, 203–4, 205n58, 210–12, 221, 224, 230–31, 233, 236; Black resistance, 120; epistemic resistance, 25, 211; feminist resistance, 225; literary resistance, 63, 206
resonance, 13, 16–18, 42, 109, 210, 227
Resonanzen festival, 15–17, 85
restitution, 203
Rezgui, Selma, 13, 17n63, 26–27, 37, 39, 43–44, 48–49, 68n33, 109–31, 187n1, 255, 258–59
rhizome, 74–75, 259

Riddle, Lucas, 171n47
Riemann, Katja, 228
Ring Petersen, Anne, 60n16, 164n11
Roca Lizarazu, Maria, 8, 9n27, 18n67, 19–21, 57–58, 63, 72, 76
Römhild, Regina, 22n93
Roma, 97–99
Rommelspacher, Birgit, 12
Rostock, 4, 149
Rushdie, Salman, 258
Russia, 3, 53, 197, 215; invasion of Ukraine, 6, 37, 212; post-Soviet Russia, 37; Russian identity, 71; Russian language, 62; war in Ukraine, 213

Sahner, Simon, 131
SAID, 18
Said, Edward, 23, 210n2, 221, 225–27
Sahebi, Gilda, 231–33
Şahin, Reyhan, 225n54
Saleh, Anja, 84
Salzmann, Sasha Marianna, 1–2, 6–8, 9n27, 11, 15, 26, 37–54, 57–59, 229, 247; open letter Iran, 228n65
Salzmann, Sasha Marianna, works by: *Außer sich*, 26, 37–38, 40–44, 49–50, 52, 56–59, 61–65, 70–72, 74–79; *Im Menschen muss alles herrlich sein*, 37, 42–44, 49–53; "Sichtbar" essay, 13, 46–47, 61
Sammons, Jeffrey L., 167n30
Sanaga, Mara, 120–21
Sandeh, Sarah, 227
Sandjon, Chantal-Fleur, 86
Sanyal, Mithu, 1, 14–15, 19, 29, 42, 241–54, 258; open letter Iran, 228n65
Sanyal, Mithu, works by: *Identitti*, 4n10, 39, 241–45, 247–48, 250, 253; *Über Emily Brontë*, 245
Savarkar, Vinayak Damodar, 250
Schami, Rafik, 18
Schapiro, Anna, 9n27
Scholz, Olaf, 3; open letter to Scholz, 213, 217, 222, 234

Schramm, Moritz, 8–9, 11, 60n16, 164n11–14, 252n23
Schwarz, Miriam, 12, 24
Schwarzer, Alice, 213
SchwarzRund, 84, 86
Schwebel, Shoshana, 190n14
Seethaler, Robert, 213
Seidler, Ulrich, 199n43
Selbmann, Rolf, 167n29, 178n64
Sestu, Timo, 163–64, 175n59, 177
sexism, 171n47, 173, 204–5
Shukla, Nikesh, 247–48
Sievers, Wiebke, 182n73
Simone, Nina, 139
Sinti, 99
Skolnik, Jonathan, 21n81–86
Slaughter, Joseph R., 167–68, 178–79
slavery, 90, 96n31, 102, 188, 192–95, 204–5
Snead, James, 94
Stanišić, Saša, 85
Steinkopf, Leander, 214, 215n21, 236
social media, 85, 149, 214, 217, 231, 233n82, 234–35
solidarity, 2, 6, 26, 202–3, 205, 247; alliances and solidarity, 7, 47, 79, 211; Black solidarity, 99, 110, 116, 124; communities of solidarity, 45, 116; cross-border solidarity, 227; international solidarity, 233; network solidarity, 212; solidarity and Iran, 209–40; solidarity and open letters, 28, 209–40
Solingen, 4, 145, 147, 149–50, 156–58
Sorani, 228, 230n71
Soviet-Jewish family history, 57, 62; Soviet-Jewish identity, 63
Soviet people, 43
Soviet Union, 49–50, 197–98
Sow, Noah, 1, 86
Sow, Noah, works by: *Die Schwarze Madonna*, 27, 84, 87, 92, 95–100
SPD, 97, 152
Spelman, Elizabeth, 258
Spielhaus, Riem, 251
Spivak, Gayatri Chakravorty, 14

Stadlober, Robert, 228n65
Stalinism, 205
Stehle, Maria, 71
Stein, Mark, 182n74
Stewart, Faye, 197n37, 198n39
Stewart, Lizzie, 22n90
Steyerl, Hito, 15n53
Strubel, Antje Rávik, 1, 48; German Book Prize, 187–88, 191; open letter Ukraine, 213
Strubel, Antje Rávik, works by: *Blaue Frau*, 28, 187–89, 194, 197–205, 258; *Kältere Schichten der Luft*, 187n3; *Nah genug weit weg*, 202n52
Sturtz, Laura Marie, 13, 17n63, 26, 37, 39–41, 45–49, 51, 53–54, 56–80, 187n1, 255
subaltern, 14
subjectivity, 2, 6, 18n67, 19, 25–27, 64, 68n33, 79, 83, 94–95, 105–6, 112, 131, 164; Black subjectivity, 92, 112, 115; Black German subjectivity, 120, 122, 259; New Subjectivity, 27, 87, 92–95, 105–6
suicide, 57, 66, 70, 72–73, 116, 174–75, 196
Suleyman, Chimene, 248n11
Sunier, Thijl, 22, 60n17
Suwalska-Kolecka, Anna, 257, 258n16
Syria, 47

Tabatabai, Jasmin, 227–28
Tawada, Yoko, 85
Taylor, Sonya Renee, 141
Third Reich, 14
Thomae, Jackie, 1
Thomae, Jackie, works by: *Brüder*, 27, 86–89, 91–92, 95
transgender identity, 41, 45–46, 57, 62, 64, 70, 72, 78, 86n7
transnationalism, 6, 10, 19, 23, 211, 231; Black transnationalism, 27, 106, 110, 115, 118, 121–22, 124, 191n19; feminist transnationalism, 28, 211
Tufekci, Zeynep, 233n82

Turkey, 152, 159, 169–70, 172–73
Turkish-German, 19–21, 73, 127, 129, 135, 152–55, 158–59, 170, 174–75; German-Turkish literature, 19–20; German-Turkish studies, 21; Turkish language, 154–55, 170
Turkishness, 181
Twist, Joseph, 18n67, 19–20, 27, 145–60

Ünsal, Nadiye, 27, 140–42, 259
Uhlendorf, Niels, 168n38, 169n39
Ukraine; post-Soviet Ukraine, 37; Russian invasion of, 6, 37, 212; war in, 47, 53–54, 213, 216, 222
USA, 13n45, 66–68, 84, 90, 92, 95, 101–2, 111, 121–26, 129–30, 248n11
Utlu, Deniz, 7n21, 40, 251; open letter Iran, 228n65

Varatharajah, Senthuran, 228n65
Vietnam, 66, 92, 102–3, 121, 126–28; Vietnamese German, 103
violence, 4–5, 7, 51, 57, 59, 71, 75, 79, 102, 146, 148, 163–64, 169, 187–206, 230, 232; anti-Black violence, 211; antisemitic violence, 6, 62; cultural violence, 258; discursive violence, 4; domestic violence, 62, 147, 174, 196; emotional violence, 179; epistemic violence, 14, 190; institutional violence, 189; linguistic violence, 48, 98, 188–91; liberatory violence, 175–77, 180–81, 183; misogynist violence, 175; neo-Nazi violence, 145–46; patriarchal violence, 76, 174–75; psychological violence, 59, 106; quotidian violence, 200; racist violence, 4, 65–66, 68–69, 73, 102, 106, 171, 195, 205; representation of, 187–90 ; right-wing violence, 4–5; sexual violence, 179, 188–90, 198–99, 201–3; structural violence, 28, 187–89, 199, 258; symbolic violence, 5, 28, 171–72, 175–77, 180
visibility, 12–15, 17, 19, 23, 27, 29, 37, 39–40, 42, 46, 54, 60, 76, 112, 118, 123, 135, 137, 139, 146–47, 149, 165, 172, 189, 194, 200, 204, 211, 233–34, 241, 246, 252–53, 259
Vlasta, Sandra, 182n73
von Haselberg, Lea Wohl, 9n27
Vowinckel, Dana, 7

Wagner, David, 228n65
Walser, Martin, 213
Waya, Chalo, 256n4
Weber, Beverly, 71, 225n54
Weigel, Helene, 228
Weiland, Severin, 174n57
Weinbach, Heike, 128n42
Weiss-Sussex, Godela, 57–58
Weimar Republic, 83
Wekker, Gloria, 23
Welzer, Harald, 213
Wels, Selma, 4, 6n16, 248n14
Wenzel, Olivia, 1, 24, 40, 85, 255, 258
Wenzel, Olivia, works by: *1000 Serpentinen Angst*, 24n101, 26–27, 56–59, 61, 64–70, 72–74, 77–79, 84, 86–87, 91–92, 95, 100–106, 109–10, 115, 120–31, 247, 256n6
West African culture, 118–19, 139, 188, 192
Weston, Kate, 77
whiteness, 10, 13, 69, 97, 116, 118, 125, 127, 129, 165, 192
white privilege, 123, 125, 127, 165n19, 170–71
white supremacy, 142, 181, 194, 203
Wiegand, Frauke, 60n16, 164n11
Windsor, Tara Talwar, 28, 187n1, 209–37, 256n4
Winkler, Josef, 228n65
Woodford, Charlotte, 256n4
working class, 94, 153, 169, 172, 181
Wright, Michelle, 90, 100n40, 111–12, 116n20, 117n21, 122, 125n37, 129, 131

xenophobia, 171n47, 71

Yaghoobifarah, Hengameh, 2; open
    letter Iran, 228n65
Yaghoobifarah, Hengameh, works by:
    Eure Heimat ist unser Albtraum, 2,
    247–48
Yakimchuk, Lyuba, 54

Yildiz, Erol, 22n92, 60n17, 61n21
Yücel, Deniz, 213

Zaimoğlu, Feridun, 85, 171n46
Zeh, Juli, 213
Zhadan, Serhij, 53
Zola, Émile, 214, 216–17, 219

Printed in the United States
by Baker & Taylor Publisher Services